T0248410

RANIS
& THE RAJ

RANIS & THE RAJ

THE PEN AND THE SWORD

QUEENY PRADHAN

PENGUIN
VIKING
An imprint of Penguin Random House

VIKING

USA | Canada | UK | Ireland | Australia
New Zealand | India | South Africa | China

Viking is part of the Penguin Random House group of companies
whose addresses can be found at global.penguinrandomhouse.com

Published by Penguin Random House India Pvt. Ltd
4th Floor, Capital Tower 1, MG Road,
Gurugram 122 002, Haryana, India

First published in Viking by Penguin Random House India 2022

10 9 8 7 6 5 4 3 2 1

ISBN 9780670091034

Typeset in Bembo Std by Manipal Technologies Limited, Manipal
Printed at Replika Press Pvt. Ltd, India

www.penguin.co.in

To my husband and son,
Vivek and Amartya,
with love

Contents

Acknowledgements

In the course of my research, numerous people have helped me, and I have accumulated many debts of gratitude. I would like to thank them for their contributions to my work.

I have fond memories of my visit to Kittur and Dharwad, with many people helping me in collecting information on Rani Chennamma. Sangamesh S. Banaladinni, librarian at Kittur Rani Channamma Sainik School for Girls (KRCRSSG), the only public sainik school for girls, gave his time and generously shared all the resources available at the library and at a small museum on Rani Chennamma. He and his wife were extremely hospitable, treating us to one of the warmest cups of tea, served with love and affection. The principal of the school, retired Colonel R.S. Khatri permitted us to use the library of the school and spared time from his busy schedule to treat us to lunch in the school mess. The hours spent at the residence of Shri Basavalingayya Hiremath, President of Janapada Samshodhana Kendra, and Smt. Vishweshwari Basavalingayya, theatre director, were the most memorable moments of the trip. The songs and lavanis sung by him transported us to Rani Chennamma's times, helping us in envisioning the period through his songs. Hours simply flew, with both of them explaining about the folk tradition and art forms. In the end, Shri Hiremath did us a great honour by singing along with my husband, Vivek. I dedicate this work to the memory of Shri Hiremath, who unfortunately passed away in January 2022. Prof. Basavaraj Naikar not only spared his time but gave many books that he has written on Rani Chennamma and other queens of the region. Prof. R.M. Shadakshari and then Head Prof. A.P. Shiladhar Mugali and the faculty of the Department of History, Dharwad University, were most hospitable, suggesting various sources to look up. Dr A.B. Vaggar sent me the published volume of the archival work which he compiled by visiting the Mumbai Archives and the Deccan Commissioner Records in Pune on Rani Chennamma,[1] which helped in reconstructing some of the events in Kittur. My special thanks to Prof. Shadakshari for insisting on my seeing the British cemetery. Mr Raghavendra at Kittur Museum gave me insights into the architectural features of Kittur Fort. Iramma Sainikop, whom I met by accident, sitting outside the Hanuman temple inside Kittur Fort, gave her perceptions of the fort. The present Swamiji of Kalmath at Kittur took interest in my research, extending all possible help to me. Stanley, the local taxi driver got involved with the research, taking us to the places associated with Rani Chennamma. I am grateful to him as well.

In Gangtok, Her Highness Hope Leezum graciously shared her hospitality and the private diary (handwritten) of Prince Sidkeong Tulku at her residence. She also gave us a tour of Tsuklakhang Royal Palace and Monastery. She is enthusiastically involved with the restoration work of the beautiful wall murals and Thangka paintings inside the chapel. Tashi Paljor, Assistant Librarian, Namgyal Institute of Tibetology, Gangtok, Sikkim,

---

[1] Kittur records are available in the Department of Archives, Elphinstone College Building, opposite Jehangir Art Gallery, Fort Mumbai (For Foreign Department volumes); Department of Archives, opposite Council Hall Pune (for Deccan Commissioner's files).

helped in getting me started with a few initial readings. My heartfelt gratitude to the students of the Department of History, Sikkim University—Vivek Thapa, Ingnam Subba, Nirnay Tamang and Anjana Tamang—for their constant companionship and unstinting help throughout my trip to Gangtok. Words fall short in expressing my affection for them. I thank Jeena Tamang for sharing information on Queen Menchi. Prof. Vijay Kumar Thangelapali and the faculty members of the Department of History, Sikkim University, not only allowed me to share my ideas with them but also made me feel at home with the sense of ease with which they interacted in the very first meeting. Anna Balikci-Denjongpa at the Namgyal Institute of Tibetology, despite her busy schedule, was forthcoming with information on many aspects of Sikkim history. She shared many articles, in particular on the queens and the political background of Sikkim. I am grateful to her for providing me important leads.

I also wish to acknowledge the assistance of the staff at the National Archives of India, New Delhi; Himachal State Archives, Shimla; Kittur Fort Museum and Bhai Veer Singh Sahitya Sadan, New Delhi. They went out of their way to help me find the material that I needed.

Dr Yadwinder Singh, Department of Punjabi, University of Delhi, and his student, Sukhchain, helped to procure a few books on Maharani Jindan at the last minute during the lockdown. My friends, Jyoti Sinha at Jaunpur and Ajit Singh at Jhansi, got hold of the much-needed folk songs on Maharani Lakshmi Bai. My friend, Aparna Vaidik, by talking about her writing experiences, sustained me in my writing when I would be stuck. Meenu and Manoj at Shimla provided comic relief from the stress during my field research and worry of finding sources.

From the Lyallpur Young Historians Club, LYHC, Tohid Ahmad Chattha and Khola Cheema helped me to understand so much more about Maharaja Ranjit Singh and Maharani Jindan.

I am very thankful to them that in the time of lockdown when we all were operating in vacuum, the discussions in the club, helped me to stay in touch with my discipline and to historicize certain aspects.

I was initially sceptical about taking up the project, but the positive responses from professors Neeladri Bhattacharya and Ramachandra Guha encouraged me greatly. Ramachandra Guha suggested the title of the book. I am grateful to Prof. I.D. Gaur, Department of History, Panjab University, Chandigarh for his help in mapping out the historiography of Maharani Jindan. It made my task simpler.

My family was unflagging in their support. My father, G.P. Pradhan, read some of my chapters and helped me with his feedback; while my mother, Asha Pradhan, always a disciplinarian, kept me on my toes whenever I would slacken at the last minute. My husband, Vivek Sachdeva, patiently read my drafts, giving his critical inputs, which were badly needed. He is my inspiration with his work discipline and his focus. I am grateful for his presence in my life, for keeping me motivated. My son, Amartya, waited patiently for the manuscript to be complete to spend some family time. He constantly missed spending time with me, and I felt bad for depriving him. My sister, Vandana Bhatnagar, her husband Deepak Bhatnagar, and my niece and nephew, Purva and Meru, reduced their phone time with me to help me stick to my commitment to finish the book. I would also like to acknowledge my students at GGS Indraprastha University, Arjun Sajeevan, Siva and Shikhar Singh for providing assistance when needed. I am grateful to my place of work, GGS Indraprastha University, Delhi, and the Vice Chancellor Prof. Mahesh Verma for accepting my leave requests so that I could go to visit the places of my research and complete my manuscript.

One individual who is instrumental in making me work on this project is Premanka Goswami of Penguin Random House

India. He was most persuasive in convincing me to take up this extremely daunting task of working on six queens. He drew my attention to the queens and that I could write about them. I had not thought of writing on the queens as I considered their narrative to be part of conventional history writing. In my previous work, I focussed on working on the regions, particularly mountain spaces on the margins and the local people's perception of history. Queens seemed to be privileged and somehow the impression was that they were well-known. I took a considered decision to work on the nineteenth century as I am familiar with this period; my previous work, *Empire in the Hills*, focuses mainly on this period. There are two queens from the hills, and one of them had caught my attention during my previous research. That had intrigued me at that time, but I didn't give it a thought later. With Premanka talking to me about the queens, I realized I can explore further about their political biographies. It was a challenge to search for the queens' stories in the archives. I thank Premanka for introducing me to this area, which has helped me grow with my sense of history. Arunima Bhatt's searching queries and rigorous editing by Aparna, Shaoni and Aurodeep helped to improve the manuscript. My special thanks to Shaoni for patiently accommodating last-minute changes, and to Rachel and Ahana for seeing the book through its final stages. My thanks to Gunjan for his enthusiastic involvement in designing the cover of the book.

In the end, I take all responsibility for the mistakes and errors in the book. I also extend my apologies in advance for certain arguments with which others may disagree or which may inadvertently cause hurt. The attempt is to understand these queens in the present context from the limited records available. While there is no dearth of the British records, the challenge has been to find other voices and versions.

Queeny Pradhan

Introduction

Traditionally, history has been telling us the stories of kings. In the long tradition of history writing, 'his story' has always dominated 'her story'. Though queens evoke a sense of romance, and their stories are told like fairy tales, in the annals of history, it has been observed that many times queens have met a tragic fate. There have been many important queens in the history of the world and India's history. Not all queens in the history of India are remembered today. Some are celebrated, while others have been almost ignored by historians. In the history of India, queens have been known for different reasons: Razia Sultan and the Maharani of Jhansi for their martial valour, Meera Bai for her spiritual quest and others for their regency and more. There are many queens about whom there are scant records, such as: Abbakka Chowta, the Kakatiya queen Rani Rudrama, Onaka Obavva, Rani of Sawunwaree, Keladi Chennamma, Belawadi Mallamma, Avantibai Lodhi of Ramgarh, Devi Durgavati and many others. Much historical research is needed to unearth information about them.

Some ruled for long, like Ahilya Bai Holkar of Indore. She probably was one of the astute state persons among the Maratha leaders of her time.[1] The Holkars belonged to a herding caste of Dhangar.[2] Ahilyabai was both a warrior and an administrator. Her devout religiosity seems to fit the mould of an ideal woman.[3] While her public persona appears to be well recorded, there are silences on her private life.

Silences on the personal lives of women and queens in history in particular poses a challenge.[4] Rani Velu Nachiyar was the first Indian queen to fight against the British in Sivagangai during 1760–90.[5] There are a few short references to the queens from

---

[1] Cathleen Cummings, 'Mapping Holkar Identity and the Good name of Ahilyabai', in Melia Belli Bose and Cathleen Cummings ed. *Women, Gender and Art in Asia, c.1500-1900,* Ashgate, (New York: Routledge, 2016), 21–40.

[2] 'The Holkars belong to the Dhangar caste', 20; and it is mentioned that in the third Battle of Panipat, Sadashiv Rao Bhau dismissed the advice of Malhar Rao Holkar by saying 'Who wants the counsel of a goat-herd', 24, in L.C. Dhariwal, *The Indore State Gazetteer,* Volume I-Text (Under the authority of the Government of His Highness the Maharaja Holkar), Superintendent Holkar Government Press, Indore, 1931; in an article written by Melia Belli Bose, 'Royal Matronage and a Visual Vocabulary of Indian Queenship' it is observed that 'Numerous Maratha dynasties were in fact of humble origins. For example, the Holkars were originally hereditary shepherds—a genealogy that hardly recommended them for rulership', 41 in Melia Belli Bose and Cathleen Cummings ed. *Women, Gender and Art in Asia, c.1500-1900,* (New York: Ashgate, Routledge, 2016), 41–62.

[3] Cathleen Cummings, 21–40.

[4] Devika Rangachari, *Invisible Women, Visible Histories: Gender, Society and Polity in North India, 7th-12th Century,* (New Delhi: Manohar Publishers & Distributors, 2009).

[5] A. Ramaswami, *Tamil Nadu District Gazetteer: Ramanathapuram,* (Madras: Director of Stationery and Printing, Madras, 1972, 100). There is a reference to Velu Nachiar for gallantly defending Sivaganga after her husband's death in 1772; A. Jekila and P. Barathi, 'Queen Velu Nachiar: First Woman against British', in *Infokara Research,* Vol. 9, Issue 3, June 2020, 891–897.

the low-caste backgrounds. Kalhana mentions in *Rajatarangini* that King Cakravarman of Kashmir (923–933) married an untouchable Domba woman, Hansi.[6] These instances are few and are briefly mentioned. It is a challenge for historians to get information about these queens who rose from the marginalized sections of society.

In post-Independence times, many queens made a successful transformation in the democratic and representative parliamentary system. Rajkumari Amrit Kaur of Kapurthala, Vijaya Raje of the Scindia royal family and Maharani Gayatri Devi of Jaipur are some of the women from erstwhile royal families to participate in the democratic process in modern India.[7]

I have selected six queens of the nineteenth century for my study. During the research, I identified certain common patterns. All the queens had to negotiate with the British Raj, either the Company, or the Crown, or even both.[8] The earliest to deal with the British authorities was the Rani of Sirmur in 1815–16, followed by Rani Chennamma of Kittur in the period of 1824–29, then Maharani Jindan in Lahore in 1844–1849, Begum Zeenat Mahal

---

[6] Jogesh Chunder Dutt, *Kings of Kashmir being a translation of the Sanskrita Work Rajatarangini of Kalahana Pandita*, (Calcutta: Trubner and Company, London, 1879). He mentions that 'The Queen and the favourites were of the low caste (literally-those who cooked dog's flesh)', 133. At another place, it is mentioned that her father Ranga, and she belonged to the 'Domva' caste. M.A. Stein in *Kalhana's Rajatarangini: A Chronicle of the Kings of Kashmir*, Vol.I, (books I-VII), Westminster: Archibald Constable & Co. Ltd, 1800, describes Queen Hansi to belong to the 'despised Domba caste.', 102.

[7] Lucy Moore, *Maharanis: The Extraordinary Tale of Four Indian Queens and Their Journey from Purdah to Parliament*, (London and New York: Viking, 2004).

[8] The period before 1857 is under the direct rule of the East India Company and post-1857, the British Crown with the Queen's Procalmation of 1858 directly took charge of India, with the Crown's representative, the Viceroy, acting on it's behalf.

in Delhi and Maharani Lakshmi Bai of Jhansi in 1857 and the
Queen of Sikkim[9] resisted the British authorities intermittently
from the 1860s to 1890s. Ranis' narratives and struggles are
conjoined with their respective regions, which have become
an integral part of their identities. The chapters are not placed
chronologically but in terms of a few similarities between these
queens. For instance, the Maharani of Jhansi and Kittur Rani
Chennamma faced the military might of the Company's armies.
Their resistance has been immortalized in Indian literature[10]
and popular culture[11], particularly films,[12] where they are seen
as 'warrior' queens. While there is a valourization of these two
queens, suspicions and doubts abound on Maharani Jindan and
Begum Zeenat Mahal. They have been vilified for their political
role in 1846 and 1857 respectively. The British archival records,
and the personal accounts of the British officers highlight the

---

[9] In the book, I discuss the debate over the name of the Sikkim Queen
under study.

[10] Subhadra Kumari Chauhan's poem 'Jhansi ki Rani' written in
Hindi in the collection of poems called *Mukul* (1930); Michelle
Moran, *Rebel Queen*, (New York : Touchstone, 2015); Sadashiva
Shivadeva Wodeyar's *Rani Chennamma*, (New Delhi: National Book
Trust, 2016); Basavaraj Naikar, *The Rani of Kittur: A Historical Play*,
2012 and many sites on the internet.

[11] Folk songs on Maharani Lakshmi Bai such as Alha Deshraj
Paterya, Jhansi Ki Rani Laxmi Bai, Vol. I and II, https://youtu.
be/JdiU48E31MQ; *Kar Gai Amar Kahani Jhansi Ki* (Rani aur Vir
Bhesh Ghoda Pe Baithi Kar Gayi Amar Kahani, https://youtu.
be/4epsK5nsPic and https://youtu:be/e-KcBNSVWKU.

[12] Films on Maharani Lakshmi Bai such as *Jhansi Ki Rani* (Sohrab
Modi, 1953), *Jhansi ki Rani Laxmibai* (Rajesh Mittal, 2012), *The
Warrior Queen of* Jhansi (Swati Bhise, 2019), *Manikarnika: The Queen
of Jhansi* (Kangana Ranaut & Krish Jagariamudi, 2019) among others;
TV series like *Jhansi Ki Rani* (Jitendra Srivastava, 2009), *Khoob Ladi
Mardaani—Jhansi Ki Rani* (Abhmanyu Singh, 2019).

ambiguous roles of these two queens in the downfall of their Kingdoms ad nauseum.[13]

The rani of Sirmur and the queen of Sikkim are peripheral in the imperial records and do not find much mention in the historiography. Both were significantly impacted by the coming of the Gurkhas[14] and subsequently the British forays in these regions in 1814–15. Both became imperial dependencies, but at different times—Sirmur in 1816 and Sikkim in 1890. Yet, both had come under the shadow of the acquisitive East India Company, ever looking to expand its commercial prospects. While in the western Himalaya, the inroads took place earlier, in the eastern Himalaya, the British had been looking to make inroads from the late eighteenth century under Warren Hastings, after acquiring Bengal in 1757.[15] The prime interest of the East India Company was commerce with Tibet and China. Mbembe observes that the 'colonial wars were wars of extraction and

---

[13] Colonel Alexander Gardner, *Soldier and Traveller: Memoirs of Alexander Gardner (Colonel of Artillery in the Service of Maharaja Ranjit Singh)*, Edited by Major Hugh Pearse & Introduction by Sir Richard Temple, (Edinburgh and London: William Blackwood and Sons, 1848); George Macdonald Fraser, *Flashman and the Mountain of Light*, (London: Harper Collins, 2005)—it is a fictional account which reinforces the negative image of Maharani Jindan. These and other accounts would be discussed in some detail in the chapters on Maharani Jindan and Begum Zeenat Mahal.

[14] In the early decades of the nineteenth century, under Prithvi Narain Shah, the Gurkha rulers of Nepal started expanding their kingdom, details in the chapter 'The Gorkha Onslaught' in Lal Bahadur Basnet's *Sikkim: A Short Political History*, (New Delhi: Chand & Company, 1974), 24.

[15] Alastair Lamb, *British India and Tibet: 1766-1910*, (London: Routledge, 1960, 1986); A.K. Jasbir Singh, *Himalayan Triangle: A Historical Survey of British India's Relations with Tibet, Sikkim and Bhutan 1765-1950*, (London: The British Library, 1988).

predation.'[16] They had heard about the gold and the minerals in Tibet,[17] but despite their repeated efforts, they could not have access to these high mountains till 1816, when the Gurkha expansion in Sirmur and Sikkim gave an opportunity to the English officers to intervene. Sirmur ruler, Karam Prakash requested the Gurkha commander to help him with his internal and external enemies. After their arrival, the Gurkhas stayed in Sirmur and the royal family of Sirmur became fugitives and finally they had to take refuge with the British authorities. In Sikkim again, due to internal troubles by the Bhutanese faction, the Lepcha faction supporting the Sikkim ruler sought the assistance of the English to fend off both the internal threats and the external threat of the Gurkhas. The British authorities seemed like the 'saviours', but as will be discussed in the chapters on these queens, tensions would emerge between them and the British. In both the places, the East India Company would take away parts of their land for economic reasons. As the records show, the Sikkim Durbar will come to resent the British movement in their land with hostilities coming out in the open in 1849 and 1860.[18] Sikkim Durbar would continue to be suspicious of their motives, especially when they insist on the settling of the Nepalese in Sikkim.[19]

Both the queens can be said to be on the margins, partly because the two regions have been peripheral to the mainstream history. In the chapters on them, I argue that these regions were of strategic importance for the British imperial authorities of the

---

[16] 'Introduction', *Necropolitics*, Achille Mbembe and Steve Corcoran, (Durham and London: Duke University Press, 2019), 4.

[17] Thomas H. Holdich, *Tibet the Mysterious*, (London: Alston Rivers Ltd., 1906).

[18] H.H. Risley, iii–iv.

[19] Ibid.

nineteenth century. These queens could assess the situation and fought the battle at the diplomatic front. What emerges from the various sources is that in both the regions, women of the royal family were influential in the politics of the state. In Sikkim, the father of Tsugphud Namgyal was challenged as the king by his half-sister. Being the elder of the two, she considered herself to be the heir to the throne and invited Bhutan to invade Sikkim. The Tibetan government aided the Sikkim king. The British records do not mention Queen Menchi initially. She is only mentioned as the fifth wife of the Chogyal, Tsugphud Namgyal. When one reads the British and the Sikkimese documents carefully, it emerges that Queen Men-chi or Menchi, who is only mentioned as the fifth queen, had an influential role in the Sikkim court politics, especially as part of the anti-British group, after her marriage to the Chogyal, Tsugphud Namgyal. The Sikkim royal records mention their marriage, intrigues by the fourth or the previous rani to prevent their union and the final culmination of marriage. She was trusted by the king, as he not only married her to his illegitimate son, Changzod Karpo, on his deathbed, but entrusted both of them with the protection of his son and successor, Thutob Namgyal,[20] in his minority.[21]

One also needs to examine the issues of sovereignty as they emerge in the two Himalayan kingdoms, Sirmur and Sikkim, at the opposite ends geographically. Their experiences with the British Raj are dissimilar, but the Raj interestingly tries to homogenize the polities of these states—by a north Indian political tradition of the plains. A homogenous term 'Raja' or 'Maharaja'

---

[20] The role of Queen Menchi of Sikkim will be discussed in the chapter on her.

[21] The details on the Sikkim Royal family are recorded by Sir Thutob Namgyal, their Highness, the Maharaja and Maharani Yeshay Dolma of Sikkim, *History of Sikkim*, Translated by Kazi Dousandup (Gangtok: 1908).

is interchangeably used for the various princely states, despite the fact that such terms were not familiar in their kingdoms.[22] For instance, the Sikkim rulers used the title of 'Chogyal' and not 'Raja'.[23] But the *Gazetteer of Sikkim* used the title 'Sikhim Raj'[24] to describe the Sikkim kingdom. The names of the queens of Sirmur and Sikkim do not find any mention in the official files of the Raj relating to these two states. Despite various efforts to trace the name of the queen of Sirmur, one finds her being mentioned as the Guleri or Goler Rani. Similarly, on Queen Menchi, Anna Balicki is of the opinion[25] that it is not her name but the name of the family, Monkyit, in Tibet from where she came. The gaps and the limitations of the colonial archives manifest in lack of clarity on the names of the queens. It is either due to the indifference or callousness of a masculine Empire or obfuscation of the facts, giving negligent attention to these queens.

Gendered History

It is essential 'to construct women as historical subjects'[26] and see the events of the nineteenth century by exploring the stories of the queens, who came in contact with the English authorities and the East India Company in particular. In many ways, it is a project of revisiting history from the point of view of women. Undoubtedly, these queens are not ordinary women and have

---

[22] H.H. Risley, *The Gazetteer of Sikhim*, (Calcutta: Bengal Secretariat Press,1894), iii.

[23] Genealogy of the Sikkim rulers in the Royal records of Sikkim.

[24] H.H. Risley, ii.

[25] Anna Balicki is a scholar at the Namgyal Institute of Tibetology in Gangtok, and during the discussion, she shared her views about 'Monkyit' being her family name, on 12 June 2019.

[26] Joan Wallach Scott, *Gender and the Politics of History* (Gender and Cultural Series), (New York: Columbia University Press, 1999), 67.

been in the limelight, but on rereading the records of the
period, it emerges that all do not have the same prominence.
Nevertheless, they play a dominant role in the politics of
their kingdoms, and in holding talks with the British. In this
respect, women emerge as active agents of history.[27] All the six
queens under study exhibit a strong 'agency', which put simply
'is purposeful action designed to have an impact.'[28] Anagol
highlights 'assertion' and 'resistance' as two aspects of women's
agency.[29] It is important to understand 'women collude with, or
benefit from, consciously upheld patriarchal norms in benign, as
well as confrontational, moments of resistance'.[30]

The research on women in history began in India in the late
1970s and 80s with the pioneering works of Uma Chakravarty
and many other women scholars.[31] Debate on the queens started

-----

[27] Joan Wallach Scott, 69.
[28] Padma Anagol, 'Agency, Periodization and Change in the Gender
and Women's History of Colonial India', in *Gender and History*,
Vol. 20, No. 3, November 2008, 6023–624, 615.
[29] Ibid.
[30] Ibid.
[31] Uma Chakravarti and Kumkum Roy, 'A Review of the
Limitations and Possibilities of the Historiography of Women in
Early India', *Economic and Political Weekly*, 30 April 1998, WS2
-WS10; Uma Chakravarti and Kumkum Roy, 'In Search of Our
Past', *Economic and Political Weekly*, Vol. 23, No. 18, 30 April 1988,
WS2-WS10; Janaki Nair, 'On the Question of Agency in Indian
Feminist Historiography', *Gender and History*, Vol.6, No. 1, April 1994,
82-100; Lata Mani, 'Contentious Traditions: The Debate on Sati in
Colonial India', *Cultural Critique*, No. 7, The Nature and Context
of Minority Discourse II, Autumn, 1987, 119-56; Tanika Sarkar,
'Nationalist Iconography: Image of Women in 19th Century Bengali
Literature', *Economic and Political Weekly*, Vol. 22, No.47, November
21, 1987, 2011-2015.

with Gayatri Chakravorty Spivak,[32] where she raises the question of 'Rani as an object of knowledge.'[33] Spivak argues that the queen, in this case, of Sirmur 'emerges in the archives because of the commercial and territorial interests of the East India Company'.[34] She states that there is silence in the imperial records on the woman as a subaltern. Arik Moran, responding to Spivak and in carrying forward the argument, asserts the agency of the Rani of Sirmur, who with adroit political manoeuvres retains the reins of power within the royal family of Sirmur. She rules as the regent for her minor son, Fateh Chand.[35] Janaki Nair writing on Indian feminist historiography observes that 'Being less powerful, after all, is not to be powerless, or even to lose all the time.'[36] The queens under study exhibit this freedom to act most appropriately 'against or despite oppressive conditions.'[37] The queens act as 'agencies of subversion, transgression or consent'.[38]

In many instances, 'cross-class collaboration'[39] emerge among women. One can identify 'networks of female friendship that provided emotional as well as physical sustenance.'[40] Maharani

---

[32] Gayatri Chakravorty Spivak, 'The Rani of Sirmur: An Essay in Reading the Archives', in *Theory and History*, 24, 3, October 1985, 247–72.

[33] Ibid., 263.

[34] Ibid.

[35] Arik Moran, '"The Rani of Sirmur" Revisited: Sati and sovereignty in theory and practice', in *Modern Asian Studies*, Cambridge University Press, 2014, 1–34.

[36] Janaki Nair, 'On the Question of Agency in Indian Feminist Historiography', in *Gender and History*, Vol.6, No. 1, April 1994, 82–100, 83.

[37] Ibid.

[38] Ibid.

[39] Joan Wallach Scott, 72.

[40] Ibid., 73.

Lakshmi Bai and Maharani Jindan had a close bond with their female companions, Jhalkari Bai[41] and Mungla[42] respectively, to whom they entrusted many delicate tasks of state affairs behind the scenes. From the beginning, royal women maintained their separate space in the patriarchal world. Maharani Lakshmi Bai had a group of women supporters as her constant companions, who belonged to different castes. Queens created a world circumventing patriarchy, but it was based on furthering their interests.[43]

Why should women be seen only as warriors to be glorified in the nationalist historiography? Somewhere, women, especially the queens, have been added to the 'list' of war pantheon.[44] War has become a symbol of pride of a nation and in politics and it is being used to highlight a particular race's martial qualities. One has to move out of the warrior mould in which the queens are slotted, and I argue throughout that women negotiated in different ways with the East India Company, but not much light has been thrown on these aspects of the history of the nineteenth century. The nineteenth century also witnessed a changing mode of production from feudal to primarily commercial capitalist mode.

---

[41] Badri Narayan, *Women Heroes and Dalit Assertion in North India: Cuture, Identity and Politics,* Chapter 5 on Jhalkaribai and the Koris of Bundelkhand', 113-132, (New Delhi: Sage Publications, 2006).

[42] Mungla's reference comes in the archival files as a close confidante of Maharani Jindan, in Foreign Department Secret Proceedings, Nos. 951-1118, 26 December 1846.

[43] The argument of Carl Deglar mentioned by Joan Wallach Scott, 73–74.

[44] Adrian Shubert, 'Women Warriors and National Heroes: Augustina de Aragon and her Indian Sisters', in *Journal of World History*, Vol. 23, No.2, June 2012, 279–313.

It will be discussed in the book how the ranis negotiated
the public and the personal boundaries, tackling both the British
aggression and that of their traditional society of the nineteenth
century. In many ways, these ranis were dealing with two
complex worldviews: modern and traditional. The question
of equality assumes importance, as the crises in many cases are
precipitated in the nineteenth century by the British refusal
to accept the widow's presence as a critical part of the state
system in the princely states. Here the patriarchal bias of the Raj
becomes apparent, where they do not see queens as necessary
in taking decisions for the people and their states. The British
imputed it on the tradition, which undoubtedly was patriarchal,
but how does this make the English officers different from the
Indian perpetrators of patriarchal prejudices?[45] On the one hand,
the British presented themselves as the harbingers of civilization,
progress and modernity, but they showed extreme patriarchal
bias when it came to these queen regents.[46] The derision of
Maharani Jindan by the English officials exposes their repugnant,
antiquated and patriarchal mindset.[47] The best weapon to
subdue a woman in a masculine society is to assassinate her
character through insinuations or propaganda. This aspect will
be discussed in the following chapters.

---

[45] A similar argument has been made by Lata Mani, 119–156.

[46] What Thomas R. Metcalf calls 'the hyper-masculine society of the
Raj', in *Ideologies of the Raj*, (New Delhi: Cambridge University Press
Foundation Books, 1998), 104.

[47] Colonel Alexander Gardner, *Soldier and Traveller: Memoirs of
Alexander Gardner (Colonel of Artillery in the Service of Maharaja Ranjit
Singh),* Edited by Major Hugh Pearse and Introduction by Sir
Richard Temple (Edinburgh and London: William Blackwood and
Sons, 1848); George Macdonald Fraser, *Flashman and the Mountain
of Light,* (London: Harper Collins, 2005)—it is a fictional account
which reinforces the negative image of Maharani Jindan.

Women, as subjects of history, have emerged as a late phenomenon. Usually, the focus has been either on events or the historical figures, mostly men and specific universal patterns in history. Women figure as an appendage. The queens are either stereotyped as romantic figures or associated with political/court intrigues—straitjacketed into slots. Yet, we find a very few of them in history. When I began my research on this area, I was surprised to see that many women, both queens and otherwise, experienced the coming of the British Raj in multitudinous ways. Queens also played their historical roles, and it was not only of warriors, as ingrained in our imagination. The public imagination is replete with the heroism of the Maharani of Jhansi. Why did both imperial and nationalist historiography consider the Maharani of Jhansi important, while other queens remain almost insignificant and obscure? The question begs an answer, but there are gaps in our historiography to arrive at a definite answer. The gap may provide a glimpse into a period—that is the nineteenth century. The first half of the nineteenth century is seen in the existing records predominantly in terms of the rise of the East India Company and the decline of the Marathas, the Sikhs and even the Mughal Empire. Another overarching event of importance in the second half of the nineteenth century is the Revolt of 1857, with rich historiography. Another strong historiographical presence of this period is the focus on the East India Company's policies and the heyday of imperialism under the British Raj, post-1858, and finally, the emergence of Indian nationalism, especially the establishment of the Indian National Congress in 1885.

In the book, while going through the British records, both official and unofficial, the queens do not always come across as romantic figures. Many are represented as scheming, manipulative and untrustworthy. In colonial fiction, some royal women are the romantic interests of the colonial masters, but only as a subject to be domesticated by the colonial masculine self.[48] Shuchi Kapila argues that 'In nineteenth-century India, romance narratives encoded a political fantasy of creating, through just government, native subjects acculturated to European values who would welcome colonial rule and ally themselves with British.'[49] These royal women were to be educated as obedient and complying subjects.[50] Their agency was to be tamed or subjugated to further the imperial interests of Britain. The two queens most reviled in the imperial records of the colonial period are Begum Zeenat Mahal, the wife of the last Mughal Emperor, and Maharani Jindan, the youngest and the last wife of Maharaja Ranjit Singh of Punjab. The imperial records suggest that they were devious and wily. What did they scheme? Why are these two queens represented negatively in the imperial records? These queens wanted to ensure the succession of their sons as their heirs. What were their vilest acts? Begum Zeenat Mahal is suspected of betraying the rebels' cause in the 1857 revolt in the nationalist historiography.[51] Maharani Jindan, in both Indian and British accounts of the time, is accused of destroying the Khalsa army which led to their massacre, giving the imperial authorities the foothold in India and Punjab. Yet, they were the most tragic figures, as they lost everything. Begum Zeenat Mahal lost her ancestors' land when she voluntarily went in exile with her husband to Rangoon. Maharani Jindan lost

---

[48] Prince Michael of Greece, *The Rani of Jhansi: A Historical Novel*, (New Delhi: Rupa, 2013).

[49] Shuchi Kapila, 'Educating Seeta: Philip Meadows Taylor's Romances of Empire', *Victorian Studies: A Journal of the Humanities, Arts & Sciences* 41, No. 2, Winter, 1998, 211–241, 212.

[50] Thomas R. Metcalf observed that in the colonial discourse 'feminized' India was to be subordinate to 'masculine' Britain, 104.

[51] Details in the chapter on Begum Zeenat Mahal.

Punjab and her only son, Maharaja Duleep Singh, who was sent to England.

Memory has also emerged as a critical discourse in the newfound interest in the queens of India. Some queens like the Maharani of Jhansi and Razia Sultan captured the popular imagination. They are still alive in people's memory. Many queens have been resurrected in iconic avatars. In post-Independence Karnataka, Rani Chennamma and her associates have been celebrated in the nooks and crannies of Kittur and its surroundings. There are both commercial and political angles in the visibility given to the rani's deeds. Maharani Lakshmi Bai emerged as an icon in northern India after the 1857 revolt. Perhaps the fact that she died on the battlefield immortalized her across India. Rani Chennamma was her predecessor, and among the first few women to resist the interference of the East India Company officials with the Indian traditions and laws. To counter the imperial narrative, especially during the national struggle, and to instil a sense of pride in the new nation, many queens, who resisted the English takeover of their principalities, were appropriated in the nationalist frame as women freedom fighters.[52] In contrast, there are queens who have been obscure or at best reduced to a footnote in the Indian history. Abbakka Chowta of Ullal, who confronted the Portuguese in the late sixteenth century, is one such queen.[53] During the early days of the British rule, the territorial negotiations and settlements were

---

[52] Prachi Deshpande, 'The Making of an Indian Nationalist Archive: Lakshmibai, Jhansi, and 1857', in *The Journal of Asian Studies*, Vol. 67, No. 3, August 2008, 855-879.

[53] Kailash Kumar Mishra, 'Abbakka Rani: The Unsung Warrior Queen', *Vihangama,* Vol. I, January February 2002, ignca.gov.in/PDF_data/Abbakka_Rani.pdf. He states: 'While Rani Jhansi has become a symbol of courage, Abbakka nearly 300 years her predecessor, has been largely forgotten.'

often conducted by queens, and one can see a specific pattern in the territorial settlement. In the cases of Sirmur and Sikkim, queens played an important role at a time when the political officers of the British Empire were expanding or consolidating the frontiers of the Empire. These queens are on the margins of history, as their presence is retrieved with difficulty from the archival catacomb. It becomes even more challenging, as they are situated in India's border regions, such as Sirmur and Sikkim.

There is a constant oscillation between the two dominant ideologies: imperialist and nationalist. The attempt in this study is to see a possibility of understanding these queens in the historical context of their times beyond the binaries. Is it possible to see them as women of their times spanning two different worlds and articulating their identity and asserting their agency under their respective circumstances? The nineteenth century is a fluid age, with the end of a medieval era and the beginning of a modern one. The regional powers that had flourished in the eighteenth century realized a new threat from the East India Company, a commercial venture of profiteering merchants and their ambitious officials, who used both diplomacy and guns to outmanoeuvre the enfeebled Mughals and the ambitious regional powers. In the nineteenth century, like the other regional powers succumbing to the Company Raj's Machiavellian machinations, the ranis also faced the imperial onslaught on their principalities. Queens are at a crucial threshold of history and may reflect the changing trajectory of their times with which their fate was intertwined in many ways. It may be worth exploring how they negotiated their existing worldview with an emerging new world.

These queens can be seen in different narrative frames— tragic, heroic and romantic. How did Maharani Lakshmi Bai, coming from an ordinary family background, respond to the rituals and restrictions of the royal family of Jhansi, where she was wedded? These questions remain unaddressed. These women battled not just the enemies outside but also the normative structure of their time. One can see Maharani Jindan and Begum Zeenat Mahal as romantic and tragic figures. They had to make some difficult choices and were condemned for doing so. Maharani Jindan took an enormously difficult challenge of accepting the Treaty of 1845. But later, more agonizing for her would be the separation from her son, Maharaja Duleep Singh. Begum Zeenat Mahal had to take a stand with the leaders of the Revolt of 1857, not only to protect her immediate family but the entire Mughal legacy. All of them were mothers who were anxious about their sons' well-being and the continuation of their dynasties. In that sense, these queens were operating in a mould of patriarchal traditions. They did not question the patriarchy, marrying men much older to them, becoming second or third wives (or even a fifth wife, in Sikkim), and conforming to the rules of segregation, principles of male succession and the traditional norms of Indian society. Yet, events of the nineteenth century centring around the ruling dynasties into which they were married thrust them into playing an active role in directing the histories of the place and its people. These queens were closely associated with the region/area in which they played a defining role in the nineteenth century. A few queens have been immortalized in people's memories, in their folk songs.

The Rani of Sirmur and the Rani of Sikkim played their part in the making of history in the regions on the Indian frontiers. They shrewdly negotiated using diplomatic skills far ahead of their age. Represented as evil and cunning, the Rani of Sikkim was portrayed to carry on with her machinations in collaboration with the Diwan of Sikkim, due to the Raja's frail health. There is a subtle hint that she was a 'foreigner', being of Tibetan origin.[54]

---

[54] H.H. Risley, iv and ix.

These political games by the East India Company are similar to today's political rhetoric, where 'outsiders' and nationalism have become a way of differentiating 'us' from 'them'.

None of these queens was aspiring to be role models, and yet they tried to live up to the expectations of their times. Sometimes they broke the normative structures and sometimes, adhered to them. Many of them came from ordinary backgrounds but lived extraordinary lives. The British projected themselves as the saviour of the upper-caste and ruling-class women.[55] But they were not the victims who needed to be rescued by the 'white man'.[56] Janaki Nair, citing Linda Gordon's argument, questions this frame of women as victims, as it makes it too simple to understand these women's complicated lives.[57] By categorizing many of these queens as 'heroines' in the modern-day propaganda and glorifying them with a halo of 'the ideal woman' traps them in a particular image. Their larger-than-life imagery deliberately obfuscates their challenges as women and as individuals. These women fought alongside men and women of different caste and creed without inhibitions. There is a need to retrieve their voices and understand the historical context to which these women, like queens and as individuals, respond.

I attempt to explore the vulnerabilities of these queens as women and their strengths as women and sovereigns. Can we look at their struggles only in patriotic or nationalistic frames? Did these women fight for the land they lived in, or for the tradition and legacy of the family they were wedded into? Were their policies people-centric or just confined to fighting for the

---

[55] Shuchi Kapila, 211–241.

[56] Ibid., 215.

[57] Janaki Nair, 'On the Question of Agency in Indian Feminist Historiography', in Gender & History, Vol. 6, No. 1, April 1994, 82–100, 83.

survival of their principalities and kingdoms? Did they fight to uphold a tradition which was no longer in keeping with the changing times? Were they trying to introduce the 'progressive' ideas by 'imitating' the English colonists? Did these queens challenge the social norms of their times? These are some of the questions that I would like to discuss.

The histories of these queens are political histories of their times. The Company Raj used inducements, coercion, diplomacy, persuasion, negotiation and manipulation to enforce their political will on the Indian rulers and legitimize their actions as reasonable and just. Like their male counterparts, the ranis were also first drawn into the mesh of alliances and the subsidiary state system, which the Company created in the early nineteenth century. The imperial officials documented the events in the files of the Political Department.[58] The records focus on the English officers adhering to the rules, and the breach of the treaty terms by the Indian rulers. An attention to the responses of the Indian rulers indicates a suppressed narrative—that treaties with the rulers were either drawn up by inducements or by the force of an unequal power equation. It is the history of the disempowerment of the princely states. The language of the treaties was English—the subtleties of language being thereby unfamiliar to the Indian rulers. The facts and arguments in the files were presented in a manner in which the point of view of the Indian rulers was either ignored or rejected or shown to be unreasonable or irrational.

The purpose was the territorial and economic avarice, in which the army of English officers acted as the frontmen for the far larger imperial designs. In the imperial archives, the Company officials came across as reasonable and paternalistic towards the

---

[58] The Foreign (Political) Department Files are available in the National Archives of India, New Delhi.

Indian people, while the Indian rulers were described as unjust, selfish, capricious, exploitative and indulgent, as happened in the case of Maharani Jindan, the widow of Maharaja Ranjit Singh. There is an orientalist stereotyping of the Indian rulers and Indian women in particular.[59] The imperial records hint at her moral transgressions, giving an impression of her incompetence as the regent and guardian of her minor son, Maharaja Duleep Singh.[60] The English justified taking over Punjab and removing Maharaja Duleep Singh from her care on these grounds. It exonerated the English authorities of any wrongdoing by separating the mother from her son. After the death of Maharaja Ranjit Singh, followed by deaths in quick succession of his successors, Maharani Jindan negotiated with treachery and intrigue hovering around her and her son, where death followed at every step. Any false step by her would have unintended consequences.

Colonial archives are also gendered, and the experiences of women are peripheral in the archival records. It is challenging to even get the proper names of the ranis in the imperial archival documents.[61] In the entire event of Kittur, Rani Chennamma is addressed very rarely by her name. Similar is the case of Maharani Jindan or the Sikkim queen. But the most obscure is Rani of Sirmur whose name is still unknown, despite attempts

---

[59] Thomas R. Metcalf argues India being defined by 'sensual indulgence', creating 'in the British view, "effeminate" men as well as "degraded" women', 104.

[60] Communications in the Political Department, 1848–49, National Archives of India, New Delhi.

[61] These are the records in the National Archives of India, especially the Foreign Department records of the British Empire. For a detailed understanding of the records of the Raj, please refer to Sabyasachi Bhattacharya's *Archiving the British Raj: History of the Archival Policy of the Government of India, with Selected Documents, 1858-1947* (New Delhi: Oxford University Press, 2019).

to trace her name in the genealogical records of the Sirmur royal family tree. She is famous as 'Guleri Rani', after the principality of Guler in Kangra, from where she came. The history of a place and its people becomes important when almost every queen is associated with the place as a principality. According to Nicholas Dirks, 'rights to landholding were political rights', intertwined with the royal honour.[62] So the queens are invariably associated with the place, that is, their marital home. Judith Bannett states that 'Women as a group are *disempowered compared to men of their group*'.[63] In India, women are bound by tradition and patriarchy, alongside the caste oppression. Queens under study had been married at a very young age to the rulers almost twice their age, who had many wives. They had the responsibility of bearing a male child as the heir to the throne and following the traditional conventions in society. They were to be the champions of tradition. Queens of the nineteenth century faced the masculinities and patriarchy of the imperial system, with the weight of the tradition of the patriarchal Indian society.

The British have left behind massive archival records compared to the knowledge produced by the Indians, especially in terms of written accounts.[64] It is a narrative of power in which

---

[62] Nicholas B. Dirks, *The Hollow Crown: Ethnohistory of an Indian Kingdom*, (Ann Arbor: The University of Michigan Press, 1996), 7.

[63] Judith M. Bannett, 'Women's history: A Study in Continuity and Change', in *Women's History Review*, Vol. 2, No. 2, 1993, 173–184, 177.

[64] The argument is derived from Michel-Rolph Trouillot, *Silencing the Past: Power and the Production of History*, (Boston: Beacon Press, 2015), (20th-century edition). Connecting history and power, he writes: 'the production of historical narratives involves the uneven contribution of competing groups and individuals who have unequal access to the means for such production', 17.

an event is recorded in detail as a testimony of what happened—
an eyewitness account. The authenticity of the archival records
is stressed. But are these narratives neutral? No. There lie some
silences and actions of individual people projected in a particular
manner to channelize into a specific way of thinking. Repetitions
reinforced a description in the other official documents of the
times like the gazetteers, and the travel accounts and memoirs.
In many ways, the archives foreground 'the agency of white,
Western, male actors' as 'manifest in much of the British
historiography'.[65] In this book, the archives have been revisited
to understand the silence, particularly in terms of gender, and
place them with the popular folk narratives to unearth the
new histories of women. The book examines certain specific
events, 'capturing exemplary moments'.[66] It does not present the
narratives of their entire lives.

But in these very imperial archives,[67] we can find the stories
of resistance by the queens in the form of petitions. The actions of
queens follow what Padma Anagol observes: 'A study of Indian
women's agency reveals that, in a majority of cases, women
started with conciliatory forms of negotiation and only when
they failed did they turn to more aggressive forms of resistance.'[68]
These queens exercise agency in different ways: through
petitions by asserting their position, resistance by challenging to
overthrow the existing power structures or by subversion, which
again can be layered. Angma Dey Jhala, while writing on the
courtly women of the late nineteenth century, makes interesting

---

[65] Priyamvada Gopal, *Insurgent Empire: Anticolonial Resistance and British Dissent*, (New Delhi, India: Simon & Schuster, 2019); Location 324 of 12705.

[66] Gopal, location 761 of 12705.

[67] Imperial Archives consulted from the National Archives of India, New Delhi.

[68] Anagol, 615.

observations, applicable to the early nineteenth-century politics. She writes: 'During the colonial period, Zenana women were significant agents in matters of state succession, dynastic alliance and the question of colonial law versus indigenous practice. They served as subtle resistors against British imperialism as well as local, patriarchal hierarchies.'[69] The inconsistency of the British policy with regard to succession comes in Dey's discussion. She cites the role of the Begum of Bhopal in choosing the successor in 1820, and in 1843, when Junkoji Rao Sindhia[70] of Gwalior died without a male heir, 'his widow fixed the adoption.'[71] She wrote quoting the Political Agent: 'the mother of each adheres to the cause of her own child as hunted tigress to her cubs.'[72] A similar unreliability and inconsistency of the British officials emerge in their dealings with Sirmur, Kittur, Jhansi or Tehree, which will be discussed at length.

Microhistory

Removed from the vast canvas of nineteenth-century India, the book examines the 'microhistories' of the events and individual queens in the nineteenth century. In the historiography, some historical characters like Maharani Lakshmi Bai and Begum Zeenat Mahal[73] (though at the margins) find their place, but what

---

[69] Angma Dey Jhala, *Courtly Indian Women in Late Imperial India*, (London: Pickering & Chatto, 2008), 2.

[70] The spelling of Sindhia in the colonial archives.

[71] Angma Dey Jhala, 51.

[72] Ibid., 54.

[73] Zeenat Mahal is peripheral to the history of her period and very little research has been done on her presence in the court of the last Mughal Emperor. The impressions about her in English records— official colonial archives, and in the works of Robert Montgomery Martin, *The Indian Empire: Illustrated,* (London: Print and Publishing

brought them into the Revolt is mentioned under the policy of Doctrine of Lapse or an issue of succession. What remains mostly missing is the arbitrariness of the Raj, be it of the 'Britannia' Company or the Crown. The work does not attempt to study each aspect of their lives from birth till their death, which has been a biographical convention in traditional history writing. The research can be placed in the realm of 'microhistory' wherein only specific events of their lives are discussed to understand how these women, seemingly in positions of power, negotiated the two worlds: Indian and the colonial, with their respective patriarchies. The 'life writings' of these queens are 'historical fragments',[74] broadly connected with specific events in their lives. From those events, I try to build an incomplete biography of these queens. An attempt is on a critical understanding of a person and events—life writings and microhistories.

In commemorative biographies[75], it seems that the work moves backwards from the actual occurrence of a historical event. The resistance of Rani Chennamma and Maharani Lakshmi Bai made them 'warrior queens'. Their martial acts became a lens through which their life stories were written, associated with qualities of bravery and courage. Using a conventional trope in biography of the fighting queens, both fight a predatory animal like a tiger or a lion to exemplify their prowess as warriors. Despite heroism in the political sphere, when it came to the social sphere it seems that they were following the social customs of their times. Though they showed a strong agency while

---

Company, 1899) and Emily Bayley, *The Golden Calm: An English Lady's Life in Mogul Delhi: Reminiscences*, (New York: Viking Press, 1980)—is ambivalent.

[74] Hans Renders, Binne de Haan, Nigel Hamilton, *Theoretical Discussions of Biography: Approaches from History, Microhistory, and Life Writing*, (Leiden and Boston: Brill Academic Publishers, 2014), 6.

[75] Ibid, 'Biography and commemoration', 12.

dealing with the matters of the state, these queens did not fight to change the social structures.

Looking from a perspective of microhistory, explained by Ginzburg,[76] the book looks for 'clues' for specific questions around these historical figures and the specific events that made them the main historical characters. There is also a partial focus on biography as the subject matter comprises the queens, but the book does not present the biographies of these queens. There is a conscious attempt to steer clear of glorifying the queens to avoid 'the danger of commemorative biography, which is based not on thorough research but largely on reputation.'[77] In this work, an attempt has been made to retrieve these ranis' voice, though none of them wrote any autobiography. Yet, some of them sent representations to the British authorities,[78] and that gives clues to their thought process. The nineteenth century is that period of Indian history where two worlds meet: the 'traditional' and the 'modern', and through the study of these queens one can trace tensions between the two in the light of the Raj, both of the Company and under the Crown.

---

[76] Carlo Ginzburg, Translated by John Tedeschi and Anne C. Tedeschi, 'Microhistory: Two or Three Things that I know About It', *Critical Inquiry*, Vol. 20, No. 1, Autumn 1993, 10–35.

[77] Hans Renders, Binne de Haan, Nigel Hamilton, 'The Limits of Representativeness Biography, Life Writing, and Microhistory', *Theoretical Discussions of Biography: Approaches from History, Microhistory, and Life Writing*, 129–138.

[78] The petitions and memorials of the ranis are discussed in the subsequent chapters to pick up the cues as to what is being missed or dismissed in the official files. In the colonial archives, through constant repetition of an argument that the imperial officials feel is most convenient, a chorus is built up from the bottom to the top of a layer of imperial hierarchy to establish that as the only 'correct' perspective. The book attempts to challenge this dominant perspective.

The terms 'tradition' and 'modern' are not seen as binaries but in a dialectical context. My research challenges the colonial assertions of carrying modernity to India. Their interactions with these princely states, especially the Ranis, reveal both patriarchy and feudal values among the colonists. The British perpetuated these regressive forces within the Indian society and even preserved them till the end of their rule.

When the English introduced the rule of law as the fairness of their rule, the indigenous rulers, including the queens, challenged the same. Queens do not wilt before a formidable opponent with its superior weaponry and machinations but show resistance and negotiate in different ways. The events referred to are about these ranis and maharanis, who rose in history in this limited time frame with differential life trajectories. Yet their histories are intertwined with a common historical factor—the British Empire. They negotiated, argued, collaborated, persuaded, yielded and rebelled like many other princely states of their times. Yet, many of them find no mention in the history of this period. These are some unexplored aspects of this period that I attempt to unearth. There are gaps in the record, and those gaps will also be there in the study. We find no papers of these queens writing about themselves. But we find their voices in the representations and petitions they wrote to the imperial authorities, and these give an imperfect insight into what the queens thought. Much could be read from their actions, as recorded in the colonial archives, and the mistrust accorded to ranis by the British authorities. This dissonance again gives us clues as to their opinions. The popular folk songs that came soon after the actual occurrence of events interestingly provide not just the answers to the silences in the imperial records, but also corroborate many events recorded in the official files. Placing the two sources together, one can gather some information on the actual events and the responses of the different historical figures involved in these tumultuous events of the nineteenth century. The events are not tumultuous only because of the overthrow of many rulers, but also because the princely states undertook changes due to the diktats of the Raj, imposed by the active interventions of the political agents or the Residents.[79] These changes do not aim at making them progressive or civilized as the imperial narratives seem to suggest, but to fall in sync with imperial designs, which has more to do with the forces of imperialism, commerce and rising capitalism intertwined together.

Continuity in Pre- and Post-1857

There is a dearth of histories of the princely states in the early half of the nineteenth century. Predominantly, the focus has been on the princely states post-1858.[80] This area requires further exploration. In the present work, the main focus will be on some queens of nineteenth-century India, who negotiated with the British Raj, both diplomatically and militarily. The focus of this study is how they perceived the Raj, a point raised by Padma Anagol.[81] They came to prominence for a brief period and disappeared. This silence is intriguing for a historian. These are tragic and heart-breaking tales of their indomitable spirit, despite the odds heavily loaded against them. As queens, they negotiated

---

[79] Michael H. Fisher, 'Indirect Rule in the British Empire: The Foundations of the Residency System in India (1764–1858), in *Modern Asian Studies*, Vol. 18, No. 3, 1984, 393–428.

[80] Barbara N. Ramusack, *The New Cambridge History of India: The Indian Princes and their States*, Volume 3, Part 6, (Cambridge: Cambridge University Press, 2004); Waltraud Ernst & Biswamoy Pati eds., *India's Princely States: People, Princes and Colonialism*, (London and New York: Routledge 2007).

[81] Padma Anagol, 610.

not only the Indian and imperial patriarchy, but also an Empire which constantly changed the rules of the game to suit their needs.

In the historiography, the eighteenth century has been described in various ways. Sometimes as a dark or decadent period,[82] and at other times, as a period of the rise of regional powers and cultural vibrancy moving to the regional centres.[83] Violence and disturbance continued in the nineteenth century as the East India Company consolidated itself. The Revolt of 1857 is projected as a landmark leading to the end of the Company Raj and the onset of the British Raj. This is said to signal the end of the commercial rapacity of the Company. But the commercial interests of the Empire reached their peak in the case of Sikkim, where the British determinedly pursued their trade interests in Tibet, finally acquiring them in 1890.[84] An impression that after 1858, under the Crown, the British Empire became more responsive to the Indian subjects[85] is a fallacy. According to Durba Ghosh, 'for all the talk of the high point of imperialism in the later nineteenth century, the basic system of British imperial domination was put in place between 1760 and 1860'.[86] In other words, by the time the period of Company ended, the British had completed their political subjugation

---

[82] The colonial historians like James Mill described eighteenth-century India as a dark age, which was replaced by order and stability of the British Empire.

[83] Historians like C.A. Bayly, Sanjay Subramaniam and Muzaffar Alam talk about the aspect of decentralization of the Mughal Empire which led to new connections and cultural growth.

[84] The Sikkim-Tibet Convention of 1890 through treaty between Britain and China was a trade treaty, safeguarding Britain's commercial interests.

[85] The Queen's Proclamation of 1858.

[86] Durba Ghosh, *Sex and the Family in Colonial India: The Making of Empire*, (Cambridge: Cambridge University Press, 2006), 10.

of India. Benton and Ford in their study commented: 'The Indian rebellion of 1857 transformed imperial governance— but it did so by ossifying some strategies of early nineteenth-century legal ordering rather than others, and we should resist the temptation to label it as a decisive break.'[87] The policy of inclusion and exclusion selectively screened the princes from the royal favour. Those rulers who openly defied the English Raj and led to killing Englishmen were never forgiven. This happened in Kittur in 1825, in the Revolt of 1857, and even in the execution of Bhagat Singh for killing an English officer. An attack against one English subject was taken as an attack against the entire nation and there was a bloody reprisal—with a massacre of Indians, including men, women and children, as it happened in 1857. Those Indian rulers who revolted against the British rule were never included under the imperial benefice. Their forts remained in ruins, never repaired—as a reminder of their act.[88]

Law and 'Orientalism'

The time frame of these ranis is 1800–1890, when most of them, like the majority of princely states of their time, fall prey to the political machinations and imperial designs of the East India Company. The Subsidiary Alliances and the Doctrine of Lapse instituted an imperial legal order, which was imposed on the princely states as a *fait accompli*. Law became an instrument of oppressing, not just the ordinary people, but also the princely states. The Raj officials impose

---

[87] Lauren Benton and Lisa Ford, *Rage for Order: The British Empire and the Origins of International Law, 1800-1850*, (Cambridge, Massachusetts: Harvard University Press, 2018), 25.
[88] Kittur and Jhansi forts.

the English legal practices, alien to the Indians.[89] The laws
and the representation of the princes either as regressive
or progressive and under an orientalist lens as debauch and
despotic, went hand in glove. They constituted what can be
termed as an 'orientalist exotica', a part of imperial regalia in
an invented British tradition of an oriental 'darbar'.[90] Imperial
darbars under the British Raj were a way of appropriating and
ordering of the princes in hierarchy. The ritual of gun salutes
bound the 'native' states in subordination to the paramount
power, the English Crown.

One has to understand the character of the Raj as it came
under the aegis of the East India Company. When we look
at the imperial archives, what we discover is the history of
Company's looting, plunder and violence without impunity.
Contrary to the caricaturing of the 'natives' as half-human,
devoid of any moral and ethical values, it is the deceitfulness of
the colonists as acquisitors that emerges. This brings in question
the very notion of civility, rationality and universality that the
colonists claim lies at the centre of their conduct. What remains
disguised and unstated is the greed of commerce and the never-
ending quest of profit for capitalism. The urge for constantly
expanding boundaries and assuming direct control of many of
these princely states is linked to the need of finances and more
revenue to rule India by its resources and to finance Britain's
imperial wars and industry.

---

[89] Macaulay Minutes of 1835 and the introduction of the Indian Penal
Code, 1860.
[90] Ronald Inden, 'Orientalist Constructions of India', in *Modern
Asian Studies*, Vol. 20, No.3, 1986, 401–446; Alan Trevithick, 'Some
Structural and Sequential Aspects of the British Imperial Assemblages
at Delhi, 1877-1911', in *Modern Asian Studies*, Vol. 24, No. 3, July
1990, 561–578.

It is also the time of transition from the indigenous legal system to the 'new' legal system, which the senior East India representatives like Lord Dalhousie attempted to use to legitimize their policies as a sound legal system on succession issues. The dominant Utilitarian ideology[91] of the early nineteenth century considered all the 'antiquated' practices to be unnecessary and hence to be done away with under the 'reformist' zeal. The princely states were an extension of those outmoded systems that had to go. The Doctrine of Lapse was an instrument to directly seize the princely states with an eye on commercial and financial resources of these states. The concept of the 'rule of law' was floated to make legal an illegal act of assuming the territories of the hapless rulers. The Company's method of entering into a formal 'legal' agreement with the rulers began with the subsidiary alliances, imposing unreasonable terms on the Indian princes. The rule of law as understood in the European context was underlined as universal and not something particular to Europe.[92] European laws were universalized under the global imperial order established by the European colonial expansion.

Like the impression of the benign nature of India's colonial rule, by constant comparisons to its predecessors, the so-called 'Muslim rule',[93] the British attempted to deny the story of

---

[91] In the early nineteenth century, the Utilitarian School of thought of Jeremy Bentham influenced many Governor Generals in India to introduce legislative reforms to remove practices like Sati. Lord William Bentinck and Lord Dalhousie were associated with such liberal underpinnings. For details, please refer: 'Liberalism and Empire', Chapter 2 in Thomas R. Metcalf, 28-65.

[92] Fredrick Cooper and Anne Laura Stoler, *Tensions of Empire: Colonial Cultures in a Bourgeois World*, (Berkeley: University of California Press, 1997), Preface, ix.

[93] James Mill in his work, *The History of British India*, (London: Piper, Stephenson and Spence, 1858) (4 volumes).

colonial violence. It is a story which has now started to emerge
in the works of Elizabeth Kolsky[94] and other historians[95] in the
recent trends in historiography. Unfortunately, these deliberate
distortions in representing ancient and medieval Indian
histories have found a place in Indian politics. While such
contemporary political ideologies lean on the imperial ideas
on Indian history, dividing Indian history under the 'Hindu'
and 'Muslim' period,[96] these phantasmagorias of the past have
come to haunt the Indian political life today. These political
views have conveniently ignored the violence unleashed by the
colonial state and that needs to be articulated and foregrounded
by today's historians.

Aime Cesaire, in his 'Discourse on Colonialism' traces
the pattern of colonial violence in the colonized countries.
The white world of the colonists ridicules and belittles the
'others', reducing them to 'animals' to justify their bestiality.[97]
Aime Cesaire states that colonization was not for the purpose
of philanthropy or civilization or to remove the tyranny of
death, disease and ignorance or evangelical pursuits.[98] It was
so in the early days led by adventurers, semi–literate merchants
and shopkeepers, mercenaries, sailors and pirates. As he says,

---

[94] Elizabeth Kolsky, *Colonial Justice in British India: White Violence and
the Rule of Law*, (Cambridge: Cambridge University Press, 2011).

[95] Jordanna Bailkin, 'The Boot and the Spleen: When Was Murder
Possible in British India?', in *Comparative Studies in Society and History*,
Vol. 48, No. 2, April 2006, 462–493, where she 'analyzes the illegal
deployment of deadly violence by Britons in India', 462.

[96] James Mill in his book, *The History of British India*, described the
periods of ancient and medieval India as 'Of the Hindu' and 'Of
the Muslim.'

[97] Aime Cesaire, *Discourse on Colonialism*, Monthly Review Press,
1972, 1–31.

[98] Ibid., 2.

the apologists came later to legitimize colonial conquest with all its violence in the frame of civilization and barbarism. The colonists superimposed their 'superior' culture on the 'barbaric'[99] pagans, thereby condoning their savagery, destruction of villages and human lives—laying waste the land and people of the colony. Their 'savagery'[100] is evident in the treaties they violated, lies they told and military expeditions they carried out with impunity,[101] subduing the colonized who voiced their objection to broken words, silencing them by military force and torturing and imprisoning those who defied them. By the process of 'thing-ification',[102] rulers and the people of the colony were debased, and their actions dismissed or violently set aside. The colonists perpetuated 'the survival of the local pasts in their most pernicious aspects'[103] by artificially supporting the feudal elite and the princely states as their loyal collaborators. These feudal elements became complicit in the colonial enterprise, 'rendering their tyranny more effective and more efficient'.[104] Those princely states that crossed their paths were suppressed with horrifying massacres. Their forts were left destroyed and desacralized to instill fear in the hearts of the colonized. In their urge of conquest, the colonized became de-civilized and criminalized.

Achille Mbembe observed that 'in the wake of decolonisation, war (in the figure of conquest and occupation, of terror and counterinsurgency) has become the sacrament

---

[99] Ibid.

[100] Ibid., 3.

[101] In the chapters, the deceptions by the British officials and military expeditions are discussed at length.

[102] Cesaire, a certain objectification of the colonized, dismissing them, 6.

[103] Cesaire, 8.

[104] Cesaire, 8.

of our times, at this, the turn of the twenty-first century'.[105]
Something was ruined forever, and the razed forts of Jhansi
and Kittur are emblematic of such ruins of colonial violence.
The bestiality and depravity of such acts remain unmatched
by any acts of the colonized. The violence on the colonized
was not chosen by these people; it was inflicted on them by
the countries[106] looking out for their commerce and profits.
It was 'the manifestation of a corrupted and impenitent
despotism, one that rested on the abject degradation of those
whom one had enslaved'.[107] Resistance resulted 'in the most
spectacular forms of cruelty [having] free rein, whether it
comes to injuring bodies, torture, or summary executions'.[108]
The Empire always remained in a state of war. 'Moreover,
the wars of conquest were asymmetrical wars from start
to finish.'[109]

The English imposed European laws as universal and
authoritative, treating the Indian rulers with a certain degree
of contempt and inferiority. The projection of Indian princes
as extensions of 'Oriental Despotism',[110] a theory that became
popular in eighteenth-century Europe, justified the European
expansion and acquisition of territories in India. The depiction

---

[105] 'Introduction', Necropolitics, Achille Mbembe and Steve
Corcoran, (Durham and London: Duke University Press, 2019), 2.
[106] All the countries in Europe that were colonizing outside Europe,
like the Spanish, the Dutch, the French and the Portuguese, along
with England.
[107] Mbembe, 18.
[108] Ibid., 19.
[109] Ibid., 24.
[110] Franco Venturi. 'Oriental Despotism', in *Journal of the History of
Ideas*, January–March, 1963, Vol. 24, No. 1, 1963, 133–142; Rolando
Minuti, 'Oriental Despotism', in *European History Online*, http//www.
ieg-ego.eu, ISSN2192-7405.

of the despotism of princes was based on the premise that these princes did not follow any law and subjects of these princely states were nothing more than beasts. Hence, the laws of the civilized world, that is Europe, were to be made applicable to stop the 'excesses' of the rulers as a 'protection' to the people. The Europeans in India had deep commercial and trading interests and a sole motivating factor for the English merchant, the soldier, an official or an individual travelling to India was to 'amass' in a short time a fortune 'what his homeland would not give him in a hundred'.[111] With a growing sense of superiority and privilege both cultural and racial, unrealistic financial expectations grew based on the practice of commerce underwritten by military power. Accounts by many such European individuals simply ignored the constraints on the capabilities of these rulers, in the form of their legal texts and interpreters. The local people, unaware as they are, do not question these depictions of the 'foreign lands'.

Lauren Benton and Lisa Ford argue persuasively how the British Empire used the 'projects of legal ethnography', that is, collecting details on the local laws, customs and practices to 'better nest eccentric local systems'.[112] This knowledge was then applied in the law of succession to the various princely states. Most of the colonial officers had no training in law. The British were 'fashioning a single, if flexible, imperial legal order'.[113] The British were welding in traditional practices into what Benton and Ford call a 'diffuse despotism',[114] in which the 'British agents manoeuvred to define a legal fore of uneven effect to multiple

---

[111] Jennifer Pitts, *Boundaries of the International Law and Empire*, (Cambridge, Massachusetts, London: Harvard University Press, 2018), 61.
[112] Benton and Ford, 14–15.
[113] Ibid., 18.
[114] Ibid., 17.

sovereignties to recognise, tolerate, or even support British intervention and commercial exploitation'.[115]

In the British actions in the princely states of the period under study, one finds that the British linked 'claims of protection with annexation'[116] in the interests of people from the supposed arbitrariness of the 'unjust legal system' in the states, or it could be the *debauchery* (emphasis mine) or the incompetence of the rulers or various other reasons. The imperial authorities attempt to portray that they were with the people against the oppressions of the princes. But many ranis were close to their people. They understood their people's plight, reeling under the taxes imposed by the British authorities on the Indian rulers. The threat of deposition of the rulers was a proverbial Damocles' sword over the heads of the rulers. The anxiety of the King of Jhansi and the Desai of Kittur on their deathbed was the successor to their gaddis. Both of them were fully aware of the British intentions to take over their states the moment they would die. Both these states were rich in their treasuries, which the British had been eyeing and felt that direct control of these states would make revenue extraction efficient. In both the places, higher officials of the Company ordered to instantly take charge of the treasury on the death of the respective rulers.[117] Benton and Ford map out patterns in the global order established by the British Empire:

'For British agents, global order outside Empire often meant conjuring other states into existence or corralling existing politics into legible regional orders. It entailed asserting authority over other states' quarrels, demanding other states'

---

[115] Ibid., 24.

[116] Ibid., 26.

[117] In the chapters on Jhansi and Kittur, details will be discussed.

orderly comportment in commercial disputes, and bullying sovereigns into protecting merchants or compensating them according to vaguely defined British commercial norms.[118]

Recent scholars of legal history have drawn a connection between law and writing.[119] Minute recordings in files became part of the rule of law and precedents. Colonial excesses questioned in the British parliament were legitimized by keeping detailed written records.[120] The debate in England over the political sovereignty exercised by the Company in India was explained in terms of what Bhavani Raman calls 'delegated *jura regalia*'.[121] Under the English law, the Company was deemed a 'franchise' which was empowered to exercise powers delegated by the Crown. This peculiar position between the English Crown and the East India Company would continue till 1858, when in the aftermath of the outbreak of the Revolt of 1857 there would be a shift. A legal fiction of the Company Raj would be replaced by the rule of the English Crown with the Queen's Proclamation of 1858. The pattern of imperial domination and acquisition would not change. Only an impression was created that with the direct control of the Crown, there was an onset of benevolent

---

[118] Benton and Ford, 26.

[119] Bhavani Raman, *Document Raj: Writing and Scribes in Early Colonial South India*, (Ranikhet: Permanent Black, 2018; originally produced by the University of Chicago Press, 2012), 2.

[120] The imperial archives were established to maintain records of all the British decisions in order to show the proceedings to the British parliament, as there was some questioning of the working of the Company in India.

[121] Bhavani Raman, the delegated rights given by the sovereign to the East India Company, 9.

despotism and enlightened administration and, by corollary, no brutality and offensive rule. [122]

The twisting of the laws to suit the convenience of the Company was rampant throughout the colonial rule. As Lauren Benton, Lisa Ford and Jenifer Pitts in their research argue, there was no accountability of the colonies' imperial policies as they did not come in the ambit of international law. Pitt states that the Europeans justified their superiority by making 'a distinction between a legitimate state and a non-legitimate one'.[123] By this distinction, the 'Europeans were perpetrating' injustices 'in the name of law and civilisation'.[124] According to Westlake,[125] international law applied to the 'civilised' countries, and India did not come under the ambit of the 'civilised' world. India, in the perception of Britain, had fallen back in the march of progress and was backward and obscurantist. The international law, Westlake writes, applied to the countries with 'common civilisation', Europe and America.[126] India was placed in the category of 'the old civilised world.'[127] In India's case, Westlake states that the East India Company 'as a technical person having an existence in law, is a technical subject of the state which has called it from nothingness into that mode of being.'[128] By this reasoning,

---

[122] The Queen's Proclamation of 1858 cited as the good intention of the British Empire; James Jaffe, *Ironies of Colonial Government: Law, Custom and Justice in Colonial India*, (Cambridge: Cambridge University Press, 2015).

[123] Pitts, 3.

[124] Pitts, 1.

[125] John Westlake, *Chapters on the Principles of International Law*, (Cambridge: Cambridge University Press, 1894).

[126] Ibid., 103.

[127] Ibid., 134.

[128] Ibid., 192.

the sovereignty rests with the British Crown, and if the company 'acquires territory, the territory and the international sovereignty over it belong to the British Crown'.[129]

A question confronted in this book is the legal position of the princely states. What was the legal standing of the princely states concerning the British Raj? Pitts raises this point, stating '. . . the political and legal status of the hundreds of Indian principalities that remained outside direct British rule was in dispute in this period. Were they, as the British parliament sometimes put it, "princes and states in allegiance with Her Majesty", whose sovereignty had to be respected under international law; or were they, as other statutes had it, under British "suzerainty" and therefore without any international standing whatsoever?'[130] As the British annexed one state after another, many legal questions arose, particularly, in Kittur, Punjab and Jhansi. The foreign department raised these legal questions while handling the princely states under the East India Company and the Crown. Did this mean that they should have been under the ambit of international law as it was developing after 1815 in Europe? Recent scholars have raised these intricate questions on the boundaries defining the then national, international and imperial laws.[131] Priyasha Saksena argues that the different

---

[129] Ibid., 192.

[130] Pitts, 180.

[131] Lauren Benton, 'From International Law to Imperial Constitutions: The Problem of Quasi-Sovereignty, 1870-1900', in *Law and History Review*, Vol. 26, No. 3, War, and History, Fall, 2008, 595–619; Antony Anghie, *Imperialism, Sovereignty and the Making of International Law*, (Cambridge: Cambridge University Press, 2004), Jeniffer Pitts, Saliha Belmessous, *Empire by Treaty: Negotiating European Expansion, 1600-1900*, (New York: Oxford University Press, 2015); Piyel Haldar, *Law, Orientalism and Postcolonialism: The Jurisdiction of the Lotus-Eaters*, (London and New York: Routledge, 2007).

actors involved in the disputes in the princely states 'articulated
differing versions of the idea of sovereignty to resolve questions
of legal status, the extent of rights, and the proper exercise
of powers, and also to construct a political order that was in
line with their interests and aspirations.'[132] Deriving from her
arguments, discussed previously by many legal scholars on global
and international laws, this involves the questions of sovereignty.
The modern states consider sovereignty to be indivisible. But
the imperial states thought sovereignty to be divisible, with the
Empire reserving the right to interfere in the internal affairs
of the princely states because the princely states were not the
equal subjects in the frame of international law on the principle
of civilized/uncivilized. The justification is given by Henry
Maine, adding his weight to the historical jurisprudence with
his many years of experience in India.[133] Before 1857, many
princely states were acquired on the grounds of ill-governance.
As revealed in their representations, the queens on behalf of
their states would argue that the states' rights were sovereign and
territorial. Before 1857, these negotiations by the princely states
failed. The British exercised absolute rights of the sovereign
to take direct control of the states on the grounds of either a
personal degeneration or misrule.

Early nineteenth-century conflicts between the East
India Company and the princely states moved away from the
relationship of equals based on the principles of international

---

[132] Priyasha Saksena, 'Jousting over Jurisdiction; Sovereignty and
International Law in Late Nineteenth-Century South Asia', in *Law
and History Review*, Vo. 38, No. 2, May 2020, 409–457, 415.

[133] Karuna Mantena, *Alibis of Empire: Henry Maine and the Ends of
Liberal Imperialism*, (NJ: Princeton University Press, 2010), 50; James
Jaffe, *Ironies of Colonial Government: Law, Custom and Justice in Colonial
India*, (Cambridge: Cambridge University Press, 2015).

law to an imperial law,[134] which increasingly defined itself under
the binary of civilized and uncivilized. In civilizational terms,
the princes came to be considered inferior. By this reasoning,
India's princely states did not come in the jurisdiction of
international law. They needed to be civilized to come under
the sphere of international law. According to Karuna Mantena,
in the aftermath of 1857, there was a questioning of the liberal,
progressive and civilizing zeal of the Empire, which aimed at
a 'radical reconstruction' of the 'native societies'.[135] Under the
garb of this 'liberal' ideology, many rulers were dispossessed. It
does not mean that the idea of progress and good governance
was completely dismissed. It continued to be a criterion for
judging and intervening in the affairs of the princes. The queens
on their part fight for power and not political independence.

It is equally important to look at the aspect of paramountcy
and the treaty relations of the East India Company with these
queens. The treaty laws which were binding on these queens
were not binding on the British. The law applicable in one case
was discarded in another case with similar facts. For instance,
Jhansi and Tehree had similar problems of succession to the
throne at the same time. The British applied the Doctrine of
Lapse in Jhansi and not in Tehree. There they searched for a
successor to the throne. In Kittur, the East India Company had
promised the Desai that he and his heirs would be protected
if they refrained from joining the Marathas against the British
in the Anglo-Maratha War of 1818. Soon after, in 1824, the
English officials reneged on their promise, eyeing the land,
markets and treasury of Kittur.

---

[134] Based on the arguments of Priyasha Saksena, 419.
[135] Karuna Mantena, *Alibis of Empire: Henry Maine and the Ends of Liberal Imperialism*, 2.

The British East India Company had signed treaties with all the princely states. While the local rulers insisted on upholding the treaties signed by the English officers, the English were only interested in imposing one-sided or commercially driven treaties. The English broke the terms of the treaty without compunction, but merely highlighted the treachery of the rulers. The British graphically described the acts of cruelty by the Indian rulers on breach of treaty, but the betrayals of the treaty by the British were justified. The official records of the English are sanitized accounts, positing a rational and judicious approach on their part in contrast to the petty jealousies, quarrels, treacheries, conspiracies and intrigues of the Indian courts or durbars. The picture that emerges from these accounts is one of all-round mistrust, and apparently, it is only the English who could be trusted to be neutral arbitrators. Punjab, after the death of Maharaj Ranjit Singh, is an illustration of this in the British accounts. In the Anglo-Sikh wars, the Sikhs were shown to be volatile and intemperate. Maharani Jindan was projected as an example of such intemperance. The stress on the lawlessness and the absence of law was used to wrangle concessions from the Indian rulers for exercising British laws. After the 'destruction' began the story of 'regeneration' under the rule of the British.

The treaty system introduced by the colonists had its inherent politics. The English colonists had a vast experience of managing treaties to their advantage amidst the intense colonial rivalries with the Spaniards, the Portuguese, the Dutch and the French in America. Treaties served many purposes. These involved an aspect of consent between the local people and the colonists. Saliha Belmessous, in her study, details the political significance of the treaty-making in colonial expansion, which was 'promoted by Europeans as a more legitimate means of acquiring land than were conquest or occupation, and therefore as a way to reconcile expansion with moral and juridical legitimacy'.[136] Commercial interests usually underlay the territorial acquisition of these states. And when the queens resisted, what was termed by the English as the 'violation' resulted in violence and dispossession at Kittur and Jhansi. In the garb of treaty-making, the English tried to project a moral, legal and hence a legitimate stand of taking over these princely states. But the flip side of the story was war and violence perpetrated on the colonized. The English stereotyped the Indian princes as 'despots' and entered into unequal treaties with them. In the case of Kittur, the English entered into secret alliances against their (Kittur's) superiors, the Peshwas, promising them political autonomy and dynastic continuity. Once the Peshwas lost and signed treaties with the British, they used the treaty to force the smaller states into submission, as the inheritors of the rights of the Peshwas. This is what the British also applied in the case of the Cis–Sutlej[137] states of Punjab in the early nineteenth century, who also entered into treaties with the British apprehending the power of Maharaja Ranjit Singh. This suited the interests

---

[136] Saliha Belmessous, *Empire by Treaty: Negotiating European Expansion, 1600-1900*, 1.

[137] The territory of the Phulkian misl of Punjab that emerged in the eighteenth century included Patiala, Jind and Nabha. The Misl is named after the first chief, Phul. The Sikh chiefs south of the Sutlej and north of Delhi came under the protection of the British under the Treaty of Amritsar signed in 1809 between Maharaja Ranjit Singh and the British. This ended the expansions of Maharaja Ranjit Singh cross the Sutlej. The name Cis- Sutlej was a British term (meaning on this side of Sutlej that is, the British side of Sutlej) to administer the territories of the Phulkian states of Patiala, JInd and Nabha, along with the other states of Kaithal, Bhadur, Malaud, Laudgahias of Rampura and Dialpura, Badrukhan and Kot Dhuna, since 1809 (www.britannica.com).

of both the signatories, but it did not mean that there was no mutual distrust and prejudice against each other. When the Sikh forces rose in rebellion against the British in the 1840s, Punjab's Phulkian or the Cis-Sutlej states tacitly supported their Sikh counterparts.

Treaties had two essential components: consent and obligation. Treaties had commercial and territorial reasons, involving trade, land resources and manpower.[138] With the treaties signed, it became an obligation to comply, and in this, the British used coercion to make the Indian rulers comply. Arthur Weststejin described the significance of treaty-making for the Dutch: 'Treaties were based on consent; consent implied obligation; and obligation, in concrete colonial practice, implied intimidation.'[139] This laid the ground for the international law that was used by the colonists to their advantage. 'The Dutch Empire by treaty claimed to be a benign empire by the rule of law, yet in the colonial arena the rule of law implied the exercise of fear, not of love.'[140] The English East India Company, in the course of expanding in India, used similar tactics. While treaties intended peace and conciliation as the watchword, in reality, the colonists actively waited for discord or dispute to expand their privileges and territories. Treaties emerged as a strategic device to legitimize possession.

According to Robert Travers, the treaties of the East India Company in India were based on the principle of equal sovereignty in the eighteenth century.[141] The East India

---

[138] Argument derived from Saliha Belmessous.

[139] Arthur Weststeijn, '"Love Alone Is Not Enough": Treaties in Seventeenth-Century Dutch Colonial Expansion', in Saliha Belmessous, 20–21. 2014

[140] Ibid.

[141] Robert Travers, 'A British Empire by Treaty in Eighteenth-Century India', in Saliha Belmessous, 133, 2014

Company was fighting for equality with the local rulers. By the 1800s, a subtle shift occurred, wherein the 'British treaties with Indian states became increasingly unequal, reflecting both a Eurocentric idea of international law limited to so-called "civilised" states and an aggressive assertion of exclusive British imperial hegemony in South Asia.'[142] What Edward Said calls the 'western tutelage of an Oriental country'[143] indicates that the Western man speaks for the Orient, knowing what is best for the Orient subject population. In the Orientalist discourse, there is no space for what the 'Orient' thinks of itself.[144] If the subject population speaks out then 'it is more likely to be "the agitator [who] wishes to raise difficulties" than the excellent native who overlooks the "difficulties" of foreign domination'.[145] The sweeping generalizations about the Orient were based on factual descriptions of the local details. For the British, it was very natural to accept that treachery was part of an oriental disposition. There was 'internal coherence'[146] in the English that the Indians lacked. Carrying forward the argument, Piyel Haldar argues that the 'deterritorialised excess' is 'fantasised' to be in the East. This 'Excess (or the fantasy of it) has an imperial and tutelary function as a necessary part of legal rationality.'[147] Such excesses also included a moral slant.

These are some of the themes that will keep coming up in the chapters that follow. The six queens have been discussed individually for the purpose of clarity. The life-stories are closely connected to the events of their time, and both have been taken

---

[142] Ibid.

[143] Edward Said, *Orientalism,* (New York: Pantheon Books, 1978), 35.

[144] Argument derived from Edward Said's work *Orientalism.*

[145] Ibid., 34.

[146] Ibid., 40.

[147] Piyel Haldar, 24.

up simultaneously. The events are enmeshed with the decisions these queens took and cannot be segregated. It is important to understand the actions of the queens in relation to the events as they unfold.

SECTION ONE

Fighting with Pen and Sword

1

Rani Chennamma of Kittur

This is a picture of Rani Chennamma's statue at the entrance of Kittur with the flag of Kittur. Kittur and its surroundings are replete with stories of valour of the rani and her supporters.

Let's look into the story of a lady warrior who was in an era even before the brave Jhansi Rani Lakshmi Bai. A warrior who was brave and immortal, yet the history overlooked her heroic deeds against the British. Kittur Rani Chennamma can be definitely called as the first female freedom fighter of India. Even though she could not win the battle against

British she definitely could create a revolution and turn into
an inspiration to the women of the future generation.[1]

The above extract is from one of the many websites that
celebrate the martial qualities of Indian women who resisted the
British, inventing a cult of women heroes.[2] 'Martial queens' has
become a standardized way of referring to queens who resisted
the takeover of their principalities by the East India Company.
These hagiographical accounts might serve the purpose of
inspiring the Indian people, but they do not give a critical
understanding of history.

Rani Chennamma was born in Kagati, in present-day
Karnataka, in 1778, to a family of the Desais of Kagati. Her
parents were Dhulappagowda and Padmavati.[3] The Adil Shahi
rulers of Bijapur gave a jagir of twenty-nine villages to her
ancestor Mariamma, and her uncle Kannagowda held the jagir.[4]

She met her husband, the Desai of Kittur, during a hunting
expedition, where she had gone to kill a tiger troubling the
villagers. Mallesarja, her future husband, also came to hunt the
same predator. He was taken with her bravery and decided to
marry her. She became his second wife. His first wife, Rudramma,
was also a warrior of repute, who fought against Tipu Sultan's army

---

[1] Sreeranjini Krishnan, 'Kittur Chennamma_First Freedom
Fighter of India', *Real Bharat*, 15 July 2018.
[2] Adrian Shubert, 'Women Warriors and National Heroes: Augustine
de Aragon and Her Indian Sisters', *Journal of World History*, Vol. 23,
No., June 2012, 279–313, 279.
[3] Sadashiva Shivadeva Wodeyar, *Rani Chennamma* (New Delhi:
National Book Trust, 1977; Reprint 2016), 36.
[4] Archana Garodia Gupta, *The Women Who Ruled India*, (New Delhi,
Hachette India, 2019), 234; Basavaraj Naikar, *The Queen of Kittur: A
Historical Novel*, (India, New Delhi: Partridge India, 2016).

and saved the fort of Desanur.[5] *Amar Chitra Katha* underlines such popular narratives, constructing the imagery of a warrior Rani, wherein Rani Chennamma encounters the tiger. It shows how from her very childhood, she was brave and trained in martial arts.

The Kittur principality was founded by two brothers, Hiremallsetty and Chikkamallasetty, in the area given by the Adil Shahis of Bijapur in 1585. From 1585 to 1682, the Desais of Kittur ruled from Sampgaon. It included 280 villages.[6] The rulers of Kittur were Veershaiva or Lingayats. In 1682, the fifth ruler, Allappagouda Sardesai, shifted to Kittur. According to the Lingayat tradition, at the behest of their Gurusiddharaja at Kalmath, the rulers moved there to find a prosperous and flourishing township.[7] 'Kittur' or '*kitturu*' means resettlement or movement (uprooting from one place and moving to another).[8] This movement gave the name Kitturu. However, there is a mention of Kittur in earlier periods. Kittur 'till then was known as Gijagana-halli (weaver-bird village)'.[9]

'The *Kalmath* at Kittur is the seat of *kalmath* Swamis, who were the gurus of the Kittur royal family.'[10] The fifth ruler also undertook the construction of Kittur Fort. After Aurangzeb annexed Bijapur in 1686, Kittur Deshagati[11] or Samusthan came under the Mughals, who appointed Rauf Khan as the Nawab

---

[5] Wodeyar, *Rani Chennamma*, 6.

[6] Ibid.

[7] Mentioned by the present Swamiji of the Kalmath temple on 4 June 2019. He also informed that 'Kal' means 'stone'.

[8] The tale was narrated by the present Swamiji of Kalmath at Kittur on 3 June 2019; M.V. Krishna Rao and G.H. Halappa, *History of Freedom Movement in Karnataka*, Vol. I (Mysore: Government of Mysore Publication, 1962), 110.

[9] Wodeyar, *Rani Chennamma*, 3.

[10] Ibid., 6.

[11] Suryanath U. Kamath, *Karnataka State Gazetteer: Belgaum* (Bengaluru: State Government of Karnataka, 1987), 128.

of Savanoor, with Kittur under him.[12] Later, with the Marathas'
ascendancy under Shivaji and subsequently the Peshwas, Kittur
chief became a feudatory chiefs of the Marathas.[13]

I

The period in which Rani Chennamma became prominent in
political history was nineteenth-century India, when the East
India Company assumed dominant political control in various
parts of India. Rani Chennamma or Desainee, the title of the
royal family of Kittur in which she was married to the Desai, was
a feudatory of the Peshwas by the eighteenth century.[14] In 1813,
on the orders of the Peshwas, Mallesarja was taken a prisoner
over a dispute on the payment of taxes.[15] In prison for almost
three years, he became unwell, and it is unclear whether he died
while in prison or was released due to his serious condition and
died on reaching Kittur. [16]

       After his death, his son Shivalingarudra Sarja succeeded to
the throne.[17] In the British operations against the Peshwa, he

---

[12] Krishna and Halappa, *History of Freedom Movement in Karnataka*, Vol. I,
106.

[13] Ibid. In 1776, the Nawab of Savanur 'ceded Kittur' to the Peshwas,
106; Suryanath U. Kamath, *Karnataka State Gazetteer: Belgaum*,
(Bengaluru: State Government of Karnataka, 1987), 117.

[14] Krishna and Halappa, *History of Freedom Movement of Karnataka*, Vol. I,
106.

[15] Ibid., 107: It is mentioned that the Desai of Kittur did not want to
pay any tribute to the Marathas or Mysore. In 1809, Mallesarja obtained
a Sanad from the Peshwa 'confirming his possession of Kittur on yearly
payment of Rs 1,75,000 and of maintaining a contingent'.

[16] Krishna and Halappa, *History of Freedom Movement in Karnataka*,
Vol. I, 107.

[17] *The South Indian Rebellions: Before and After 1800* (By South Indian
History Congress Session), NAI, New Delhi,100.

helped the Company, much against the wishes of his stepmother, Rani Chennamma. He had his reasons, as the Peshwas were the immediate enemies of the Kittur royal family.[18] The oppressive tax extraction of the Peshwas resulted in rebellions by many of the chiefs of the 'Southern Mahratta'[19] country. In November 1817, the British commissioner in the Deccan wrote to Shivalingarudra before the war against the Peshwa asking him not to join the Marathas. Elphinstone, the commissioner of the Deccan, wrote: 'There is no quarrel between the English and you. The Peshwa will not be able to fight long. You don't participate in the war. Remain at home. Recall your troops from the Peshwa . . . '.[20] He also said that if the chief of Kittur stayed away from the war, he was assured of retaining his possessions and would not suffer under any settlement made after hostilities ended. After the end of the war with the Marathas, the British accorded high honour to Shivalingarudra Sarja for supporting General Munro against the Peshwas. Elphinstone recommended to the governor-general that 'this Chief ought to be invested with his ancient character of a tributary prince, that his arrears ought to be remitted and future tributes ought to be fixed on a liberal consideration of his ability to pay, but on no account exceed what he was bound to pay to the Peshwas'.[21] However, while the Kittur Samusthan (or principality) paid a tribute of Rs 70,000 to the Peshwas in 1792, they had to pay an annual tribute of Rs 1,70,000 to the British authorities in 1818, to retain the

---

[18] Krishna and Halappa, *History of Freedom Movement in Karnataka*, Vol. I, 103. The chiefs or the Desais and Deshmukhs of Karnataka 'maintained an attitude of semi-independence of the Peshwa, who was bent on their ruin.'
[19] Krishna and Halappa, *History of Freedom Movement in Karnataka*, Vol. I, 101–02. Both Marhatta and Mahratta are used in the British records.
[20] Ibid., 110.
[21] Ibid.

Kittur Samusthan. They also took from Kittur the lucrative area of Khanapur. [22]

In the war with the Peshwas, Shivalingarudra Sarja helped with men and money. Rani Chennamma lost her son, Sivabasavaraja, thereby losing a possible heir to the Kittur Samusthan. [23] After the war, a sanad was granted to Shivalingarudra whereby, in return for an annual tribute of Rs 1,70,000, the Samusthan[24] would be continued in his family. Under the agreement reached between Munro and the Kittur Desai in 1818 regarding the Kittur Samusthan, the Kittur family was allowed to retain all the possessions since the time of the Bijapur Sultans and the Peshwas; the Kittur chief was allowed to continue with 'all the privileges, titles and other marks of royalty' enjoyed from the past; the Desai was treated very favourably by the British and high tributes were paid to him, according him a higher status than the Patwardhans and other Jagirdars; and all feudal obligations of providing cavalry and infantry to the Peshwas were removed, thus giving them autonomy. [25] This accord seems to have strategically exploited the fissures between the Kittur Desai and the Peshwas to bring the Kittur Raja on the British side. The strategy of the British was to divide a united confederacy against them by playing on the differences. The British promised, clear from the terms of the settlement, the Desai of Kittur that the Kittur Samusthan would continue in perpetuity as a hereditary title to him and his future generations. It seems that he accommodated the

---

[22] Wodeyar, *Rani Chennamma*, 23, 30; Saketh Rajan (Saki), *Making History: Karnataka's People and their Past: Colonial Shock, Armed Struggle (1800-1857)*, (Bangalore: Vimukthi Prakashan, 2004).

[23] Basavaraj Naikar, *The Rani of Kittur: A Historical Play*, Gnosis, New Delhi, 2012, 40; Krishna and Halappa, *History of Freedom Movement in Karnataka*, Vol. I, 110.

[24] Wodeyar, *Rani Chennamma*, 15. There were 286 villages in the Kittur samusthan.

[25] Krishna and Halappa, *History of Freedom Movement in Karnataka*, Vol. I, 113.

British demands to a large extent. Rani Chennamma and the councillors around her, including Guru Siddhappa, were not happy with the agreement as the Desai was asked to surrender Khanapur taluka to the British to maintain the Company army. This deprived the state of a substantial part of its income and strategic advantage.[26] Khanapur was an important trade centre, located on the road to Belgaum and Goa. It had rich agricultural produce, with crops such as sugarcane, rice, millet, gur (jaggery), puffed rice and jackfruit. Meanwhile, owing to Shivalingarudra Sarja's deteriorating health, Rani Chennamma took up the running of the administration at Kittur.[27]

In 1824, the crisis in Kittur aggravated, with Shivalingarudra dying without a natural heir. Just before his death in September 1824, Shivalingarudra adopted a son of a distant relative by the name of Shivalingappa[28] as his heir and successor. He wrote to the political agent at Dharwad, John Thackeray, informing him about his decision. The details exist in the Deccan Commissioner Records. Shivalingarudra highlighted the tenth paragraph of the sanad given by Thomas Munro to the Desai of Kittur on 28 July 1818, stating that 'An annual *Peshcush* of Shapoor Rupees 1,75,000 will be taken from you and the *Samusthan* continued to your children and their children (*pootrapautra*) from generation to generation.'[29] In the letter, he informed Thackeray about his feeble health and adopting Shivalingappa, renamed as Mallasarja, Pratapa Rao Shamsherjung Bahadur, as his successor. He requested Thackeray to continue the Samusthan to his

---

[26] Wodeyar, *Rani Chennamma*, 30.

[27] Ibid.

[28] Krishna and Halappa, *History of Freedom Struggle of Karnataka*, Vol. I, 109.

[29] Political Department 1824 V. No.18/162, 13–14 (S-73.M73), Deccan Commissioner Records, V. No. 393, No.3509, 96. Translated by William Chaplin.

successor.[30] The letter was dated 10 July 1824 but received on 12
September 1824, after the death of the Desai. John Thackeray
cast doubts on the antedated letter as 'the Deshai's signature . . .
is scarcely legible, and that the characters are quite different
from his usual handwriting, which was remarkably good and
distinct'.[31] The British mistrusted Desai's family and questioned
the descent of the adopted child, whose selection they blamed
on 'a manoeuvre of the Deshai's servants, whose only object
was, to perpetuate their own influence'.[32]

John Thackeray immediately sent Dr Bell to examine
the Desai, but on the way, he was informed of his death. He
continued with his journey to Kittur, ostensibly to diagnose
the reason for Desai's death, but more particularly to collect
information for the British political agent about the happenings
at the Kittur royal court. Thackeray was looking for reasons
to annex Kittur directly under the East India Company.[33] He
immediately set aside the succession, conspiring with a few local
conspirators, Konnur Malappa Setty and Haveri Venkata Rao. [34]

---

[30] Desai's letter of 10 July 1824, received 12 September 1824, in
Political Department 1824 V. No. 18/162, 13–14 (S-73.M73), Deccan
Commissioner Records, V. No. 393, No. 3509, 96. Translation
by Warden.
[31] John Thackeray, Political Agent, Southern Maratha Country, to
William Chaplin, Commissioner, Poona, Political Department, dated 14
September 1824, Camp Kittoor, V. No. 18/162, 3-12 (S-63 M-63),
Deccan Commissioner Records, V. No. 224, No. 925 of 1824, 413.
[32] Ibid.
[33] Krishna and Halappa, *History of Freedom Movement in Karnataka*, Vol I,
114.
[34] John Thackeray, Political Agent, Southern Maratha Country, to
William Chaplin, Commissioner, Poona, Political Department, dated
14th September 1824, Camp Kittoor, V. No. 18/162, 3-12 (S-63 M-63),
Deccan Commissioner Records, V. No. 224, No. 925 of 1824, 413.

Thackeray's severity in handling the affairs of Kittur precipitated the political disquiet.

With Thackeray's rejection of the succession of the adopted heir, trouble began in Kittur. The two queens of Kittur were Chennamma and Veerawwa, the latter being the widow of Shivalingarudra Sarja and a minor of eleven years of age. Queen Chennamma spearheaded the negotiations with the British authorities. She wielded power and commanded the Kittur army. She accused the English of breaking the agreement of 1818, which had assured the right of succession in perpetuity to the Kittur Samusthan.[35] The petition of the two queens reiterates that the Desai was promised his land's safety for not participating in the decisive Anglo–Maratha War of 1818. The correspondence between the Kittur Samusthan and the Company authorities besieging the fortress underline the centrality of the 1818 agreement.[36]

Based on his various informants, both English and Indian, Thackeray sent his version of the political happenings at Kittur to Chaplin, the commissioner of the Deccan, preparing the ground for annexing Kittur. To complicate the matter, Thackeray alleged that there were two rival factions within the royal household. One section wanted to adopt a male child from the widow of the previous Desai, Veerawwa, while Rani Chennamma wished to have the child from her family be the heir apparent.[37] He introduced a legal complication by claiming that the succession took place after the Kittur Desai's death, meaning that the letter

---

[35] A letter from Chennawwa, and Veerawwa, translated by T. Warden, to N. Chaplin, Deputy Commissioner of Bombay Presidency, 3 December 1824.

[36] Ibid.

[37] John Thackeray to Chaplin, Commissioner of Deccan in a letter of 14 September 1824.

was forged and did not have the Desai's consent. He further questioned the legitimacy of the boy adopted by the Kittur Samusthan because he belonged to a remote collateral branch of the family.[38]

John Thackeray then proceeded to seal the royal treasury, which contained about Rs 8 or 9 lakh.[39] In another version, the sealed treasury amounted to about Rs 15 lakh. He placed his sentries to guard the treasure and the jewels.[40] Thackeray further appointed the two of his collaborators, Konnur Malappa Setty and Haveri Venkata Rao, to guard the sealed treasury. After that he reached Kittur Fort, camping outside the fort walls, intimidating and threatening to take over the principality, triggering the first round of confrontation. Thackeray ordered 'the two guns of the horse artillery, and a company of infantry' to enter the fort. 'The people refused to admit them.'[41] After waiting for some time, he asked Captain Black to proceed with blowing open the fort's gates with artillery. The Kittur army under the control of Rani Chennamma retaliated and 'opened tremendous fire'.[42] The official British records only state that John Thackeray was killed by the 'rebels' on 23 October 1824. Thackeray came out of his tent, and while moving towards the fort, he was shot, 'receiving a ball in his groin'.[43] In the local version, John Thackeray was shot dead in an open area in front of the fort by Amatur Balappa, Rani Chennamma's trusted bodyguard.

---

[38] Ibid.

[39] Ibid.

[40] 'Disturbance at Kittor, Death of Mr. Thackary', *The Asiatic Journal and Monthly Register for British and Foreign*, Vol. 19, in Asian Intelligence, Miscellaneous, Bom. Cour. Nos. 3, 1825, 474–5, 474

[41] Ibid.

[42] Ibid.

[43] Ibid.

He opened fire on Thackeray. Thackeray fell from his horse, and his body was cut to pieces.[44] The popular version in circulation in Kittur is that his beheaded body was dragged to Dharwad and left there.[45] Captain Black and Lieutenant Dighton also lost their lives. Lieutenant Sewell was severely wounded. Avaradi Virappa, Guru Siddhappa and Amatur Saidannavar Balappa led the Kittur forces in this round of confrontation. Virappa was the commander-in-chief of the Kittur army, and Guru Siddhappa was the diwan. On the same day, Thackeray's Indian collaborators, Kannur Mallappa, Kannur Veerappa and Sardar Malappa, were also executed by the Kittur Samusthan.[46]

During the first round of unprovoked confrontation due to aggression by John Thackeray, the Kittur authorities took a few hostages, Messrs Stevenson and Elliot of the Madras Civil Service. To stop the English troops from firing, both were brought in front of the British forces.[47] By keeping the two Englishmen as hostages, the Samusthan asked the British to honour their commitment. The British commanding officer insisted on the release of the two English prisoners as a sign of goodwill on the part of Kittur. But Chaplin was non-committal about honouring the agreement and instead wrote to N. Newnham, chief secretary to Fort Bombay, about how the English authorities had shown 'utmost forebearance' with Kittur, 'notwithstanding a continued firing of Cannon shot from the Fort, at our Posts and into our Camp, at intervals

---

[44] Krishna and Halappa, *History of Freedom Movement in Karnataka*, Vol. I, 134.

[45] In Dharwad, there is a famous Chennamma Park, which is said to be where Thackeray's body was left.

[46] Krishna and Halappa, *History of Freedom Movement in Karnataka*, Vol. I, 133–134

[47] *The Asiatic Journal and Monthly Register for British and Foreign*, 475.

throughout the day, and till a late hour, . . . and no firing whatever returned on our part'.[48]

Meanwhile, the English kept exerting pressure by 'repeated communication to the Chiefs' throughout the day, 'intimating that the period fixed in the Proclamation was expiring'. The English threatened 'that unless our Prisoners were released before evening, no part of the garrison could escape with their lives'.[49] The passage creates an impression that the British were being reasonable against the intransigence of the Kittur authorities. The choice of words like 'forbearance' on the one hand seemed to convey the positive intent of the British, while for the chiefs, they used terms like 'insurgents' and 'rebels'. Such description in the official colonial archives, if read uncritically, would paint an impression of the local chiefs being irrational. The colonial records claim to be tolerant, but in their language, the East India Company officials show hostility.

On the persistent British request and subtle intimidation, the Kittur Samusthan, in consultation with the rani, agreed to release the two prisoners unconditionally, hoping for a positive response from the Company authorities. Under the negotiations, the two English prisoners were released at nine in the morning of 2 December 1824 as stipulated.[50] Despite the release of prisoners,

---

[48] To N. Newnham, Chief Secretary to Fort Bombay by N. Chaplin, 2 December 1824, Political Despatch, No. 146, 7 January 1825.
[49] Ibid.
[50] Foreign Political Proceedings, 7–28 January 1825, No. 14, Chief Secretary to the Government at Bombay, No. 350, Political Department, Bombay Castle, 11 December 1824, to the Secretary in the Secret Political Department, Fort William. N. Newnham wrote to the secretary to the Secret Political Department at Fort William informing him about the commissioner's despatch in the Deccan dated 2 December 1824, 'reporting the release of Messrs Stevenson and Elliot, from their confinement in the Fort of Kittoor'. In

the British authorities did not withdraw the Madras regiment or the cannon. Reading the Company correspondence available in the National Archives, Foreign Department files, one finds that contrary to the English opinions, the Kittur officials were acting honourably, acceding to all the English authorities' demands. One reason could also be that they were aware of the might of the British guns and wanted to avoid war. The Kittur principality representatives again pleaded the cause of continuing the old system. [51] They continually make the request that the right to decide on the succession was the prerogative of the Kittur royal family. It was a reasonable request in conformity with the British assurance of maintaining the internal autonomy of Kittur, which was repeated time and again.

Despite the release of hostages, the British authorities under Chaplin insisted on the surrender of the Kittur chiefs.[52] This suggests that the Kittur royal family had the support of the chiefs and the local population were willing to resist. The British authorities also admitted that despite their efforts by the proclamation to discourage the nearby villages to support the royal family, they were only 'partially successful'.[53] The people continued to support the cause of the Kittur Samusthan. In the proclamation, the English authorities also asked the Kittur chiefs to come to their side, but Rani Chennamma's close aide, Guru Siddhappa, foiled these attempts. Chaplin stated that 'no paper' was 'allowed to reach the inside without first passing through the hands of the Leader Goor Siddapa, who has, of course,

---

Political Department, to the Secretary of State in the Secret Political Department, Fort William, Bombay Castle, 11 December 1824.

[51] 'At the present, however, the Vaqueels plead that the *Samusthan* may be continued', No. 1, Pol. Dept. No. 146, 7 January 1825, Foreign Department file.

[52] Ibid.

[53] Ibid.

suppressed all the copies that have come into his possession'.[54]
For this reason, the British were particularly hostile towards
Guru Siddhappa, and this attitude is apparent when Chaplin
wrote that 'he being the only person excepted from the general
amnesty'.[55]

Stevenson and Elliot described to Colonel Deacon the
fair treatment given to them at the fort. Most likely, they
informed him that Guru Siddhappa was the chief authority
acting under the control of the dowager Rani Chennamma.
'Before the abovementioned gentlemen were allowed to
quit the Fort, they were sworn to intercede on behalf of
the *Samusthan*, and they have accordingly said everything
about the good treatment by Goor Siddappa.'[56] He exercised
restraint in 'committing devastations as he might have
done since the chief authority has been in his hands'. The
British inflexibility became evident when they refused to
commit, while the Kittur authorities 'must' honour the
British demands. This intimidation is being done by a show
of strength in their superior weaponry, particularly their
battering guns. Colonel Deacon arrived with the battering
guns within four miles of the camp.[57] They wanted nothing
short of complete surrender of the Kittur principality. They
kept communication channels open as a strategy to delay
so that they could first get the English officers' release, and
second, to gather their army from Madras and Bombay, with

---

[54] Ibid.

[55] Ibid.

[56] To N. Newnham, Chief Secretary to Fort Bombay by N.
Chaplin, 2 December 1824, Political Despatch, No. 146, 7 January
1825.

[57] 3 December 1824 by Chaplin, No. 15, Chief Secretary to the
Govt of Bombay, No. 1366, Political Department Bombay Castle, 14
December 1824, to the Secretary to the Supreme Govt, Fort William.

the guns and ammunition.[58] Chaplin allowed till 1 December 1824 for the final surrender by the Kittur chiefs, failing 'which if they still continued contumaciousness it is declared that they would be treated as Rebels'.[59]

On 3 December 1824, the British army, under Col. Deacon, attacked the Kittur Fort.[60] Kittur Fort had a five-metre enclosed wall.[61] Despite the superiority of the cannons and battering guns of the British, the Kittur chiefs in their final communication before the attack refused to surrender. Yet, inexplicably, the chiefs surrendered in the course of the night. Here the English official records do not give any reason. One possibility, which is narrated in the popular folk saga, is the betrayal by somebody inside the fort, purportedly Mallappa Shetty and Venkata Rao, British collaborators, who covered the Kittur cannons with cow dung. Due to the moisture, the entire gunpowder was spoilt. The local chiefs had no choice but to surrender.[62] 'In the course of the night,' Chaplin informed, 'the Principal of the Insurgent Chiefs surrendered themselves in a condition of their

---

[58] No. 16, to N. Newnham, Esq. Chief Secretary to the Govt., Bombay, Copy of a letter with Enclosures by Col. Deacon, Political Department, No. 149 of 1824.

[59] Ibid.

[60] No. 15, Chief Secy to the Govt. of Bombay, No. 1366, Political Dept. Bombay Castle. To the Secretary to the Supreme Govt., Fort Williams, 14 December 1824.

[61] According to the curator at the Kittur Fort Museum on my visitin June 2019: Kittur Fort wall had a thickness of 5.4 metres on one side and 4.3 metres on the other side.

[62] This is mentioned in the oral tradition, recounting the betrayal by the insiders, as the British maintain silence on the sudden surrender. The colonial records are silent in which the English are complicit.

lives being spared . . . Both upper and lower forts were in consequence occupied by the British troops at about 8 am this morning.'[63]

Chaplin reported on the successful termination of the operations against Kittur; properties were 'captured in the Fort, and claimed as Prize by the Army'.[64] With the English victory, Rani Chennamma with her daughters-in-law, Veerawwa, widow of Shivalingarudra and Jankibai, widow of Rani Chennamma's son, were taken prisoners and kept at the fort of Bailhongal. The rani did not give up her hopes of regaining Kittur and inspired others to continue their resistance. The people's resistance against the East India Company was carried forward by the rani's trusted subordinate, Sangolli Rayanna.[65] Avvardi Veerappa, who headed the soldiers, escaped, 'accompanied by Kinkery Venkuna and three Gumasthas, Govind, Naraen and Yasovantha'.[66]

Rani Chennamma remained in the palace for a week in detention along with the Jankibai and Veerawwa. They had to sign a document ceding Kittur to the British. A pension of Rs 40,000 per annum was fixed for the three, and the British sent them to prison at Bailhongal.[67]

---

[63] No. 16 Political Department, Chaplin, Camp at Kittoor, 4 December 1824, 5 PM, No. 143 of 1824, to Newnham.

[64] Ibid.

[65] Bombay Political Letters to the Court of Directors, for affairs of the Hon'ble United Company of Merchants of England trading to the East Indies, London, Cons. 2 of 1830 from the Political Department.

[66] Chaplin to Newnham, 5 December 1824, in Political Department V. No.18,/162, 425–30 (S-487 M-483), Deccan Commissioner Records, V. No. 393, No. 3635, 200.

[67] Wodeyar, *Rani Chennamma*, 170.

II

From the above details, one can question the efficacy of the official Company records. The official descriptions were purposely silent on crucial aspects of the acquisition of Kittur. The Company records give no hint of any foul play, as these records would be scrutinized by the British Parliament and questions could be raised on the means by which Kittur was taken over. Despite their repeated assurances, the East India Company officials did not act honourably.

The queens made repeated attempts to address the British authorities, Chaplin and Elphinstone, to fulfil their commitment, the agreement of 1818 for succession to continue in perpetuity. Kittur's position becomes clear from a letter of Rani Chennamma. She had hoped that the senior British officers would intercede fairly to 'investigate' the matter which precipitated the events in Kittur. Instead, they came with the military force and battering guns to pressurize the royal family and their supporters into surrender. The rani wrote: 'You wish the fort to be evacuated—to that we reply that we considered you as our superior and could not have believed that we should have been brought to this condition. You wrote that if we did not surrender and declare ourselves loyal subjects of the govt by 10 o'clock today, you would commence an attack upon us. We were before told by you, that there should be no war, and we're satisfied that an investigation should be made respecting Mr. Thackeray's proceedings that the *Samusthan* would be confirmed on us.'[68]

---

[68] A letter from Chennawwa and Veerawwa, translated by T. Warden, to N. Chaplin, Deputy Commissioner of Bombay Presidency, 3 December1824.

Thackeray comes across as a person of dubious character, who could be unscrupulous and ruthless in attaining his objectives, showing the greed of Company officials for wealth and territory. His associate, Eden, confirmed his rash behaviour. Eden expressed these sentiments to Chaplin: 'I am inclined to think the melancholy affair (referring to Thackeray's death) which occurred at Kittur had not been premeditated and had not Mr. Thackeray prematurely directed an attack with a very inadequate force, nothing of the kind would have occurred.'[69] John Thackeray wanted to take advantage of the confusion over the question of succession to the Kittur Samusthan to acquire a prosperous state, well aware of the English military domination over these small princely states. He arrived at Kittur with a force and battery to intimidate the royal family into submitting to his authority.[70] His men seized the treasury and put their lock, uncaring of the sentiments of the grieving young widow or other family members who had suffered a grievous blow. This lack of sensitivity repeatedly underlines British rule, where the British behaved and acted like conquerors, uncaring about fine human sentiments, which they accorded to their fellow white officers. For a single white life lost, they retaliated with a disproportionate vengeance. They not merely pounded forts, but killed thousands of people, rupturing livelihoods and families.[71] The desire for commercial and territorial acquisition, combined with brute force without any accountability, made a heady combination. There was a complete non-existence of any

[69] Krishna and Halappa, *History of Freedom Movement in Karnataka*, Vol. I, 134, in a letter dated 29 October 1824, from Eden to Chaplin.
[70] *The Asiatic Journal and Monthly Register for British and Foreign*, Vol. 19, 1825, 474–475, 475.
[71] In both Kittur and Jhansi, they continuously used cannons to force the ruling family and the people in the fort to surrender.

international law, and the Indian rulers were treated unequally and without regard to their customs and practices. The English interpreted and decided the Indian rules of succession.[72] The British legitimized their claim under the 'Doctrine of Lapse',[73] an exercise in opportunism. Under the garb of this policy, used arbitrarily, the East India Company took direct control of some of the lucrative Indian states by declaring that they did not accept an adopted son's rights. Other princely states would face similar situations.[74]

The Kittur Samusthan, since the time of Lord Wellesley, supported the British in all their campaigns, particularly the last Anglo–Mysore War against Tipu Sultan.[75] In their representation to the East India Company officials at Bombay, it is understood that the help of the chiefs of 'Southern Marhatta country'[76] was

---

[72] In the Indian princes' petitions to the British authorities, they constantly mention the custom of succession by adoption, but the British constantly deny this assertion by interpreting the custom according to their understanding of the line of succession among the princely states.

[73] The policy of Doctrine of Lapse was aggressively pursued by Lord Dalhousie, Governor-General of India from 1848-1856. But instances of principalities lapsing to the East India Company exist prior to his period.

[74] In the state of Gwalior and later Orchha, the principle of the Doctrine of Lapse was not enforced, although there was no direct heir to the throne. But in many other states, the Doctrine of Lapse was applied on the ground when there was no direct successor to the throne, Kittur being an early instance.

[75] A letter from Chennawwa and Veerawwa, translated by T. Warden, to N. Chaplin, Deputy Commissioner of Bombay Presidency, December 1824.

[76] Political Letters from Court, 1814–15, Governor General in Council from Fort William. In the political letters, the settlement of the Peshwa with the southern territories called the Southern Mahratta country is

of strategic importance to the British during their conflict with
Tipu Sultan. Subsequently, the British adopted the same strategy
to co-opt them in their fight with the Marathas, as many of these
chiefs in the Kannada land resented the demands of revenue by
the Maratha Sardars and the Peshwas.[77] The queens reminded
Chaplin of these acts:

> We can perceive in your last letter no demonstrations of such
> a result you desire us today to declare an allegiance to the
> British govt but from the beginning have been on friendly
> terms with the British govt. We accompanied and assisted
> Governor Genl. Wellesley with our Armies. We acted as allies
> to Maj Genl Munro at Belgaum, which he feeling satisfied with
> the assistance that we had afforded, gave us a *Sunnad* for the
> continuation of our *Samusthan* from generation to generation,
> which *Sunnad*, by your kindship, has been in force up to this
> day – what can be written in reply to your communication
> that, putting aside investigation, you will attack us. You are
> our superior. Let it be on your part to acquire to yourself
> renown by supporting us, the 100,000 dependents who are
> with us, by this course you will be esteemed. You disregarding
> this feeling show a disposition to be hostile. When the period

---

recorded. The claims of the Peshwa over his Southern Jagirdars was for
'regular serinjams'. The Peshwa was 'hostile to Jaghirdars', considering
them enemy and traitors. The governor general stepped in as intermediary
to 'purposely' conceive 'our interference between the Peishwas and his
Jaghirdars with a view to place them in a state of direct submission to his
authority and thereby to give strength and efficiency to his Government,
to be not merely expedient, but even essentially necessary to the
preservation of an important branch of our political interests in India'.
[77] Krishna and Halappa, *History of Freedom Movement in Karnataka*
Vol. I, 107. It is mentioned how Mallasarja was confined by the
Peshwa to get the revenues of the Kittur Samusthan.

given us have expired what remedy have we. It is according
to your own pleasure. Let your favorable disposition towards
the *Samusthan* continue undiminished.[78]

Chaplin ignored the reasonable and repeated petitions of the
queen. Nowhere did Rani Chennamma talk in an aggressive
or threatening language. Rather, she pleaded for the security of
the people dependent on the Kittur principality and constantly
asked Chaplin to investigate the matter.

The East India Company seemed to have no other motive
than sheer avarice, and the term 'lapse' is applied as early as 1824,
for taking over the Kittur principality. The first thing Thackeray
took charge of was the treasury, containing cash and all jewellery.
There was no questioning of the greed and rapaciousness of
the British. The dominant narrative was that of a brutal attack
and death of the collector of Dharwad, John Thackeray, by the
Kittur principality. The official political department records do
not go into the reasons for such attacks, and it is only through
the petitions of the queens that we understand their objections.[79]
Kittur was essential to the Marathas, the Portuguese in Goa and
also the English. The Lingayat spiritual mentor of the Kittur
royal family chose the site and felt that Kittur would be a better
place for their rule. Economically, there are references to the
trading opportunities due to Kittur's strategic location.[80]

The British officials in Bombay disagreed with Thackeray's
hasty action, as they knew that Veerawwa, the widow of the
Desai, had the rights over the principality. While reporting the

---

[78] A letter from Chennawwa and Veerawwa, translated by T. Warden,
to N. Chaplin, Deputy Commissioner of Bombay Presidency,
December 1824.
[79] Ibid.
[80] Wodeyar, *Rani Chennamma*, 16–7.

matter of Kittur in the 'Southern Maratha' country to the Court
of Directors of the East India Company, it was recorded as follows:

> [The state of Kittur] has of late been disturbed by a body of
> insurgents who have carried off with them the person who
> on the death bed of the late Dessoy was attempted to be
> imposed upon as his adopted child; the disorder, occasioned
> in the Kittoor province, by these misguided people, has
> been considerable, but the military detachments sent against
> them have met with signal success, and this with the prudent
> measures taken by Mr. Nisbet of confining the Desainee in
> the fort of Koosoogul, have, we are happy to say broken the
> bond of union, which held the insurgents together, and we
> trust restored tranquillity in this province.[81]

The British denied Kittur the right of succession and the
principality was taken under direct British hold. The claims of
adoption were set aside, and Kittur was incorporated directly
under British rule. The term province in the passage above is
crucial in signifying the changed position of Kittur from an
independent principality to the conquered one. The resistance
of the people of Kittur was dismissed as misguidance by a few
people with vested interests. The rural region of Kittur to this
day remembers Rani Chennamma and her loyal supporter
Sangolli Rayanna. The songs lauding the bravery of Sangolli
Rayanna, even after the imprisonment of the rani, to carry out
her wishes, are recited in detail.[82]

---

[81] Bombay Political Letters to the Court of Directors, for affairs of the
Hon'ble United Company of Merchants of England trading to the East
Indies, London, Cons. 2 of 1830 from the Political Department.
[82] The famous folk singer, Hiremath, estimates that these lavanis
emerged in the late 1820s, after the Kittur battle. Interview with the

III

Rani Chennamma played a critical role in trying to prevent the East India Company from annexing Kittur, which was strategically important due to its trading networks with the Portuguese in Goa and the Dutch. 'The agricultural products together with well-established trade contacts between the country below the Western Ghats and plateau made it a flourishing trade centre and prosperous state.'[83] Nandgadh was an important trade centre for Kittur as 'All articles and products grown or produced in the Konkan region were to pass through Nandagada before they could reach other producing centre'.[84] Mallasarja constructed a fort there for protecting the internal trade. Desanur was a centre for textiles and jute, with close trading links with the Konkan. Sugar cane called bella or gur was grown. Cotton, textile goods, clothes like sarees and *dhotis* were produced at Bailhongal and Sampagaon. They were also marketing centres. Glass bangles were also made at various places in Kittur.[85] Many items made at Kittur were sold to the vyapar kendra at Goa. Kittur in the local narratives is described as a samruddh, that is, a rich area with fertile land. Being in the vicinity of Goa, merchants from Arabia and Europe also visited Kittur.[86] Kittur was located on important trade routes between Goa and the Deccan, with five main roads crossing Kittur. Two roads went to Poona, and one to Kaladgi and Sholapur and one road to Goa.[87] Its location made Kittur

---

famous Kannada folk singer Hiremath and his wife, 4 June 2019.
[83] Wodeyar, *Rani Chennamma*, 16.
[84] Ibid., 17.
[85] Ibid.
[86] Basavaraj Naikar, *The Rani of Kittur: A Historical Play*, (New Delhi: Gnosis, 2012), 17; field research records, 3 June 2019.
[87] Wodeyar, *Rani Chennamma*, 16.

prosperous, with flourishing trade and industry, with an annual revenue of about Rs 3, 50, 000. The Kittur ruler had his mint.[88]

The British realized the economic and military prospect of Kittur at the beginning of the nineteenth century. Lord Wellesley laid out Kittur's strategic prominence in 1804, by mapping out the geographical position of Kittur as crucial for defending the British territories. The location of Kittur on the eastern side of the Western Ghats made the movement of the English troops difficult, as Kittur 'is situated in a defenceless point of the Company's frontier'.[89] The Fort of Hullihalli was without garrison, as the troops were drawn from there to complete the corps at Goa. The British waited for the opportune time to strike at Kittur. As early as 1804, they could see that Kittur's location, in case of conflict, would allow the Desai to 'secure communication and entrance into Canara and Bidnur, both provinces entirely defenceless; and the former, upon the resources of which Bombay and Poona and the army depend entirely for subsistence . . .'.[90] The British also wanted to keep an eye on the other European powers in the region. Kittur's proximity to the Portuguese, French and Dutch settlements, with its two watchtowers to watch movements from Dharwad (the watchtower was called Garha da Maradi) and other roads would be useful for the English. East India Company officials were perhaps waiting for the opportune time to strike at Kittur and place it under Company control. It was difficult to do so under Mallasarja, who ruled Kittur for thirty-four years. His son and successor did not keep good health and was easily swayed. The British were waiting for him to die, not anticipating the strong

---

[88] Wodeyar, *Rani Chennamma*, 17.

[89] Wellesley wrote this to the Peshwas on 6 May 1804, who were seeking dispossession of the Kittur rulers, in Wodeyar, *Rani Chennamma*, 12.

[90] Wodeyar, *Rani Chennamma*, 13.

reaction from the widow of Mallasarja, Rani Chennamma. She emerged as a formidable foe to thwart the colonial-capitalist designs of the Company. Unlike her stepson, Shivalingarudra Sarja, the rani was a strong administrator. Consolidation of power by her led to unease in the British minds, who were waiting for the ailing Desai to die to seize Kittur. They tried to interfere in Kittur in 1822 on the frivolous accusation that Kittur harboured robbers and thugs, creating a law-and-order problem in the region. But it was not a very strong ground to attack Kittur.[91]

Popular lore around Rani Chennamma and the imperial records of that time have differing versions of the events in the 1820s. The two, when taken together, help reconstruct the chain of events at Kittur, as the English records are silent on specific questions. Kannada lavanis (folk songs) fill the gaps in the official imperial documents on vital questions, as a crucial corroborative source.[92] The narratives run parallel to each other, but there are silences on the role of the company officials and their Indian agents in the English accounts and there are no Indian records available accept the folklore. Hiremath retells Rani Chennamma's story, sung in a traditional Kannada lavani, translated by his wife.[93] In the song, two officers in the service of the Kittur royal family, Konnur Malappa Setty and Haveri Venkata Rao, were working for John Thackeray. The betrayal of the two is part of the oral narratives of Kittur. It seems they deliberately delayed giving the letter to the English collector at Dharwad to suggest that the succession occurred after Desai's death and gave an

---

[91] Wodeyar, *Rani Chennamma*, 13.

[92] The famous folk singer, Hiremath, estimates that these lavanis emerge in the late 1820s, after the Kittur battle.

[93] Interview with the famous Kannada folk singer Hiremath and his wife, 4 June 2019.

impression to the British authorities at Dharwad that the Kittur family acted independently of the British authorities in naming the successor. The English also raised the dispute on succession on two grounds: first, no succession took place before Desai's death, and second that the Kittur royal family did not seek their permission. Rani Chennamma had anticipated trouble from the British about adoption, and she had appealed to all the chiefs of Kittur to stand in solidarity at the time of the royal succession. Sardar Mallappa, in their testimony to the English, confirmed Desai's intention to adopt a son and their participation in the ceremony after his death.[94] He asked Guru Siddhappa to search for suitable candidates, who were brought to the court. Finally, Shivalingappa was chosen, and a rite of succession took place at Desai's deathbed on 11 September 1824. The boy took the *Mangala snana*, a purifying bathing ritual, and the Kittur royal family's seal was suspended around the child's neck.[95]

The second issue is the right of the Kittur royal family to decide on the successor. Under the agreement of 1818, Kittur Samusthan enjoyed internal autonomy, and they did not need to seek permission for succession, given that the agreement stated that their right to rule was granted in perpetuity. Further, there was no such condition in the agreement or in general social practice that stated that the successor had to be from the immediate family and be chosen before the ruler's death. Mallasarja, Rani Chennamma's husband, had been adopted by Parvatevva, the wife of Desai Veerapagouda, while he was in exile, without seeking the permission of the

---

[94] Political Department V. No. 18/162 81–84 (S–165 M–165), Deccan Commissioner Records Vol. No. 224 of 1824, 283, Surdar Mullappa to Thackeray on 25 September 1824.
[95] Ibid.

Peshwas.[96] Ganachary Shivapa[97] in his testimony to Walter Elliot mentions the connection between Shivalingappa and the Kittur royal family, from the brothers of the Desais of Kittur. In their records too, the British admitted that Shivalingarudra Sarja's widow could be considered his heir and there existed a possibility of sanad being given to her.[98] Yet, inexplicably this line of reasoning was not pursued. Not just Thackeray, but Chaplin and Elphinstone, the Bombay governor, were keen to annex Kittur.[99]

The entire correspondence[100] between Chaplin, deputy commissioner of Bombay Presidency, and Newnham, indicates a complicated story—a trail of broken promises, intimidation, betrayal and the ultimate surrender by Kittur. There is no rule of law and no proper justification for attacking Kittur. Rani Chennamma mentions Thackeray's high-handedness and the complicity of some of the close associates of the Kittur Samusthan in her letter of 11 October 1824.[101] Thackeray ordered the removal of Shivalingappa from Kittur to prevent claims to the throne. Rani Chennamma objected to this and threatened to proceed to Poona or elsewhere with her daughters-in-law. Thackeray told her to go, leaving behind the widow of Shivalingarudra Sarja. This prompted Rani Chennamma to write to Chaplin. When no response came from Chaplin, the rani decided to muster her

---

[96] Wodeyar, *Rani Chennamma*, 56.

[97] Political Department 1824, V. No. 18/162, 236–40, (S-229 M-227), Deccan Commissioner Records V. No. 224, No. of 1824, 269.

[98] J. Thackeray to Chaplin, 14 September 1824.

[99] Ibid.

[100] To N. Newnham, Chief Secretary to Fort Bombay by N. Chaplin, 2 December 1824, Political Despatch, No. 146, 7 January 1825.

[101] Political Department 1824 V. No. 18/162, 202–5 (-193M-193), letter from Chennamma and Veramma to Chaplin on 11 October 1824.

chiefs and other military officers to report to Kittur and prepare for the battle with the British. The mood in Kittur was defiant, with the people also joining in.[102] From the English records too, it becomes evident that the rani had widespread support. The British observed that the 'that the soldiers . . . are bent upon resistance' and the 'people are evidently under no sort of discipline'.[103] In other words, the people of Kittur did retreat under the threats issued by the English proclamations. In the war with the British, the people of Kittur were on the side of their queen, Rani Chennamma.

It is difficult to find much mention of the rani of Kittur in the Company records. The voice of the colonized is muted, and the political importance of the queen is barely mentioned in the English records. There are very few references to her by name in the Company archives. She appears as a mere shadowy presence, surrounded by the local chiefs making decisions. The rani comes alive in the Kannada lavanis, which seem to have been composed soon after her death in 1829–30, glorifying her skill as a warrior. Based on these sources, there is an attempt to reconstruct her life story. The entire attention of the British records is focused on Guru Siddhappa and on breaking the confederacy of the local leaders of Kittur. Guru Siddhappa is the chief conspirator in these records, and the rani seems to be influencing the conflict from the background. The petitions by Rani Chennamma and Veerawwa to the English authorities claiming their right of adoption under the terms of the Samusthan contradict this view. They displayed their unhappiness by accusing the English of breaking the trust of the Kittur royal family. The Kittur Samusthan, under the patronage of the powerful Lingayat sect and its influential leader Guru Siddhappa, was also upset at

---

[102] No.1, Pol. Dept. No.146, 7 January 1825, NAI, New Delhi.
[103] Ibid.

this breach of trust by the English authorities at Dharwad. The English records focus exclusively on pinning the blame on Guru Siddhappa, as it would be difficult to prove the rani to be equally guilty without proof. Further, 'The punishment of a woman of her Rank would be highly unpopular'.[104]

The rani played a crucial role in mobilizing the chiefs and people of Kittur to fight for the Samusthan. She sent emissaries to the nearby Jagirdars and the raja of Kolhapur to come to the aid of Kittur. British intelligence reported that 200 Arabs had 'marched from Sawantwadi on their way to Kittur'.[105] The Raja was looking for reasons to move closer to Kittur,[106] but British intelligence came to know of his intention. They had always considered him 'a malcontent'.[107] The ruler of Kolhapur collected his whole force to march.[108] According to the observation of Chaplin, the raja pretended to be ill but marched from Kolhapur with 5,000 foot soldiers, 1,000 horses and seven guns. Chaplin sent a communication to the raja of Kolhapur to wait for him, forcing him to stop his advance.[109]

---

[104] Political Department, V. No. 18/162, 263–75 (S-263 M-261) Poona, 31 October 1824, by M. Elphinstone.

[105] R. Eden to William Chaplin, dated 29 October 1824, in Political Department 1824, V. No. 18/162, 3290332 (S347 M-343), Deccan Commissioner Records, V. No. 224, No. 943 of 1824, 351.

[106] The raja of Kolhapur was not happy with the control of the Company over him and was waiting for an opportunity to defy the Company.

[107] Krishna and Halappa, *History of Freedom Movement in Karnataka*, Vol. I, 348.

[108] To William Newnham by Assistant Collector in Konkan, dated 1 November 1824, in Political Department, V. No.18/162, 289-291 (S-295 M-291), No. 21 of 1824.

[109] From Chaplin to William Newnham, 29 November 1824, in Political Department 1824, V. No. 18/162, 523–6 (S-631 M-627), Secret Counsel: 32/1824.

The British accounts describe the Kittur resistance as an 'insurgency'.[110] The term 'insurgents' applied to unlawful combatants. Under the terms of the agreement of 1818, the Kittur family had the right to oppose the takeover of their principality. The ruling family was simply following what the other local principalities were doing at that time. It was not a question of unity among the Indian rulers, but a realpolitik of survival amidst two powers. The Peshwa did not respect the Kittur chief, Mallasarja, which weighed heavily on his son and successor's mind. Mallasarja, the husband of Rani Chennamma, was kept prisoner by the Peshwa, and it seems he suffered many hardships, due to which he was near death. The Peshwa released him so that he did not die in Poona. Within two days of his arrival in Kittur, he died. It devastated the royal family and his first wife, Rudramma, left Kittur on a spiritual quest. This probably impacted Shivalingarudra Sarja, leading to his pact with the English against the Peshwas.

Rani Chennamma belonged to the Lingayat sect. According to Romila Thapar, 'Some of the larger sects became castes, such as the Lingayats.'[111] The close association of the Kittur royal family with the Kalamath, the seat of the Lingayat sect, has political significance. In the 1824 conflict, the political and temporal groups resisted the English intrusion in their internal affairs.

---

[110] Bombay Political Letters to the Court, Cons. 2 of 1830, No. 2 of 1830, Political Department, To, The Hon'ble the Court of Directors, For Affairs of the Hon'ble United Company of Merchants of England trading to the East Indies, London, para 9, on prudent measure taken by Mr. Nisbet of confining the Kittur Desainee in the fort of Koosoogul, breaking the bond of union with the 'insurgents'. But they managed to take the adopted child.

[111] *Talking History: Romila Thapar in Conversation with Ramin Jahanbegloo with the Participation of Neeladri Bhattacharya*, (New Delhi: Oxford University Press, 2017), 226.

Kittur had a history of conflicts and resistance against the regional powers like Tipu Sultan and the Peshwas.[112] There is also the Kittur family's story revolting against Chhatrapati Shivaji and his army's excesses while crossing Kittur.[113] These narratives reveal a tale of resistance to the powers with imperial ambitions[114] such as the Marathas and regional potentates like Tipu Sultan. Shivaji's tensions with local chiefs in the Kannada lands were mostly on the question of revenue and tributes. In the post-Aurangzeb period, regional states like Mysore rose, and smaller states like Kittur tried to maintain their autonomy vis-à-vis the regional powers and the imperial powers like the Marathas.

One cannot read the story in the frame of Indians against the English as such a consciousness did not exist. Rani Chennamma was only fighting to continue the Kittur Samusthan and the right to decide on the successor. The lavanis[115] and some of the nationalist works glorify Rani Chennamma as a brave woman and a warrior. In the course of India's freedom struggle, these women were presented as fighting for the freedom of India, but what also needs to be underlined is that most of them did not fight for a modern nation, but their individual principalities and kingdoms. Basavaraj Naikar, in the first lines of the preface to his historical play on Rani Chennamma, states that Rani Chennamma 'happens to be one of the patriotic and heroic

---

[112] Krishna and Halappa, *History of Freedom Movement in Karnataka*, 106: 'Neither the conquering Mysore despots nor the invading Marathas were well-wishers of Kittur.'

[113] Wodeyar, *Rani Chennamma*, 22.

[114] The Marathas were expanding their territories, and after the period of the great Mughals, their ambitions were no longer regional but imperial.

[115] Sung by Hiremath.

women of India'.[116] His depiction of the Kittur royal family
is ideal. There is no tension between Mallasarja's two wives,
Rudramma and Chennamma. Chennamma, the second wife,
assures Rudramma, that she will live like a younger sister and
never be a rival. The writer mentions Mallasarja's court poet,
Amriteswara, who compares them to Shiva, Parvati and Ganga.
Such depiction continues in nationalist writings. The nationalist
sentiments portray conflicting images of these women as symbols
of an idyllic Indian domesticity as well as of a warrior and in
many ways the ideal of Hindu womanhood.[117] In a similar vein,
in the first post-independent work on Karnataka,[118] it is written
that 'Rani Channamma of Kittur was the first Indian warrior to
take up arms against the British, forestalling Rani Laxmibai of
Jhansi by a generation'.[119] They claim precedence for her in the
annals of India's freedom struggle, along with 'the patriotic sons
of Kittur'.[120]

Rani Chennamma was not as well-known as Maharani
Lakshmi Bai all over India during the nationalist struggle.
In recent postcolonial historiography, we find more details
of Rani Chennamma, especially after Karnataka became a
separate state. The nationalist narrative focuses on her marital
qualities to include her in the war pantheons of India's heroes.

---

[116] Basavaraj Naikar, *The Rani of Kittur: A Historical Play*, (Bangalore:
CVG Books, 2015), vii, 19.

[117] Badri Narayan, *Women Heroes and Dalit Assertion in North India:
Culture, Identity, Politics*, 114 writes: 'An interesting point to be noted
is that the celebrations around Rani Laxmibai focused on her feminine
qualities, which are much admired by upper castes, such as sacrifice,
self-effacement, sense of honour and beauty.'

[118] Krishna and Halappa, *History of Freedom Movement in Karnataka*,
Vol. I.

[119] Ibid., 98.

[120] Ibid.

In nationalist literature,[121] she is celebrated for her martial qualities, which prepared her for her role in fighting the East India Company right from her childhood. Rani Chennamma was well known locally as a queen who dared to take on the East India Company, much before Maharani Lakshmi Bai. The question is, why did Maharani Lakshmi Bai of Jhansi capture the nationalist imagination on a larger scale than Rani Chennamma?[122] Maharani Lakshmi Bai died on the battlefield fighting the Company, refusing to give in, thereby getting immortalized in the nationalist literature. Rani Chennamma remained in prison at Bailhongal for almost six years, a nearly forgotten figure at the time of her death on 2 February 1829.[123] It could also be that Maharani Lakshmi Bai belonged to the highest caste in a Brahminical society.[124] Rani Chennamma was an adherent of the Lingayat community, which challenged the varna-divided Brahminical society and in many ways claimed the status of a separate sect.[125] In post-Independence India, the creation of Karnataka as an independent state with a few prominent leaders from among

---

[121] *Amar Chitra Katha* and booklets by National Book Trust on queens like Rani Chennamma and Maharani Lakshmi Bai contribute to the image-making as nationalist warriors and heroines.

[122] Badri Narayan argues that during India's freedom movement, Savarkar included Maharani Lakshmi Bai among the pantheons of freedom fighters, and later Jawahralal Nehru included her among the freedom fighters in his discovery of India. In post-Independence India, publications such as *Amar Chitra Katha* and history textbooks also added to her image, 116.

[123] Suryanath U. Kamath, *Karnataka State Gazetteer: Belgaum*, 129.

[124] Prachi Deshpande, 855–79.

[125] To read more on the Lingayats, see K. Ishwaran, *Speaking of Basava: Lingayat Religion and Culture in South Asia,* (London and New York: Routledge, Taylor and Francis, 2019).

the Lingayats led to a 'resurrection' of Rani Chennamma as a woman leader.

There is a tradition of strong queens in the area, which the English called the 'southern Mahratta' or the Kannada country. There is a famous story of the queen of Belvadi, who challenged Shivaji when his army attacked the milkmen to procure the rations.[126] Rani Rudramma fought against the commander of Tipu Sultan, Badrul Zaman Khan, to defend the Fort of Desanur.[127] There are instances of capable queen regents and queens in the nineteenth century. The Begums of Bhopal ruled for a long time. Also, in the Travancore royal family, there was a long period of rule by the queens: 'Two Attigal Ranis, in fact, came to rule the whole of modern Travancore in the nineteenth century. The first was Gowri Lakshmi Bayi who came to power in 1810 when there were no male princes in the royal house.'[128] Despite bearing two sons and a daughter, on her death in 1814, she was succeeded by her sister Gowri Parvathi, who ruled for fourteen years.

What is equally significant is the support the rani received from the people from different caste backgrounds. In the recorded histories, sacrifices and resistances of lower castes are not mentioned. But they remain in the memories of the people in the form of folk songs, myths and stories. The folk

---

[126] Suryanath U. Kamath, *Karnataka State Gazetteer: Belgaum*, 117, where it is mentioned that in 1678, Shivaji arrived in Sampgaon. There was a conflict of the camping army with the local guard over the supply of ration and in the ensuing conflict, the Deshagati of Belvadi, Ishaprabhu, died. His wife, the princess of Sonda, Mallavya, strongly defended the fort for twenty-three days. Later Belvadi was merged in Kittur in 1686 by the Mughals.

[127] Wodeyar, *Rani Chennamma*, 22.

[128] Manu S. Pillai, *The Ivory Throne: Chronicles of the House of Travancore*, (Noida: Harper Collins India, 2015), 64.

subverts the silences in the recorded histories by remembering
their acts in the folk or janapada tradition. Sangolli Rayanna
belonging to the lower caste Kuruba community, which was a
shepherd or goat-rearing group, is significant in this context.[129]
Sangolli Rayanna's commitment to the cause of Kittur royal
family remained steadfast despite their deportation from Kittur.
In many medieval Indian narratives, lower caste loyalists support
the rulers during challenging times, even sacrificing their lives if
necessary. In times of political necessity, rulers and people came
together under the oath of fealty and service. Sangolli Rayanna
followed a similar tradition of loyalty to the queen.[130] Instead of
seeing it as insurgency, one finds a tradition of resistance by the
Jagirdars in Karnataka rising against the excessive taxation and
atrocities of the overlords.[131] A Marathi record of 1809 termed
the Kittur Desai 'as a powerful rebel in Karnataka'.[132] The late
eighteenth century was a period of constant warfare between the
Peshwas on one side and Haider Ali and Tipu Sultan of Mysore
on the other side. The Jagirdars of the region were caught in
between these two regional powers. The people of these areas
also sided with their Jagirdars.[133]

The songs of the janapada have immortalized not just Rani
Chennamma, but also Guru Siddhappa, Sangolli Rayanna and
Rani Veerawwa. Their songs mention how Guru Siddhappa
was immediately hanged, cut into pieces or blown up by the

---

[129] V.V. Kare, *Historical Marathi Records*, Vol. XV, 8054, Bhartiya
Itihas Mandal, Poona, cited by Wodeyar, *Rani Chennamma*, 25.
[130] Ajay Skaria, *Hybrid Histories: Forests, Frontiers and Wildness in
Western India* (New Delhi: Oxford University Press, 1999), talks
about the political presence of the lower castes, tracing it from the
medieval times.
[131] Suryanath U. Kamath, *Karnataka State Gazetteer: Belgaum*, 117.
[132] Kare, *Historical Marathi Records*.
[133] Ibid.

canon at Belgaum. The songs also tell of Sangolli Rayanna's
visit to Rani Chennamma in Bailhongal prison dressed as a
swami or guru.

Rani Chennamma was kept in prison in Bailhongal and ultimately
buried there. After Independence, a park in her memory was
developed as Rani's Memorial Park, Bailhongal.

The tales are an emotional account of long guerilla warfare
carried out by Sangolli Rayanna.[134] Long after his death, the

---

[134] *Kranthiveera Sangolli Rayanna*, a film available on Disney Hotstar
in Kannada released in 2012. The director of the film is B. Naganna

people in Veedi, Nandgaon and Sampgaon carried on with the fight up to 1834. The folk songs mention the resistance of Rani Veerawwa, the young widow.[135] She did not give up the hope of regaining Kittur and sent money to a few chiefs of Kittur to carry on the fight, but the British learnt of it and sent her to Kusugal.[136] The rani became unwell and was sent to a relative at Dharwad. According to the folk songs, she was poisoned by the collector of Dharwad. Her last wish was apparently to see Kittur by climbing up on the roof of Chennabasaveshwar temple.[137]

Rani Chennamma's story is a living memory in Kittur and its surroundings. She is the legend in Kittur and Karnataka in the songs of janapada. Local people respect her as a goddess, and no

---

working in Kannada cinema. The film begins with Rayanna's location in a village on Malaprabha river in Kittur principality, emerging victorious in a wrestling match in his village. He is mentioned to as belonging to the Kuruba caste and said to be the doorkeeper by Thackeray. There is a strong regional nationalism of Kannada consciousness in the film. There are historical inaccuracies in the film with Lord Dalhousie's Doctrine of Lapse being mentioned, while historically Lord Dalhousie comes in much later in the 1850s. Rayanna had the divine benediction when the goddess appears in front him, giving him a sword. In the battle, while the Kittur soldiers fight with swords, the British fight with rifles and canons. Rayanna is hailed as a 'powerful warrior', and his loyalty is to Rani Chennamma. The problem with such hero cult is that many other historical characters recede in the background.

[135] Suryanath U Kamath, *Karnataka State Gazetteer: Belgaum*, 1987, 130. He was hanged in 1830 at Nandgadh.

[136] Bombay Political Letters to the Court, Cons. 2 of 1830, No. 2 of 1830, Political Department, To the Hon'ble the Court of Directors, For Affairs of the Hon'ble United Company of Merchants of England trading to the East Indies, London, para 9, on prudent measure taken by Mr. Nisbet of confining the Kittur Desainee in the fort of Koosoogul, breaking the bond of union with the 'insurgents'.

[137] Wodeyar, *Rani Chennamma*, 177.

one can enter her memorial wearing footwear.[138] Folklore has immortalized her action of not submitting to the Company's decision till the last moment, ending her life in prison. Every place associated with the rani and her associate Sangolli Rayanna has become a place of memory. Many folk songs narrate a curse on those who betrayed Rani Chennamma and Sangolli Rayanna. In the rendition of the folk songs by Basava Hiremath,[139] the Inamdar Gowda families of Neginal and Khodanpur informed on Sangolli Rayanna and were cursed. Due to the curse, the local people believe that the Gowda families cannot eat food at night as the food gets spoilt, or ants start crawling on the food. According to a folk song, Sangolli Rayanna was captured by betrayal on 26 January 1829 on Dori Benichi Halla (a small river) where he was bathing. He was hanged along with five other members in Nandgarh, with a cry of 'Jai Bhuwaneshwari' on his lips. His last wish, as narrated in the folk song on him, was that 'in every house, there will be Sangolli'. He was kept in Khanapur prison and hanged from a tree in public in Nandgarh. Hundreds of civilians died in the reprisals by the army of the East India Company. For the death of a few Englishmen, they shed the blood of thousands of civilians, whose only fault was that they were defending the land and the rulers of the land that they had known for centuries.[140]

The vengeance of the English officers for killing the white officers was not only reserved for Guru Siddhappa and Sangolli Rayanna. How they pounded the three-storeyed palace of

---

[138] A field visit to Kittur, June 2019. The park with the rani's bust is located at Bailhongal. The prison where she remained for the remaining years of her life, unfortunately, could not be traced.

[139] Interview with Shri Basavalingayya Hiremath and Smt. Vishweshwari Basavalingayya on 5 June 2019.

[140] Ibid.

Rani Chennamma, holding a history of the Kittur Desais for generations, shows the mindless violence and mayhem caused by the English. With its three bhavis (wells), the palace, durbar hall, the rani's place of worship and many other beautiful and ornate structures with intricate doorways were utterly destroyed as a reminder to the people of Kittur of what would happen if they dared to resist the English again. Today, the ruined fort symbolizes Rani Chennamma's resistance to the anarchy unleashed by the Company and its soldiers in Kittur. The English cemetery, where there are beautiful cenotaphs for Thackeray and other English officers who died in the battle, now lies in a state of utter neglect, with cows lying on top of the graves. The beautifully carved graves, smeared with cow dung, are located in the 'machli bazaar' today, and no one can visit the place due to the unbearable stench. The hatred of the people towards the English in the colonial times has turned into indifference and is represented in the neglect of the English cemetery, which tells its own story in postcolonial times. The English colonists, like their cemetery, are fading out of people's memory. What is remembered are the rani's tales of resistance. Many of the residents today have no idea about the existence of this English graveyard, as the local Christian population use another cemetery.

2

Maharani Lakshmi Bai of Jhansi

The statute of Maharani Lakshmi Bai on horseback, with her son and
a sword, typecasts her as a warrior queen, imprinting
on the minds of the viewers her martial qualities, which
overshadows the historical context of her resistance.
This is a celebration of her warrior image.

On 5th June 1857, the mutiny broke out at Jhansi. At about 3 pm yesterday, a lot of Sepoys having raised a clamour that the Magazine was being attacked by Dacoits made a rush for the place (Star Fort). A number of men not implicated directly got in with the Mutineers, and at once loaded the guns and put them in position. The good or rather the lukewarm men got out again in the evening, but the Magazine is still held by about 50 men and the two guns.[1]

From the inferno of 1857, rose the maharani of Jhansi, Lakshmi Bai, who attained the position of eminence in the annals of the history of 1857. She was pushed to the forefront by circumstances and events that were not of her making. The cataclysmic events that rocked north India in 1857 thrust Maharani Lakshmi Bai in a position of a 'rebel leader'. The story of her rebellion is not very clear in the official records. What emerges from the archival catacomb in the official British records is that before the revolt of 1857, the maharani fought a long legal battle for her adopted son to be the successor to Jhansi's gaddi and for the right to be his regent.

Maharani Lakshmi Bai was born to Moropant (Moreshwar Tambe) and his wife, Bhagirathibai, from the Sapre family of Karar, on 21 November 1835 at Assi Ghat, Banaras. 'The mother named her Manikarnika, or Manu for short.'[2] When she was two years old, her mother died. Moropant was in the service of Chimanji Appa, Peshwa Baji Rao II's youngest

---

[1] An account of the mutiny in a letter written by Captain Gordon, deputy superintendent of Jhansi, 6 June 1857, Foreign Political Department, Nos. 280–8, Supp. (New Delhi: NAI, 30 December 1859).

[2] Mahasweta Devi, *The Queen of Jhansi*, trans. Sagaree and Mandira Sengupta, (Calcutta: Seagull, 2010), 21; Lebra Joyce Chapman, *The Rani of Jhansi: A Study of Female Heroines in India*, (Honolulu: University of Hawaii Press, 1986), 15–6.

brother. After Chimanji Appa's death and on the invitation
of the last Peshwa, Baji Rao II, he moved to Bithur, near
Kanpur, in 1838. Baji Rao fondly called Manu Chhabeeli.[3] At
the age of seven and a half, she received a marriage proposal
from Gangadhar Rao through Tatia Dikshit. The wedding
took place in Jhansi, most likely in 1842. In 1843, the British
acknowledged Gangadhar Rao as the independent king of
Jhansi, with a condition to keep an English battalion there. The
maharani was considered lucky. For the upkeep of the English
army, Gangadhar Rao gave away Dulio, Talganj and two other
districts worth Rs 2,55,891.[4] In 1851, the maharani gave birth
to a son who died in three months. This affected the maharaja
adversely. His health gradually deteriorated. On 20 November
1853, Gangadhar Rao adopted a boy, Anand Rao, whose name
was changed to Damodar Rao. Gangadhar Rao died on 21
November 1853 of blood dysentery.[5] The English massacre on
8 June 1857 at Jhansi [6] and the subsequent arrest warrant issued
by the Calcutta government against the maharani led to a chain
of events resulting in Maharani Lakshmi Bai's rebellion. On 18
June 1858, she died on the battlefield in Gwalior.

---

[3] Vishnu Bhatt Godshe Versaikar, *1857: The Real Story of the Great Uprising*, trans. Mrinal Pande (New Delhi: Harper Perennial, 2011), 83.

[4] Mahasweta Devi, *The Queen of Jhansi*, 30.

[5] Major Ellis on 21 December 1853, Foreign Department, (New Delhi: NAI).

[6] Charles Ball, *The History of the Indian Mutiny: Giving a Detailed Account of the Sepoy Insurrection in India; and a Concise History of the Great Military Events which have tended to Consolidate British rule in Hindostan*, Vol. I, (London and New York: The London Printing and Publishing Company Limited, 1858–59 (Volume I)), 274–5. In between the two pages, there is a picture graphically illustrating the brutal massacre of men, women and children at Jhansi.

The maharani's story begins with the death of Gangadhar Rao. Of the following sections, the first discusses the maharani's long fight, not with a sword as the weapon but a pen. She sends representations, files and counter replies substantiated with documentary proof for each demand that the British declined. Having no answers, they took refuge in technicalities and administrative obfuscations to deny her claim. The second section deals with the events during the revolt of 1857, particularly the Jokhum Bagh Massacre. Many stories of the maharani's association with the Jokhum Bagh Massacre emerged in the English media, viciously attacking her as a fanatic or a Jezebel.[7] A section of the contemporary British writers say that the maharani jumped the bandwagon, seeking revenge soon after the outbreak of the rebellion. The English write her story as one of vendetta.

On the contrary, the maharani showed a lot of restraint in the early days of the rebellion when the soldiers were clamouring for her to join the revolt. She continuously stayed in touch with the English authorities at Jubblepore. Erskine asked her to take charge of administration at Jhansi. To ease the pressure on her, she repeatedly sent letters to Erskine and Hamilton requesting reinforcements when Jhansi's borders were attacked by Duttia

---

[7] Jezebel is a biblical reference to an evil or wicked queen in the Hebrew bible. Major Erskine, the commissioner of Jubblepore Division, made it clear to Mr Muir, secretary to government, Allahabad, that the ladies who were murdered at Jhansi had been dishonoured, contradicted', Home Public, GGS, No. 90, April 1858, that the letter in the newspaper *Bombay Times* 'purporting to be written from Jhansie stating, contrary to the evidence I had received that all the European ladies murdered at Jhansie had been dishonoured by the direct orders of the Ranee, I requested the Superintendent of Jhansie to make particular enquiries.' Charles Ball, *The History of the Indian Mutiny*, Chapter XV, 270–5.

and Orchha. These details will be subsequently looked at to give an alternative viewpoint to the imperialist and a nationalist one.

The third section tries to get all the narratives together, with the maharani taking up the sword to fight.

I

There are multiple representations of Maharani Lakshmi Bai of Jhansi. In historiography, she is described as a warrior queen. There is no shortage of literary and archival material on the maharani of Jhansi. Imperial historiography describes Lakshmi Bai in different ways. The English writers underline revenge to be the prime motivation behind her rebellion. Forrest reduces her position to that of an 'unyielding' queen, indulging in 'the stern passions of anger and revenge'.[8] According to his narrative, the news of 'Mutiny at Meerut on 18th May inspired her with the hope of gratifying her revenge'.[9] The raja of Jhansi, which is a small Maratha state in Bundelkhand, died in November 1853 having written on his death bed a letter to the governor general, requesting the acceptance of his adopted child as his successor and of Maharani Lakshmi Bai to officiate as the child's regent, according to the custom of the country.

> The British agent, in forwarding this appeal, bore Witness to the fidelity of the Jhansi Government to the English, as having been maintained under circumstances of considerable temptation; and he described the maharani as being "highly respected and esteemed," and "fully capable of doing justice,

---

[8] George W. Forrest, *A History of the Indian Mutiny* (Reviewed and Illustrated from Original Documents), (Edinburgh and London: William Blackwood and Sons, 1912), 4.
[9] Ibid.

to such a charge." It was no new thing among the Hindoos for a woman to bear rule, and no sovereign ever governed more successfully than the excellent Mahratta princess, Ahaliya Bye, of Indore. Lord Dalhousie did not, however, listen to these arguments, but acted in this case as he had done in others. The disappointed Rani, a young, beautiful, and resolute woman, made a vow of vengeance, and kept it.[10]

Vendetta was underlined. The imperial narratives on Maharani Lakshmi Bai admire her fighting spirit but reduce it to a fanatic zeal of an intemperate oriental woman. She is described unkindly as a Jezebel. In 1903, Forrest states that the maharani was no 'Indian Joan of Arc', as stated by John Latimer, fighting at Jhansi, which 'is indeed a libel on the fair fame of the Maid of Orleans'.[11] Forrest and Charles Ball accuse her of the Jokhum Bagh Massacre.[12] Charles Ball accuses her of instigating the soldiers to kill the English in the fort before departing from Jhansi.[13]

During the course of India's freedom struggle, the maharani was praised as a valiant fighter who laid down her life for India's Independence. She is immortalized in the folklore of Bundelkhand. The saga of her bravery in

---

[10] Robert Montgomery Martin, *The Progress and Present State of British India* (A Manual for General Use, based on Official Documents, Furnished under the Authority of Her Majesty's Secretary of State for India), (London: Sampson Low, Son, & Co., 1862), 30–1.

[11] George W. Forrest, *The Indian Mutiny 1857-58*, (Selections from the Letters, Despatches and other State Papers Presented in the Military Department of the Government of India, 1857-58), Vol. IV, (Calcutta: Superintendent Government Printing, 1912), 162; Forrest, *A History of the Indian Mutiny*, 282.

[12] Ibid.; Ball, *The History of the Indian Mutiny*, 274–5.

[13] Ibid., 274.

the battlefield, with her adopted son, Damodar Rao, tied at her back, is sung all over Bundelkhand. A new trend in these songs is the description of her fight and valour in a chronological sequence.[14] Another aspect that comes to the fore is that in post-Independence India, many of these women rulers are deified as the symbols of India's glorious past. Maharani Lakshmi Bai's resistance, fight and martyrdom at an early age have made it to the hallowed portals of India's freedom fighters—a nationalist icon.

In the post-Independence period, the *Amar Chitra Katha* and the National Book Trust retrieved the tales of heroism of India's women leaders. Unconsciously, a sense of nationalist pride seeped in. Their tales are heroic, but their appropriation as the pride of the Indian womanhood needs to be seen with care. Nationalists appropriated the ranis as national icons—as symbols of resistance against the colonists.[15] But nationalism as understood in terms of India as a nation did not figure in the imagination of the Indian princes of the nineteenth century.

There has been a resurgence of an aggressive nationalism in the popular literature on the internet and print media in recent decades. Maharani Lakshmi Bai is described as follows in the article, 'Unknown qualities of "Ranaragini Jhansi ki Rani—Rani Lakshmi Bai!"', quoting Vishnupant Godshe, who travelled to Jhansi in 1857. What is interesting in the passage are the allusions to her caste and the varna system, which ascribes certain qualities to a particular varna. Celebrations of such varna consciousness are being underlined in the passage below:

---

[14] Alha Deshraj Paterya, 'Jhansi Ki Rani Laxmi Bai', Vol. I and II, https://youtu.be/JdiU48E31MQ, accessed on 25 May 2022.
[15] See Prachi Deshpande, 855–79.

Fearless fight with the British is what one remembers when one hears the name of Rani Lakshmibai. This "Kshastra vrutti" was created in her due to her following certain things in a much-disciplined manner. Besides, she was also a strong administrator. There are a number of her qualities about which many of us have no knowledge. Late Vishnubhatt Godshe from Varsai (Taluka Penn, Dist. Raigad)[16] had written down travelogues of his journey to North India and since he had met Rani Lakshmibai, we are able to know these details. He has thus obliged his future generations by writing down these things. A section of the Society is trying to destroy history out of their hatred towards Brahmin community and they are trying to devalue contribution of Brahmins in history. This article by Godse Guruji, will help us to know how it is necessary to foil attempts of such devaluing of Brahmins and in fact, how this community has obliged society.[17]

In a similar vein, a recent film on the maharani of Jhansi, titled *Manikarnika*, is steeped in patriotic fervour. The film shows the maharani's relationship with her husband and her immediate family to be ideal. She is projected as larger than life, a perfect ideal of womanhood. Such an idyllic picture in the film is contrary to what Vishnu Godshe, describes during his visit to Jhansi in 1857. He indicates a picture of an unhappy domesticity.[18]

---

[16] Versaikar, *1857: The Real Story of the Great Uprising.*

[17] 'Website of Hindu Janajagruti Samiti with the Copyright of Sanatan Sansthan'. The same website mentions her fighting the First War of Independence.

[18] Versaikar, *1857: The Real Story of the Great Uprising*, 87; Lebra Chapman, in her work on Maharani Lakshmi Bai, quotes V. L. Verma, who admired the rani for her resistance to the British, on the unhappy marital front: 'maharaja was not only aging and suspicious but also short tempered, capricious and unbalanced in his political judgements', 18.

Maharani Lakshmi Bai is acknowledged as an important leader of the 1857 revolt in India's historiography. In celebration of her bravery and martial skills, the point that is usually missed is the reason for her rebellion. One needs to understand the continuity in the patterns of the East India Company in acquiring territories in India from the early nineteenth century to the late nineteenth century. In the history of this period, the story of Jhansi and of Maharani Lakshmi Bai is associated with Dalhousie's Doctrine of Lapse. Yet, this resonates with the Kittur story. I argue that there is a continuity in the policy of the British Raj throughout the period of its rule with regard to the political acquisition of princely states. The pattern of the Company and its officials is similar: signing a treaty but later breaking the promises, culminating in treachery. The pattern is visible in the case of Kittur Chennamma, then with Maharani Lakshmi Bai and much later in the case of Queen Menchi of Sikkim. An attempt is made to explore the reasons for their rebellion, beyond the imperial and the nationalist frame and beyond the actual battle. The ranis' continuous petitions to the English officials show their determination to challenge the British decisions on their turf by getting into a protracted war of words in their official correspondence. These queens come across as women with an agency of their own and with clarity of purpose in what they considered right. The names of the queens are rarely mentioned in the colonial archives, but the focus is on the correctness of the English venture.

The voice of Maharani Lakshmi Bai isn't discussed, but her acts are constantly foregrounded by the British for her fierceness in war and by the nationalist for her martial valour. On the contrary, the maharani does not immediately jump into war. She does a tightrope walk by holding the rebels in check, while simultaneously seeking the assistance of the English. She even informed the mutinous sepoys' leader, Bukshish Ali, according to the English intelligence, that she will hand over the territory of Jhansi to the English once they reach Jhansi.[19] After this, the rebel sepoys left Jhansi. There is no frenzy in the actions of the maharani of Jhansi. She does what is right for Jhansi, and one needs to understand her actions before and during the revolt.

These petitions by Lakshmi Bai, reveal the inconsistency and arbitrariness of the East India Company, euphemistically called the 'Company Raj'. It raises questions regarding the imperial claims of 'fairness'. The correspondence of the Company officials focusses on the local rulers' eccentricities as compared to the proper and disciplined conduct of the English officers. The English officers of the company had their experiences and prejudices about India, and the princes in particular.[20] In the case of Jhansi too, there are subtle hints about the effeminacy of Raja Gangadhar Rao of Jhansi, with his theatrical inclinations bordering on 'absurdity'.[21] But not all English officers were alike. Major Ellis, who closely worked with Maharaja Gangadhar Rao and later with Maharani Lakshmi Bai, had a strong moral obligation to do the right thing for Jhansi.[22] But as we will

---

[19] Foreign Political, Supp., 30 December 1859, Nos. 267 & KW.

[20] Col G.B. Malleson (ed.) *Kaye's and Malleson's History of Indian Mutiny of 1857-8*, In Six Volumes, Vol. I, (London, New York and Bombay: Longman, Green And Co., 1898). There was a member of the Supreme Council, Colonel John Law, who 'knew what were the vices of the Indian Princes and the evils of native misrule', 56–57. But he too objected to the Doctrine of Lapse, arguing 'that the extinction of a loyal native State, in default of heirs, was not appreciable in any part of India', 58.

[21] There are references that the Political Agent F.D. Gordon asked the maharaja of Jhansi why he wore bangles. There are also references to his liking for women's dresses in D. V. Tahmankar, *The Ranee of Jhansi*, (London: Macgibbon & Kee, 1918), 20.

[22] In the correspondence of the 'Political Letter to the Secretary of State to the Hon'ble Court of Directors of East India Company',

see, his voice would be overpowered by his seniors within the
colonial state's highly stratified administrative machinery. The
maharani's abilities as an administrator are admired, but the
East India Company was determined to annex Jhansi. It was an
imperial design based on commercial interests.

The story of the maharani's presence of mind and her agency
emerges in 1854. Before that, she hovers in the margins, with her
husband, Gangadhar Rao, who was conducting the negotiations
with the British. The maharaja, a title given to the Jhansi ruler in
1832 by William Bentinck,[23] was well aware of the intentions of
the British to take direct control of Jhansi after his death. He was
anxious to secure the reins of power in the hands of his wife,
Maharani Lakshmi Bai, who would act as a regent, by securing
succession through adoption. On his deathbed, Gangadhar Rao
sent for the British resident, Gordon, requesting him to allow
the young maharani to adopt a son as per the Indian custom,
'from one of the families of his close relatives to succeed him'.[24]
On denial of this request by the authorities, the maharani
was confined to a part of the fort, while Gordon took over
as the chief administrator of Jhansi.[25] It seems that the British
wanted to directly control the revenues of Jhansi, reportedly
amounting to twenty-five lakh rupees annually.[26] The maharani
was pushed to the margins—away from political hold on Jhansi,
to a life of obscurity and oblivion—by the English authorities

---

dated 4 March 1854, Fort William, Foreign Department, 1854.

[23] 'Translation of a Khureeta from Her Highness the Lukshmi
Bai, the widow of Gunagadhar Rao late Maharaja of Jhansi to the
address of the Marquis of Dalhousie the most the Most Noble
Governor General of India, dated 16th February 1854', in Foreign
Department, Nos. 94-96, FC, 18 August 1854, (New Delhi: NAI).

[24] Versaikar, 1857: The Real Story of the Great Uprising, 90.

[25] Ibid., 88.

[26] This is an amount stated by Versaikar, 91.

after the maharaja's death. However, she was not permitted to leave Jhansi to perform the obligations of a widow,[27] as she was important to the people of Jhansi, and the British knew that. She was denied all her husband's property, and her adopted son's rights under the Hindu Personal Laws were also taken away till he attained majority. Instead of giving up hope, the maharani began sending petitions, memorials and representations to the various Company authorities in India and Britain. She even sent a representation to the British Crown. Her memoranda to the highest officers of the East India Company were all in vain. In a letter of 1 August 1855, the secretary of state informed the governor-general of India in Council of their 'approval of the annexation of the territory of Jhansi to the British possession'.[28]

The English authorities were explicitly instructed to take immediate charge of the fort and the treasury as soon as the raja died.[29] The British brushed aside the adoption to immediately seize control of Jhansi in 1854. The officials justified the takeover of Jhansi based on the law of escheat, wherein the property reverts to the Crown on the death of a ruler dying without a natural heir:

The Chief of the State of Jhansi, which was created by the British government as a tributary and dependent principality, adopted a son the day before his death. We have decided in accordance with a precedent in the case of the same State, that

---

[27] Ibid., 88.

[28] Foreign Department, Political Letter from the Secretary of State, Cons. 1 August 1855, No. 17 of 1855.

[29] Foreign Department, Political Letter to the Secretary of State, Cons. 4, No. 21, 4 March 1854 to The Hon'ble Court of the Directors of East India Company, dated Fort William, 4 March 1854, 'Cases of Jhansi and Tehree two small principalities of Bundelkhand, where the chiefs have lately deceased'.

this adoption shall not be recognised as conferring any right to succeed to the ruler of the Principality, and that as the Chief has left no descendants of any preceding Chief of this State and in existence, the State has lapsed to the British government.[30]

Based on this logic, Lord Dalhousie exercised the Doctrine of Lapse to directly acquire Jhansi, breaking all the previous understandings with Jhansi and justifying the takeover with the help of the official records by stating that he followed 'the trend of his predecessors, Auckland, Ellenborough and Hastings'.[31] The law of escheat or taking the hereditary principalities of the nobility directly by the Crown was never an acceptable practice in India despite the claims of the rulers in theory. When Jodhpur's Maharaja Jaswant Singh Rathore died without leaving an heir-apparent, Aurangzeb tried to insist on exercising the law of escheat by bringing the Rathore lands under the Khalisa or the crown land directly under the control of the Mughal Emperor,[32] the Rajputs led by Durga Das strongly resisted the move. Aurangzeb had to give in to the sentiments of the Rathores.[33] There existed in Indian society a long-standing practice of adoption.[34]

---

[30] Ibid.

[31] Tapti Roy, *The Politics of a Popular Uprising: Bumdelkhand in 1857*, (Bombay: Oxford University Press, 1994), 98.

[32] Satish Chandra, *Medieval India*, (New Delhi: Orient Blackswan, 2018), 366.

[33] Robert C. Hallisey, *The Rajput Rebellion against Aurangzeb: A Study of Rajput-Mughal Relations in Seventeenth-Century India* (Columbia: University of Missouri Press, 1977), 49, 55–57.

[34] Col. G.B. Malleson, ed. *Kaye's and Malleson's History of the Indian Mutiny*, 55: 'According to the law and usage of his country (the Maratha Prince of Satara), an adoption by his widow would have been as valid as an adoption by himself.'

Lakshmi Bai's voice is secured in the imperial records, but her pleas fell on deaf ears. The tales of her courageous fight and battle with the English army have been written about in detail. It is also a well-known fact of history that injustice happened, but what was that injustice? What is puzzling is that in the case of Jhansi, the English authorities were insistent on taking direct control, setting aside the claims of the maharani of Jhansi on behalf of her adopted son and also of a raja's cousin, while in the adjacent state of Tehree (Orchha), which was in a similar situation as Jhansi and had no direct heir of the deceased raja, they did not take charge. Major Ellis questioned this inconsistency in the decision-making of the English authorities. In Orchha, they viewed the claimants to the throne, before finalizing the successor.[35] We need to re-examine the details of the correspondence between the maharani, through her vakeel and the East India Company to understand the arbitrariness of the imperial policies. This record strips the English of their posturing of being just and ethical. Their commercial and imperial interests are apparent in their decisions.

Major Ellis strongly supported the maharani's cause on the grounds of justice. He wrote these observations in a letter dated 24 December 1853:

The intent of the treaties with Jhansi and Orchha is common. So allowing one to adopt a son and denying other to have it will not be in the interest of justice. In the order of the Court of Directors, dated 27th March 1836, it has been admitted

---

[35] Foreign Department, Political Letter to the Secretary of State, Cons. 4, No. 21, 4 March 1854 to The Hon'ble The Court of the Directors of East India Company, dated Fort William, 4 March 1854, 'Cases of Jhansi and Tehree two small principalities of Bundelkhand, where the chiefs have lately deceased'.

that the rulers of Indian states have full rights to adopt a son.
It would be a serious contempt of the orders of the Company,
in my opinion, if today it is said that the rajas, who have been
made rulers in return of their services are not as old as other
royal families and for this reason their claim to adopt a son is
not accepted.[36]

In contrast to Jhansi, where the adoption occurred smoothly,
in the case of Tehree, there was a greater disturbance and
political turmoil.[37]

But Major Malcolm raised the issue of disputed succession
in Jhansi to deny the claims of the maharani and her adopted
son, Damodar Rao. 'Since the death of the Raja of Jhansi two
persons have advanced claims of rights of succession to the *gadi,*
namely Kishen Rao and Sadasheo Narain.'[38] He gave no grounds
for rejecting the claim of the first. He admitted to Sadasheo

---

[36] Letter dated 14 December 1853 from Major Ellis, political
assistant, Bundelkhand, to Major D. A. Malcolm, political agent for
Bundelkhand and Rewah, in which Major Ellis, while forwarding the
Khureeta of Sadasheo Narain, the son of Narain Rao of Parola in the
Deccan, rejected the claim by stating that his 'pretensions to the Jhansi
succession' appear 'to be utterly void of all just foundation'; No. 34
of H. 31 March 1853, No .1/14, 1854, Foreign Political, Political
Agency Office, Camp Kotra, 31 December 1853.

[37] Foreign Department, Political Letter to the Secretary of State, Cons.
4, No. 21, 4 March 1854 to The Hon'ble The Court of the Directors
of East India Company, dated Fort William, 4 March 1854, 'Cases of
Jhansi and Tehree two small principalities of Bundelkhand, where the
chiefs have lately deceased'.

[38] Secretary to the Government of India, Foreign Department, Fort
William, a letter dated 31 December 1853 No. 34 of 1853: The
first claimant was Ramchunder Rao's sister's son, and his claim was
rejected in 1835. In the case of second claimant, Sadasheo Narain,
Major Ellis considered the man's claim as inadmissible.

Narain's claim based on the genealogical tree, which made him the nearest relative left to claim the gaddi.[39] The Secretary to the Government of India in the Foreign Department I.P. Grant also challenged the succession of Damodar Rao on the grounds that he belonged to the collateral family, whereas the succession has only been recognized among the family members of the last two Subadars.[40] A subadar was an administrator of the Peshwa and the first charge was given to Sadasheo Rao Bhao to administer Bundelkhand as their subordinate.

But the case of Orchha was more complicated, and yet the same officer was willing to consider adoption. From the correspondence of Major Malcolm, it seems that in Tehree (Orchha), there were different parties for succession to the throne.[41] Tehree seems to be in a disturbed state after the death of its ruler. In his letter dated 21 December 1853, Major Ellis mentions 'around 10 and 1,100 armed men under Jahan Beg, the Koomendar of the Cannoniers and Kadir Khan reported to be bent on creating disturbances'.[42] His letter reveals the

---

[39] Letter dated 14 December 1853 from Major Ellis, political assistant, Bundelkhand, to Major D. A. Malcolm, political agent for Bundelkhand and Rewah, i; No. 34 of 1853, H. 31 March No.1/14, 1854, Foreign Political, Political Agency Office, Camp Kotra, 31 December 1853.

[40] Note by the Secretary, I. P. Grant, to the Government of India, Foreign Department,1854.

[41] In his letter to the officiating secretary to the Foreign Department of the Government of India, dated 31 December 1853, he states that 'I have learnt that the widow of late Soojan Sing has not joined her late husband's party but remains with her relative the Laraie Ranee'. No. 55 of 1853, from the Office of the Political Agent to Bundelkhand and Rewah, Major D. A. Malcolm to the Officiating Secretary, Foreign Department, GOI, Fort William, 31 December 1853.

[42] No. 55 of 1853, from the Office of the Political Agent to Bundelkhand and Rewah, Major D. A. Malcolm to the Officiating

tensions between different groups at Tehree. Even when the raja
of Tehree was alive, there were conspiracies and intrigues by the
widow of the previous ruler, Laraie Ranee. The raja, who was
also adopted, was poorly treated 'during his minority . . . by
the party of the Ranee'.[43] The raja of Tehree nominated his
successor only a few hours before his death on 16 December
1853. Ellis writes, 'It is agreed upon that the Raja has lived
many hours on the 16th of the month and therefore his note of
the same date nominating Deva Sing to succeed can be supposed
to have been dictated by him before the hour of his death.'[44]
Ellis considers the possibility of Tehree lapsing to the 'Supreme
Government' unless the Government 'choose to show much
liberality in this case for some political purpose'. In such a
scenario, Ellis considers it 'prudent' to give it to the old rani
for life as 'nearly all the subjects and forces of the influential
Jagheerdars' are 'friends of the old Ranee'.[45]

The correspondence shows that during the political vacuum
in Tehree, after the death of the ruler, there were tensions
between the various claimants to the throne, which were patiently
considered by the English authorities. In Jhansi, the Company
authorities took direct control immediately after the demise of
Maharaja Gangadhar Rao. Major Ellis notes this arbitrary act
in his letter to Major Malcolm of 24 December 1853, raising

Secretary, Foreign Department, GOI, Fort William, 31 December
1853. The letter suggests that the money and other valuables were
removed by the Laraie Ranee to another palace. On his deathbed,
those present with the raja, that is Seeta Ram Kamdar and his party,
said that the raja was suspicious of people trying to kill him when he
stated 'that two persons are performing the fatal prayers for his death'.
[43] Ibid.
[44] Major Ellis on 21 December 1853, Foreign Department,
(New Delhi, NAI).
[45] Ibid.

strong objection: 'I beg leave to observe that we have a Treaty of alliance and friendship with the Jhansi as well as the Urcha state and that I cannot discover any difference in the terms of the two which would justify our withholding the privilege of adoption from one state and allowing it to the other.'[46] He goes on to mention the policy of the Court of Directors of the East India Company 'most clearly acknowledge in paragraphs 16 and 17 of despatch No. 9 of 27th March 1839' to allow the 'right of native states to make adoption'.[47] He also questions the inconsistency of the imperial policy and its lack of credibility. He opposes this disparity in 'the spirit of enlightened liberality', arguing that there is a stronger case for the continuity of the Jhansi principality, as a privilege and 'a reward for the services rendered to the British govt' by Jhansi rulers. He questions the reasoning 'that they were not of so ancient an origin as others', questioning Charles Metcalfe's Minute of 1837, which was used as the ground for taking of Jhansi.[48]

Major Ellis's views and the language used provides a critical insight into the Company's machinations in acquiring territories. His defence of Jhansi reveals the manner in which the colonial officers won over the smaller principalities to their side against their stronger adversaries, like the Marathas, and formed treaties with them. They then broke the treaty once the purpose was served. The Jhansi family was appointed as the Subadars of Jhansi under the Peshwas. The British argued that as the Jhansi principality was created by the Peshwas, it was a dependency of the Peshwas, unlike the Maratha chiefs, who led military-territorial expansion, carving out semi–independent

---

[46] Major Ellis to Major Malcolm, No. 36, Camp Jhansi, 24 December 1853.
[47] Ibid.
[48] Ibid.

principalities.[49] Yet, the colonial authorities entered into a treaty in 1817–18 with Jhansi to keep peace and prevent rebellions. At that time, they assured the rulers of Jhansi that their successors would be allowed to rule Jhansi, the very issue that Maharani Lakshmi Bai raised with the Company officials. Once the English consolidated their hold and the threat from the Peshwa or the Maratha chieftains ended, they ultimately reneged on their agreement with Jhansi in 1853.

The Company officials were inconsistent in their policies. The officers projected the modern rational outlook of the English authorities in comparison to the traditional mindset of the princes. Yet, they often contradict themselves in their acts. Modernity, as projected by the colonists, exhibits a depletion of values at the political level. The English political interests based on short-term vested interests contradict their claims of establishing a just system. White officers acted like gods, giving what Kolsky calls 'white justice', based on their privileged position.[50] The posturing of being enlightened rulers of India, bringing modern ideas, becomes untenable in the light of the fact that they preserved Indian society's most regressive elements—many princes with their outdated and outmoded structures and ideas. It was only a political manipulation to keep the smaller principalities on the Company's side as long as it suited their purpose. One questions the 'modernity' that the British imperialists claimed to bring to India and what is alluded to by Ellis in the use of the term 'enlightened liberality', based

---

[49] Appendix No. 2615, No. 1, from G. J. Edmonstone, Esquire, Secretary to the Government of India to I. Lang, Esquire, Fort William, dated 21 June 1854, Foreign Department, 1854. A copy of the translation of a letter from General Lake to Subadar Sheoram Bhow, dated 28 November 1803, (New Delhi: NAI).

[50] Kolsky, *Colonial Justice in British India,* 12.

on the perceived notion of rationality and civilized behaviour which differs from the 'primitive' Indian rulers of the past. The projection of the universalist rationality as presented in the imperial archives is itself open to question. It seems to convey that the Indian rajas and queens were irrational in their reaction.

The Secretary to the Government of India in the Foreign Department I.P. Grant[51] further complicates the matter. He raises two grounds of objection to the succession at Jhansi: 'First, was Jhansi an independent sovereign state?' Second, they raise the question on the lineal and collateral ancestors to dispute the adoption. Grant further raises issues of the sovereignty of Jhansi and states that the British, as 'the paramount power', were within their rights to take Jhansi. Grant argues that Jhansi state was created by the Peshwas after separating it from the state of Tehree. The Peshwa appointed Sadasheo Rao Bhau as the Subadar of Jhansi for the administration of Bundelkhand. He was not a Maratha chief expanding Maratha power through military expeditions, but a subordinate of the Peshwas in Bundelkhand assigned for administrative purposes. Since the territory was bestowed as a gift and not given to the ruling family of Jhansi by their conquest, it continued to be under the sovereignty of Peshwas. In 1817, after the Peshwas surrendered Bundelkhand to the East India Company, Jhansi came under the paramountcy of the English Raj. Paramountcy entitled the British to directly take control of Jhansi, ignoring all the previous treaties signed. The Company officials rake up all possible issues to justify their takeover.[52]

Grant's narrative foregrounds what he claims is the history of the relationship of the British with Jhansi, which, according

---

[51] Note by the Secretary, I. P. Grant, to the Government of India, Foreign Department, 1854, (New Delhi: NAI).
[52] Ibid.

to him 'goes no further back than Ramchund Rao the 3rd Subadar'.[53] He endorses the views of Major Malcolm, political agent to Bundelkhand and Rewah when he states, 'Major Malcolm reports that this adoption by the late Chief of Jhansi on his deathbed has taken everyone at his Court by surprise and that officer does not appear to recognise the right of the Raja to nominate an heir to his principality by adoption'.[54] This viewpoint stands contrary to Major Ellis, who was based in Jhansi and had direct access to the political developments in Jhansi. Gangadhar Rao called him to the court and briefed him about the adoption. Major Malcolm, his superior, chose to ignore this, and even 'forgets' to send Major Ellis's letter, which supports the claims of adoption.

To further strengthen the case against Damodar Rao, Grant raised the point that in Jhansi the ruler's right to declare their successor was not established from the beginning. He wrote that the English disallowed the claims of a boy adopted by Ram Chand the day before his death as it was done without 'enquiry in the fact of adoption or nomination (which was doubtful) as though it was an immaterial circumstance'.[55] The boy's claim was set aside in favour of the second son of Sheo Rao Bhow, and the uncle of Ram Chand. Rao Raghunath was considered the rightful successor to the estate by the agent Mr Begbie. Raghunath Rao died in 1838 leaving behind four claimants: Gangadhar Rao, the only surviving son of Sheo Rao Bhow; Krishna Rao, the adopted son of Rao Ram Chand; Allu Bahadoor, an illegitimate son of Raghunath Rao and the widow of the late Raja. They created a precedent of not allowing Rao Ram Chand's adopted

---

[53] Ibid.

[54] Ibid.

[55] Foreign Department, Political Letter from the Secretary of State, Cons. 1 August 1855, No. 17 of 1855.

son to be the successor and later use it at the time of Gangadhar Rao's death.

Grant raised another issue not addressed by Ellis or Malcolm. He not only discussed the British relations with Jhansi but also of Bhow's (a title to address the Jhansi rulers) relations with the Peshwas. Grant wrote that the status 'of the Bhow has been more that of an amil or governor of the Subadaree of Jhansi than of a chief possessing a "proprietary right" on the soil'.[56] The governor-general was of the opinion that the documents furnished by the Bhow designate also indicated the charge of 'Collector and the accounts which he has transmitted of receipts and disbursement corresponded with that designation'.[57] Sheo Rao Bhow died in 1814 and was succeeded by his grandson Rao Ram Chand, who applied to the British Government for a Khelat of investiture. The British government refused on the ground that investing Ram Chand with a Khelat 'might imply the recognition of his title by the British government and might have the effect of giving umbrage to the Paishwa by appearing to bar his pretensions to the superiority of the soubah of Jhansi'.[58] In 1817, the Peshwa finally 'ceded' to the British government 'all his rights, feudal territorial, social and pecuniary in the province of Bundlecund'.[59] Noting the 'fidelity and attachment of the Subadars of Jhansi', it was resolved to 'declare the territory of Jhansi to be hereditary in the family of the late Sheo Rao Bhow to perpetuate with his heirs the Treaty concluded with the late Bhow and to relinquish all claims to tribute on

---

[56] Note by I.P. Grant, 1854.
[57] Ibid.
[58] Orders of Govt., 24 March 1815, Foreign (Political) Department, (New Delhi: NAI)
[59] Ibid.

condition of the Chief furnishing at all times when required
by the British government a small body of good horses'.[60]

The British authorities used complicated technical and
administrative language to justify the annexation of Jhansi. But
the English officials could not give any rationale for the promises
made earlier in 1804 and 1817, assuring the Jhansi rulers of
hereditary succession. Grant himself wrote, 'The Governor-
General in Council directed that the above stipulation should
be reduced to the form of a supplemental article professedly
founded on the transfer to the British Government of the
Paishwa's supremacy over Jhansi and reciting the motives for
the commission in favour of the chief of that state.'[61] In the
treaty concluded with Rao Ram Chand dated 17 November
1817, giving reference to the previous treaty of 1804 with Sheo
Chaund Bhow, Rao Ram Chand, his heirs and successors,
were 'constituted' as the hereditary rulers of the territory under
Article 2.[62] In 1832, the title of maharaja was conferred by
the Governor General William Bentinck on the Subadar of
Jhansi.[63] The names of the governor generals are not mentioned,
giving an impression that the policies were seamlessly followed
irrespective of who held the title. Both Lord Minto in 1812 and

---

[60] Ibid.

[61] Govt. order of 29 July 1817.

[62] Appendix No. 2615, No. 8, from G. J. Edmonstone, Esquire to I.
Lang, Esquire, Fort William, dated 21 June 1854, Foreign Department,
Treaty with Row Ramchund Row the minor Soubadar of Jhansi1854,
(New Delhi: NAI).

[63] Memorial of Luchmee Baee to Court of Directors, 2 March 1855,
75 & KW, F. C. Foreign (Political) Department, 1854; A memorial
of Rani Lukshmi Bai by her Vakeel to G.F. Edmonstone, Secretary to
the Government of India, Calcutta, Foreign (Political) Department,
Nos.94–96, 18 August 1854.

Lord Hastings in 1817, before Lord Bentinck, continued with the same line of argument, without mentioning their names.

It seems that the intent was always to dishonour the treaty with Jhansi and take direct control of Jhansi. The policy of territorial acquisition was in place from the beginning of British rule. They kept changing their narratives to deny the Jhansi rulers the right of succession. Gangadhar Rao was declared the successor by the British officials in Bundelkhand, citing Raghunath Rao's precedent: 'The Commissioners declared an opinion in favour of Gungadhar Rao's right to succeed. This was a conformation of the principle acted upon in 1835. Gungadhur Rao being the youngest brother of the late Rajah.'[64]

Another twist is added in the British narrative to legitimize the direct takeover of Jhansi by the British government. Grant cites the history of Jhansi principality after the end of the Peshwas rule to show that 'Jhansi falls within the class of those who hold by a gift from a sovereign or Paramount power'.[65] Grant asserts that the Subadars of Jhansi were given hereditary rights as a favour or a 'gift' first by the Peshwas, and later by the Company.[66] Grant cites Sir Charles Metcalfe's minute on the question of adoption in respect of Bundelkhand chiefs dated 28 October 1837. These debates bring in the problems of sovereignty. According to Metcalfe's minutes, 'the power

---

[64] Foreign Department, Political Letter from the Secretary of State, Cons. 1 August 1855, No. 17 of 1855.

[65] Administrative Note of Grant, Secretary to the GOI, Foreign Department, Political Letter from the Secretary of State, Cons. 1 August 1855, No. 17 of 1855.

[66] There is a contradiction in the British position. They first suggest that Jhansi was given as an administrative assignment, but later they themselves give the hereditary rights to the rulers of Jhansi. Then they argue that as they had given this as a gift or a favour, they can take it back.

which granted and the power standing in its place would have a right to resume on the failure of heirs male of the body'.[67] He justifies the British taking control of Jhansi as there 'is now no male heir . . . of any Raja or Subadar of Jhansi'.[68] As the Sovereign power, the Company decided to withdraw the favour, conveniently ignoring the previous treaties signed with the successive rulers of Jhansi.

The British repeatedly mentioned the inefficiency and inadequacy of the last two rulers of Jhansi. The secretary to the Foreign Department states that Raghunath Rao 'was a leper' and that the 'late Raja Gangadhar Rao was kept out of real power till 1843 owing to his incompetency and the bad State of the country. The revenue of Jhansi once yielded eighteen lacs but had fallen in 1832 to 12 lacs and in 1838 owing to gross mismanagement to 3 lacs' and 'under our management it rose next year to seven lacs and a half'.[69] If this was the case, then why was Gangadhar Rao allowed to succeed Raghunath Rao? The maintenance of the English political resident and troops at Jhansi was a substantial financial burden on Jhansi. Taking a territory to the value of Rs 227, 458 for the maintenance of half the Bundelkhand Legion was a loss of revenue to Jhansi. The secretary of state observed, 'The Settlement of 1844/45 for the remainder of the territory was at a Jumma of Rs. 5,91,970.'[70] What remains unclear is whether it was the principle of sovereignty or the maladministration which was applied in taking direct control of Jhansi.

Maharani Lakshmi Bai's petition cites the cases of adoption allowed in Orchha, Duttea and Jaloun as examples favouring

---

[67] Ibid.
[68] Ibid.
[69] Ibid.
[70] Ibid.

her claim. The British government's deception is revealed in their statement that Orchha and Duttea were independent principalities before the Marathas entered Bundelkhand. But these states accepted Maratha sovereignty and became subordinate rulers. They came under the British after the Marathas. Their political position before the Marathas carried no weight in the light of the fact that they accepted Maratha authority. In Jaloun, the situation was similar to Jhansi, and here the British defended the adoption of 1832 saying it was 'agreeable to the wishes of the people'.[71] Later they usurped the state in 1840, at the death of the adopted son, stating that the rule of the minor was 'extremely disastrous' as he was under the tutelage of his sister and her minister.

As a last resort, the British government used their superiority entitling them to take Jhansi. Grant wrote that 'the Paramount power has' in any case 'discretion to authorise an adoption if it conceives that measure best for the public good the fact of authorisation in the case of any particular state is no proof that authorisation was accorded as of right far less can it be accepted as a proof that authorisation can be claimed as right in the case of any other state'.[72] By their admission, the British government states that the grant to an adopted son of succession to the ruler of a Bundelkhand state would depend on the 'public good'.[73] In the case of Jaloun they relied on the widow to represent the people's interest. If the people's interests were the cornerstone, did Maharani Lakshmi Bai not command such respect among the people of Jhansi? Why was the widow's position not given countenance, while the same was done in the case of Jaloun?

---

[71] Ibid.

[72] Ibid.

[73] Ibid.

In his minutes, Lord Dalhousie (dated 27 February 1854) applied the rules of lapse or escheat under the general principle laid down by the court of directors in 1849 regarding the dependent states. He also made mention of the particular minute laid down by Lieutenant Governor Sir Charles Metcalfe regarding the succession of the petty states in Bundelkhand in 1837.[74] Both the dates were after the treaty with Jhansi that had been signed with Rao Ram Chand in 1817 and could not be applied retrospectively. They were also detrimental to the interests of the rulers of Jhansi. The rules were made and unmade for the convenience of the 'Paramount' authority, who was brazen enough to use them to acquire territories from the local chiefs. By creating an intricate web of rules, the British government deprived the princely states of their rights of succession according to Hindu law. Sometimes they used the argument of paramountcy, or of a gift or a dependency and finally of their knowledge of the Hindu law to exclude the collateral heirs. They made a distinction between those who got the grants by conquest and those who were assigned a grant and hence a dependency. How was Tehree not a subordinate of the Peshwa when the governor general himself observes that 'a portion of Tehree was separated from it by the Paishwa the superior of Tehree' to create Jhansi? Tehree (Orchha) was as much a Peshwa dependency as Jhansi. It is stated in the minutes:

> Jhansi is a dependent principality in like manner as and even more distinctly than Satara. It was held by a chief under a very recent grant from the British govt as sovereign. It is therefore liable to lapse to the govt that gave it on the failure of heir male. The dependent nature of the Chiefship of Jhansi does

---

[74] Referred in Foreign Department, Political Letter from the Secretary of State, Cons., 1 August 1855, No. 17.

not admit of dispute. It never was a Sovereign State, even
in the sense in which Tehree was so regarded. It was in fact
a portion of Tehree separated from it by the Paishwa the
superior of Tehree and placed under the superintendence of
a Subadar.[75]

In those very official records, a parallel story of Jhansi's political
position emerges. The Maharani Lakshmi Bai gave point
by point answers to the arguments put forth by the British
officials. A careful reading of the maharani's *Khureeta*[76] to the
Company authorities' offers insights into the issues involved
between Jhansi and the Company. She sent all the records
and supporting documents to buttress her claims on Jhansi on
behalf of her adopted son. There were three important issues
that emerged from the maharani's petition: first was the right to
adopt according to the Hindu laws of succession; the second was
the status of Jhansi under the Peshwas and later the English and
the third was the question about the proper administration and
governance by the rulers of Jhansi.

The maharani answers all these questions with proper
documents. Regarding the first point on adoption, she writes
that this was a widely practiced policy followed by the princes
and the ordinary people in India. In her memorial, she
submitted 'that the Hindu right of adoption' applied equally to
'Ranee or peasants' and 'is indispensable'.[77] On the second point
regarding the political position of Jhansi in northern India since

---

[75] Ibid.

[76] *Khureeta* of Rani Lakshmibai, trans. Major R. R. W. Ellis,
Political Assistant to Bundelkhand.

[77] No. 1, From G. J. Edmonstone, Secretary to the Government
of India to J. Lang, Fort William, dated 21 June 1854, Appendix No.
2615, Foreign Department, 1854, translation of a memorial by Rani
Lakshmibai of Jhansi.

the time of the Peshwas the maharani's representations, along
with Vishnu Bhatt's accounts, make the position clear. As the
Maratha power expanded in north India under the Peshwas,
the command of the army was given to Mahadji Shinde, based
in Gwalior. To control the substantial revenues,[78] and to keep
a check on the power of Maratha military chiefs, the Peshwas
sent another noble, a Brahmin like them, Rao Sadasheo Bhau
Parulekar, as their second representative in the north, at Jhansi.
He was given the charge of the area in and around Bundelkhand
to collect taxes on the Peshwa's behalf. The Jhansi Subadar sent
a designated sum annually to the Peshwa.

After the agreement between the Peshwas and the British
in 1803, a separate treaty was signed with the Subadar of
Jhansi. She provided a copy of the treaty between the British
government and Sheo Rao, Subadar of Jhansi, with all the
terms of articles as concluded on 6 February 1804.[79] Captain
Baillie was asked to 'present to Sheo Ram Bhao in the name
of His Excellency the most noble the Governor-General
a suitable *Khelat* as a mark of His Excellency's esteem and
confidence'.[80] As a consequence of the treaty of 13 June 1817,
concluded between the Peshwas and the British government,
the principality of Jhansi was transferred to the British, making
the former treaty signed in 1804 virtually obsolete.

---

[78] Versaikar, *1857: The Real Story of the Great Uprising*, 83.
[79] It was given as Appendix No. 5, with 9 articles in the treaty.
No. 1, From G. J. Edmonstone, Secretary to the Government of
India to J. Lang, Fort William, dated 21 June 1854, Appendix No.
2615, Foreign Department, 1854, translation of a Memorial by Rani
Lakshmibai of Jhansi.
[80] B. Edmonstone, Persian Secretary to Captain Baillie, 27
June 1804, Agent to His Excellency, the Commander-in-Chief,
Bundelcund, No. 6, Appendix.

In the light of the changed status, another treaty was signed on 17 November 1817 between the British government, through its emissary John Wauchope, and Rao Ram Chand. The 1817 treaty was 'made in considerations of the very respectable character borne by the late subadar, Sheo Rao Bhao and his uniform and faithful attachment to the British government in deference to his wish expressed before his death that the Principality of Jhansi might be confirmed in perpetuity to his grandson Ramchund Rao'.[81] According to the maharani, 'with the view of confirming the fidelity and attachment of the government of Jhansi', the second article acknowledged and constituted Rao Ram Chand and his heirs and successors hereditary rulers of the territory enjoyed by the late Sheo Rao Bhao.[82] It meant that the British government would accept any party he adopted as his son as his successor to perform the necessary funeral rites over his body. The adopted son would preserve the name and the interests of the Jhansi royal family. With the treaty of 1817, the English authorities entered into a new political arrangement with Jhansi. It is on this agreement between Jhansi and the then governor general that Jhansi became independent, with a right to choose the successor to the throne. The ruler was honoured with khillut for his services to the British government, with a 'permission to adopt the British flag'.[83] In 1832, Bentinck honoured him with the title of 'maharaja' for his 'exertions to suppress the Thugee, apprehending two hundred and ninety

---

[81] Appendix, No. 8, part of the enclosures submitted by the rani to the British. Treaty of 1817 with 10 articles, Foreign Department, 1854.

[82] Ibid.

[83] Ibid. *Khillut* is a robe of honour in recognition of the services rendered by the Jhansi ruler as a subordinate of the British. The British followed the practice of the Mughals.

thugs, tracing out the property plundered and the bodies of
the persons murdered'.[84] The right of hereditary succession
given in the treaty of 1817[85] was guaranteed in 1843 by the
political agent in Bundelkhand.[86] Colonel Sleeman reiterated
'the continued existence of all the benefits claimable' by the
Jhansi Government under Gangadhar Rao.[87]

The maharani refuted the third issue raised by the British
that the decision to take direct charge of Jhansi was due to the
poor administration by Gangadhar Rao and the unhappiness
of the people. The people of Jhansi were 'contented with the
Government' of the maharani and her husband, which was
as good as the one 'under British rule, and did not desire a
change of government'.[88] In a letter of 20 December 1853, Col.
Sleeman, the resident of Lucknow,[89] congratulated the maharaja
for regaining his health, complimenting him on his excellent

[84] Letter from J. Remain, Secretary to William Bentinck, 20 December
1832 and later a Translation of a Letter from the Governor-General
to Maharajah Ramchunder Rao, grandson of Sheoram Baho, dated
1833, given in Enclosure 11.
[85] Translation of a letter from Colonel Sleeman to Maharaja
Gangadhar Rao, cited in Appendix, Encl. No. 13.
[86] Enclosure No.12, 'Translation of a letter from the Political Agent in
Bundelcund to Maharaja Gungadhar Rao, Chief of Jhansi, dated 20
September 1843. This letter mentions that in the boundary disputes
between the states in Bundelkhand, 'it is proper to prefer the case to
the British Court where a fair decision thereof will be made'.
[87] No. 362, in Foreign Political Department, Nos. 362–5, 2
December 1853.
[88] 'Subject – People of Jhansi did not desire to be the subjects of the
East India Company', in Foreign Department, Political Branch, Cons.,
2 March 1855, No. 75, K.W.
[89] Translation of a letter from Colonel Sleeman to Maharajah
Gangadhar Rao, cited in Appendix, Encl. No, 13.

qualities. The British officers arriving from Jhansi praised 'the good management of the affairs' of the state.[90]

Maharani Lakshmi Bai and Gangadhar Rao were well within their rights under the terms of the treaty of 1817 to invoke the Hindu law of succession as mentioned in the shastras, stating 'The Hindoo Shastras inculcate the doctrine that the libations offered to the names of a deceased parent are as efficacious when performed by the adopted son as by a real son and the custom of adoption is accordingly found prevalent in every part of Hindoostan'.[91] She also underlined the fact that the rules of succession as laid down in Hindu law were followed under the instructions of her husband, Gangadhar Rao. She, along with Narasingh Rao Appa, Lalla Lahori Mull and Lalla Yutti Chand, the minister, were 'told to consult the shastra and such a duly qualified child from his own "gote" clan to succeed him as ruler of Jhansi'[92] as his health was worsening. They summoned Ram Chand Babu and 'at his recommendation out of several children of the gote it was agreed that Anand Rao a boy of five years of age, the son of Basdeva was the best qualified for the purpose'.[93] Gangadhar Rao asked for the performance of the rites of adoption by the Shastri. Pandit 'Benaich' (Vinayak) Rao 'performed the Sanglalpa' in which the boy's father poured water into the hands of Gangadhar Rao with the accompanying ceremonies. The 'boy was renamed as Damodar Rao Gungadhar', and this completed the ceremony of adoption.[94]

---

[90] Ibid.

[91] It was given as Appendix No. 5, with 9 articles in the treaty. No. 1, From G. J. Edmonstone, Secretary to the Government of India to J. Lang, Fort William, dated 21 June 1854, Appendix No. 2615, Foreign Department, 1854, translation of a Memorial by Rani Lakshmibai of Jhansi.

[92] Ibid.

[93] Ibid.

[94] Ibid.

On 19 November 1853, the ministers of Jhansi 'by the orders of the Raja' wrote to Major Ellis and Major Martin, the officer commanding the station, encamped six kos from Jhansi, 'requesting their attendance at the palace with the view to bearing witness to what had been done'. On 20 November 1853, the two officers came to the palace, and Raja Gangadhar Rao handed a letter to Major Ellis, 'requesting him to obtain the sanction of government to the adoption'. On 21 November 1853, Maharaja Gangadhar Rao died and 'the different funeral rites required to be performed by a son have all been discharged by Anand Rao styled Damodar Rao Gungadhur'.[95]

Despite refusals by the British officials, the maharani was persistent. She gave all the documents in support of her adopted son's succession. She mounted a strong campaign through documents and agreements between the Jhansi royal family and the English, to which the English officials gave weak administrative replies.[96] They had no logical arguments to refute the manifest evidence she provided. The maharani is rational in her conduct throughout, while the British are throughout irrational and unyielding. In the official record the British maintained that 'no reason is shown in the document for altering the just and reasonable decision, which the Government of India was led to form'.[97] The maharani relentlessly pursued the

---

[95] Ibid.

[96] 'Translation of a Khureeta of Ranee of Jhansi', to A. S. R. E. Wilikinson, Bheel Agent and Political Assistant In charge of Residency, in Foreign Department, Political Letters from Secretary of State, Cons., 1 August 1855, No. 17.

[97] Appendix No. 2615, from G. J. Edmonstone, Secretary to Government of India to J. Lang, Fort William, 21 June 1854, in 'People of Jhansi did not desire to be subjects of the East India Company', in Foreign Department, Political Branch, Cons., No.75, K.W., 2 March 1855.

British authorities, and on 19 July 1854 asked for 'the copies of the Papers showing the grounds on which the state of Jhansi has been resumed' to 'be furnished to her, to enable her to submit a fresh settlement of her claims'.[98] This was a reasonable request she made to prepare her reply. The government denied her request, ordering 'that the memorialist be informed in reply that her requests are wholly inadmissible, and that she be further told that the orders for the resumption of Jhansi will not be revoked by the govt of India', without giving any reason.[99] On 21 December 1854, Maharani Lakshmi Bai wrote to the governor general of India, with a request to submit her representation to the Court of Directors of the East India Company in London, on her and Damodar Rao's behalf. She further requested him to reconsider his decision 'even at the eleventh hour' to alter the direct takeover of Jhansi and to put in a favourable recommendation of her case to the Court of Directors.[100]

II

In 1859, a detailed account of what transpired at Jhansi was recorded in the imperial files.[101] The Agent to the Governor-General for Central India Sir Robert Hamilton had started

---

[98] No. 3607, Office Memorandum, No. 2, from G. J. Edmonstone, Secretary to the Government of India, Fort William, Foreign Department, 18 August 1854.

[99] Ibid.

[100] Memorial from Maharani Lakshmi Bai to the Marquis of Dalhousie on 21 December 1854, in Foreign Department, Political Branch, Cons., 2 March 1855, No. 75, K. W.

[101] No. 171, A letter from Sir Robert Hamilton, AGG for CI Indore Residency, Camp Jhansi, 24 April 1858, to G. J. Edmonstone, Secretary to the GOI with GG, in Foreign Political Supp., 280–8, 30 December 1859.

making enquiries into the events at Jhansi in 1857. He quoted
a letter dated 6 June 1857 by late Captain F. D. Gordon, the
deputy superintendent of Jhansi, to Major Erskine.[102] The letter
stated that a portion of the 12th Native Regiment broke out in
open mutiny, seizing the star fort containing the magazine and
'all the treasure amounting to about four and a half lakhs of
rupees'. This started at 3 p.m. on 5 June 1857 with a clamour
raised by the soldiers 'that the Magazine being attacked by
Dacoits', and they rushed to the fort.[103] Gordon reported that
the English officers and their families took shelter in the fort:
'The whole of Europeans, are safe, at present and we are all in
the fort, which we shall endeavour to defend.'[104] They had sent
express messages to Gwalior and Kanpur for assistance, but they
were losing hope and were preparing to rely on their resources.
Hamilton underlines that 'no allusion is made in any way to the
Ranee or her party'.[105] Hamilton's inquiry made it clear that the
maharani of Jhansi was not involved in the outbreak that started
in 1857 in the cantonment of Jhansi, a claim that the maharani
had been repeatedly making in her correspondence to the
English authorities at Jabalpur. She appealed to these authorities
to send reinforcements as she did not have sufficient resources to
withstand the pressure from the soldiers for long.[106]

Captain Gordon, in his correspondence before his death,
referred to Mrs Mutlow, the wife of a clerk in Captain Skene's
office. Mrs Mutlow later would escape and be a witness to
the incidents at Jhansi and the massacre at Jokhum Bagh on
the afternoon of 8 June 1857. Mrs Mutlow, in her testimony,

---

[102] Ibid.

[103] Ibid.

[104] Ibid.

[105] Ibid.

[106] Ibid.

confirmed the outbreak in Jhansi at 3 p.m. after a great noise
by the sepoys rushing to the magazine. She took refuge in
the fort at 6 p.m. On 6 June, Captain Gordon and Captain
Skene sent messages to the maharani, and she sent 'about 50
of her own sepoys'.[107] She further states that during the day,
Mr Taylor of the cavalry reached the fort wounded, 'and soon
after the Rani withdrew her sepoys after which they joined
the Mutineers'.[108] It is difficult to ascertain if Mrs Mutlow's
statement was an accusation against the maharani of being
complicit or if it said that, as the mutiny spread, the maharani
was under heavy pressure from the rebels. On 8 June, Captain
Gordon was killed by a shot, which struck him in the head,
while he was inspecting the fort in the morning. Mrs Mutlow,
in her account, mentioned that 'overture were then made' to
the mutineers, 'and under a solemn promise of safety and oaths
of the Soobedars, Hindoo and Moosulman, and the signature
of the Ranee they left the fort and were taken, surrounded by
Sepoys and Police Burkundaz to the Jokhum Bagh, about 400
yards beyond the Oorcha gate of the city'.[109] Mrs Mutlow, her
ayah and child were able to escape unnoticed into the crowd
as she was wearing 'her ayah's native dress, which enabled
her to escape into one of the many old *chuttrees*/tombs/at the
Jokum Bagh, she, however, saw no more of the unfortunate
party'. All English men, women and children were massacred
at Jokhum Bagh at Jhansi.[110]

---

[107] Ibid.; 'Release of Mrs Mutlow and her children', in Foreign
Department, SC, Nos. 43–4, 16 July 1858.

[108] No. 171, A letter from Sir Robert Hamilton.

[109] Ibid.; 'Release of Mrs Mutlow and her children', in Foreign
Department, SC, Nos. 43–4, 16 July 1858.

[110] From Captain Pinkney, Superintendent of Jhansi to W.C. Erskine,
Home Public, No. 94, dated 13 April 1854.

Maharani Lakshmi Bai has been maligned in the British
media in India and Britain on the 'Jokhum Bagh Massacre'.
Hamilton asked Captain Pinkney to enquire into the matter.[111]
Captain Pinkney found that murder of the European and Anglo-
Indian residents of Jhansi happened under circumstances that did
not involve the maharani in any way.[112] He wrote:

> After J. D. Gordon was shot dead over the gateway of the
> fort, the other officers and residents who were inside being
> in want of provisions agreed to surrender on the lives of
> themselves, their wives and children being spared. This the
> mutineers and rebels swore to do, and the Europeans then
> allowed them to enter, but though indeed police and the
> Ranee's armies followed and rebels immediately bound the
> men, took them, their wives and children to Jokhum Bagh,
> outside the fort and the walls, and separating the men from
> the women, first murdered the men. Buckshish Ally, the
> Jail Darogah, commencing the slaughter by cutting down
> Captain Skene with his own hands and they then killed the
> women and children with swords and spears.[113]

---

[111] Major Erskine, the commissioner of Jubblepore Division, made
it clear to Mr Muir, secretary to government, Allahabad Statement
of *Bombay Times* that the ladies who were murdered at Jhansi had
been dishonoured, contradicted', Home Public, GGS, No,90, April
1858, that the letter in the newspaper *Bombay Times* 'purporting to be
written from Jhansie stating, contrary to the evidence I had received
that all the European ladies murdered at Jhansie had been dishonoured
by the direct orders of the Ranee, I requested the Superintendent of
Jhansie to make particular enquiries.'
[112] From Captain Pinkney, Superintendent of Jhansi to W.C. Erskine,
Home Public, No. 94, dated 13 April 1854.
[113] Ibid.

Both Erskine and Pinkney declared an anonymous letter sent to the newspaper *Bombay Times* to be false, and Erskine wanted to publish Captain Pinkney's letter in the *London Times* to ease out the 'great pains to the friends in Europe of the deceased'.[114] Captain Pinkney clearly stated that 'The European and Anglo Indian females were not brought before the Ranee and stripped, their faces were not blackened nor were any of them dishonoured'.[115] These accounts indicate rani's non-involvement in the Jokhum Bagh Massacre.

The narratives also highlight the injustice done to the maharani and her attempt to govern Jhansi, seeking British assistance for her state. Even here, the duplicity of the English officers thwarted the maharani's efforts of keeping her rationality in the face of adversity, after her husband's death and during the mutiny by the soldiers.[116]

Another testimony was given by Shahaboodeen, the servant of Capt. Skene, the political agent at Jhansi. He corroborated the alarm of dacoits by the sepoys. He mentioned how Captain Skene sent his family in Captain Burgess' carriage and later drove to the fort with Captain Gordon. The Indian servants transported milk and bread to the fort, where under the fort wall, Captain Skene threw a rope to receive the supplies. Shahaboodeen indicts the maharani and her father in his testimony. He says that while returning from the fort he was arrested by a servant of the maharani, Ghonee, who took him to 'Mama Sahib the Ranee's father by whom he was sent to Lall Bahadoor Soobadar, and the Risaladar (Fyze Ali, 14th Irregular) to be put to death', but for some reason, the order was suspended and later in the hustle and bustle he escaped. He says that the English people were taken

---

[114] Ibid.
[115] Ibid.
[116] No. 171, A letter from Sir Robert Hamilton.

by the sepoys and the maharani's people to Jokhum Bagh and were murdered. It seems that Shahaboodeen did not witness the Jokhum Bagh episode. He said that after the event 'Buxish Ali and his accomplices came to the risaldar [cavalry officer] before whom Buxish Ali publicly boasted that he had killed the "Burra Sahib" (Captain Skene) with a cut'.[117] All Indian servants were set free.[118]

A sepoy of 12 NI (Native Infantry), who was made prisoner after the capture of Jhansi, also gave his statement. He stated that 'a letter was received from Delhi, stating that the whole of Bengal Army had mutinied and that as the Regiment at Jhansi had not, the men of it were outcasts, and had lost their faith'.[119] He said that this immediately triggered four sepoys, 'Daibu Singh of Banoda of Lucknow, Nooring Singh of Baiswara, Jey Singh of Bhojpoor and Jeydan Singh of Mongair', to revolt. As Major Dunlap left the parade, he was shot at, pursued and killed. Lieutenant Taylor was shot at the door of the Quarter Guard. 'Captain Gordon was killed by a matchlock ball and that his body was sent on a Charpoy by orders of the Ranee to be interred [this is corroborated by other statements] with other bodies as the Jokhum Bagh.'[120] It seems that the maharani was trying her best to keep doing whatever she could for the British despite the extreme hostilities of the soldiers of the Company. Many eyewitnesses asserted that she was reluctant to side with the rebel sepoys.[121] The maharani sent repeated requests to the British to help Jhansi and that she was holding the charge till the British authorities could take control.[122]

---

[117] Ibid.

[118] Ibid.

[119] Ibid.

[120] Ibid.

[121] Foreign Political, Supp., 30 December 1859, Nos. 267 & KW.

[122] 'Application from Jhansi Rani to be placed under British control', Foreign Department, Nos. 29–32, F. C. 28 February 1856.

Another soldier, Aman Khan,[123] described how 'The *Pulthunwalas* suspected that the cartridge newly received were covered over with hog's or cow's skin, and that their religion would be encroached upon. 50 sepoys broke out in open rebellion'.[124] They had fifteen gunners with them. After attacking the magazine and killing the two English officers, 'all went to the palace of the Ranee with loaded guns and demanded assistance and supplies. She was obliged to yield and to furnish guns, ammunition and supplies'.[125] The maharani ordered the body of Captain Gordon to be brought in from the fort and buried. Aman Khan joined the services of the maharani, while most of the mutineers left. According to Aman Khan, the maharani was able to raise an army of 30,000 soldiers. Besides this force, 100 soldiers were from Jhansi, 80 men from the Scindias' contingent that was 'disarmed and disbanded at Aseer, who came to Jhansi for employment under Rani'. He states that 'there were about 300 Wilaytees, 500 mutinous sowars and about 500 Boondaila sowars. Each Zemindar of the Jhansee district furnished his quota of men. The total number of these men both within the town and on outpost duties amounted to about 30,000 men'.[126]

Aman Khan's testimony also reveals that Company rule was intensely disliked. It states, 'The Cantonment Bungalows were I am told, burnt by the people of the town and not by the mutinous sepoys.'[127] There was evidence with the British in Jhansi that no 'indignity was offered to any single one of

---

[123] 'Abstract Translation of the Statement of Aman Khan, son of Kureem Khan aged 35, Resident of Ahmadpoor, near Agra, a Sepoy of the 8th Company 12th Regiment, Bengal NI, 14 April 1858', in No. 171, A letter from Sir Robert Hamilton.
[124] Ibid.
[125] Ibid.
[126] Ibid.
[127] Ibid.

the unfortunate sufferers . . . on the contrary it may be safely asserted that not one of the bodies was afterwards mutilated or ill-treated'.[128]

The most incriminating evidence against the maharani was given by Captain Skene's khansama, Shahaboodeen.[129] He had packed all silver in one box and a box of other utensils. In the list, most of the items mentioned are the silver and porcelain pottery. According to him, the queen's father carried off four boxes. The treasurer Akheymull, in whose safekeeping these boxes were to be kept, joined the maharani's services, suggesting that 'possibly the silver jewellery entrusted to him taken'. The most damaging accusation made by him was as follows: 'One day before the murder of the officers it was proclaimed in the Town by the beat of the drum that "the country belonged to the King, the Ranee held the right and that the officers will be killed tomorrow". After the murder no proclamation was issued.'[130] He further states that the maharani opened her mint on 25 March 1858. His account is in conflict with the other testimonies, and it would be difficult to say if the maharani actually issued the proclamation or she was taking charge of Jhansi as the British authority was violently removed.

The maharani's helplessness is mentioned in many depositions. In his deposition, Sheikh Hingun Shookaburdar mentioned a letter sent by Captain Gordon to the maharani to say that it was her raj and the English would leave. A servant then brought her answer stating her helplessness before the sepoys: 'What can I do Sepoys have surrounded me, and say

---

[128] No. 171, A letter from Sir Robert Hamilton.

[129] 'Abstract Translation of the Statement of Shahaboodeen Khansamah of Major Skene, 23 March 1858', in No. 171, A letter from Sir Robert Hamilton.

[130] No. 171, A letter from Sir Robert Hamilton.

I have concealed the gentlemen, and that I must get the fort evacuated, and assist them, to save myself I have sent guns and my followers, if you wish to save yourself abandon the fort, no one will injure you.'[131] He also disclosed how Mr Andrew disguised as Sudder Allah went to the maharani to get the carriage. But he was identified and 'killed by Ranee's sepoys. Ranee raised 2 companies of Sepoys, and gave the command to 3 mutineers who had remained behind'. She also gave the Sultanpur mutineers a feast at Jokhun Bagh.[132] He confirmed that she became the ruler of Jhansi: 'I saw it all. All police and other business in the city was carried on in the Ranee's name. Neeladhur, who was formerly Kotewal still continues so under the Ranee. A proclamation was made in the city that the Ranee was governing, but the *guddee* belonged to the adopted child.'[133]

The reprisals from the British were quick and brutal. Moro Bulwunt or the Mama Saheb, the father of the maharani, was arrested. He was tried by Hamilton, sentenced to death, and executed 'on the tree in the Jokhum Bagh the scene of atrocities'.[134]

The British did not spare the people of Jhansi, and for three days after the capture of Jhansi, there was mayhem in the city. The British lost 227 men while capturing the fort, while around 3,000 Indians were killed, including civilians.[135] On the

---

[131] 'Deposition of Sheikh Hingun Shookaburdar', in Foreign Political, in No. 171, A letter from Sir Robert Hamilton.

[132] Ibid.

[133] Ibid.

[134] No. 171, A letter from Sir Robert Hamilton; 'Execution of the father of Ranee of Jhansie', Governor-General's Despatch to Secret Committee, No. 15 of 1858.

[135] Captain S.W. Pinkney, Superintendent of Jhansi to W. Muir, Secretary to the Government of NWP, No. 83 of 1858, dated 7 April 1858, Foreign Political, No. 55, 15 October 1858.

night of 4 April 1858, 'the Ranee and a large body of rebels made a dash out of the Fort, but were driven back . . . they then changed their course and got through the picket towards Bhandere, they were followed up by Lieutenant Dowker' of the Madras Army with a small body of cavalry. They inflicted some losses, capturing many of the maharani's followers, but the queen herself departed from Jhansi.[136]

What emerges from the many testimonies is that Maharani Lakshmi Bai was trying to keep a fine balance between the demands of the revolting soldiers and the English authorities. She assisted the British officers by providing munition. In her deposition, Mrs. Mutlow recalled that Skene and Gordon 'went to Ranee and got 50 or 60 guns and some powder and shots and balls and 50 men on the fort to assist us'. Yet, she also mentions that the maharani had issued an order that 'if anyone catch us going out of town' she will 'give one hundred rupees as a present'.[137] Her contradictory acts underline the precariousness of her position. Bhugwant Brahmin,[138] in his testimony, stated that 'sepoys in the service of the Ranee got a blacksmith who broke open the lock', and 'the mutineers entered the city' from the Sayer gate.[139] He said that the bodies of all English men, women and children amounted to about 80. He exonerated the maharani by stating, 'I did not hear that the Europeans were killed by the orders of the Ranee.'[140]

---

[136] Ibid.

[137] Account of Mrs. Mutlow, in Foreign Political, in No. 171, A letter from Sir Robert Hamilton.

[138] 'Translation of the Statement of Bhugwant Brahmin, son of Bukhta', aged 29 in Resident of Cawnpoor District, in No.171, A letter from Sir Robert Hamilton.

[139] Ibid.

[140] Ibid.

Madan Bux[141] narrated the sequence of events in Jhansi from 5 June 1857. Captain Gordon asked him to meet Duttiah Vakeel Soondur Lall, with a request for two guns and assistance, while Nuthoo Singh Jemadar was sent to Orchha vakeel with a request for help. They heard noise and disturbance at the maharani's house and found that instead of 14 men, there were 1,400 men with the maharani's man Gulam Khudabaksh and her other retainers. Later he was approached by a servant of Nawab Ali Bahadur to secure the English officials' safely to the servants' house by some means. But they were caught by the 'Teelingas' (mutinied regular sepoys of the Company in 1857) and the maharani's men. The risaldar then asked the tehsildar to write a letter to the English officers saying that if they came out they would not be hurt.[142] He took it to the fort but was 'abused by Rani's men and was not allowed to approach the fort'.[143] He went to the maharani's residence, and after much persuasion, was given a harkara (messenger) to go to the fort. He gave the letter to the English officers, tied to a rope. The English gave a letter to him for the maharani. Here his account seems to suggest deception on the part of the maharani. He says that she sent the letter to the risaldar through her vakeel, Adjudia Purshad, but Zabita Khan also went on horseback. Madan Bux says that at that point, the maharani's chobdar, Sumoo Moosulman told him that 'Ranee had sent Adhudia Purshad for outward show, but that Zabita Khan was the bearer of another message and that I would not succeed what I wanted'.[144] He also said that while

---

[141] 'Deposition of Jemadar of Orderlies, Madan Bux attached to Captain Gordon of Jhansi', 23 March 1858, in Foreign Political, No. 171, A letter from Sir Robert Hamilton.

[142] Ibid.

[143] Ibid.

[144] Ibid.

carrying the risaldar's letter to Gordon, he saw Mr Scott and
two Purcells[145] being led as prisoners by the maharani's sepoys
and heard about their killing afterwards at the parade ground.
The maharani also coined money, and after the killing of the
English, she proclaimed that 'the world is God's, the country's
the Padshah, and the Raj's Rani Luchmee Bai'.[146] According to
him, the sepoys and the maharani were in communication. The
sepoys asked her to give them Rs 1,25,000 for the gaddi, which
she agreed to do so, and gave them 15,000, but at night they
got the news that the Gwalior contingent was coming, and the
mutineers left Jhansi. According to Madan Bux, the bodies of
the English were buried towards the Sayer Gate near the Muttia
Sovera, though no one knew by whom.[147]

Deo Keemundeen Lohar[148] described the events at Jhansi.
He mentioned that the maharani's men immediately sided
with the mutineers. He stated that the subadar misinformed
the English officers that only thirty-two sepoys had mutinied,
and they told him to inform the soldiers 'that if they wished to
serve Government they were to do so properly if they did not
wish to serve, they might return, but that they must not commit
mutiny. Subedar pretended to be satisfied'. He also informed
that the tehsildar of Purwar, Kashunath, had also come to Jhansi
without informing the British, but the reason was that he was
the maharani's relative as his 'brother's son has been adopted by
the Rani'.[149] He remained in Jhansi for one and a half months,

---

[145] C. Purcell was a Head Clerk at the Superintendent's Office and
J.Purcell was a clerk at the Commissioner's Office.
[146] Ibid.
[147] Ibid.
[148] 'Deposition of Deo Keemundeen Lohar, formerly Orderly of
the late Lieutenant Gordon of Jhansee, 11 March 1858', in Foreign
Political, No. 171, A letter from Sir Robert Hamilton.
[149] Ibid.

and 'In that time the Ranee proclaimed in the town that her reign had commenced and that the English Raj was over. She erected her flag on the fort, assembled the Mahajuns to present her with a "Nuzzerana" and set going a mint. The day of the murder the Ranee gave the sepoys an elephant and some money'.[150] After the sepoys left Jhansi, the maharani took out two guns, one of which was mounted on the fort. Lohar also mentioned that he was not allowed to meet the maharani and give the message of the English officials seeking her help, by her father and Bugoley Lal Tehsildar. Again, the maharani's role in the early days of the revolt is unclear. She doesn't seem to have been on a mission seeking revenge.

On 23 January 1858, Hamilton told Col R. Strachey, secretary to government, the Central Province, Allahabad that he did not reply to the khureeta of the maharani of Jhansi.[151] It seems that the maharani was still trying to reach out to the British to explain her position. But the British relied on their intelligence in their refusal to acknowledge her. Hamilton informs Strachey that on 5 January 1858, he had received the news that the maharani 'continued to rule over Jhansi – that all disaffected and mutinous men that go to Jhansie are kept by the Ranee. Bukhshsish Alli, the last Jail *Darogah* of Jhansi who was at the bottom of the whole mutiny at that place with about 50 *sawars* and as many footmen (All mutineers) has taken refuge with the lady – the brother and the whole family of the *Darogah* have been, for some time, protected by the Ranee'.[152] But in the same report, Hamilton writes:

---

[150] Ibid.
[151] Foreign Political, Supp., 30 December 1859, Nos. 267 & KW.
[152] Ibid.

It is reported that Bukshis Allee, the *Darogah* of Jhansie Jail asking Ranee whether she would fight or not with the English forces was informed by the Ranee that she would not, but will return all the districts under her to the British officers when they came to Jhansi. On getting this information, the Darogah did not take service with the Ranee.[153]

It is apparent that the maharani tried her best to negotiate with the British, but the British mistrust stonewalled all her efforts at conciliation. On 28 June 1858, the news of the death of the maharani of Jhansi came from Gwalior.[154]

In the dispatch of the governor general, there is a one line of confirmation of the maharani's death.[155] The accounts of Martin and Forrest claim that she died on 17 June 1858, in a surprise attack by the squadron of the 8th Hussars. She was wounded by 'a shot in the side, and a sabre-cut on the head'.[156] The maharani and Sir Hugh Rose did not have a confrontation. Hugh Rose and Tantia Tope's forces met, but by the time Hugh Rose entered Jhansi, the queen had left the place.[157]

In the English account, the final moments of the maharani are described as follows. On 17 June 1858, Brigadier Smith reached Kotah-Ki-Sarai, three or four miles south-east of Gwalior. From there, he moved with a squadron of 8th Hussars, two divisions of horse artillery and one troop of the 1st Lancers

---

[153] Ibid.

[154] R. Simson, Secretary to the GOI with the Governor General, 28 June 1858.

[155] 'Death of Ranee of Jhansi', Governor General's Despatch to Secret Committee, No. 26 A of 1858.

[156] Montgomery Martin, *The Progress and Present State of British India*, 77.

[157] 'Capture of the town and fort of Jhansi by Sir Hugh Rose and escape of the Ranee', in Foreign Department, No. 55, 15 October 1858, F. C.

closer to Gwalior against the rebels near the Phoolbagh palace, under the command of Tantia Tope. 'Smith ordered the squadron of Hussars to charge them. Led by Colonel Hicks and Captain Heneage, they dashed at full speed, sweeping the enemy before them, and they never drew rein until they had ridden through the enemy's camp in the Phoolbagh two and a half miles away.'[158]

At the end of this attack, 'Among the slain, that day was the Ranee of Jhansi'.[159] Forrest claims in his account that her servant informed him of this. The maharani was drinking sherbet with the 'Brahminee concubine of her husband' near the Phoolbagh batteries when the Hussars suddenly attacked. She was in 'a soldier's attire of a red jacket, trousers, and a white turban on her head, which made it impossible to tell her sex.'[160] Around 400 soldiers from the 5th Irregular were near them. Most of them fled, except about fifteen. Her horse 'refused to leap the canal, when she received a shot in the side, and then a cut on the head, but rode off. She soon after fell dead, and was burnt in a garden close by'.[161] Sir Hugh Rose 'declared, that the high descent of Lakshmi Bye, her unbounded liberality to her troops and retainers, and her fortitude, which no reverses could shake, rendered her an influential and dangerous adversary; and he announced her death to the Government as that of the bravest and best military leaders of the rebels'.[162]

---

[158] Ibid.; George W. Forrest, *The Indian Mutiny 1857*-58, (Selections from the Letters, Despatches and other State Papers Presented in the Military Department of the Government of India, 1857-58), Vol. IV (Calcutta: Superintendent Government Printing, 1912), 161.

[159] Forrest, *The Indian Mutiny 1857*-58, 161.

[160] Ibid., 161–2.

[161] Ibid. 162.

[162] Montgomery *The Progress and Present State of British India*, Martin, 77–8.

III

The third section deals with some of the unanswered questions about the maharani, her family life, the direct rule of the British and the events as they occurred in Jhansi in 1857.

From Vishnu Godshe's account, it seems that the maharani was always a suspect in the eyes of the British, despite her efforts to dispel such suspicions by keeping the lines of communications open with the British. She kept them informed about the developments in Jhansi at the peak of rebellion in 1857 regularly and appealed for assistance to rescue the beleaguered Jhansi. The enemies of Jhansi, especially the Bundelkhand Rajput states, who were unhappy with the only Maratha state amidst them, were keen to take advantage of the turmoil to drive out the maharani. The maharani, Mughal ruler Bahadur Shah Zafar, Nana Saheb of Bithur and the begum of Awadh were excluded from an emergency conclave organized by the British in Calcutta in June 1857, as mentioned in Vishnu Bhatt Godshe's account. Godshe writes, 'The Governor-General had summoned the heads of all the princely houses to Calcutta', except the rulers mentioned above.[163] He states that the maharani patronized 'many Brahmins from Brahmavarta'.[164]

Vishnu Bhatt narrates this about Gangadhar Rao:

> When the urge struck him, he would suddenly go to the roof of the palace, remove his male attire and return dressed as a woman in a resplendent *zari* choli and sari, with a colourful silken braid attached to his topknot, bangles on his wrists, pearls around his neck, a nose ring and jingling anklets.[165]

---

[163] Versaikar, *1857: The Real Story of the Great Uprising*, 40.

[164] Ibid., 80.

[165] Ibid., 86–7.

He also shunned the company of men and observed 'four days of untouchability each month, as menstruating women do, and attend court only after he had performed the ritual cleansing bath on the fourth day'.[166] Due to this, he was not considered a suitable suitor. Vishnu Bhatt exonerates the ruler of his eccentricities by stating that the king told the English resident that he dresses as a woman as he was emasculated by the English, who entered their land and made them subservient to them and exacted taxes from all 'native' rulers.[167] He admired Gangadhar Rao's administrative skills, handling Jhansi with a firm hand and maintaining law and order.

In the nationalist and literary accounts, Maharani Lakshmi Bai symbolizes an ideal woman. Such accounts do not explore the controversial aspect of her domestic life. Writing from his visit to Jhansi in the middle of the revolt of 1857, Vishnu Bhatt delves into her unhappy marital life. He writes:

> Lakshmi Bai's marriage was not a happy marriage. As a husband, Gangadhar Baba was a stern and suspicious man who allowed his wife very little freedom, Lakshmi Bai was confined within the walls of the palace and was mostly kept under lock and key, with her chambers guarded day and night by armed women. No male was allowed to enter her quarters. Under such exacting circumstances, the poor girl began to lose much of her earlier glow and, as a recluse, acquired a few strange habits.[168]

In her representation, the maharani cited the adoptions of Parashuto (Paricchat), the late Raja of Datia, that of Balu Rao

---

[166] Ibid., 86–7.
[167] Ibid., 88.
[168] Ibid., 90.

(most likely Balarao), the last chief of Jaloun (Jalaun) and that of Tej Singh, the last raja of Orchha (Tehree).[169] Respecting her contention, Major Ellis forwarded the letter to Major D. A. Malcolm, the political agent of Gwalior, Bundelkhand and Rewah, to be sent to Governor General Lord Dalhousie. Previously, 'in 1825 the adopted son of the Raja of Kotah as heir to that principality was recognised, and on that occasion, the Government of India was understood to admit the right of all Hindoo Sovereigns to perpetuate their succession by adoption'.[170] In another instance, in 1827, Maharaja Daulat Rao Scindia died without a male heir. His widow Baiza Bai adopted Junkojee Rao Scindia as his successor. As late as 1853, the same year as Maharaja Gangadhar Rao's death, on 7 February 1853, Junkojee Rao died without an heir, and his widow Tara Bai adopted Jiyaji Rao with the consent of the Government of India. Maharani Lakshmi Bai, as the widow of Gangadhar Rao, had a similar right of adoption.[171] Unlike their assertions, the British were inconsistent in applying the rule of law and uphold

---

[169] Foreign Department, Political Letter to the Secretary of State, Cons. March 1854, No. 21, to the Hon'ble The Court of the Directors of East India Company, Fort William, 4 March 1854.

[170] Ibid.

[171] Maharani Lakshmi Bai cites other instances of succession by adoption in her memorial. The previous chief of Jaloun in Bundelkhand who, like the raja of Jhansi, was of a Brahmin family, was adopted by his sister, the widow of Bhale Rao, former chief of Jaloun, after the death of Bhale Rao. This adoption was sanctioned by the Government of India. Similarly, Khandy Rao, Brahmin Jageerdar of Algi in Bundelkhand, died in 1839 without issue. 'Mr. Fraser, the Agent to the Governor-General, confiscated his State, but Colonel Sleeman, his successor in office, taking a more liberal view of the case obtained the sanction of Government to the widow of Khandy Rao to adopt a son, and she adopted a son of a very remote ancestor of the deceased. Further, the revenue collected during the four years during

fair play. Both the rulers died in 1854, without a son of their own, but different rules applied to them.

In March 1854, the cases of Jhansi and Tehree (Orchha), two small principalities of Bundelkhand, emerged after the death of the chiefs in both principalities. Major Ellis cited these instances, pointing to the inconsistency in applying the Doctrine of Lapse. The Foreign Department observed that in Jhansi, the British decided 'that as the Chief has left no descendants of any preceding Chief of the state, and, in existence, the state has lapsed to the British government'.[172] In the case of Tehree state, 'We have come to a contrary decision . . . where too the Chief of this state having died without issue and without having adopted a son, we have directed such measures to be taken for its continuation under a Native Ruler'.[173] The maharani gives in detail the case of Orchha, while the British officials are not forthcoming:

In 1837 the Government of India acknowledged the late Soorjan Singh the adopted son of the Raja of Oorcha as his successor. In 1841 an attempt was made to question the right of that Rajah to adopt a son and successor on the ground that he would not have been permitted to experience such a right under the Moghul Emperor, but Lord Auckland, the Governor-General of India in Council, decided in favour of the adoption. On the death of Soorjun Sing in the present year 1854, the Government of India again allowed the right

which the state was confiscated was made over to her as the guardian of the adopted heir.'

[172] Foreign Department, Political Letter to the Secretary of State, Cons. March 1854, No. 21.
[173] Ibid.

of adoption by his widow; so that State is governed by the
Ranee during the minority of the adopted infant Rajah.[174]

Their explanations were logical only to them, but they could
not convince the local rulers, whose principalities they were
taking, of the unjustness of their decision-making. Maharani
Lakshmi Bai, in this case, had a reason to be aggrieved. If the
British had a stated policy of dividing princes under a hierarchy,
this should have been informed to the princes at the time of
signing such treaties. How could the British authorities take
recourse to an unstated rule, as they accorded the importance
to the written document to be legal and authentic? Both were
also under the Maratha suzerainty that was cited as the reason
for the takeover after the Marathas signed a treaty with the
East India Company.[175] Both were allowed to continue in
their respective territories, recognizing their traditional rights
under the previous rulers. Yet, Rani Chennamma in 1824 and
Maharani Lakshmi Bai in 1854 were denied their principalities
and the traditional rights of the rulers to adopt their successors.
If the argument was that it was done under the Doctrine of
Lapse, a policy introduced by Lord Dalhousie in the 1850s,
then how was that applicable in the case of Kittur in the 1820s?
If it was being followed from the earlier times by the Company,
then how was Jhansi annexed under the policy of the Doctrine
of Lapse, but in the adjacent principality of Orchha (Tehree),
the widow was permitted to adopt a successor, and the throne
remained unoccupied for a while? The excuse offered in the
imperial records is that the Thakurs had ancient ruling rights. If
that was the case, then why were the rights of succession given
to Jhansi raja from the 1820s and 1830s?

---

[174] Ibid.
[175] Ibid.

In her final memorial to the court of directors, the maharani was unequivocal in claiming sovereignty for Jhansi by stating that Subadar Sheoram Bhow and his family 'had, and have independently of the British Government or the East India Company an absolute and indefeasible right and property in and to the territory and Government of Jhansi subject only to certain tribute payable originally' to the Peshwas, 'which tribute has been compensated and satisfied by the cession of territory made by Raja Gungadhur Rao to the East India Company'.[176] Interestingly, she challenged the fact that Jhansi had not been taken by any war or conquest, thereby reasoning that 'this absolute and indefeasible right was not, and has not, been transferred by Treaty, or otherwise to the East India Company, nor has it been lost or forfeited . . . by any breach of Treaty, or in the course of War or by conquest, and it has not been in any way acquired by the East India Company'.[177] She challenges not only the disowning of the adoption, but the Company's title to Jhansi:

> Does it confer on them a right to govern, and a right to possess and enjoy the territory and revenues of that State? Does it entitle them to seize the government and territory of Jhansi? Does it authorise them to capture the treasury – "to pension off" the Rani on a pittance of the state's revenues and depriving her and his heirs of "their entire inheritance except for the petty reversion of his personal estate?"[178]

The maharani's questioning this decision was valid, but the British refusal to answer her by using high moral language but

---

[176] The Memorial of Rani to the East India Company, 1855, Foreign Department, (New Delhi: NAI).
[177] Ibid.
[178] Ibid.

administratively weak responses such as 'just and reasonable decision' was simply another one of their unaccountable acts in the colony. If these were independent principalities, then they should have been under the ambit of the international treaty system. The despotic nature of the colonial state could not have been more evident. Their adamant refusal in no way reflects fair play and justice. The British authorities quote the Hindu Law of Succession, which technically should have been taken up as a legal matter by the competent courts of law. The Company policy did not permit the princely states to pursue legal procedure. They could only take up the matter with the court of directors of the East India Company and the British Crown. Hence the maharani petitioned first the governor general,[179] then the court of directors and finally the Crown. The matter was administratively handled by the Foreign Department of the Company throughout. The British had made up their mind to take direct control of Jhansi for the purposes of revenue, much before the demise of the ruler Gangadhar Rao. In a note of 1853, Sleeman claimed that the 'adoption would render her miserable. The Pandits will, no doubt, besiege him and her right and say to adopt in order to secure the revenues of the estate for themselves. They will force the adoption if they can'.[180] Posing as the saviour and protector of a widow from the greed of the Brahmins, he went on to write: 'I think the Raja himself told me one day, that all he cared about was, in case of his death that his

---

[179] Memorial of Rani Luchmee Baee, 2 March 1858, No. 75, K. W., Foreign Department, (New Delhi: NAI): 'Lakshmi Bai's demand for the restoration of Jhansi was broad-based on solid popular support. In her memorial to the Court of Directors in view (on View) she stresses the fact that her people do not want a change of rulers.'

[180] No. 362, 15, Sleeman, Foreign Political, Nos. 362–5, Foreign Political Department, 2 December 1853.

widow should be made happy and comfortable.'[181] According to Sleeman, the raja paid a private visit to him, where no one was present, and told him that he had no relative that he cared strongly about.[182]

The British decision to take Jhansi directly under their control was a breach of the treaty between the two, and the maharani points this out forcefully.

> The Government of India is expressly bound by its own treaties, and the repeated acts and promises of its servants, to maintain and preserve inviolate the rights and interests of the heirs and successors of Sheoram Baow Soubadar of Jhansi and Ramchund Rao Maharaja of Jhansi, whose lawful heirs and representatives your memorialist and her ward at present are.[183]

The maharani gave instances beginning with General Lake's assurance to Sheoram Bhow in 1803 of the British support for those who remained devoted to the British government being allowed to retain their possessions. In 1804, Lord Wellesley, with reference to the treaty concluded on 6 February 1804 between General Lake and the subadar, sent a letter to Sheoram Bhow assuring him of protection for the confidence 'judiciously reposed in the justice and liberality of the British Government'.[184] The same was reiterated in a treaty signed on 17 November 1817 between the Marquis of Hastings and Ramchand Rao, agreeing to maintain and protect the 'Subadar, his heirs and successors as hereditary rulers of Jhansi'.[185] In

---

[181] Ibid.

[182] Ibid.

[183] The Memorial of Rani to the East India Company, 1855.

[184] Ibid.

[185] Ibid.

return, the Subadar and Ramchand rendered assistance to Lord Amherst, supplying 5,000 Bunjarree bullocks at the cost of Rs 70,000 for service in the Burmese War.[186] The fidelity of the Jhansi state to the British government was constant. In 1843, Lord Ellenborough also acknowledged the loyalty of Gangadhar Rao, when apprehending an outbreak of rebellion at Gwalior, assuring him that 'the Government will never depart from the terms of the Treaties concluded'.[187] The maharani concluded her memorial on this note: her dispossession 'are in the express and gross violation of the Treaties of the Government of India, and of its promises and pledged faith by its servants, and if persisted in, they must involve the gross violation and negation of British faith and honor'.[188] She demanded the restitution of her rights at the earliest based on the treaties she provided in detail and also on popular support. These concluding observations tear into the British image of justice and fair play.

Both Kittur and Jhansi were confronted with the brutal acquisitiveness of the Company Raj. The commercial aspect plays an important role in both the places but has been underplayed in the imperial records. Both Kittur and Jhansi were flourishing trade centres, and the East India Company, with their trade interests, desired the two principalities for their strategic importance. Jhansi's location was important for

---

[186] Translation of a letter from the Political Agent in Bundelcund to Ramchunder Rao Bahadoor, dated 16 December 1824, No. 9, Foreign Department. He was given a 'Khellat of distinction' for his loyalty to the British. Lord William Bentinck, in a letter dated 20 December 1832, gave Ramchunder Rao the title of Maharajadheeraj, No. 2645, Appendix No. 10, Foreign Department.
[187] Memorial of Rani Luchmee Baee, 2 March 1858, No.75, K.W., Foreign Department, (New Delhi: NAI).
[188] Ibid.

controlling the region of Bundelkhand.[189] Jhansi was a flourishing trade centre under Gangadhar Rao. Despite the caricaturing of raja as effeminate and effete, it seems he was able to introduce sound economic policies, providing stability to Jhansi, which continuously faced succession issues. Gangadhar Rao was able to increase the revenue of Jhansi from Rs 3 lakh under Raghunath Rao to Rs 6 lakh, excluding the territory ceded to the East India Company for the maintenance of the Bundelkhund legion.[190] This cessation of territory more than adequately compensated for the tribute paid by Jhansi to the Peshwas. The maharani denied any debts left by Gangadhar Rao as he 'paid off debts contracted by the former Rajas to the extent of about twenty-five lacs'. The people of Jhansi were contented under Maharaja Gangadhar Rao and Maharani Lakshmi Bai. 'Public Works were not neglected by Raja Gungadhar Rao. Good roads, tanks and Bridges were constructed and spacious Bungalows were erected for the accommodation and comfort of travellers passing through the territory and a large mansion with a garden was constructed at the expense of upwards of lac of Rupees and given to the Agent to the Governor-General, without rent. No tax is levied on grain, cattle etc., passing through Jhansi and there was effective police'.[191] Vishnu Bhatt confirms the prosperity of Jhansi on his visit in 1857, describing

---

[189] Lebra Joyce Chapman, *The Rani of Jhansi: A Study of Female Heroines in India*, 15: 'Jhansi town became known throughout Bundelkhand for the manufacture of spears, bows, and arrows, all essential for the martial lifestyle of the Bundelkahnd Rajputs. Jhansi was moreover at the convergence of five roads leading to Agra, Kanauj, Nowhong, the Nerbudda Valley and Indore. Their roads were heavily travelled by trades in cotton, grain, sugar and the salt.'

[190] Foreign Department, Political Branch, Cons., 2 March 1855, No.75, K.W.

[191] Rani's Memorial, 1855.

it as prosperous 'with its grand fort and beautifully laid out gardens'. It had 'a population of about fifteen lakh' on the eve of the revolt.[192]

Tapti Roy writes, 'With increasing economic problems, the British actually did come to acquire larger and larger territories in the 1840s.'[193] Towards the last decades of the eighteenth century and the early decades of the nineteenth century, 'one of the primary interests in this region was the export of raw cotton produced here. It found the cotton grown in Bundelkhand, especially in Jalaun and villages adjacent to Kalpi, to be better than that of the Doab'.[194] Many nearby towns like Jhansi, Kalpi Jalun and Kunch emerged as important trading marts. 'Jhansi and Jalaun were the major areas that supplied cotton to the East India Company'.[195] The increase in the trading activities and the British commercial interests connected Bundelkhand to the 'growing market network operated by the East India Company and foreign private traders'.[196] The rulers lost control over the new economic patterns, and the British interventions increased in their states. The collapse of this raw cotton boom in the 1820s hit the Bundelkhand countryside, creating disturbances. The British calculated that direct control was the only way to control the countryside and manage the revenues.[197]

They ruthlessly set aside the claims of the queens of Jhansi and Kittur to their principalities and annexed the states. But the inconsistency of their policy is revealed in the strong case prepared by Maharani Lakshmi Bai. The maharani's memorial

---

[192] Versaikar, *1857: The Real Story of the Great Uprising*, 84.

[193] Roy, *The Politics of a Popular Uprising*, 97.

[194] Ibid., 86.

[195] Ibid., 90.

[196] Ibid., 85.

[197] Ibid.

underlined the financial angle and the English rapacity about jewels and treasury. She mentioned that not just the hereditary state and inheritance of Damodar Rao was 'taken possession of' and their affairs were now managed, the revenues of Jhansi were collected by the officers of the East India Company.[198] In 1853,

> a four per cent Promissory note of the East India Company for Company's Rupees one lac eighty-three thousand and six hundred was issued to Raja Gungadhur Rao for tribute payable to him from revenues of the Chirgong district, which district formerly was held by a Chief who was tributary to the Jhansi state whose possessions having been occupied by the East India Company, the tribute fell due by them to the Raja of Jhansi.[199]

The East India Company gave a promissory note for the debt to be paid by the chief to the maharaja of Jhansi. 'This Promissory note was ordered by the Government of India to be given to the late Raja after the payment by him of the debt due from Jhansi to the Government of India, which amounts to about Company's twenty thousand.'[200] The maharani did not receive the promissory note, from which she was willing to pay the balance of the debt. In a letter of Major Ellis,[201] an offer of seven articles was made in consultation with Major Malcolm to the maharani to pay to her a sum of Rs 5,000 per month and a barah or palace at Jhansi for her to stay. Major Ellis also

---

[198] Foreign Department, Political Branch, Cons., 2 March 1855, No. 75, K.W.

[199] The Memorial of Rani to the East India Company, 1855.

[200] Ibid.

[201] Translation of a letter from Major Ellis to the Maharanee of Jhansi dated 28 April 1854, a friendly offer by Major Malcolm, Political Agent in Bundlecund of seven articles.

suggested giving the charge of late Maharaja Gangadhar Rao's property to the maharani so that she could take care of it on behalf of her minor son. In addition, he requested that she be also pardoned from attending the British court and that all the gems that formed the personal property of the maharaja, with every other kind of property, and all the income after due calculation be deposited with the maharani. She repudiated this offer on 29 April 1854 as she wanted to ensure the right of succession to the gaddi of Jhansi and asked for thirty days to represent her case to Lord Dalhousie. On 8 June 1854, she filed her response.[202]

Many questions come to the fore. Despite Maharani Lakshmi Bai's valour and heroism that have immortalized her in the canons of the nationalist historiography, she was hemmed in by patriarchy at every stage. From being Manu Bai to her marriage into the royal family of Jhansi, she was only following the prevailing norms of society, marrying a man twice her age, becoming his second wife and trying to adjust to a traditional household and a husband with his eccentricities. She did not challenge patriarchy in any of this. Her fight was also to perpetuate the old order, to maintain the rulers' right to choose their successor and her right to be a guardian of that tradition. In the process, she did expose the patriarchy of the Company authorities. They only recognized Gangadhar's right to decide, but her claims were indifferently dismissed. She raised her voice against the inconsistency of the Company's decision making regarding succession. Her letter to the various English authorities, right up to Queen Victoria, provides important clues as to the East India Company's working.

---

[202] Foreign Department, Political Branch, Cons., 2 March 1855, No. 75, K. W.

Another aspect that emerges is how the event, with all its characters, unfolds in its occurrence and subsequent iconization. Rani Chennamma and Maharani Lakshmi Bai become icons or heroes in the ensuing nationalist struggle from the latter decades of the nineteenth century. But this representation as national icons decontextualizes these historical characters from the period in which they were located, which had no nationalist colour. The romanticization of Rani Chennamma and Maharani Lakshmi Bai gradually emerged out of popular songs and lavanis, where they are seen as heroines. Political leaders appropriated these ranis in a nationalist frame to legitimize their politics, decontextualizing these historical figures.[203] We need to place them in their historical period. Herein Romila Thapar mentions the use of the phrase 'heard history' by Romi Khosla,[204] in which people use 'the past indiscriminately to legitimise his activities in the present'.[205] The idea of the nation in nineteenth-century India was tied up with 'socio-religious revival' and 'the idea of Indian civilisation being defined as Sanskrit-speaking and Hindu in religion'.[206] As a Brahmin under the Peshwas,[207] Maharani Lakshmi Bai captures the nationalist imagination first. These two queens, taking a cue from Romila Thapar's reading of Shakuntala, were 'well placed in society, faced with an event that forces a choice' on them, as also 'the social values involved in her choice and reactions to it'.[208] Neeladri Bhattacharya makes the pertinent observation that it is important to understand 'the cultural politics of recording and forgetting, of foregrounding or

---

[203] This argument has been made by Romila Thapar in conversation with Thapar and Jahanbegloo and Neeladri Bhattacharya, 274.

[204] Thapar and Jahanbegloo, 275.

[205] Ibid., 276.

[206] Ibid., 278.

[207] Chapman, *The Rani of Jhansi*, 15–6.

[208] Thapar and Jahanbegloo, 282–3.

understating'.[209] In the case of Rani Chennamma and Maharani Lakshmi Bai, one can read such 'cultural politics' with an overarching focus on their martial qualities, ignoring their other political acts.

If there is a glorification of the British rule in the colonial records, in the nationalist frame, there is the demonization of the 'traitors' in the tragic fall of the rulers of the times. The rulers were not weak, but it is treachery which led to the fall of kingdoms. Can we possibly read a counter-story, shorn off the celebrations on both the sides? As Ann Stoler says, we have remnants of Empire that the present age historians have to resolve.[210] This should not let the present weigh heavily on the past but attempt to understand history from the evidence available.[211] Are these stories of national valour, or an anti-imperialist struggle? It was certainly in many ways an anti-imperial struggle, where both the kingdoms of Kittur and Jhansi resisted the imperial designs of a colonial-capitalist state, looking to extract the resources of such places through direct annexation. The events stopped short of being part of a nationalist struggle as these rulers are only safeguarding the interests of their principalities and ensuring the continuation of their dynasties. The British officials highlight the 'imbecility' of the Indian princes or their profligacy to bring the princely states under the direct control of the Company, for order and discipline in these states.[212]

---

[209] Ibid., 302.

[210] Ann Laura Stoler (ed.), *Imperial Debris: On Ruins and Ruination*, (Durham and London: Duke University Press, 2013), 2.

[211] Ibid.

[212] Col. Malleson ed., *Kaye's and Malleson's History of the Indian Mutiny of 1857-8*, Vol. III,119: 'Baba Gangadhar Rao was not the man to remedy this state of things. He, too, was an imbecile, and it was conjectured that under his sway, disorder, far from being checked, would be increased tenfold.'

Elizabeth Kolsky, in her work on *Colonial Justice in British India*, wrote that 'whiteness was monolithic'.[213] In many ways, the colonial authorities' relationship with the princes was also defined by total impunity with which the 'imperial whiteness' disregarded the treaties and laws they made with the local rulers. Their interpretations of such treaties could not be challenged. 'The notion of the rule of law as a system of principles designed to govern and protect equal subjects – a notion introduced into India by Britons themselves – was blatantly contradicted.'[214] The white imperialist laws dominated and controlled the local rulers as also their subjects. The rule of law's idea as imposed by the colonist to justify their control over the Indian people comes across as ambiguous and arbitrary. Kolsky argues 'that colonial law and colonial justice, when viewed through the prism of white violence, were both unjust and ambiguous'.[215] 'The promise of equal justice' followed by the practice of going against this very promise created the tension between the colonists and the colonized.

As revealed in the archival records, the cases of succession were seen as political matters and not as legal issues. Even the laws of succession were conveniently interpreted by the colonial authorities to suit political exigencies. Many English officers involved with the takeover of Jhansi in 1854 cited Charles Metcalfe's Minutes of 1837, wherein he discusses dependent states, such as Jhansi, which was a subordinate of the Peshwa. Once the powers of the Peshwa devolved upon the British government as the lord paramount, Metcalfe reasoned that the paramount power was 'entitled to limit succession according to the limitations of the grant, which in general confirms it to heirs

---

[213] Kolsky, *Colonial Justice in British India,* 11.

[214] Ibid., 12.

[215] Ibid., 13.

male of the body, and consequently preludes adoption.'[216] All these discussions on the territorial claims of the Company were carried out by non-legal administrative officials, who were either military officers or civil servants. They simply complied with the policy that the then governor general of India implemented. The patriarchal bent of mind of the British further reinforced the patriarchy of traditional Hindu society. In denying the right to adopt his sister's son to Rao Ram Chand, they only confined the succession to the male line and the male members of the family.

On the contrary, in the Hindu laws of adoption, no such restriction is mentioned, which is further confirmed by the acts of the British in the case of Jaloun. Tapti Roy's study on Bundelkhand[217] notes the succession in Jaloun—in 1842, they declared the minor brother of the maharani as the successor on the death of her husband.[218] The fact that they did not take up such matters legally is that such a succession would not withstand scrutiny in the court of law, as under the Hindu law, adoption is permissible in different ways and is not merely confined to the collateral line. The British refusal to allow Indian rulers to make decisions autonomously was the source of angst and retaliation in Kittur and Jhansi. Even if the king had not declared a successor before his death, the queen could decide, as stated by Sleeman in the case of Jaloun.

---

[216] Quoted by Lord Dalhousie and mentioned in Foreign Department, Political Branch, Cons., 2 March 1855, No. 75, K.W.

[217] Roy, *The Politics of a Popular Uprising*.

[218] Colonel Sleeman, political agent to Bundelkhand, mentions that the widow of the Jhalana Raja adopted her brother as the successor, in Political letter to the Secretary of State, Cons. 4, No. 362, in a letter dated 2 December 1853, Foreign Political Department, 1854, Nos. 362–5.

Maharani Lakshmi Bai's decision to join the revolt of 1857 was not based on anger or revenge as reasoned by Forrest. She took her decision when the British did not respond to her distress calls, after the attack by Dutia and Tehree on Jhansi's borders. She refused to be swayed by the rebellious soldiers in Jhansi, despite the mounting pressure they exerted on her. She believed that the British would be able to see her rationale. The British officers refused to respond to her letters even though Erskine had asked her to take the reins of Jhansi after the outbreak of revolt.

On the contrary, Erskine encouraged Tehree to attack Jhansi, as recorded in the official files.[219] It is important to mention here that the recent folk songs on the maharani and Jhansi in Bhojpuri recite the events with dates—something unusual in the popular rendition of the events in Jhansi. The maharani's close female companions' constant presence and their loyalty to her, and their deeds of bravery are recited alongside those of the maharani. The Dalits in modern times take pride in the participation of a lower caste Dalit woman alongside the maharani who took her mantle, due to her close resemblance to the maharani, to help her escape.[220]

The British perception of the acts of the Indian rulers in the aftermath of 1857 reveals their bias as conquerors. Sir Robert Hamilton, AGG to Central India, wrote that 'punishment has been inflicted in a manner never before contemplated, all classes have learnt to their cost that rebellion is not a game in which only the Chiefs can lose but is a crime

---

[219] No. 36, from Sir Robert Hamilton to AGG to Central India, 5 June 1858, Foreign Department Secret Proceedings, 30 July 1858.

[220] Badri Narayan, 'Jhalkaribai and the Koris of Bundelkhand' in *Women Heroes and Dalit Assertion in North India: Culture, Identity and Politics* (New Delhi: Sage Publications, 2006), 113-132.

for participation in which every individual of a community will meet punishment. I have from the first advocated stern justice'.[221] Vishnu Bhatt Godshe also recounts the merciless killing by the white men on entering the city of Jhansi. He had received some Rs 250 from the maharani that the white men snatched.[222] 'For three days, the white men shed blood in Jhansi plundered the city, finally left, carrying all the gold, silver and precious' stones they could.'[223] He also describes the destruction of Maharaja Gangadhar's library, which had a rare and rich collection of Vedic and Puranic texts, sutras, treatises on Ayurvedic medicine, etc. 'The books had all been embellished with beautiful handcrafted bindings.'[224] The use of the term 'wicked marauders'[225] for the English is ironical, as the English who prided themselves on discipline and professionalism of the white army indulged in the most savage behaviour in Jhansi.

There are some gaps in the imperial records or deliberate silence on the events as they unfold in Kittur. The use of subterfuge, betrayal of promises and arbitrary rulemaking mark the British takeover of India. The story resonates in the case of Jhansi, and the glaring inconsistencies and arbitrariness of the British policies stand exposed, as revealed in Maharani Lakshmi Bai's vigorous defence of her case. The legitimacy of British rule in India was based on the claim that they were fair and just, and this stood exposed in the manner in which they took over the principalities of Kittur and Jhansi. They behaved like conquerors

[221] No. 36, from Sir Robert Hamilton to AGG to Central India, 5 June 1858, Foreign Department Secret Proceedings, 30 July 1858.
[222] Versaikar, *1857: The Real Story of the Great Uprising*, 136.
[223] Ibid., 139.
[224] Ibid., 139.
[225] Ibid., 140.

and continuously acted dishonourably. But the official records have a tone of self-righteous indignation on the 'impropriety' of the Indian rulers and the 'morality' of the Company's cause. Official records need to be revisited to peel off the projection of objective and faithful recording of the events as they occurred. An eyewitness account in history always has a ring of authority, but we also need to examine the authorship of the source and for what end these records were written and maintained. The British colonizers were the ones writing these official papers from their point of view.

The pardon of Queen Victoria in her famous proclamation of 1858[226] had no meaning, as the announcement conveniently ignored the extremities committed by the British officers, and the princes and people of India were pushed into taking an extreme position. In one stroke, she exonerated the excesses of the British officials, beginning a phase of benevolent despotism by proclaiming 'amnesty' for the Indians, but making it clear that it was not for those who had committed offences against the English. The political control of India now passed to the Crown and the British parliament. However, as I will discuss in the last chapter, the nature of the British Raj in India did not change with the change of power. It only became subtle when it suited them, but the commercial avarice and acquisitive spirit of capitalism reached its apogee in the handling of affairs in

---

[226] From the Secretary of State to the Government of India, to the Secretary to the Government of Fort St. George, No. 521, and to the Secretary to the Government of Bombay, No. 522, dated Allahabad, 8 November 1858, No. 75, 'Copy of the Royal Act of amnesty, pardon, and obedience, which they command of the Queen has been promulgated to the people of India, and conveying instructions for the guidance of all officers entrusted with judicial powers, in dealing with persons charged with political offenses', in Home Public, 20 November 1858, Nos. 75–92.

Sikkim. Susan Buck-Mors argues that, moving 'away from the nostalgic European gaze upon ruins',[227] one needs to 'treat them as symptoms and substance of history's destructive force', leaving the 'traces of violence' linked to capitalism. Stoler wrote that 'the "rot" of colonial men and their murderous acts remain'[228] in ruins left behind.

The colonized subject was the persecuted one, and the violence wreaked by the white colonists were sites of remembering the white terror so that the subjugated people did not dare to rise up against the authorities. The Kittur and Jhansi forts were pummelled to smithereens as a reminder of the white colonists' savagery against those who revolted. The white man was possessed with ruthless and absolute brutality. As a counter to the imperial view, the nationalist perspective spins a 'phantasy'[229] in the tales of confrontation and resistance, 'of magical, supernatural powers' which 'prove to be surprisingly ego-boosting'.[230] These women are appropriated with that magical halo to identify it with a nation's glory. These myths are in the songs of Bundelkhand,[231] which till date sing of the glories of not just the queen of Jhansi, but her female companions, especially Jhalkari Bai, the maharani's

---

[227] Susan Buck-Mors, in ed. Ann Laura Stoler, *Imperial Debris: On Ruins and Ruination*, (Durham and London: Duke University Press, 2013), ix.

[228] Stoler, *Imperial Debris*, 2.

[229] Frantz Fanon, *The Wretched of the Earth*, trans. Richard Philcox (New York: Grove Press, 2004), 211.

[230] Fanon, *The Wretched of the Earth*, 211.

[231] Alha Deshraj Paterya, 'Jhansi Ki Rani Laxmi Bai', Vol. I and II, https://youtu.be/JdiU48E31MQ, accessed on 1 June 2022; 'Kar Gai Amar Kahani Jhansi Ki Nar' (Rani aur Vir Bhesh Ghoda Pe Baithi Kar Gayi Amar Kahani), https://youtu.be/4epsK5nsPic and https://youtu:be/e-KcBNSVWKU, accessed on 1 June 2022.

lookalike from a lower caste, who sacrificed herself to allow the maharani to escape from Jhansi. Today, the Dalit pride and the maharani's tale are sung together in the region's local songs.[232]

[232] Badri Narayan, *Women Heroes and Dalit Assertion in North India*, 119-120.

SECTION TWO

Queens in Controversy

3

Maharani Jindan of Punjab

There are many portraits available of Maharani Jindan. In this particular portrait, more than her beauty, one can see a sense of determination on her face.

All I have written may appear to show the instability of present arrangements at Lahore; it does show that much improvement is requisite; and it is not improbable that there may be, and it would be desirable indeed that there should be, considerable changes, may even a radical change, in the constitution of the Durbar, whether the Maharajah's Government will stand or fall, no man can tell; but I see nothing that can injuriously affect it, except the misconduct of the Maharanee and ministers themselves.[1]

The biographical accounts of Maharani Jindan mention her to be the daughter of 'Kennel officer Manna Singh'[2], an Aulakh Jat from a village of Chachar in district Gujranwala.[3] Her father served as a junior officer (kumedan) in Maharaja Ranjit Singh's household, looking after the department of hunting dogs.[4] She married Ranjit Singh in 1835. In 1838, Maharaja Duleep Singh was born. By the Treaty of Bhairowal, 16 December 1846, the maharani was separated from Duleep Singh and sent to Sheikhupura fort in 1847. The mother and son would meet after fourteen years in February 1861 in London.[5]

[1] Henry Lawrence, the Agent to Governor General, North West Frontier to Fredrick Currie on 21 July 1846 at Simla Foreign Department, No. 992 (Cons.), Fort William, 26 December 1846, para 32.
[2] M. L. Ahluwalia, *Maharani Jind Kaur (1816-63)*, ed. Prithipal Singh Kapur, (Amritsar: Singh Bros, 2001), 13.
[3] Bakhshish Singh Nijjar, *Maharani Jind Kaur: The Queen Mother of Maharaja Dalip Singh*, (Delhi: NBS Revised Edition, 2003), 8
[4] Ibid.
[5] Christy Campbell, *The Maharajah's Box: An Imperial Story of Conspiracy, Love and a Guru's Prophecy*, (London: Harper Collins, 2000), 119-123.

I

Maharani Jindan is one of the most controversial historical characters in Indian and imperial historiography. One of the recurring themes is an 'image of sexual voracity'[6] associated with her. Henry Lawrence described Maharani Jindan as 'a woman of most dissolute character'.[7] Mrs Login wrote: 'Duleep Singh's mother was the beautiful and notorious Maharanee Jinda (or "Chunda"), sometimes known as the "Messalina of the Punjab"'.[8] Mrs Login's statement has strong connotations of immorality She was only repeating what was said about Maharani Jindan in the official English circles. Many of these representations were supposedly based on the eyewitness accounts of the English and European officers, whose credentials themselves are of doubtful integrity.[9] Some were mercenary soldiers. Their description of Maharani Jindan's morality is accepted unquestioningly. There are references to Lal Singh as her 'paramour' in the imperial records.[10] In an official file, Henry Lawrence wrote, 'The Maharanee indulges herself as

---

[6] Antonia Fraser, *The Warrior Queens: Boadicean Chariot*, (London: Phoenix, 2002), 12.

[7] J. J. McLeod Innes, *Sir Henry Lawrence: The Pacificator*, (Oxford: Clarendon Press, 1898), 49.

[8] E. Dalhousie Login, *Lady Login's Recollections: Court Life and Camp Life, 1820-1904*, (London: Smith, Elder & Co., 1916), 85. This was a name given by Henry Lawrence to Maharani Jindan. Messalina was the third wife of a later Roman Emperor Claudius, characterized as promiscuous.

[9] One such account, in yellow page journalism, is George Macdonald Fraser's *Flashman and the Mountain of Light* (From the Flashman Papers, 1845–46). It circulates a stereotype of Maharani Jindan as an oriental consort with a voracious appetite for men.

[10] Major Herbert B. Edwardes, *A Year on Punjab Frontier in 1848-49, Vol. I* (London: Richard Bentley, 1851), 6. He described Maharani

usual. Her latest amusement is to push her slave girls into the ponds and fountains of the palace gardens, and laugh at them as in her own and Lal Sing's presence, they duck and dive in their efforts to get out.'[11]

In the imperial historiography, there is a constant questioning of the marriage of Maharani Jindan to Maharaja Ranjit Singh and Duleep Singh's paternity. Major Carmichael Smyth wrote: 'I do not mean to assert, however, that Duleep Sing is the offspring of the old impotent sinner, but he certainly is his mother's son, and that may give him some small claim to the Guddee.'[12] He emphatically wrote that

> Dulleep Sing's mother, Mai Chunda, was not, however, one of Runjeet Sing's wives; he was only married to two women, Metab Kour, the daughter of Suda Kour and Mai Nekee, the mother of Kurruck Sing; and he only performed even the Chadardalna with three women, namely, the two widows of Sahib Sing, of Guzerat, and Gool Begum, and Kunchenee of Lahore.[13]
>
> Besides Mohran, Gul Begum and Jind Kalan, three other Muhammedan Ranees are named – Teiboo, Junnut Bibi and Gobe.[14]

Jindan as 'able and unscrupulous' and Prime Minister Lal Singh as 'her paramour'.

[11] Foreign Department, No. 992, Fort William, 26 December 1846, para 22.

[12] Major G. Carmichael Smyth, Third Bengal Light Cavalry, *A History of the Reigning Family of Lahore, with some Account of the Jummoo Rajahs, the Seik Soldiers and their Sirdars* (Calcutta: W. Thacker and Co., 1847), xviii.

[13] Ibid.

[14] Khushwant Singh, *Ranjit Singh: Maharajah of the Punjab*, (London: George Allen & Unwin Ltd., 1962), 185.

In Sikh history, Maharani Jindan, as the mother of the young ruler, is called Mai Jindan. She was considered a heroine and a freedom fighter.[15] Meenakshi Rajan writes, 'Today she is regarded as the first female freedom fighter in the struggle to drive the British out of India.'[16] There are many accounts of the family background of Maharani Jindan and her meeting with Maharaja Ranjit Singh. Khushwant Singh gives an interesting though an unsubstantiated version of her being a Muslim (Aulakhs were both Hindus and Muslims):

> She and her mother had been summoned by Ranjit Singh about 1832 to answer the complaint of one named Abdul Samad Khan who stated that Jind Kalan was betrothed to him, but her mother refused to fulfil the engagement. Ranjit Singh cancelled the betrothal and kept Jind Kalan and her mother in his own seraglio.[17]

Nationalist historiography has not focused on her much. She is almost obscure in mainstream nationalist historiography. In more recent times, many works on her have come out, which throw a different light on her. Priya Atwal considered Maharani Jindan well-equipped in handling Punjab's affairs after Maharaja Ranjit Singh:

---

[15] Ahluwalia, *Maharani Jind Kaur (1816-63)*; Nijjar, *Maharani Jind Kaur*, among others.

[16] Meenakshi Rajan, 'Spiritual Warriors: The Role of Women in the Sikh Religion', in *Proceedings of the Indian History Congress*, Vol. 68, Part Two, 2007, 1445–6, 1446. There are other scholars celebrating Maharani Jindan as a freedom fighter: M. L. Ahluwalia & Kirpal Singh, *The Punjab's Pioneer Freedom Fighters*, (Bombay: Orient Longman, 1963); Mahinder Kaur Gill, Harbans Kaur Saggu, trans. Jagjit Kaur, 'Punjab ki Pratham Nari Swantrata Senani: Maharani Jindan', in *Punjab Ki Raniyan*, (New Delhi: Vijay Publication, 1997), 39–68.

[17] Singh, *Ranjit Singh*, 208.

Jindan's politics were impenetrable due to her skilful deployment of purdah and manipulation of gendered rhetoric. She may not have been the unsullied heroine that some historians from our [Sikh] community would have her be. Still, she was certainly an extremely sharp, capable leader, who was well suited to deal with the politics of her momentous era.[18]

In her latest study, Atwal[19] places her in the frame of gender studies, drawing attention to women's importance in the politics in the Lahore durbar of Maharaja Ranjit Singh. Many contemporary English and Indian writers mention[20] what were considered the indiscretions and amours of the queens, be it the grandmother and mother of Maharaja Ranjit Singh and Maharani Jindan. Sikh historiography countered such negative representations by citing the strength of these women in adversity. Maharani Jindan only followed the line of such illustrious women. In the context of late medieval or early modern times in South Asia, the strong presence of women and their regard in political matters is certainly important. These studies negate the impression that the women were mere wallflowers in the history of these times. Many scholars of gender studies have disproved with their research such an ahistorical understanding of the period.

---

[18] Priya Atwal, 'Politics Behind the Purdah: Maharani Jind Kaur and Anglo-Sikh Relations, 1839-1863', Sikolars 2013 Presentation, (Presented at Queen Mary's University, London on 18 May 2013, http://www.sikholars.org.

[19] Priya Atwal, *Royals and Rebels: The Rise and Fall of the Sikh Empire* (London: C. Hurst & Co., 2020).

[20] Smyth, *A History of the Reigning Family of Lahore*; Syad Muhammad Latif, *History of the Panjab: From the Remotest Entity to the Present Time*, (Calcutta: Calcutta Central Press Company Limited, 1891).

II

Maharani Jindan was not known before the 1840s. Only when the successors of Maharaja Ranjit Singh died one after another did one faction under Raja Dhian Singh Dogra prop up Duleep Singh, son of Maharani Jindan, the maharaja's youngest wife, as the successor to the Punjab throne. There are many versions of her early days. It is certain that she was the daughter of a lower-level officer of Maharaja Ranjit Singh and had come to his court at a young age of nine. Syad Latif has recorded Maharaja Ranjit Singh's marriages and even his grandson with meticulous precision, but somehow his marriage to Maharani Jindan has not been mentioned. The silence is intriguing.

English accounts describe the maharani as charming and as a 'seductress'. It is puzzling that the British authorities find her their most dangerous adversary. An English military officer directly involved with Punjab's affairs in the crucial period of 1838 to 1846 is Joseph Davey Cunningham. For eight years, he worked closely with the Sikhs, under Colonel Claude Wade, the political agent to the Lahore durbar. Cunningham first met Maharaja Ranjit Singh in 1838, during his meeting with Lord Auckland, then governor general of India. In his introduction to Cunningham's work, H.O. Garrett feeds his ideas too, highlighting the constant conflicts between the Mughals and the Sikhs, comparing them to the Roman Empire's tensions with Christianity.[21] These are sweeping generalizations, without getting into the dynamics of the Mughal–Sikh relations. The Mughal–Sikh history is complex. The Mughal Prince Khusrau was closely associated with Guru Arjan Dev in his revolt against his father, Jahangir.[22]

---

[21] Joseph Davey Cunnigham, *A History of the Sikhs,* ed. By H.L.O. Garrett, (Lahore: Oxford University Press, 1915; revised edition), Oxford, 1918, vii.

[22] Satish Chandra, *Medieval India*, Part II, A textbook of class XI (Old series), (New Delhi: NCERT, 1983) (Reprint), 206

Syad Latif provides detailed histories of the Sikh misls. Ranjit Singh was born to the chief of Sukerchakia Misl, Maha Singh, and Mai Raj Kaur on 2 November 1780.[23] Mai Raj Kaur was the daughter of Gajpat Singh of Jhind, and 'being from Malwa, she came to be popularly called 'Mai Malwain, or the Malwa mother'.[24] According to Latif, Ranjit Singh was afflicted with virulent small-pox at the age of five. He lost one eye, became 'kana', and his face had become so disfigured that he looked repulsive.[25] In 1800, Ranjit Singh took Lahore, with the active support of his mother-in-law Sada Kaur. In 1801, he 'formally assumed the title of Maharaja, or Raja of Rajas, and, in a public darbar held on the occasion, declared that, in all public correspondence, he should be styled "Sarkar", signifying power and state'.[26] In 1802, he married Moran 'according to the Mahomedan rites'.[27] In 1802, Rani Nakain,[28] or Raj Kaur gave birth to the first son of Ranjit Singh, Kharak Singh. In 1807, Rani Mahtab Kaur 'presented the Maharaja with Sher Singh, and Tara Singh as her twin sons'.[29] Latif clearly states that Rani Mahtab Kaur 'never bore any children to the Maharaja. Sada Kaur knew well that the only way of increasing her power with her son-in-law was through her daughter'.[30] According to Latif, 'Ranjit Singh was never deceived; but as he liked the idea of

[23] Latif, *History of the Panjab*, 341.

[24] Ibid., 340.

[25] Ibid., 341.

[26] Ibid., 353.

[27] Ibid., 358.

[28] In 1808, after Ranjit Singh took Sheikhupura and gave it to Prince Kharak Singh as jagir and his mother, Rani Nakain as his guardian. The rani lived in the fort until her death, and seldom came to Lahore. (Latif, 370).

[29] Latif, *History of the Panjab*, 370.

[30] Ibid.

being called a father, he treated both as sons, and called them Shahzadas, or princes'.[31]

On 25 October 1809, a treaty was signed between C. T. Metcalfe, on behalf of Governor-General Lord Minto, and Maharaja Ranjit Singh, 'by which Ranjit Singh agreed not to attempt conquest, or occupy territory south of the Sutlej, and to withdraw all claims of sovereignty over the Sikhs inhabiting that territory'. [32] In 1814–15, Shah Shuja was made prisoner by Ranjit Singh, and the Kohinoor was forcibly taken from him.[33] In 1815, Shah Shuja left Lahore. In 1819, Latif mentioned the birth of Multana Singh to Rani Rattan Kaur, and Rani Daya Kaur had two sons, Kashmira Singh and Pishora Singh.[34] In 1821, Nau Nihal Singh, the first grandson of Maharaja Ranjit Singh, was born to Kharak Singh and Chand Kaur.[35]

The first mention of Maharani Jindan and Duleep Singh in both Cunningham[36] and Latif's account is in Sher Singh's time. The relationship between Maharaja Sher Singh and his Prime Minister Dhian Singh was deteriorating, due to the ascending influence of the Sindhianwala, Attar Singh, Ajit Singh and Lahna Singh. Sher Singh pardoned them for fighting on the side of Chand Kaur, and they heavily influenced Sher Singh.[37] Latif states that Dhian Singh.

---

[31] Ibid.

[32] Ibid., 379.

[33] Ibid., 399.

[34] Ibid., 419.

[35] Ibid., 425.

[36] J. D. Cunningham, *A History of the Sikhs,* ed. By H.L.O. Garrett. (Oxford: Oxford University Press, 1918), 216.

[37] Latif, *History of the Panjab*, 510.

began to show great consideration to the child Dulip Singh,
a five-year-old son of Maharaja Ranjit Singh. He treated the
child as the legitimate and rightful heir to the throne and
showed him great respect. He started taking out the young
prince in public proclaiming his lineage as the son of the great
Maharaja by his highly-favoured queen, the Rani Jindan.[38]

Cunningham also writes in his account that the English authorities
thought that the official line of Ranjit Singh's family ended
with Nau Nihal Singh, and the British were not aware of the
existence of Duleep Singh. He writes that Sher Singh's claim was
treated with 'scorn and the English authorities were reminded
of what perhaps they had never known, viz. that Rani Jindan, a
favourite wife or concubine of Ranjit Singh, had borne to him
a son named Dalip'.[39] Cunningham is doubtful about the validity
of the marriage between Maharani Jindan and Maharaja Ranjit
Singh.[40] However, Lala Sohan Lal Suri, vakeel of the Lahore
durbar, mentions Duleep Singh's birth in his Persian work,
Umadat-i-Tawarikh.[41] Lala Sohan Lal Suri writes, 'On the 23rd of
Bhadon Sambat 1895 (6th September 1838 A.D., the glorious
Sahibzada was born of Mai Jindan (Jind Kaur) at Lahore.'[42] The
maharani sent the information to Maharaja Ranjit Singh through
Munshi Gobind Ram Sahai. The maharaja 'expressed unlimited
pleasure'. Raja Kalan Bahadur (Dhian Singh), 'according to the

[38] Ibid.
[39] Cunningham, 216.
[40] Ibid.
[41] Lala Sohan Lal Suri, *Umdat-ul-Tawarikh, An Original Source of Punjab History, Chronicles of the Reign of Maharaja Ranjit Singh, 1831-1839*, Daftar III, Part V, trans. V.S. Suri, 1972, 525.
[42] Suri, *Umdat-ul-Tawarikh*, Part III, V, 525.

custom of the hilly region, put fresh things (fruits or vegetables) over the head of the Munshi'.[43]

The British, it seems, were taken aback with the elevation of Duleep Singh as the maharaja. Lieutenant Colonel A. J. Richmond, agent to the governor general in the North-West Frontier, wrote to J. Thomason, secretary to the Government of India,

> Raee Kishen Chund did not touch upon the birth of Duleep Singh who has been styled Maharaja, nor did I allude to the day. I talk at present only of the Durbar, or Court, in the abstract, and treat the Vakeel as the agent of a de-facto government. Hereafter should Raee Kishan Chund broach the subject of the hereditary right of Duleep Singh, I propose to say to him that whoever the Sikh people generally, and the leading men of the country, regard and obey as the children of their late ruler, will not perhaps be objected to by the British Government, and that I am aware that Duleep Singh has for several years been talked of as the child of Runjeet Singh.[44]

The British doubted the paternity of Maharaja Duleep Singh, questioning the character of Maharani Jindan.[45]

---

[43] Suri, *Umdat-ul-Tawarikh*, Part III, v, 525; Khushwant Singh mentions the birth of his seventh son, Duleep Singh, from Jindan, just before his meeting with Lord Auckland, 186.

[44] No. 179. Letter from Lieutenant Colonel A. J. Richmond, AGG, NWP to J. Thomson, Secretary to GOI, dated 26 September 1844, in Foreign Secret, nos. 487-94, 23 March 1844.

[45] Major Edwardes writes in his account on Duleep Singh as a 'child, not of Runjeet Sing, but of the water-carrier of his bath and a girl in the harem, whom, between drunkenness and dotage, the monarch had called his "wife"'. Edwardes, *A Year on Punjab Frontier in 1848-49*, 7.

According to Major Carmichael Smyth, the conspiracies and bloody deaths of Maharaja Ranjit Singh's successors were planned by the Dogra brothers, Dhian Singh and Gulab Singh. Gardener,[46] who served both Ranjit Singh and after his death Raja Gulab Singh, narrates in his account the ambitions of the Dogras that Heera Singh, the son of Raja Dhian Singh, would succeed Ranjit Singh, as the latter preferred him over his sons. Gardner writes that Ranjit Singh loved Heera Singh 'like a son from his birth'.[47] He 'could hardly bear the boy to be out of his sight, and he from infancy was sedulously taught to call the monarch *taba* (papa)'.[48] This affection emboldened the Dogra brothers, leading 'to successive deeds of violence by which it seemed to them that their ambitious design might be gratified. This dream was that Hira Singh, the heir of their family, or at least the most promising of its rising generation, might eventually succeed to the throne of Ranjit Singh.[49] Gardner gives the account of the conspiracy hatched by the Dogra brothers to discredit Kharak Singh, the son and successor of Maharaja Ranjit Singh, by spreading rumours among the Khalsa army that his minister Chet Singh was in the service of the British, and Kharak Singh too intended to go under the protection of the British.[50] The Dogra brothers were also able to influence his wife Chand Kaur and his

---

[46] Gardner was married to a girl from Dhian Singh's family, making him privy to all the happenings of the Dogras, 244–45. Colonel Alexander Gardner, *Soldier and Traveller: Memoirs of Alexander Gardner* (Colonel of Artillery in the Service of Maharaja Ranjit Singh), Edited by Major Hugh Pearse & Introduction by Sir Richard Temple, (Edinburgh and London: William Blackwood and Sons, 1848).

[47] Gardner, *Soldier and Traveller*, 212.

[48] Ibid.

[49] Ibid.

[50] Ibid., 226.

son Nau Nihal Singh against the maharaja. According to the Dogra brothers' conspiracy, at night, the ladies' door of the palace was deliberately left open for them to enter the palace. They killed Chet Singh, and Kharak Singh was made prisoner. He was slowly poisoned in prison, and he died in nine months. Kharak Singh's cremation ended with the fatal accident of his son, Nau Nihal, when the pillar of the doorway fell on him and the son of Dhian Singh. The Dogra brothers were suspected of being involved in his death, but Gardner cited Latif's reasoning that if the Dogra brothers had planned it, then Dhian Singh's son, Udam Singh, who also died on the spot, would not have accompanied Nau Nihal Singh. 'Dhyan Singh himself also appears to have narrowly escaped being crushed, his arm being severely contused. This certainly points to an accident.'[51] Gardner states that after this episode, the Dogra brothers deliberately divided themselves into two camps, one supporting the widow of Kharak Singh, Chand Kaur and other supporting Sher Singh.[52] Dhian Singh supported Sher Singh. Gardner describes the elevation of Sher Singh to the guddee and his betrayal by the Sindhianwalas in September 1843.[53] Cunningham also states that by the summer of 1843, Dhian Singh perceived his influence on Sher Singh on the wane, and he 'began to talk of the boy Dalip Singh, to endeavour to possess the minds of the Sindhianwala' chiefs.[54] The Sindhiawalas killed Sher Singh, his young son, Partap Singh and Raja Dhian Singh.[55] Then there is a mention of Duleep Singh and Maharani Jindan. According to Gardner,

---

[51] Ibid.

[52] Ibid., 227.

[53] Ibid.

[54] Cunningham, 230.

[55] Ibid.

Maharani Jindan was a protégé of Dhian Singh. When she was thirteen, Maharaja Ranjit Singh gave Maharani Jindan to Raja Dhian Singh with an allowance of Rs 5,000.[56] He treated her with dignity and 'ultimately effected the celebration of the *Karewa,* tantamount to the *chadar dalna*[57] marriage ceremony, between her and Ranjeet Singh'.[58] Gardner wrote that from that time, 'Her ascendancy over the Maharaja was soon gained, and never lost.'[59] The role of the English will be discussed in a subsequent section.

According to Latif and Cunningham, at the age of eight, 'Dulip Singh was proclaimed Maharaja of Punjab in September 1843'.[60] Dhian Sing's son Hira Singh was appointed as his wazir at twenty-five. Hira Singh was under the influence of Jalla Missar, 'a crafty and fanatic Brahmin from the mountains'.[61] A rivalry existed between Hira Singh and Suchet Singh, his uncle, the younger brother of Dhian Singh. Maharani Jindan preferred Suchet Singh for the *wazirat,* 'and induced him to aspire' to the post. Hira Singh was regarded 'as a stripling, inexperienced in business and incapable of discharging the duties of the office entrusted to him'.[62] Suchet Singh had the support of Maharani Jindan and her elder brother, Jawahir Singh.[63] Hira Singh won over the army by 'adding two and a half rupees to the pay of the common soldiers'.[64]

---

[56] Gardner, *Soldier and Traveller,* 253.

[57] *Chadar dalna* or throwing the sheet was considered legitimate, and the offspring had the right of inheritance.

[58] Gardner, *Soldier and Traveller,* 253.

[59] Ibid.

[60] Latif, *History of the Panjab,* 520; Cunningham, 231.

[61] Latif, *History of the Panjab,* 521.

[62] Ibid.

[63] Ibid.

[64] Ibid.

Suchet Singh, conspiring with Jawahir Singh, decided to inflict a blow to Hira Singh's powers. 'At a review of the *Khalsa* troops, Jawahir Singh was induced to mount an elephant, with the young Maharaja in his arms, and to complain to the troops of the harsh treatment to which the royal boy and his mother had been subjected at the hands of the minister and his party.'[65] His threat of taking refuge with the British, aimed at getting sympathy for the young ruler, earned the ire of the Khalsa, who found the thought of British protection repugnant. The command of the Khalsa troops was under Missar Jodha Ram, a Brahmin, father-in-law of Jalla. He gave Jawahir Singh a blow on his face, and both Suchet Singh and Jawahir Singh were 'declared traitors to the State'.[66] Duleep Singh was brought back to Lahore fort and handed over to his mother, while Jawahir Singh was put in confinement in the haveli of Maharaja Kharak Singh. The Khalsa spared his life at the request of the soldiers as the maternal uncle of the maharaja. Suchet Singh died fighting bravely against the much larger forces of the Lahore durbar.

Maharaja Ranjit Singh had two other surviving sons—Kashmira Singh held Sialkot as his patrimony from the maharaja while Pishora Singh held Gujranwala.[67] However, Duleep Singh's claim was considered superior to those of these two adopted sons. Hira Singh felt insecure about his position and wanted to remove the threat from these two.[68] The Khalsa troops 'were averse to the reputed sons of the old Maharaja being subjected to ignominy'.[69] According to Latif, the Sikhs 'had the profoundest

---

[65] Ibid.
[66] Ibid., 522.
[67] Ibid., 522.
[68] Ibid., 523.
[69] Ibid., 523.

esteem for even the adopted sons of a man whom they universally revered, and that the great Khalsa was from the first averse to waging war with the reputed sons of the late Maharaja'.[70] On this issue, serious differences arose between Hira Singh and the Khalsa troops. However, he was able to win them over with offers of money. But Hira Singh's blind adherence to Pandit Jalla proved to be his undoing. Pandit Jalla, according to both Cunningham and Latif, treated Maharani Jindan and her brother, Jawahir Singh, with contempt. Cunningham had a low opinion of Lal Singh as he observes at one place in his account that Pandit Jalla 'raised unworthy Lal Singh, a Brahmin, and a follower of the Rajas of Jammu (in 1844) but who was understood to have gained a disgraceful influence over the impure mind of Rani Jindan'.[71]

Both Cunningham and Latif mention Maharani Jindan's closeness to Lal Singh. Lal Singh, the treasurer, was Raja Dhian Singh's protégé. According to Latif, 'The cunning Rani Jindan and her lover, Lal Singh, entered into a conspiracy to overthrow the power of the Dogra element, and with it the ascendancy of the Misser Jalla.'[72] Jawahir Singh was supplied with money to win over the discontented Nihangs, other fanatics and the disgruntled regular troops to join on the maharani's side. Pandit Jalla gave the soldiers a reason to be angry with him by publicly insulting Maharani Jindan, while she was distributing 'golden *butkis*' (butki is a gold coin, also called temple coins, which bring good luck, generally weighing about 8 grams) as alms to the poor.[73] According to Latif, the 'incensed queen and her injured brother appealed to the children of Khalsa'[74] for

---

[70] Ibid., 523–4.

[71] Cunningham, 240.

[72] Latif, *History of the Panjab*, 529.

[73] Ibid.

[74] Ibid.

this insult to the relative of the great Maharaja. The soldiers demanded the presence of Pandit Jalla. Hira Singh, sensing the danger, left his private residence on 21 December 1844[75] with Pandit Jalla and his followers. They were chased by Sardar Sham Singh Attariwala and General Mewa Singh Majithia. Pandit Jalla was caught and cut to pieces when he stopped out of exhaustion. With a body of General Ventura's Dragoons, Jawahir Singh ordered the little village where Hira Singh had stopped to quench his thirst to be set on fire, and Hira Singh and his soldiers were killed while trying to escape.[76] Jawahir Singh became the wazir.

According to Latif, if Duleep Singh was supervised by the Sindhianwalas, being of the direct lineal descendants of the common ancestors with Ranjit Singh, then the Dogra influence could have been removed. The interests of Sindhianwalas naturally aligned with Duleep Singh. Latif felt that the 'extirpation of the Sindhianwalas and the restoration of the Dogra family, whose interests could never have been identical with those of the legitimate rulers, was a death-blow to the kingdom of the great Maharaja'.[77] After the death of Hira Singh and Pandit Jalla, Jawahir Singh became the wazir on 14 May 1845. Lal Singh was given the title of raja at the same time,[78] occupying the crucial positions in the Lahore durbar. According to Latif, the maharani offered the office of wazir to Gulab Singh, showing political acumen, but Jawahir Singh's will prevailed. On 10 July 1845, Maharaja Duleep Singh was betrothed to the daughter of Chattar Singh, chief of Attari.[79]

---

[75] Ibid., 530.

[76] Ibid.

[77] Ibid., 531.

[78] Ibid., 532.

[79] Ibid.

It seems that the ambitions of the Dogra family of controlling Lahore didn't end. According to Latif, Gulab Singh Dogra of Jammu played a dangerous game. On the one hand, he encouraged Pishora Singh, who in the words of Latif was 'a vain person of inadequate capacity, with nothing but his relationship with the great Maharaja to recommend him'.[80] On the other side, Gulab Singh instigated Jawahir Singh to remove him as a threat and rival to Duleep Singh. Pishora Singh had the support of the Khalsa troops, Jawahir Singh was not on good terms with the army. Maharani Jindan showed sagacity and maturity in offering the wazir's position to Gulab Singh, though thwarted by her brother. She also showed diplomatic skills and maturity in inviting Pishora Singh to the Lahore durbar, where he 'was received with open arms and treated with honour as the equal of Dulip Singh, her own son'.[81] Latif writes that this aroused the jealousy of her brother, who was cold to Pishora Singh and was also disrespectful to him in the durbar.[82] Pishora Singh became distrustful of this treatment and decided to stay with General Avitabile. Pishora Singh was initially supported by the army, but later the rani and her brother won over the soldiers with promises of gold and other things. The army told Pishora Singh to withdraw to his estates in Gujranwala, which he did. Raja Gulab Singh, who had conspired to bring about the rupture between Pishora Singh and the Lahore durbar, seeing his plans fail, advised Jawahir Singh to assassinate Pishora Singh, for the interests and stability of the kingdom of Lahore. Pishora Singh had taken the fort of Attock. Jawahir Singh sent Sardar Chattar Singh Attariwala and Fatteh Singh Tiwana to punish Pishora Singh, without the aid of the Khalsa troops. They induced

---

[80] Ibid., 533.
[81] Ibid.
[82] Ibid.

Pishora Singh to capitulate by agreeing to his terms, thus putting him off guard. He was 'treacherously made prisoner and thrown into a dark dungeon, or tower called *Kala Burj*, in the fort of Atok, where he was strangled at night and his body thrown into the Indus'.[83]

The Khalsa troops did not take the news well and swore vengeance on Jawahir Singh. Gulab Singh Dogra also stoked the fire of the Khalsa. He had ingratiated himself with all the parties in the Lahore durbar, 'save Jawahir Singh, whom he may have despised as of no capacity'.[84] Jawahir Singh and Maharani Jindan tried their best to drop the matter by various inducements. The Dogra faction had already bribed the deputies of the army. The Khalsa army remained unmoved, demanding the appearance of Jawahir Singh before them. On 21 September 1845, taking Maharani Jindan and Maharaja Duleep Singh, he appeared before the Khalsa. The maharaja was in his uncle's lap on an elephant, with Maharani Jindan on another elephant, with the slave-girl Mangla and other members of the zenana and slave girls. Maharani Jindan again made promises of lavish rewards to the soldiers in the hope of saving her brother.[85] However, the Khalsa army did not hear anything that Jawahir Singh had to say, and he was stabbed with a bayonet and dragged down from the elephant. Latif described the rani's 'shrieks lamenting over the death of her beloved brother',[86] cursing the Khalsa. The next morning, she flung herself and Duleep Singh on her brother's body and her painful cries on seeing the mangled body of her brother 'touched the sympathies of the most callous

---

[83] Ibid., 535.

[84] Cunningham, 232–3.

[85] Latif, *History of the Panjab*, 535.

[86] Ibid., 536.

spectator'.[87] With great difficulty, the maharani was persuaded to return to Lahore by noon. For weeks, she was inconsolable, making the Khalsa feel guilty and uncomfortable. Sikh troops sought to make peace with her, and the maharani convened a meeting of the panches and sardars at the Summum Burj. When all had assembled, she declared that she would be satisfied if her enemies were seized and delivered to her.[88] Jawahir Mal was taken and given to her. Pirthi Singh and other Dogras were quietly made to leave. Under the advice of Lal Singh, 'who was generally understood to be her paramour',[89] Jawahir Mal was also released.

Maharani Jindan now assumed direct charge of the administration and held daily durbars, at which orders were passed. She was declared regent of the state after the Dussehra, and frequently appeared in public, consulting Diwan Dina Nath, Bhai Ram Singh and Missar Lal Singh on state affairs.[90] But the real power rested with the panches, or delegates of the army, who were inclined to give the office of wazir to Gulab Singh, though he declined. Tej Singh, nephew of Khushal Singh, was offered the wazirat, but he too declined. The maharani then tried to make Lal Singh the wazir. Five slips of paper were prepared, and the young maharaja was to pick a slip. Lal Singh's name turned up, but the Sikh army refused to accept him. The maharani continued as the regent, assisted by Lal Singh as her executive minister and Tej Singh as the commander-in-chief.[91] The rani could see how precarious her situation was, with control in the hands of the turbulent

[87] Ibid.
[88] Ibid., 537.
[89] Ibid.
[90] Ibid.
[91] Ibid.

Sikh soldiery. With an empty treasury and the resources of the kingdom drained, she was unable to meet the soldiers' constant demands for money. The soldiers openly talked of making an infant son of Sher Singh the maharaja of Punjab. According to Latif, faced with such challenges, the rani devised a plan to divert the Khalsa's attention and thus break their union and weaken their hold on the Lahore durbar. They mooted the 'proposal of crossing the Sutlej to make war on the British Government'.[92] However, the plan was temporarily shelved, as there was no munition for war and inadequate military provisions. In November 1845, Lal Singh openly took up the charge of wazir 'and conducted the business of State under the control of the queen-mother'.[93]

In Latif's account,[94] it is suggested that there was a deliberate attempt by the Lahore durbar to spread the news that the British army was advancing to the south and east of the Sutlej. Lord Hardinge, in a letter to his wife, dated 3 December 1845, wrote that the queen, 'in fear of her own life from the ferocity of the troops (but above all anxious to save the life of her lover Lal Sing, whom she had appointed her minister) had been using all exertions to induce the army from Lahore to move down upon our advanced stations and invade our provinces'.[95] The letters from the Sikh governors of the territories beyond the river were produced to show that British officers were interfering with Sikh subjects and causing all sorts of trouble. This was sufficient to rouse the Khalsa army to agitation. At this moment, Lal Singh convened a council of the sardars, panches of the state's army

---

[92] Ibid., 538.
[93] Ibid.
[94] Ibid.
[95] Dr Kirpal Singh, (ed.), *Hardinge Papers relating to Punjab*, (Patiala: Publication Bureau, Punjabi University, 2002), 3.

and officers at the Shalimar Garden. Diwan Dina Nath read them a letter, purporting to have been sent by the Sikh officers beyond the Sutlej, informing them about the mistreatment of the subjects of the durbar by the British authorities and demanding tribute from them. He also informed that Peshawar and Kashmir had ceased to remit a single rupee to the durbar and anarchy reigned throughout the country. Dina Nath 'reminded them that their sovereign was but a child, that the whole Sikh nation were, as loyal subjects, bound to defend his rights, and that, unless arrangements were speedily made for the maintenance of Sikh rule and power, its utter collapse would be the inevitable result'.[96] He also conveyed the maharani's wishes to make Lal Singh the wazir and sardar Tej Singh the commander-in-chief of the Sikh armies. 'This eloquent speech made such an impression on the *panches* of the Khalsa and the sardars assembled, that there was a unanimous cry for war, and the appointments proposed by the Maharani were acceded to with loud acclamations.'[97] They were appointed at the samadh or a mausoleum of Maharaja Ranjit Singh on 8 November 1845.[98] The Khalsa pledged their fidelity to the young maharaja and obedience to Lal Singh and Tej Singh.

On 17 November 1845, a formal declaration of war against the British Government was made, on the following grounds 'alleged by the darbar':

First, the advance of bodies of British troops towards the Sutlej and the adoption by the British for defensive measures, in anticipation of the outbreak of hostilities in the Panjab, which

[96] Latif, *History of the Panjab*, 538.
[97] Ibid., 538.
[98] Cunningham, according to the *Lahore Newsletter*, 8 November 1845, 263.

were looked upon in the light of aggressive preparations; secondly, the refusal of the British authorities to restore eighteen lakhs of rupees in the Ferozepur treasury, claimed by the Sikh Government as the property of the late Raja Suchet Singh; thirdly, the confirmation, by the British Government, of the escheat of the village Morwan to the Raja of Nabha; and lastly, the refusal of the British Government to allow a free passage to the Sikh troops into the Khalsa possession south of the Sutlej.[99]

Rumours circulated that the English were getting the boats ready at Bombay to make a bridge across the Sutlej and that troops were being equipped in Sindh for an advance on Multan. Latif writes: 'All these allegations were, of course, mere pretexts to lead the uncontrollable and obnoxious Khalsa army into collision with a power which was sure to destroy their influence, if not their existence, and so make it possible to establish a Sikh government in Punjab unrestrained by the censorship of the army.'[100]

According to Sita Ram Kohli, 'The use of artillery and the employment of large masses of disciplined infantry were recent innovations in the Indian system of warfare.'[101] The Indians despised foot soldiers and were accustomed to fighting on horseback. Gradually, Maharaja Ranjit Singh introduced a disciplined infantry with regular drills. He paid his soldiers in cash, and some senior officers were given revenue grants. In

---

[99] Latif, *History of the Panjab*, 538–9.

[100] Ibid., 539.

[101] Sita Ram Kohli, *Catalogue of Khalsa Darbar Records*, *Volume I* (Lahore: Superintendent, Government Printing, 1919), 1. After the transfer of the administration of the Punjab in 1849, the Khalsa durbar records, consisting of official papers dealing with the ministerial details of the several departments of the government of Maharaja Ranjit Singh and his successors.

his lifetime, 'the Maharaja kept the size and expenditure of his army within proper limits, and [. . .] within seven years after his death, both the strength of the army and the amount paid on account of salaries, were very considerably increased'.[102] The Sikh soldiers mastered 'all the tactics of European warfare' and all the complicated manoeuvres of a European army.[103] This army, trained by the most efficient European officials like Allard, Ventura, Court and Avitabile[104] among others, became all powerful after Maharaja Ranjit Singh's death, forcing his successors 'to increase their pay'.[105] Finance was a contentious issue that Maharani Jindan also had to face. There are accusations against the maharani that she deliberately sent the Khalsa to fight the British in the First Anglo-Sikh War, to ease off the pressure on the Lahore durbar.[106] The treachery of the Sikh generals, Tej Singh and Lal Singh is also attributed to this conspiracy. A few British records loosely accuse the maharani of wreaking vengeance on the Khalsa army for executing her brother, Jawahir Singh. It cannot be said with certainty that the maharani was complicit, as discussed later.

The English blamed the First and the Second Anglo-Sikh Wars on the indisciplined Sikh army. But Sohan Singh Suri's description of the professional training of the Sikh soldiers under Maharaja Ranjit Singh refutes such claims. Cunningham was equally critical of the Governor Generals Lord Ellenborough and Lord Hardinge, as their decisions created situations that

---

[102] Kohli, *Catalogue of Khalsa Darbar Records*, 5.

[103] Ibid., 6.

[104] Ibid., 8.

[105] Ibid., 5.

[106] Major Edwardes writes: 'It was to divert the Sikh army from dethroning him' (Duleep Singh) that Maharani Jindan had 'thrust them on the invasion of British India'. Edwardes, *A Year on Punjab Frontier in 1848-49*, 6.

compelled the Sikhs to fight. He wrote that the Sikhs had a reason to feel threatened by the British.

> Many circumstances, unheeded or undervalued by the English, gave further strength to this conviction. It had not indeed been made known to the Sikhs that Sir William Macnaghten and others had proposed to dismember their kingdom by bestowing Peshawar on Shah Shuja when Ranjeet Singh's line was held to an end with the death of his grandson.'[107]

He felt that the British aggravated the situation with the Sikhs with Major Broadfoot's appointment as the political agent on the Punjab Frontier, which 'greatly increased the probabilities of a war with the Sikhs'.[108]

Cunningham wrote that Lal Singh's closeness to the English was 'common knowledge'.[109] According to him, Lal Singh was 'in touch with Captain Nicolson, the British Agent at Ferozepore',[110] citing the *Calcutta Review* of June 1849, which

> admits that the former was not only in communication with Captain Nicolson, as stated, but that on 7th February 1845, he was understood to have sent a plan of the Sikh position at Sobraon[111] to Colonel Lawrence, and that on the 19th

---

[107] Cunningham, 250-51.

[108] Ibid., 255.

[109] Cunningham, he cites Dr. Macgregor's *History of the Sikhs* where he mentions the close contact between Lala Singh and the British, 263.

[110] Cunningham, 263.

[111] Battle of Ferozehah on 21 December 1845, 28 January 1846, the Battle of Aliwal under Sir Harry Smith victory for the English, Battle of Sobraon on 10 February 1846: Tez Singh deserted, but the fiercest battle took place under Sham Singh Attariwala, with the Sikhs refusing

December 1845, the day after the battle of Mudki, Lal Singh's
agent came to Major Broadfoot.[112]

Cunningham seems to support the treachery of Tej Singh on
the following grounds: 'As regards Tej Singh's treachery it
may be stated that according to a reliable tradition, that officer
discovered early in the operations that his artillery ammunition
had been tampered with and much of it rendered useless. Such
treachery on the part of his own side doubtless had considerable
effect upon his subsequent conduct.'[113]

On 20 February 1846, Governor General Lord Hardinge
entered Lahore. The Treaty of Lahore was signed on 9 March
1846, marking the end of the First Anglo-Sikh War. Duleep
Singh was recognized as the maharaja, with Maharani Jindan as
the regent and Lal Singh as the executive minister. Sardar Tej
Singh, Ram Singh and Diwan Dina Nath were also present.
Jammu was taken by the British and given to Maharaja Gulab
Singh, recognized by Maharaja Duleep Singh.[114]

The giving of Jammu and Kashmir to Maharaja Gulab Singh
increased the tensions between him and the Lahore durbar. Raja
Lal Singh and other ministers visited the agent to the governor
general, North-West Frontier, on 9 April 1846, complaining

---

to surrender and in the carnage that followed, his body was found
amidst a heap of bodies. His servant, coming all the way from Attari
'placed the body on a raft and swam with it across the river'. His wife
had already immolated herself, with his clothes that he had worn on
his wedding day. Their Samadh is outside the village of Attari.

[112] Cunningham, 263.

[113] Ibid.

[114] Article 12 of the Treaty of Lahore. The detailed Treaty is available in
C. U. Aitchison, *A Collection of Treaties, Engagements and Sanads relating
to India and Neighbouring Countries*, Vol. IX, (Calcutta, Superintendent
of Government Printing Press, 1892), No. XVI, 39–43.

against 'aggression and retention of districts in the plains' by Gulab Singh.[115] The political agent squarely blamed the Sikh delegation for not supplying 'accurate information as to the lands in question'.[116] He also informed Fredrick Currie, 'The Maharanee continues very unwell, indeed I am inclined to think her life in danger. She has desired Rajah Lal Singh to take up his quarters in the palace so as always to be at hand.'[117] It seems more likely that the maharani did not wish to entertain the British. The British were disappointed with Maharaja Gulab Singh for not accommodating British expectations, as observed by the political agent. Financial concerns were the reason for this, as the agent writes, 'He still affects poverty. He seems to expect everything and to be little disposed to give in return.'[118]

The British officials did not hold the maharani in high esteem. Henry Lawrence, A. G. G., North–West Provinces, wrote to Fredrick Currie on 3 July 1846:

I perceive that Sirdar Heera Sing, the Maha Ranee's brother, though himself "a worthless debauched character, is indignant at the intimacy between his sister and the minister and loudly declared that if the latter continues to make the place his residence, he shall be made to repent". Sirdar Heera Sing is not singular in this expression of opinion, and I see in the profligacy of the parties, the most probable stepping stone to the destruction of the present administration.[119]

---

[115] Foreign Department, Secret, No. 800, 26 December 1846, from AGG, NWF to Fred Currie, Secretary to the Government of India with Governor General, Lahore, 9 April 1846.

[116] Ibid.

[117] Ibid.

[118] Ibid.

[119] No. 952, from H. M. Lawrence, AGG, NWP to Currie, Secretary to GOI with GG, Headquarters, Simla, 3 July 1846.

As the wazir and the trusted advisor of Maharani Jindan, Lal
Singh was trying to consolidate his position in the Lahore
durbar. As observed by Henry Lawrence, 'In the Durbar, Raja
Lall Sing carries himself with a high hand.' The British official
files highlight his feud with the maharani's close confidante
and slave girl, Munglee, also referred to as Mangla. Lal Singh
wanted to eliminate all his rivals. 'He has for the present,
expelled the slave girl Munglee, from the Summum Burj, and
has contrived to place his own people almost entirely around
the Maha Ranee.'[120] But Munglee was also a spirited woman.
As H. M. Lawrence wrote, she 'has by no means given up the
contention for authority'.[121] Here the maharani is again referred
in unflattering terms:

> She continued to rival her mistress in debauchery when
> Raja Lal Sing bars the admittance of her lovers to the court
> precincts, she goes almost openly out to them. The woman
> aims at the *Unzarat* (treasury). She tells the Maha Ranee
> that, if armed with authority, she will arrange the affairs of
> the Provinces, and the arrears of the troops and guarantee
> that henceforward the latter are regularly paid, month
> by month.[122]

Munglee and Lal Singh were fighting to control the finances of
the Lahore durbar.

The British watched with concern the rise of the French
army officer, Colonel Cortlandt, under the regency of Maharani
Jindan and encouraged by Lal Singh. Lawrence reported:

[120] Ibid.
[121] Ibid.
[122] Ibid.

Colonel Cortlandt has lately risen to great power at Lahore. It is discovered that he is a very faithful servant and accordingly, from leaving the command of our one Regiment, he received two and has now been informed that he is to have four, with 25 guns and 12000 horsemen. This force is a sort of bodyguard, and having few or no Sikhs in its ranks, is expected under all circumstances to be faithful.[123]

From the English official records, it seems that the British felt that Lal Singh was encouraging Cortlandt to protect the Lahore durbar from the unpredictability of the Sikh army of the past. Lawrence is sceptical about this move: 'I much doubt whether Colonel Cortlandt is the man to restrain household troops from the practices of their predecessors, indeed if they are always kept at Lahore, they cannot fail to become dangerous to the Durbar.'[124]

Similar observations were made by F. Currie, secretary to the Government of India with the governor general. He reports as the items of intelligence, the consolidation of powers by Lal Singh, enlisting 'foreigners and *mussulmans* from his own native place. He is lavish in his praise of Colonel Cortlandt'.[125] He kept himself surrounded with the Afghan mercenaries, 'well-armed and watchful'.[126] He was afraid of the Khalsa, who was dissatisfied with him. The agent was critical of the officers at the Lahore durbar and he stated, 'It is lamentable to think that there is not one man in the Durbar honestly working for the state, but that individual aims only at

---

[123] Ibid.

[124] Ibid.

[125] Agent to Governor General, N. W. Frontier to F. Currie, Secretary to the Government of India, 26 December 1847, No. 1008, Fort William, Foreign Political Department.

[126] Ibid.

his own aggrandisement and enrichment.'[127] He found Diwan Deena Nath the 'most patriotic man among them',[128] though bitterly opposed to the British.

Henry Lawrence,[129] in the aftermath of the First Anglo-Sikh War, 'dreaded . . . the machinations of the Rani and her party in the Council'.[130] Lal Singh was trying to consolidate his power. The maharani was aggrieved with the transfer of Kashmir to Gulab Singh. Sheikh Imamuddin the governor of Kashmir, and the representative for the Sikh durbar, opposed Gulab Singh's assumption of power in Kashmir and revolted. After his surrender, Imamuddin informed the British that he was acting on the orders of the Lahore durbar, under the written instructions of Raja Lal Singh. Lal Singh was tried and removed to Firozepore in December 1846. Under the changed circumstances, a fresh agreement was signed between the British government and the Lahore durbar on 16 December 1846 known as the Treaty of Bhairowal.[131] Under the terms of the treaty, a British officer was stationed as resident at Lahore, with 'full authority to direct and control all matters in every department of the State'.[132] This arrangement was to continue during the minority of Maharaja Duleep Singh. It was to cease when he turned sixteen. A Council of Regency was constituted, which included Sardar Tej Singh, Sher Singh Attariwala, Diwan Dina Nath, Fakir Nuruddin, Sirdar Runjore Singh Mujeetheea, Bhai Nidhan Singh, Sirdar Utter Singh

---

[127] Ibid.

[128] Ibid.

[129] During the period of March to December 1846.

[130] Innes, *Sir Henry Lawrence*, 61.

[131] Details of the treaty are available in Aitchison, *A Collection of Treaties, Engagements and Sanads relating to India and Neighbouring Countries,* Vol. IX, Treaty No. XVIII, 45–8.

[132] Cunningham, 417.

Kaleewalla and Sirdar Shumsher Singh Sindhanwalla, 'acting
under the control and guidance of the British Resident'.[133]
The Lahore State was to pay Rs 22 lakh per annum to the
British government for the upkeep of the army and other
administrative expenses. The maharani was removed from the
regency, and a sum of Rs 1.5 lakh was to be set aside for her
and her dependents.[134]

The maharani realized that the British had taken over the
reins of power at Lahore. With the Treaty of Bhairowal, she
became an implacable enemy of the British in Punjab. She
was in communication with the Sirdars to remove the British
from Punjab and is said to have thrown her bangles at them
for giving away the state.[135] In February 1847, a conspiracy
(called the Prema Conspiracy) was unearthed with an intent to
murder Henry Lawrence and Raja Tej Singh. On inquiry, the
maharani's servant was implicated, but no concrete evidence
could be found against the maharani.[136] The British authorities,
from Lawrence to Lord Hardinge and Fredrick Currie, were
anxious to remove her. They did their best to tarnish her
character, associating her with anyone who visited her. She was
kept virtually a prisoner in the Summum Burj of the palace.
The stories of her persecution, meanwhile, started agitating the
people of Punjab. The British knew that she was a formidable
threat. They got an opportunity to remove her from Lahore on
7 August 1847. Tej Singh was given the title of raja of Sialkot
for his loyalty to the British, but Maharaja Duleep Singh, on

[133] Innes, *Sir Henry* Lawrence, 69; Cunningham, 417.
[134] Cunningham, 419; Aitchison, *A Collection of Treaties, Engagements
and Sanads relating to India and Neighbouring Countries*, Vol. IX, Treaty
No. XVIII, 45–8.
[135] Khushwant Singh, *A History of the Sikhs, 1839-1964*, Vol. II,
(London: Oxford University Press, 1963), 63.
[136] Ibid. This is called the Prema Conspiracy.

the advice of his mother, objected to Tej Singh's investiture and refused to dip his finger in the saffron to put the saffron mark on the forehead of Tej Singh. This was an insult to Tej Singh and infuriated Henry Lawrence. The maharani's influence on Duleep Singh became evident, and on 19 August, Lawrence sent her to Sheikhupura fort, about 40 miles to the south-west of Lahore.[137]

The Lahore durbar had to put up with the British's incessant demand for payment of the troops. The main council of the Lahore durbar included Tej Singh, Fakir Nooroodin, Ram Singh and Diwan Deena Nath. The English behaved like an occupying force. John Lawrence, commissioner and superintendent on duty at Lahore, informed H. M. Elliot, secretary to the governor general, on 21 August 1847, 'I have this morning moved the Durbar to arrange for the payment of the troops in the Province, and will take care that no delay takes place in their doing it.'[138] They kept pressuring the Lahore durbar for the 'punctual returns of the revenue' as 'urgently necessary'.[139] Further, Henry Lawrence disbanded many of the Sikh regiments and carried out disarmament in Punjab, further disaffecting the disbanded soldiers of the Khalsa and creating unease among the people. Henry Lawrence was succeeded by Sir John Lawrence for a brief period.

In 1848, Lord Dalhousie became the governor general of India. On 6 April 1848, Sir Fredrick Currie became the resident of the Lahore durbar. The taxes on the people of Punjab increased excessively, and Multan raised the banner of revolt

---

[137] M. L. Ahluwalia, *Maharani Jind Kaur (1816-1863)*, 68.
[138] Foreign Secret, No. 104, 1847, No. 129, From, John Lawrence, Commissioner and Superintendent on duty at Lahore to H. M. Elliot, Secretary to the Governor General, dated Lahore, 21 August 1847.
[139] Ibid.

under Diwan Mulraj.[140] His father, Diwan Sawun Mull, was loyal to the Lahore durbar, and he would never revolt against 'a Sikh government'.[141] Mulraj was also equally loyal to the Lahore durbar. The British accused Mulraj of being oppressive to the people. Mulraj offered to resign. On his repeated request, the British sent Sirdar Kahn Singh to take up the governor's charge, accompanied by two English officers, P. A. Vans Agnew and Lieutenant W. A. Anderson. [142] According to Latif, on 19 April 1848, Diwan Mulraj handed the keys of the fort to the two English officers. Agnew and Anderson were attacked at the gate of the fort towards Idgah. Despite the injury, Agnew informed the resident of Lahore, with letters to General Cortlandt at Dera Ismail Khan and Lieutenant Edwardes at Bannu. Agnew asked Mulraj to meet him. Mulraj replied that the entire garrison had revolted, and he could neither come nor give up the guilty. The British should take care of their safety. His soldiers urged him to declare independence. On 20 April 1848, Mulraj declared war. All the Sikh soldiers deserted on the side of Mulraj. Kahn Singh was left with a few soldiers. The Lahore durbar delayed taking a decision, expressing their inability to put down Mulraj's rebellion. In the first battle at Dera Ghazi Khan, Mulraj lost his trans-Indus dependencies. On 18 June 1848, the battle of Kaneri was fought. Mulraj's army was put to flight. Mulraj was joined by Bhai Maharaj Singh, a revered Sikh guru. On 1 July 1848, at the Battle of Saddasam, Mulraj, commanding in person, was thrown from his elephant and fled to the city on a horse.[143]

---

[140] William Dalrymple and Anita Anand, *Kohinoor: The World's Most Infamous Diamond*, (New Delhi: Juggernaut, 2018), 125.

[141] From the AGG, NWF, to F. Currie, Officiating Secretary to Government with Governor General, in Foreign Department, Secret, Cons., No. 530, 23 March 1844.

[142] Latif, *History of the Panjab*, 538.

[143] Ibid., 562.

The siege of Multan began on 7 September 1848. Mulraj's troops fought well, but on 12 September 1848, they suffered reverses. At that point, the English received the news of the rebellion of Sardar Chattar Singh Attariwala at Hazara in August 1848, whose daughter was engaged to Duleep Singh. The Sikh troops at Hazara killed Colonel Canora, an American under the employment of the Sikh government. They attacked Attock but were repulsed by Lieutenant Nicolson.[144]

Meanwhile, on 14 September 1848, Raja Sher Singh, son of Chattar Singh and the member of the Council of Regency, ordered the *Dharam-ka-Dhosa* or religious drum to be beaten in the name of the Khalsa and joined the rebels. It was declared a war for religion and faith, and not against Mulraj. The Khalsa joined Mulraj. On 27 December 1848, the siege of Multan was resumed under the direct command of Lord Gough, the commander-in-chief. Mulraj's army was much depleted by many soldiers joining the rebellion of Chattar Singh. The resources at his disposal were also strained. On 27 December 1848, the English had taken many important areas in the suburbs. On 2 January 1849, two breaches were made in the city. By 3 January 1849, the town of Multan was battered. Mulraj was now cornered.[145] The 'rebel' Diwan Moolraj of Mooltan sent an urzee (a request) to the British, translated by Major Edwardes. According to the urzee, 'the garrison of Mooltan is now in the last extremity –the gunners are unable to secure their guns from incessant shelling; the buildings are almost all unroofed from the

---

[144] Foreign Department, Secret, 27 January 1849, 764. 'Papers relating to the affairs of Mooltan, Punjab and the Huzarah country'; No. 176, No. 7. From Major Herbert B. Edwardes, Assistant Resident to the Hon'ble F. Currie, Resident at Lahore, from Camp Mooltan, 6 January 1849; *Political Diaries of Lieut. H. B. Edwardes*, Assistant to the Resident at Lahore, 1847, (Allahabad: Pioneer Press, 1911), 49.
[145] Ibid.

same course and afford but little shelter'. Edwardes further stated that Diwan Moolraj had

> sought refuge in the gateway of Leikhee Gate, and every soldier is obliged to grind the wheat for his own dinner, all the flour having been blown up in the explosion of the Jumma Musjeed. In this state of things Moolraj's chief advisors are urgently preparing him to surrender, and he has promised either to do so or take poison if no succour reaches him in the course of three days.[146]

Major Edwardes concluded from this that it was a sign that Moolraj's 'pride is broken down at last, and he wants the courage to play out his part'.[147] Multan surrendered on 22 January 1849.[148]

Lord Dalhousie wrote at length to justify that the English did not make an issue of the killing of the English officers.

> The murder of the British officers at Mooltan, and the open rebellion of the Diwan Moolraj, were not made a pretext for a quarrel with the Government of Lahore. On the contrary, the offence of the Diwan Moolraj was sedulously distinguished from national wrong. The Sikhs were called upon to punish Moolraj as a rebel against their own sovereign, and to exact reparation for the British Government, whose protection they had previously invoked.[149]

---

[146] Ibid.

[147] Ibid.

[148] *Private Letters of the Marquess of Dalhousie*, 52; also available at www.archive.org.

[149] Ibid., 24.

In his Minutes, Dalhousie claimed that the war was 'due to no precipitation or fault of ours'.[150] Lord Dalhousie justified the British involvement as 'national safety'.

> But when it was seen that the spirit of the whole Sikh people was inflamed by the bitterest animosity against us—when chief after chief deserted our cause, until nearly their whole army, led by Sirdars who had signed the treaties, and by Members of the Council of Regency itself, was openly arrayed against us—when, above all, it was seen that the Sikhs, in their eagerness for our destruction, had even combined in unnatural alliance with Dost Mahomed Khan and his Mahomedan tribes—it became manifest that there was no alternative left. The question for us was no longer one of policy or expediency, but one of national safety.[151]

The Sikhs under Chattar Singh and Sher Singh joined hands with Dost Mohammad against the British and had to be subdued. Sher Singh took up his position at Rasul for the confrontation with the British. The judicious selection made by Sher Singh reflected on his skill as a general. Entrenchments were erected at Chillianwala. On 13 January 1849, the Battle of Chillianwala took place. It was bloody, and many Sikh soldiers on the side of the English deserted. The English did not obtain a decisive win as the Sikhs retreated. On 1 February 1849, the Battle of Gujarat began, with Chattar Singh and Sher Singh on one side and the British under Lord Gough on the other. The Sikhs lost, and on 12 March 1849, Sher Singh surrendered.[152] On 21 March 1849, Punjab was annexed to the East India Company.[153]

---

[150] Ibid., 23. Final Minute of the Marquess of Dalhousie.

[151] Ibid., 24.

[152] Latif, *History of the Panjab*, 571.

[153] See the details of the Treaty of 1849 between Lord Dalhousie and Maharajah Duleep Sing in Aitchison, *A Collection of Treaties, Engagements*

Evans Bell underlines three main reasons for the Second Anglo-Sikh War: 'the exile of the Maharanee, the refusal to fix a day for the Maharajah's marriage, and the treatment of Sirdar Chuttur Singh'.[154] Henry Lawrence had reservations about Sirdar Chattar Singh. He considered Sher Singh to be 'a bold and intelligent young man, his sister being betrothed to the Maharaja . . . His father (Chutter Singh) is however a creature of Maharajah Golab Sing's, and his great claim upon the Ranee is that he was the murderer of Prince Pishora Sing, her son's rival'.[155] There has been speculation in the English records that the diwan was a loyalist of Maharani Jindan and that she was behind his rebellion. In a recent work on the maharani, M. L. Ahluwalia mentions letters found on Mohan, a servant of Misr Shiv Dayal, the family priest of the maharani, revealing her secret plans.[156] The maharani was careful to have no direct hand in the conspiracies, so it was difficult to pin anything on her. In a letter of 16 May 1848, the resident wrote to the secretary to the Government of India that though 'there is no proof' of her involvement, 'but it is certain, at this moment, the eyes of Diwan Moolraj, of the whole Sikh army and military population are directed to the Maharanee as the rallying point of their rebellion or disaffection'.[157] In June 1848, Mohan and Shiv Dayal were arrested on the information given by Gama Beg of the Intelligence Department of the British Magistracy at Lahore and about thirty letters recovered from

---

and Sanads relating to India and Neighbouring Countries, Vol. IX, Treaty No. XIX, 49–50.

[154] Major Evans Bell, The Annexation of the Punjab and the Maharaja Duleep Singh (London: Trubner & Co., 1882), 12.

[155] Foreign Department, No. 992 (Cons.), Fort William, 26 December 1846, para 24.

[156] Ahluwalia, Maharani Jind Kaur (1816-63), 75.

[157] Sardar Ganda Singh, 'Three letters of Maharani Jind Kaur', in Proceedings of the Indian History Congress, Vol. 13, 1950, 304–13.

Mohan.[158] Therefore, it was decided to send the maharani from Sheikhupura first to Ferozepur and then to Banaras to remove any threat from her end. In both the Anglo–Sikh Wars, the maharani's presence was strongly felt in the background. The English dreaded her power over the Sikh chiefs and troops, and the Sikhs found her and Duleep Singh's trials and tribulations a source of inspiration. The maharani did not give up. She sent her vakeel, Sardar Jiwan Singh to represent her case to the governor general in Calcutta in December 1847.[159]

III

The British were always interested in Punjab. Their intentions were evident in the early 1800s. They justified their interference in Sikh affairs with the following reason: 'Our right of supremacy over the Seik Chiefs is that country we acquired when we became possessed of the powers formerly exercised by the Marhatta government in the North of Hindustan.'[160] The British established a military post at Sutlej under the command of Lieutenant Colonel Ochterlony.

Despite the denials by the British, they actively participated in the court intrigues at Lahore after Maharaja Ranjit Singh's death. The British were keeping a close eye on Ranjit Singh and his successors.[161] At the time of the accident of Nau Nihal, the British were present there. Cunningham, in his account, stated

---

[158] Ahluwalia, *Maharani Jind Kaur (1816-63)*, 75.

[159] Ganda Singh, 'Three letters of Maharani Jind Kaur', 310.

[160] Secret Letter from the Court, 13 February 1811 to 26 October 1816, to the Governor General in Council, Fort William in a letter of 18 September 1811. Correspondence with the Court available at National Archives, New Delhi.

[161] This is mentioned in many English and Indian accounts, Sohan Singh Seetal, *Maharani Jindan*, (Ludhiana: Lahore Book Shop, 2020).

that in the 1840s, the British policies regarding Punjab were changing. He wrote that 'further enquiry will show that the policy pursued by the English themselves for several years was not in reality well calculated to ensure a continuance of pacific relations; and they cannot, therefore, be held wholly blameless for a war which they expected and deprecated, and which they knew could only tend to their own aggrandisement'.[162] In July 1844, Lord Hardinge had succeeded Lord Ellenborough as governor general. The commander-in-chief at the time of the First Anglo-Sikh War was Sir Hugh Gough.[163] Cunningham is critical of both Hardinge and Gough for engaging in 'a desperate and, perhaps, useless struggle'.[164] The British assigned Major Broadfoot to take advantage of differences and factionalism at the Lahore durbar. Cunningham considered Major Broadfoot to be a bad choice as he was rash and abrasive. Cunningham criticized the English vulnerabilities in the battle as he stated that Tej Singh had the reserve and could have quickly taken the English as 'at a moment when the artillery ammunition of the English had failed, when a portion of their force was returning upon Fereozepore, and when no exertions could have prevented the remainder from retreating likewise if the Sikhs had boldly pressed forward'.[165] He criticized the decision of the British forces to fall back on the night of 21 December 1845. In Cunningham's estimate, there were a large number of casualties: 694 soldiers were killed and 1,721 were wounded, 103 English officers including Major Broadfoot were killed. As many as 2,000 Sikh soldiers were also killed.[166]

---

[162] Cunningham, 258.

[163] Ibid., 262.

[164] Ibid., 267, 22 December 1845.

[165] Ibid., 264.

[166] Ibid., 268.

It would be incorrect to say that the maharani wanted the decimation of the Sikh army as a revenge for the Khalsa killing her brother, as insinuated in the English accounts. On the contrary, Maharani Jindan did not give up at this stage and gathered around 500 Sikh soldiers to go to the battlefield to fight. The fact that the rani sent reinforcement to help the Sikh soldiers despite the soldiers suffering losses shows that Maharani Jindan did not want the decimation of the Sikh army.[167] She knew well that the extermination of the Khalsa would mean the end of Maharaja Ranjit Singh's dynasty. The maharani was negotiating at many fronts. She had to ward off the threat to her small son, Maharaja Duleep Singh and, in that case, the Khalsa army was the best protector against the intrigues of the Lahore durbar, which had seen some gruesome deaths in the last few years. She could only turn to her family, in particular, her brother Jawahir Singh. The rani showed political maturity in treating the remaining sons of Maharaja Ranjit Singh with love and warmth in 1845. She knew that the Khalsa army was strongly attached to the sons of Maharaja Ranjit Singh. Jawahir Singh did not show this political sagacity, betraying his reservations for Pishora and Kashmira Singh, angering the Khalsa. The Khalsa did not want the blood of scions of the erstwhile maharaja to be spilled. The last straw was the killing of Pishora Singh by treachery at night by the generals sent by Jawahir Singh at Attock, that too after he had surrendered. For this, Jawahir Singh was asked to appear before the Khalsa military court and executed.[168]

The maharani was able to use the outpouring of grief to move the most hardened of the Sikh generals and garner the sympathy as well as the support and loyalty of the army. Setting her grief aside, she entered the political business of running the

---

[167] Ibid.
[168] Latif, *History of the Panjab*, 638–9.

empire, holding the court herself. Her grief was palpable to the people of Lahore, as every time she visited the place where her brother was cremated, she crossed the entire bazaar. With her skilful oratory, knowing well what would rouse the Khalsa army, she was able to control them and could negotiate to appoint the officers of her choice at the Lahore durbar.[169] She may have been romantically associated with Raja Lal Singh, but she did not lose sight of her son's interests as the ruler of Punjab, and that remained a priority.

Cunningham also had a different view on the personal affairs of Maharani Jindan. He showed disapproval of her brother and her behaviour, but he also mentioned that 'decency was seldom violated in public; and the essential forms of a court were preserved to the last, especially when strangers were present'.[170] He also provided his insights into how the powerful behaved and the moral righteousness of the ordinary people:

> The private life of princes may be scandalous enough, while the moral tone of the people is high, and is, moreover, applauded and upheld by the transgressors themselves, in their capacity of magistrates. Hence the dominant vices of the powerful have, comparatively little influence on the public affairs. Further, the proneness of news-mongers to enlarge upon such personal failings is sufficiently notorious; and the diplomatic service of India has been often reproached for dwelling pruriently or maliciously on such matters. Finally, it is well known that the native servants of the English in Hindustan, who in too many instances are hirelings of little

---

[169] Ibid.

[170] Cunningham, 257, Enclosures to the Governor General's Letter to the Secret Communication of the 31 December 1845 (Parliament Papers, 26 February 1846).

education or respectability, think they best please their
employers, or chime in with their notions, when they traduce
all others, and especially those with whom there may be a
rivalry or a collision. So inveterate is the habit of flattery, and
so strong is the belief that Englishmen love to be themselves
praised and to hear others slighted, that even petty local
authorities scarcely refer to allied or dependent princes, their
neighbours, in verbal or in written reports, without using
some terms of disparagement towards them. Hence the scenes
of debauchery described by the Lahore news-writer are partly
due to his professional character, and partly to his belief that
he was saying what the English wanted to hear.[171]

Maharani Jindan's voice is recorded in the three letters[172] she
wrote to the British government. They are a testimony to her
eloquence, asserting her rights over Punjab and her son. The
British officers were also aware of her capacity to organize the
Sikhs in the cause of Maharaja Ranjit Singh's family. According
to Herbert Edwardes, 'the Ranee Jhunda, . . . had more wit and
daring than any man of her nation'.[173] On 7 December 1846,
Lord Hardinge wrote to Fredrick Currie 'in any agreement
made for continuing the occupation of Lahore, her deprivation
of power is an indispensable condition'.[174] The British wanted
to take over the young maharaja's guardianship and wean him
from the influence of his formidable mother. They accomplished
this through the treaty of Bhairowal on 16 December 1846. The
maharani was to withdraw from the Lahore court with an annual

[171] Cunningham, 257.
[172] Ganda Singh, 'Three letters of Maharani Jind Kaur'.
[173] Quoted by Bell, *The Annexation of the Punjab and the Maharaja Duleep Singh*, 13.
[174] Ganda Singh, 'Three letters of Maharani Jind Kaur', 305.

allowance of Rs 1.5 lakhs. The reason they used, mentioned in Mrs. Login's[175] recollections, was that she 'instigated her little son to offer an open insult to the Resident, Sir Henry Lawrence, and the native Durbar'.[176] This gave them an excuse to separate the maharani from her son, and on 19 August 1847, she was 'removed to Sheikopoora, twenty-five miles from Lahore' as a prisoner.[177] The British still suspected the queen of creating havoc in Punjab as long as she continued to be there. She was accused of another conspiracy, when 'On the 8th May 1848, she was discovered to be implicated in a plot to poison, and otherwise dispose of, the Resident and other prominent British officials, so she was removed from Sheikopoora to Ferozepore, and ultimately to the fortress of Chunar', the fort of Sher Shah in the past, near Banaras.[178] Mrs. Login's account is silent on Tej Singh. Bell states that the decision to send the maharani to Banaras was taken by Resident Fredrick Currie, without the Cabinet of Regency's approval. In a dispatch dated 16 May 1848, the resident reported that it was by his orders that the rani was removed from Sheikhupura because 'Her summary banishment from the Punjab, and residence at Benares, under the surveillance of the Governor-General's Agent, subject to such custody as will prevent all intrigue and correspondence for the future, seems to me the best course which we could adopt'.[179]

In one of the letters, the maharani raised concerns about the safety of her son and his fears. She wrote: 'The Maharaja came to me today and wept bitterly for a long time. He said that Bishan

---

[175] She was the guardian of Maharaja Duleep Singh, along with her husband Dr Login, after the young prince was removed from the side of his mother, Maharani Jindan.

[176] Login, *Lady Login's Recollections*, 86.

[177] Ibid.

[178] Ibid.

[179] Bell, *The Annexation of the Punjab and the Maharaja Duleep Singh*, 14.

Singh and Gulab Singh had been frightening him. If something happened to the Maharaja through fright, then what shall I do?'[180] He was kept separately from his mother in Shalimar, and that aggrieved the mother and son. She then mentions the betrayal of the British by taking 'possession of the kingdom by underhand means'. She questions their pretence of friendship by putting her in prison and not letting her meet her son. She threatens to appeal to the London headquarters against the injustice. She also highlights the British mode of operation by preserving 'three or four traitors, and put the whole of Punjab to the sword at their bidding',[181] underlining the violence unleashed by the British.

Her pleas only strengthened the resolve of the British officials such as Henry Lawrence to banish her from Punjab to Kangra. This was suggested by him to the secretary to the governor general.[182] The maharani was finally imprisoned in the fort of Sheikhupura as the 'first step to the final banishment of Ranee Jhunda from the country'.[183] In her second letter, the maharani recorded her anguish at her separation from her son. In a letter dated 23 August 1847, John Lawrence admitted to the secretary to the governor general that the young maharaja was upset with his mother's removal from Lahore. The sadness was visible on young maharaja's face.[184] Her third letter written on 30 August 1847 in Persian to John Lawrence is the most poignant one, where she described her separation from her son and accused the British of the worst kind of backstabbing: 'Weeping, he was torn away from his mother, and taken to

---

[180] Ganda Singh, 'Three letters of Maharani Jind Kaur', 142.

[181] Ibid.

[182] Ibid., reference to the letter of 16 August 1847 between Henry Lawrence and the Secretary to the Governor General.

[183] Governor General to the Secret Committee, Punjab Papers, 1847–49, 143–4.

[184] Ganda Singh, 'Three letters of Maharani Jind Kaur', 143.

Shalimar Garden, while the mother was dragged by her hair. Well has the friendship been repaid.' She asked how a child would live happily without his mother. Then she asserted, what has come to be the testimony of the British insensitivity: '*Meri izzat abru aur tumhara zaban ka sukhan gaya* (I have lost my dignity, and you have lost regard for your word).'[185] The maharani's words are a moving testimony on the devastation wreaked by the imperial process of taking over Punjab. Her letters challenged the British records, and her defiance in her son and Punjab's interests showed courage in the face of the formidable propaganda unleashed by the British against her. She did not give up and sent Sardar Jiwan Singh to represent her case to the governor general at Calcutta and to the secretary to India's government on 2 January 1849.[186] She demanded justice and full and impartial investigation of the charges against her 'but imperfectly known even to herself' under which 'she has been condemned to incarceration'.[187] Her petition tore through the British sense of justice. She dared to question the narrative put forth by the British officers involved in the conquest of Punjab. Despite her request for fair trial, it was not conducted as they would have to acquit her if no evidence was found against her. This was voiced by Major Evans Bell when he quoted the resident of Lahore, stating that 'Legal proof of the delinquency of the Maharanee would not, perhaps, be obtainable'.[188]

Maharani Jindan was constantly referred to as a formidable enemy. From Camp Ferozepure on 31 January 1849, Lord Dalhousie wrote to Brigadier Mountain: 'The pretences of Sikhs of their anxiety to get back the Ranee whom they

---

[185] Singh, 'Three letters of Maharani Jind Kaur', 144.

[186] Ibid., 145.

[187] Ibid., 145–6.

[188] Bell, *The Annexation of the Punjab and the Maharaja Duleep Singh*, 15.

were perpetually seeking to destroy when she was there, are preposterous.'[189] He further stated his apprehensions about the maharani, writing, 'She has the only manly understanding in the Punjab, and her restoration would furnish the only thing which is wanting to render the present movement (Second Anglo-Sikh War) truly formidable, an object and a heap.'[190] The maharani was in correspondence with Chattar Singh and Mulraj through letters enclosed in tahveez (a protective amulet).[191] On 1 May 1849, Lord Dalhousie wrote that he was annoyed to hear the news of the maharani's escape from confinement at Chunar.

> She was under strict guard at Benares, and on suspicion being excited was removed by the agent into the fortress at Chunar. Thence she affected her escape alone, nobody knows how. It seems impossible that it could have been done without the connivance of her guard, and a Committee of Inquiry is now going on. The thing in itself is of no great importance now. I have confiscated her nine lac worth of jewels, and she has no money of her own, so that she can't do much harm. If she flies to Nepaul and keeps quiet there, it will be a clear gain, for she will lose her pension, of course. If she goes to the Punjab, she can do no great mischief there now. Three months ago it would have been less agreeable.[192]

Mrs. Login gives a dramatic description of her escape to Nepal: 'on the 18th April, 1849, she managed to escape, in the disguise of a *fakirnee* (female mendicant), and took refuge in Nepal'.[193]

---

[189] *Private Letters of Lord Dalhousie*, 68.

[190] Ibid.

[191] Ahluwalia, *Maharani Jind Kaur (1816-63)*, 95.

[192] *Private Letters of Lord Dalhousie*, 68.

[193] Login, *Lady Login's Recollections*, 86.

The maharani was escorted to Banaras under Major Macgregor. At Banaras, she carried out a rehearsal of her escape, by involving her maid Hargo, who escaped in disguise by mixing with the servants. On this, the maharani was removed to Chunar, under the supervision of Captain Rees. She knew that the British had no idea how she looked as she maintained a strict purdah with them. They recognized her by the distinct tone of her voice. At Chunar, she asked for a tailor-woman (seenewali) to get some clothes stitched. Most likely, it is in disguise that she left the fort.[194] She did not stay in Chunar for more than fifteen days, leaving behind a cryptic letter: 'You put me in the cage and locked me up. For all your locks and sentries, I got out by magic.'[195] It was a long letter, in which she asked the British authorities not to punish her servants as they had no knowledge of her escape and could not be blamed. She again asked for the reason for her confinement: 'I told you plainly not to punish me too hard. What crime had I committed that you brought me to the fort of Chunar.'[196]

With the maharani's escape to Nepal, Lord Dalhousie heaved a sigh of relief. He wrote: 'She may stay if she likes. A native State, as a point of honour, cannot on-demand give up anyone who takes refuge. So I have not demanded her, but I have called on them to see that she does no mischief. All quiet in the Punjab.'[197] Accordingly, the government put forth its power: 'After a prolonged campaign, and a struggle severe and anxious, the Sikhs were utterly defeated and subdued, the

---

[194] Ahluwalia, *Maharani Jind Kaur (1816-63)*, 99; Nijjar, *Maharani Jind Kaur*, 41–2.

[195] Ahluwalia, *Maharani Jind Kaur (1816-63)*, 99.

[196] Ibid.

[197] *Private Letters of Lord Dalhousie*, 77.

Afghans were driven with ignominy through the mountains'[198] and Punjab became a British province. Latif described Maharani Jindan as 'turbulent', 'whose ambition and intrigues had mainly conduced to the rapid fall of the Empire of Ranjit, having become nearly blind, broken in heart and subdued in spirit', she died in Kensington in 1863.[199]

---

[198] Latif, *History of the Panjab*, 574.
[199] Ibid.

4

Begum Zeenat Mahal —
The Mughal Queen

'A Miniature of Begum Zeenat Mahal painted on ivory by the
portrait painter for the King of Delhi'; reproduced in Montgomery
Martin's *Our Indian Empire and the Adjacent Countries of Afghanistan,
Balochistan, Persia, and Depicted and Described by Pen and Pencil*,
Vol. II, The London Printing and Publishing Company Ltd.,
London & New York, 1879-81, 1879. The young queen
in her royal finery.

The time at length arrived for carrying the sentence of the court into effect; and the ex-king, accompanied by Zeenat Mahal, her son, and one other of the wives of the prisoner, were removed from Delhi to Allahabad, from whence they were conveyed by steamer to Calcutta, and there placed on board H. M.'s ship Megaera, for transportation, to their future home. Availing herself of the permission granted by government, Zeenat Mahal had, as we have seen, with true woman's fidelity, determined to share the destiny of her husband. Her father had already paid the debt of nature; but the youngest of her sons, Jumma Bukht, remained to her, and, like herself, was free to choose a path through the future intricacies of life; and each made a noble choice, that might atone for many faults. The wife and the son descended from the steps of a throne to the deck of a convict ship, that the few remaining years of him to whom they owed affection and obedience, might not be utterly without solace amidst the desolation that had over whelmed him.[1]

Begum Zeenat Mahal was born in 1821 in Faizabad to the influential nobleman Ahmad Kuli Khan, serving in the Mughal court at Delhi. In William Dalrymple's words, she was 'his only consort to come from an aristocratic background'.[2] Emperor Bahadur Shah succeeded Akbar Shah II to the Mughal throne in 1837. He married Zeenat Mahal on 18 November 1840. She was the youngest queen of the Mughal emperor. She was nineteen, and he was sixty-four at the time of their marriage.

[1] Robert Montgomery Martin, *The Indian Empire: Illustrated*, Vol. III, (London: Print and Publishing Company, London, 1899) Mayur Publications, Delhi, Reprint 1983, 192.
[2] William Dalrymple, *The Last Mughal*, (London: Bloomsbury Publication, 2009), electronic publication; location 134 of 11750.

She died in Rangoon on 17 July 1886. She had one son, Mirza Jawan Bakht.

An attempt is made to understand Zeenat Mahal's story from the limited sources, both imperial and nationalist, available on her. Of late, moving away from these two perspectives, are the works on the people on the margins. It is a rich historiography on 1857.[3] Unfortunately, discussions of women's agency are still limited. In the first section, the begum's early life story is traced; in the second section, the events of 1857 as they unfold and her presence in them is presented; and in the third section, the last few months of the queen and the emperor in India and their ultimate move to Rangoon are described.

I

There are few accounts of Zeenat Mahal, the woman who married an old Mughal emperor, giving him the fifteenth out of sixteen sons. Begum Zeenat Mahal is important in the nineteenth century for two reasons: One, she was the favourite wife of Bahadur Shah Zafar; two, she was in the eye of the storm when the revolt reached Delhi in 1857.

Montgomery, who was critical of a few English officers for the killing of Mughal princes and indulging in senseless slaughter in 1857, still has his biases about the Mughals. He saw Zeenat

---

[3] A few of them are: Eric Stokes, *The Peasant Armed: The Indian Revolt of 1857*, ed. C. A. Bayly (London: Clarendon Press, 1986); Crispin Bates (Series Editor), *Mutiny at the Margins: New Perspectives on the Indian Uprising of 1857* (New Delhi: Sage Publications, 2013) (7 volumes); Dirk H. A. Kolff, *Naukar, Rajput, and Sepoy: The Ethnohistory of the Military Labour Market of Hindustan, 1560-1850* (Cambridge: Cambridge University Press, 1990); Biswamoy Pati, ed., *The Great Rebellion of 1857 in India: Exploring Transgressions, Contests and Diversities* (New York : Routledge, 2010).

Mahal from an imperial lens. Writing about her early life, Martin portrayed her father and her as ambitious aspirants to the Mughal throne.[4] His narrative, nevertheless, provides a peek into the early years of this relatively unknown historical figure. Begum Zeenat Mahal's father, Ahmad Kuli, was a friend of the Mughal emperor for many years when the latter was still a prince and called Mirza Aboo Zaffar, eldest son of the emperor. Shah Akbar died in 1837 and was succeeded on the *musnud* by the Mirza, who thereupon assumed the name and title of Mahomed Suraj-oo-deen Shah Ghazee, being then between sixty and seventy years of age. 'The father of Zeenat had long, previous to the accession of his royal friend, held an important position at the court of Delhi, and was known to possess great influence among the princes of Hindoostan.'[5] The English writer suggests that the Emperor possibly had some 'vague' idea of a future struggle for re-establishing his ancestors' empire.[6] He entered into the matrimonial alliance with the daughter of this powerful noble to rally all Muslims 'through the exercise of his influence throughout the Mohammedan states of India'. Zeenat Mahal was 'therefore demanded in marriage and was shortly afterwards conveyed, with great pomp . . . to the imperial residence at Delhi'.[7]

There was the disparity of age between the two. Marriage was an honour for

> an alliance with the imperial house of Timur was of itself
> sufficient to counterbalance any objection that might be

---

[4] There is a separate chapter on Begum Zeenat Mahal in Martin, *The Indian Empire: Illustrated*, 188–9.

[5] Ibid., 189.

[6] Ibid.

[7] Ibid.

supposed likely to arise on the part of the young lady or
her sire, both of whom were flattered by the prospect thus
opened to the ambition of the one, and the girlish aspiration
of the other.[8]

It was a marriage of convenience for the emperor and the begum
and her father. All aspired to further their interests.

After the marriage, Begum Zeenat Mahal earned the trust
of her husband, becoming his closest confidante. Her political
eminence is evident from the observation in *Dastan-e-Gadar*,
'Sixteen horses were used to pull the carriage of the emperor and
eight horse employed to pull the carriage of Nawab Zinat Mahal
Begum Sahiba.'[9] She gave birth to a son, who was named Mirza
Jawan Bakht. The records discussed later suggest that from the
time of her son's birth, her singular ambition was to safeguard his
interests. She was keen that the privileges and rights of the Mughal
emperor, after her husband, be transferred to her son, Mirza Jawan
Bakht. In a post-Independence historical novel, Khushwant Singh
described Mirza Jawan Bakht in most unflattering terms. Presenting
a typically orientalist character,[10] Singh wrote: 'The boy had not
been taught how to behave in the company of ladies. He kept
chewing betel-leaf and spitting the horrible, bloody phlegm into a
silver spittoon which a eunuch carried everywhere he went. And
like common natives he kept scratching his privates.'[11]

---

[8] Ibid.

[9] *Dastan-e-Gadar,* Location 426 of 4391.

[10] There is a stereotyping of the people of Asia as 'Oriental', and
in this discourse the people of the 'Orient' are represented pejoratively.
Edward Said's work *Orientalism* highlights the discourse where there is
an 'otherization' of Asia by the West. The princes are stereotyped in a
particular way.

[11] Khushwant Singh, *Delhi: A Novel* (New Delhi: Penguin
Books, 1990), 281–2.

To promote her son's interests with the British, Begum Zeenat Mahal planned a grand wedding for him in 1852. The spectacle also displayed her influence over her husband. The celebrations were a visible emblem of her power and prestige in the Mughal court. The marriage of Prince Jawan Bakht took place on 2 April 1852, and William Dalrymple has given a vivid account of the wedding procession. The turrets of the Red Fort were illuminated, and there were many fireworks. The chobdars or macebearers led the parade. Six well-decorated imperial elephants followed. Behind them came the palace servants laden with gifts for the bride's family. A squadron of camels and drumbeaters followed them.[12] The British soldiers led by Captain Douglas, the commandant of the palace bodyguards, was also part of the procession passing through Chandni Chowk.[13] A band of kettledrummers, shehnai players, etc. followed. After this, on horses were the young princes, including Mirza Jawan Bakht. He was only eleven at the time of his wedding.[14]

Behind him on an elephant, seated on a golden howdah, was the Mughal emperor.[15] Begum Zeenat Mahal carefully planned the spectacle to project her son as the heir apparent. Dalrymple states: 'The exceptionally lavish wedding she planned was intended by her to raise the profile of the Prince, and also to consolidate her own place in the dynasty.'[16] Zafar had sixteen sons, and Zeenat Mahal knew that the task of making her son succeed to the throne would not be easy. Jawan Bakht's wife was Zeenat Mahal's niece, Nawab Shah

---

[12] Dalrymple, *The Last Mughal*, locations 768, 775 of 11750.

[13] Ibid., locations 775, 903 of 11750.

[14] Ibid., description of wedding procession on location 781 of 11750.

[15] Ibid.

[16] Ibid., location 801 of 11750.

Zamani Begum. Jawan Bakht's wedding celebrations eclipsed the weddings of his brothers. Begum Zeenat Mahal was aware of the competitive rivalry among the consorts of the emperor. Her marriage had displaced Begum Taj Mahal, who was his chief wife for fifteen years. The tension between the two would continue till the end. Begum Taj Mahal would leave the royal entourage at Allahabad, while moving to Calcutta to go to Rangoon in exile, and there was a parting of ways between the two queens.

Despite the show of grandeur at the wedding of her son, Begum Zeenat Mahal was unable to impress the British agent and later, the political resident since 1835 at the Mughal court, Thomas Metcalfe, to consider her son for the Mughal throne. By 1852, 'the British and Mughals found themselves in an uneasy equilibrium'.[17] One of the reasons for the tension was the issue of succession to the throne. In 1849, the emperor's oldest living son Mirza Dara Bakht died of a fever. Martin R. Montgomery wrote that Zeenat Begum wanted her son, Mirza Jawan Bakht, to succeed the Mughal emperor, but the British agent, especially Thomas Metcalfe, wanted Mirza Fakhruddin, as the eldest, to succeed.[18] Zeenat Mahal refused 'to accept the succession of Mirza Fakhru',[19] the eldest surviving heir. Dalrymple further mentions the mysterious deaths of Mirza Fakhru and all the English officers who signed the succession deed in 1853.[20] Emily

---

[17] Dalrymple, *The Last Mughal*, location 2262 of 11750.

[18] Martin, *The Indian Empire: Illustrated*, 189; Nigam says something similar. N. K. Nigam, *Delhi in 1857* (New Delhi: S. Chand & Co., 1957), iv. Bahadur Shah 'wanted his son by Zinat Mahal to succeed him but this request was made at the instance of the wily queen and was rejected by the British authorities and the King kept quiet.'

[19] Dalrymple, *The Last Mughal*, 2262 of 11750.

[20] 'This balance was, however, broken most dramatically in 1853, by a series of deaths. By the end of that year all three British officials who

Bayley, Thomas Metcalfe's daughter, had her suspicions about
Begum Zeenat Mahal's role in her father's unexpected collapse
and subsequent death.[21] Her description of Zeenat Mahal was
most unfavourable, suggesting that there was a clique at the
Mughal court

> headed by the Queen – a clever, wicked woman . . . Her
> rage, therefore, when she heard that the Heir Apparent
> had consented to the arrangements was unbounded and she
> determined to take her revenge. My father knew her character
> well, and that she would not let any obstacle stand in the way
> of her ambition. My Father knew also that her revenge would
> not stop, and he said to us, 'The first act in the drama is played
> out – what will be the next?'[22]

The British always suspected Begum Zeenat Mahal of conspiring
to kill Thomas Metcalfe by poisoning him on 1 November
1853, 'of symptoms believed to have been the result of vegetable
poison'.[23] She considered Thomas Metcalfe as an obstacle to her
son's succession to the Mughal throne.

From Dalrymple's account, it seems that the emperor came
to know of a secret meeting which was held between Metcalfe

had signed the succession agreement with Mirza Fakhru were dead, all
in suspicious circumstances. The most suspicious – a straightforward
case of poisoning, according to the doctors who attended him – was
the slow and lingering death of Sir Thomas Metcalfe.' Dalrymple, *The
Last Mughal*, location 2262 of 11750.

[21] Emily Bayley, *The Golden Calm: An English Lady's Life in Mogul
Delhi: Reminiscences* (New York: Viking Press, 1980). (It has beautiful
miniatures and excerpts from *Delhie Diary* of Thomas Metcalfe).

[22] Dalrymple. *The Last Mughal*, location 2297 of 11750.

[23] Charles Theophilus Metcalfe, *Two Native Narratives of the
Mutiny in Delhi* (London: Archibald Constable & Co., 1898), 19.

and Mirza Fahkru, in which the prince agreed to shift from the Red Fort to Mehrauli and drop the Mughal claim of superiority to the governor general.[24] This news infuriated the emperor. It is possible that the emperor had reservations about Mirza Fakhru's succession due to his proximity to the English resident of Delhi. The emperor had apprehensions that Mirza Fakhru would surrender all the Timurid dynasty's privileges and pride to the British. Mirza Fakhru was stripped of all honours and privileges at the Mughal court by the emperor.[25] The British remained unmoved and declared Mirza Fakru as the successor. Showing his unhappiness with the English political resident's decision, the emperor threatened to leave for Mecca for Haj. Thomas Metcalfe accused Begum's 'baleful influence'[26] on the emperor for his changed behaviour. In her reminiscences, Emily Bayley mentions that the emperor was not interested in the negotiations, but 'his wife the Queen would not be persuaded'.[27] Zeenat Mahal prevailed over the emperor to negotiate for her son's proposal as the successor to the Mughal throne. Bayley and Dalrymple make allusions to the begum's role in Thomas Metcalfe's death, as he thwarted her son's succession. She had 'always hated the British, and now she raved and threatened, and swore that she would be revenged upon all who had planned this thing—they die by poison, everyone!'[28]

---

[24] Dalrymple, *The Last Mughal*, location 1114 of 11750.

[25] Metcalfe, *Two Native Narratives of the Mutiny in Delhi,* 18. It is mentioned that 'a Board was appointed to discuss and report on the course to be followed with regard to the retention of the Royal Family at Delhi. To this committee were nominated Shahzada Fakir-u-din, heir-apparent and the eldest of nine princes.' The other members were Sir Henry Elliot, Mr Thomason and Sir Thomas Metcalfe (Resident at Delhi), 18–9.

[26] Dalrymple, *The Last Mughal*, location 1133 of 11750.

[27] Bayley, *The Golden Calm*, 216.

[28] Ibid.

But on 10 July 1856, Mirza Fakhru died and once again, Begum Zeenat Mahal's aspiration for her son to become the heir apparent rose. Mirza Fakhru died of cholera or as the English suggested, of poisoning,[29] and he was to be succeeded by his son Abu-Bakr. It was intolerable to Begum Zeenat Mahal, and Montgomery wrote:

> When at length it was formally announced, by the resident at the court of Delhi, that his government had determined that the son of the deceased Prince Furruk-oo-deen, and grandson of the king, should inherit all that yet remained of imperial power at Delhi, as the heir in a direct line of the existing sovereign, the hostility of the begum to British influence became intense.[30]

Montgomery deduced that it was natural for Begum Zeenat to influence the Mughal emperor to overturn the English Raj and get her son to succeed to the throne. But Montgomery also admitted that throughout the rebellion and the later trial, there was no evidence of her involvement against the British.

II

On 11 May 1857, the soldiers from Meerut reached Delhi and declared themselves under the Mughal emperor's sovereignty. From the beginning of the rebellion, there were simmering undercurrents of tension and resentment among the soldiers on one side, and the emperor and the begum, with their councillors on the other. At times, the soldiers' uncouth and rough behaviour addressing him rudely as an old

---

[29] Metcalfe, *Two Native Narratives of the Mutiny in Delhi*, 19.
[30] Martin, *The Indian Empire: Illustrated*, 189.

man (*buddha*) disturbed the royal family's pride.[31] Troubles began from the outset with the mayhem on the streets of Delhi, and there was a large-scale massacre of white men, women and children against the wishes of the emperor and his advisors. At the time of the outbreak of the mutiny, English officers had sought refuge for Miss Jennings, daughter of the Chaplain and another young English lady, Miss Clifford, and a few other English women at the begum's palace for protection. They were all stuck at the palace of the emperor, and before they could move, they were all killed, despite the protestations of the emperor.[32] Fifty-two British were killed by the soldiers and the palace guards under a peepul tree in front of the palace.

What made Begum Zeenat Mahal controversial was that she was neither trusted by the British officials nor by the rebels in 1857. She was constantly looked at with suspicion by the rebels. Throughout the period, when the soldiers were in Delhi, they accused her of collaborating with the British.[33] On 29 May 1857, they confronted the emperor, contending 'that the King's Begum had arranged' for the powder and shot 'in collusion with Mahommed Saur Ali Khan' to be sent to the English.[34] Both the emperor and the begum's feelings were ambivalent about the mutineers and were expressed when Jeewan Lal said that 'The King sent for Mirza Mogul Beg, Mirza Abu Bakr, and Mirza Abdulla, and expressed his anger at their sympathy with the Sepoys, warning them that one day they would be hanged,

---

[31] Metcalfe, *Two Native Narratives of the Mutiny in Delhi*, 80.

[32] Ibid.

[33] Mahmood Farooqi, *Besieged: Voices from Delhi 1857*, (New Delhi: Penguin Books, 2010), 98–9.

[34] Metcalfe, *Two Native Narratives of the Mutiny in Delhi*, 'Narrative of Munshi Jeewan Lal', 107.

as soon as the English entered the city'.[35] The fear of the British reprisals played on the minds of the royal couple.

Munshi Jeewan Lal, the agent of the governor general at the Mughal court, maintained a daily diary (roznamcha) that was sent to the British officers. He wrote that the soldiers were getting restless for payments and the begum feared that they might plunder the palace. 'She sent thousand rupees worth of jewel to the King, and asked him to give it to the Sepoys, but the King refused, remarking with a touch of sarcasm, that as long as he lived let the burden of indigestion and trouble fall on him.'[36] The emperor was already showing his impatience with the demands of the soldiers.

On 16 May 1857, the sepoys went to the emperor's palace 'in great anger, as they said they had seized a messenger with a letter cursing the mutineers'.[37] The sepoys threatened to kill Ahsanullah Khan and Nawab Mahbub Ali Khan, and also threatened to take away Zeenat Mahal Begum Sahiba and keep her as 'a hostage for the King's loyalty.'[38] There was a great uproar and to appease the mutineers, 'Mahabub Ali Khan took an oath that he was not the author of that letter, nor had it been written with his knowledge'.[39] On 29 May 1857, the sepoys were agitated again. 'They contended that the King's Begum had arranged' powder and granary 'in collusion with Mahmud

[35] Ibid., 111.

[36] Metcalfe, *Two Native Narratives of the Mutiny in Delhi*; this is in the Narrative of Munshi Jeewan Lal, 217.

[37] Metcalfe, *Two Native Narratives of the Mutiny in Delhi*, 93. In his narrative, Munshi Jeewan Lal mentioned how the sepoys seized a letter 'cursing the mutineers' and accused the emperor of being complicit. They 'threatened to take away Zinat Mehal Begum Sahiba and keep her as hostage for the King's loyalty', 93.

[38] Ibid.

[39] Ibid.

Sadur Ali Khan' to be sent to the English'.[40] At another place, during his trial, Bahadur Shah Zafar mentioned how the rebel soldiers mistrusted Zeenat Mahal and accused her of colluding with the British.[41] The translation of Urdu records on 1857 by Mahmood Farooqui stated that the rebels claimed that Hakim Ahsanullah Khan, Mahboob Ali Khan and Zeenat Mahal sent 'letters to the English and are in league with them, therefore we will kill them'.[42] He went on to reveal that they arrested Zeenat Mahal's father Samsamuddaula with the 'announcements that they 'will depose the king and crown Mirza Mughal king'.[43] They pressured the emperor 'to handover Zinat Mahal Begum to them, adding that she is colluding with the English and so they wanted to arrest her'.[44] Bahadur Shah expressed his helplessness, saying that he could not prevent the rowdy behaviour of the soldiers. He also narrated how '[o]ne day, they assaulted Zinat Mahal's house and wanted to loot it, but they could not break open the gate'.[45] The emperor expressed his helplessness by stating,

> One should consider that if they were under my control or if I was conspiring with them, then why would these things have happened? Furthermore, nobody asks even a poor defenseless man to give up his wife, nor does anyone say to him hand us over your wife so that we can arrest her.[46]

---

[40] Ibid., 107
[41] Farooqui, *Besieged*, 98–9.
[42] Ibid., 98.
[43] Ibid.
[44] Ibid.
[45] Ibid., 99.
[46] Ibid.

The thanadar stated to Kotwal Guzar Qasimjan on 5 August 1857 how the soldiers stationed outside Zeenat Mahal's house 'forcibly took away the carriages of the *barqandazes* of the thana and even abused them.'[47] They later apologized to the father of Zeenat Mahal, promising not to do it. Interestingly, a document of this period 'mentions a court which deliberated on crowning Prince Jawan Bakht as king, provided his mother Zinat Mahal paid enough money'.[48] The soldiers were continuously negotiating for money with the Mughal family members, in particular, Begum Zeenat Mahal, as she had considerable wealth of her own. On 20 July 1857, Bahadur Shah Zafar gave some of the property belonging to the deceased Europeans forwarded to him by the thanadar of Nigambodh 'to be made over to the Begum'.[49]

To raise money for the soldiers, according to Jeewan Lal, 'On 24th July 1857, Mirza Akbar Sultan summoned all the wealthy bankers of the city and extorted a sum of 8,000 rupees from them. In this matter, the principal movers were the Begum Zeenut Mahal, Ahsanullah Khan, her minister, and Mahmud Lal.'[50] On 8 August 1857, Begum Zeenat Mahal sent word to Bahadur Shah Zafar, that she, like Ahsanullah, 'was suspected of negotiating with the English, and that she had been warned that the soldiers intend to plunder the Palace. The King sent two hundred troopers to guard her house and Ahsanullah's'.[51] On 16 August 1857, petitions were sent by the raja of Ballabhgarh —'one was addressed to the Begum, another to the King asking pardon for any offence he might have given to His Majesty'.[52]

---

[47] Ibid., 236.

[48] Ibid., 255.

[49] Metcalfe, *Two Native Narratives of the Mutiny in Delhi*, 157.

[50] Ibid., 164.

[51] Ibid., 190.

[52] Ibid., 196.

The sepoys were keeping an eye on the movements of Begum Zeenat Mahal and other advisors of the emperor as they were suspicious of them. All their activities were regularly reported. For instance, on 23 August 1857, 'Begum Zenut Mehal went to the Lal Koti',[53] and her movement was again viewed with suspicion by the soldiers. In Delhi, the soldiers who had revolted against the British constantly pressurized the Mughal Emperor for money and support. On 3 September 1857, it was reported that the soldiers offered to enthrone Begum Taj Mahal in place of Zeenat Mahal Begum, 'whom they intended to imprison unless their pay was forthcoming within fifteen days'.[54] The soldiers showed an awareness of the Mughal court's power dynamics, negotiating with political acumen and shrewdness to play up one camp against the other within the royal family. On 14 September 1857, a 'severe fight took place in the Begum's garden, where four hundred men fell'.[55]

Many of these bits of information indicate Zeenat Mahal's active role as Emperor Bahadur Shah Zafar's advisor. Montgomery mentioned,

> There is no doubt, from the revelations made by Mukhun Lall, the private secretary of the King, in the progress of the trial of his fallen master, that, during the siege, Zeenat Mahal took an active part in the deliberations of the royal council, and that, upon several occasions, her advice animated and encouraged the princes in their efforts to avert the catastrophe

---

[53] Ibid., 207.

[54] Ibid., 218; On 3 September 1857, Jeewan Lal wrote, 'It was reported to-day that the Sepoys had proposed to the Taj Mehal Begum to enthrone her in the place of Zinat Mehal Begum, whom they intended to imprison unless their pay was forthcoming.'

[55] Metcalfe, *Two Native Narratives of the Mutiny in Delhi*, 'Narrative of Munshi Jeewan Lal', 230.

that, nevertheless, was inevitable. At the private conferences of the King, Maibhoob Ali Khan, the prime minister; Hussun Uskeeree, the astrologer; the Begum, Zeenat Mahal; and, generally, two of the King's daughters, were present, and by their councils, he was understood to be guided.[56]

What emerges is that the queen played a vital role to protect the royal family; it does not indicate her complicity with the mutineers. She seemed to have been trying a balancing act between the mutineers and the Mughal court on one side and at another level trying to keep communication open with the British authorities. But it creates an ambivalent and at times a controversial position for the begum. Even in the end, she was negotiating ultimately with the British for the lives and safety of her husband and her son. She seems clear-headed in the way she steered the family through the crisis to survive.

Zeenat Mahal was not happy with the Mughal emperor joining the rebels, and probably for the first time, he did not heed her advice.[57] She moved to her haveli at Lal Kuan. But when she realized that the emperor could not handle the political turmoil, with the constant pressure of the soldiers, she decided to be at his side. The emperor wanted to restore the house of Timur to its former glory and saw in the revolt an opportunity to do so. He may have been unhappy with the conduct and perceived indiscipline of the soldiers, but their anti-British sentiments and hostility towards Christianity gave him a glimmer of hope for reviving his fortunes.[58] In his report, Hodson stated that during his secret negotiations with Zeenat Mahal, in return for assisting the English, she demanded 'that

---

[56] Martin, *The Indian Empire: Illustrated*, 190.

[57] Dalrymple, *The Last Mughal*, 273.

[58] Ibid., 406.

her son should be pronounced heir apparent and the succession of the throne guaranteed to him, while on the part of the King that it was demanded that his position should continue undiminished, and the arrears for the five months subsequent to the outbreak in May paid up at once'.[59]

Hodson told the begum about the reality of her situation and the precariousness of the emperor's political position. Montgomery Martin observed,

> The King made repeated overtures to the British, and the Queen Zeenat Mahal was extremely anxious to obtain terms for the life of the King, and for their young son; but her proposals were rejected, it having been well ascertained, at an early period of the siege, from the reports of spies and in other ways, that the King and Queen had really no power to procure the surrender of the city.[60]

Hodson stated that the emperor had lost all rights to the Mughal throne after joining the soldiers. The begum realized 'that not only the liberty, but also that the lives of the King and her son were at stake', and according to Hodson, he was able to convince Zeenat Mahal to persuade her husband to surrender. She agreed on the condition that the lives of her husband and son would be spared.[61] Zeenat Mahal's loyalty and sense of purpose and pride in the house of Timur stayed with her till the end. She was a woman of her times, caught between the unravelling of

---

[59] Ibid.

[60] Robert Montgomery Martin, *The Progress and Present State of British India (A Manual for General Use, based on Official Documents, Furnished under the Authority of Her Majesty's Secretary of State for India)* (London: Sampson Low, Son, & Co., 1862), 45.

[61] Dalrymple, *The Last Mughal*, 406. 'On this condition alone would she consent to use her influence with the King.'

the Mughal dynasty and a mother's ambition for her son. To say that she was scheming is to judge her and will not be a proper assessment of her personality.

The British did not show much sensitivity in handling the proud successors of the house of Timur, and till 1857, Mughal sovereignty continuously diminished. The ambivalent attitude of Bahadur Shah Zafar towards the English and his joining the revolt in 1857, albeit reluctantly, can be explained in terms of his diminishing sovereignty when the court of the East India Company used the defeat of the Marathas in 1803 to reduce the Mughal title to the 'King of Delhi' and assert the position of the East India Company. To announce the changed sovereignty, the court approved 'alteration in the impression of the coinage of British India, by substituting the designation of the Company for that of the King of Delhi'.[62] The reasoning was that 'the pre-eminence of the Company' had to be asserted by 'doing away with every mark of authority in the King of Delhi which could render him a rallying point of the Mahomedan power'.[63] They further reasoned that this would make the King realize 'the hopelessness of any attempt on his part to assert an authority over the former Moghul Empire, or assume any characteristic but that which was accorded to him by the arrangement of 1803'.[64]

Lord Amherst was 'prepared to admit the superiority of rank on the part of the King of Delhi, as the titular and acknowledged representative of an ancient and illustrious

---

[62] To the Governor General in Council from the East India House, London, 4 January 1815, in Secret Letter from the Court, 13 February 1811 to 26 October 1816. Available at the National Archives, New Delhi.

[63] Ibid.

[64] Ibid.

dynasty of Sovereigns observing that the Governor-General has always used in his correspondence with the Monarch of Asia a style of address which distinctly concedes this point and that between the crowned head as alone could exact equality be claimed or maintained, in the form either of epistolary or personal intercourse. It appeared to Lord Amherst, however, of essential importance that he should decline to accede in person to any ceremonial which could be supposed to admit the King of Delhi sovereignty over the British Government or imply a tenure on his pleasure.'[65] It was further underlined that the court of the East India Company was

> aware that all intercourse by the letter between the Governor-General and the King of Delhi had been dropped since 1819/20 chiefly in consequence of a resolution which was taken at that period by the Marquis of Hastings to discontinue in his correspondence with the native princes of India the use of the seal having inscribed on it the humiliating design of 'Fidun Akbar Shah' or 'vassal of King Akbar'.[66]

Under these circumstances, the Mughal Emperor broke the deadlock by proposing to the resident at Delhi, Sir Charles Metcalfe,[67] that the emperor relinquished 'all demands for Nuzzur',

> a seat was to be provided for the Governor-General in front of the throne, and the King offered to return Governor

---

[65] Foreign Political 'Letter to Court 1828-29' Pt I, 52, Delhee and Rajpootana. Foreign Department Files at the National Archives, New Delhi.

[66] Ibid.

[67] Sir Charles Metcalfe was the elder brother of Thomas Metcalfe and the Political Resident at Delhi before him. In 1835, he briefly became the governor general after Lord William Bentinck.

General's visit. The minor arrangements were all of a nature
calculated to do honour to the head of the British government,
with one or two trifling exceptions which formed the subject
of further discussion and correspondence . . . the relation of
the Sovereign and Vassal had ceased to exist even in name,
between the representative of the House of Timoor and the
British Government in India.[68]

Emperor Bahadur Shah till the end wanted to keep the dignity
of the Mughals.

III

On 16 September 1857, Delhi fell into the hands of the British.

The palace of the Mughals was captured, and the king, with
his favorite wife, Zinat Mahal, and two sons and a grandson
(Mirza Mughal, Mirza Kuresh Sultan and Mirza Abu Bakr,
son of the late heir-apparent), the chief inciters of the late
atrocities, who had betaken themselves to the mausoleum of
Humayun, surrendered themselves to Captain Hodson.[69]

They 'gave themselves up to Captain Hodson on receiving a
pledge of personal safety'.[70] Hodson

with his own hands shot the princes dead on the way back
to Delhi[71] and ordered their bodies to be conveyed to the

---

[68] Ibid.

[69] Latif, *History of the Panjab*, 580.

[70] Martin, *The Progress and Present State of British India*, 46.

[71] Telegram from Adjutant-General, Dehlee, to Chief Commissioner,
Lahore; Mr Barnes, Umballa; Major Lake, Jullundhur; and

kotwali, the mayor's court, where they were thrown on the
chabuttra, or raised terrace, and exposed to the scoffs and jibes
of the gallant soldiers and the avenging Sikhs, for on the same
spot, 180 years before, Tegh Bahadur, one of the two martial
gurus of the latter, had fallen a victim to the relentless hatred
of Aurangzeb.[72]

By referring to the Sikh Guru and Aurangzeb, Hodson showed
his solidarity with the Sikhs to keep their loyalties with the
English. Hodson stated that he was 'fortunate enough to capture
the King and his favourite wife'.[73]

The Mughal princes expected a fair trial, which was denied
to them as recounted in the passage below.

On leaving the tomb, the princes saluted Hodson, and
remarked that their conduct would, of course, be investigated
in the proper court. He bowed assent. Then, notwithstanding
the vehement opposition of the faithful Mohammedans, the
princes went away with Hodson and the Seiks in a 'ruth'
or covered vehicle drawn by bullocks. The Mohammedan
soldiers, in obedience to the orders of their unfortunate
masters, did not attempt to follow them; but when the ruth
reached within a mile of Delhi, a mob gathered round the
guard, and seemed disposed to attempt a rescue. Whereupon

Lord W. Hay, Simla, 23 September 1857, Enclosure (2) to 103,
in Mutiny Records Correspondence, Part II (Lahore: Punjab
Government Press, Lahore, 1911), 73.

[72] Latif, *History of the Panjab*, 580.

[73] George Hodson, (ed.), *Twelve Years of a Soldier's Life in India: Being
Extracts from the Letters of the late Major W.S.R. Hodson (including a
Personal Narrative of the Siege of Delhi and Capture of the King and Princes)*,
(London: John W. Parker and Son, 1859); On 21 September 1857 the
city of Delhi was finally captured by the English, 297.

(according to Lieutenant Macdowell) Hodson made the princes descend, and after seizing their arms, compelled them to 'strip and get into the cart; he then shot them with his own hand.'[74]

Hodson wrote with satisfaction that 'I have seized and destroyed the King's two sons and a grandson (the famous, or rather infamous, Abu Bukt), the villains who ordered the massacre of our women and children, and stood by and witnessed the foul barbarity'.[75] Montgomery Martin is critical of the English officers' conduct, in particular Hodson, who did not abide by his words. But he considered this a shameful act by one or two Englishmen, Hodson and Lieutenant Macdowell, thereby trying to exonerate the other English officers of this deceit. But the fact was that the bodies of the princes remained in an open courtyard, with the Europeans spitting on the corpses. Finally, after three days, when the stench became unbearable, the bodies were unceremoniously disposed of. It did not reflect well on other English soldiers.[76] It clearly showed the brutal vengeance of the English, merciless in the retribution.

---

[74] Martin, *The Progress and Present State of British India*, 46–7.

[75] Major Hodson, 297. In Hodson's account there is a reference that on the 'Chiboutra' (courtyard) in front of the Kotwali (Police station) where 'the head of Gooroo Teg Bahadoor had been exposed by order of Aurungzebe, the Great Mogul, nearly 200 years before. The Sikhs considered that in attacking Delhi they were "paying off an old score". A prophecy had long been current among them, that by the help of the white man they should reconquer Delhi.' 302. The reference to the Sikh guru by the English officers was a strategy of showing solidarity with the Sikhs and keeping their loyalty with the English.

[76] Martin, *The Progress and Present State of British India*, 47.

Martin admitted to the mercenary character of the English soldiers of fortune, who came to India to amass wealth, uncaring about the lives of the people of India.

> Captain Hodson's vexation at being compelled by General Wilson to makeover to the prize agents a considerable portion of the property taken by him from the persons of the King and princes was forcibly expressed. His passion for "loot" was notorious. In Europe, his conduct was stigmatised in terms rarely applicable to a British officer, as that of an executioner who looked sharply after his perquisites, and stripped his victims before slaughtering them.'[77]

While the English accounts usually highlighted the barbaric acts of the Indian soldiers and princes during 1857, Montgomery on the contrary highlighted the British barbarities:

> Besides the princes slain by Hodson, many others surrendered or were captured by the British. Among the prisoners were seven sons or grandsons of the King, who all escaped. The majority of them were retaken, summarily tried, hung, and thrown into the Jumna; but others remained at large, including Prince Feroze Shah, who became a noted general.[78]

The pledge given by Captain Hodson to the king and queen of Delhi for 'freedom from personal indignity',[79] was not honoured, and the king and the queen were kept in an unhygienic and dirty chamber above one of the archways of the Red Fort, with no privacy. The king had to face a public

---

[77] Ibid.
[78] Ibid.
[79] Ibid., 83.

trial which went on for twenty-one days and ended in his being pronounced 'a false traitor to the British Government, and an accessory to the massacre in the palace'.[80] King Bahadur Shah Zafar pleaded helplessness in dealing with the soldiers and asserted that he and his wife tried to prevent the massacre of the English on three occasions at the risk of their lives; and 'there is reason to believe this was really the case, for the Queen and one of the princes had been rendered exceedingly unpopular in Delhi by their efforts on behalf of the English and Native Christians'.[81]

Major Hodson's wife's description of her visit to the Red Fort where the Mughal Emperor and his family were imprisoned was of 'pity', with a sense of conquest. She described Zeenat Mahal sitting in a 'smaller, darker, dirtier room' with 'eight or ten women, crowding round a common charpoy (bedstead), on which was a dark, fat, shrewd, but the sensual looking woman'.[82] From the brief conversation, which apparently occurred between Mrs Hodson and the begum, it seems that the begum had not lost her spirit. She told Mrs Hodson that if the British had not promised to spare the emperor and her son's life, 'the king was preparing a great army, which would have annihilated us'.[83] Mrs Hodson exhibits only contempt and disgust for the begum and the emperor, refusing to sit next to the begum, humbling the mighty Mughals by this act.

Ommaney, Zafar's jailer, wrote about Zeenat Mahal, 'who . . . henpecked her ailing and senile husband; but of the sixteen harem women at his disposal, only she seemed to look

---

[80] Ibid.

[81] Ibid.

[82] Ibid., 190.

[83] Ibid.

after the old man'. Zafar, wrote Ommaney in his diary, 'is kept greatly in order by his favourite wife, Zeenut Mehul, who if she is speaking and he puts in a word, tells him to keep quiet as she is speaking. He is always wanting trivial things, which if they do not please him, he throws away, which at times, enrages the Ex-Queen who holds the purse'. He further wrote that Zeenat Mahal 'talks prettily, but with difficult language for a novice'. Later he wrote, 'Zeenut Mehul I have never seen, [though] one day I saw her hand and arm which she showed to let me see part of her clothing at the time she wanted money. She talks nicely, but I believe she is not good looking. She strikes me as being a very clever and intriguing woman'.[84]

During the course of his trial towards the end of January 1858, which took place at the Diwan-i-Khas of the Red Fort, Bahadur Shah Zafar's oral testimony was recorded. From these records, one finds that the last Mughal emperor attempted to minimize his role in the rebellion. He projected his helplessness before the rebels. He shared how the soldiers 'often humiliated him and persecuted his closest companions, his favorite wife Zinat Mahal and his physician Ahsanullah Khan, included'.[85] It seems from his testimony that the emperor was at pains to prevent the massacre of the Europeans, but the trial did not consider this. The purpose of the trial was to discredit him in his people's eyes and make an example of him. By exiling him to Rangoon, the British were removing all remnants of their predecessors, the Mughals, so that they could not again become a rallying point for any future rebellion. The king's defence did not prevent the infliction of the severest penalty, which the primary condition of his surrender permitted. The connection between the East India Company and the house of Timur ended

---

[84] Mahmood Farooqui, *Besieged*, 94.
[85] Ibid.

in the last of the Company's representatives sentencing the last Mughal ruler 'to be transported across the seas as a felon'.[86]

The British themselves prided on their sense of justice, but the Indians did not appreciate it.[87] The English courts were unpopular as seats of corruption. The white violence unleashed in Delhi after its recapture, leaving it desolate and devastated, questions the English notions of justice and the rule of law. 'Of all the notable persons who had joined the rebellion and had its short-lived "greatness thrust upon them", none paid a heavier penalty than the octogenarian king of Delhi and his beautiful queen, Zeenat Mahal'.[88] After the capture of the city, in the words of Montgomery Martin, 'judicial measures of extreme severity followed the military excesses committed there'. Then Commissioner Mr Greathead was a reasonable man, who was not clouded by a spirit of revenge. But his death due to cholera resulted in a reign of terror unleashed by the triumphant British arrival in Delhi, inflicting 'capital punishment with such indiscriminate fury, that the first act of Sir John Lawrence on receiving the charge of Delhi and Meerut "was to put a stop to civilians hanging from their own will and pleasure, and to establish a judicial commission to try offenders"'.[89]

---

[86] Martin, *The Progress and Present State of British India*, 81.

[87] Nigam, *Delhi in 1857*, 23. Charles Metcalfe wrote: 'We should deceive ourselves if we were to suppose that the system of justice which we have introduced is acknowledged to be such a blessing as we conceive it to be . . . it has its attendant evils. These are felt more than its benefits and our courts of justice are generally spoken of with disgust, with ridicule or with fear, and seldom if ever, with cordial approbation and respect.'

[88] Martin, *The Progress and Present State of British India*, 82.

[89] Ibid., 82–3.

Saunders' communications also reveal the destruction and desolation wreaked on Delhi to suppress the rebellion of 1857. There are two different narratives of the killing of the Mughal princes, which was the beginning of the violence, and throwing their bodies in the open at the same place as Guru Tegh Bahadur's execution. A chronicler of Maharaja Narinder Singh of Patiala tries to justify the Sikh support of the British by linking the execution of the guru with the Mughal Emperor Aurangzeb and popularizing a purported prophesy of the guru that the Mughal empire would come to an end within 150 years. Latif mentioned that the Mughal Emperor 'sent him a letter, asking his aid against the British Government, and promising rewards; but the Maharaja forwarded the letter in original to the British authorities'.[90] The maharaja 'sent a contingent to Delhi under Sardar Partab Singh, which did excellent service during the siege and assault of that town, the hot-bed of the mutineers. The assistance rendered by the Maharaja was warmly acknowledged by General Wilson'.[91]

According to another chronicler, Jeewan Lal, the same spot was the site of the massacre of the English women and children in 1857 by the sepoys.[92] Today, the place is famous as the Khooni Darwaza. While describing the elephant ride of Mirza Jawan Bakht, Saunders highlighted the massacre of the people of Delhi, 'while perambulating the desolate streets of Delhi, deserted by almost every living being, except a few stray cats in a state of starvation the dead bodies of

---

[90] Ibid., 328–9.

[91] Ibid., 329.

[92] Metcalfe, *Two Native Narratives of the Mutiny in Delhi*, 'Narrative of Munshi Jeewan Lal', 71.

our enemies, and here and there a guard of our victorious troops'.[93]

After regaining Delhi, Captain C. B. Saunders was appointed the officiating commissioner, Delhi and the agent to the lieutenant governor, North West Province. The Company questioned his conduct in giving honour to Mirza Jawan Bakht. They sought an explanation from him regarding 'Colonel Hogge having been allowed to take Mirza Jawan Bukht out occasionally for an airing, such act directly contravening the order of the Government'.[94] The authorities at Calcutta were referring to the temper of the public opinion and the newspapers agitated by such display of honour to the Mughal prince. The king and members of his family were to be kept in 'closed custody'. Saunders denied receiving any such order. The English authorities were also concerned that the prince was in the custody of a single British officer. At the time of capture of the Mughal royal family from Humayun's Tomb, two or three of the elder princes caught there were made over to the custody of the Sikh soldiers by the officer in command.[95] The Sikh soldiers showed sympathy to the princes, knowing that they would not be spared, and allowed them to escape. These princes remained at large.

Saunders considered Mirza Jawan Bakht in the custody of the British officer 'as the best guarantee of his security'. He looked upon Jawan Bakht as 'a mere youth, and one who had not personally embraced his hands in the blood of

[93] Foreign Despatch (Secret), No. 12, From Saunders to E. H. Parke, Officiating Secretary on 26 January 1858 to send a copy of his reply explaining his conduct be forwarded to Calcutta; No. 13, No. 2, of 1858 from Saunders to G. F. Edmonstone, Secretary to the Government of India, Fort William, dated 26 July 1858.
[94] Ibid.
[95] Ibid.

our countrymen or taken any part in the war'.[96] He did not credit Jawan Bakht with any attachment or humanity for the British. He could not play a prominent role as he was relegated to the background by his elder brother, who 'at once gained more or less personal influence with the mutineers'. He exonerated him of any involvement in the bloodbath at Delhi in 1857. According to him, the king and Jawan Bakht's mother Zeenat Mahal 'at the very first commencement of the outbreak were anxious to instal him in the *wazirat* or Office of Prime Minister but without success'. He allowed him some relaxation from his confinement, and in this regard, he mentioned that 'the Sikh Chieftains Chutur Singh and Shere Singh Attariwala, the leaders of the last Seikh campaign who were sent down in strict confinement as state prisoners to Calcutta',[97] were allowed to go out for fresh air in a carriage attended by a European.

Saunders had an ulterior objective in allowing Colonel Hogge to take Jawan Bakht outside. He wanted Colonel Hogge to gather information from Jawan Bakht regarding the war and the events in Delhi in 1857, as mentioned in a semi-official letter dated 24 September 1857. Four days after the surrender of the emperor and his consort, John Lawrence wrote, 'Try and get out of the King now that he is alarmed all that you can. Tell him that much will depend on his making a clean breast.'[98] In compliance with that instruction, Saunders visited the king and tried to get information from 'the King and his more loquacious consort, the Begum Zeenut Mahal'. He could not get anything of value from their conversation, 'their chief object evidently being to avoid criminating

---

[96] Ibid.

[97] Ibid.

[98] Ibid.

themselves and at the same time, to endeavour as little as possible to inculpate others'.[99] But Jawan Bakht was different. In front of his parents 'he was perfectly taciturn on all subjects on which we desired to obtain information'. However, he signalled to the British that if 'he were allowed to go out for an airing, he would tell us anything we wished to know. He kept his word and a great deal of useful and important information was elicited from him on subjects bearing upon the mutiny, the conduct of the war and the complicity of the native chiefs in the Rebellion'.[100] He also mentioned the treasures his mother kept and which were later taken by the British. After this, he was kept in strict confinement and no honours were given to him.[101]

Montgomery Martin elaborated on the plight of the Mughal royals due to the policies of the East India Company. It seems from his narrative that the Mughal princes were caged and bound from all sides, with nothing to do. They were not allowed to be properly educated or get into service. He wrote that the Calcutta government

> hedged them in with restrictions, forbade their entering the service of the army or the state, and made no effort whatever either for their moral or physical welfare. The ignorance and sensuality of the 'Sullateen,' as the younger members of the family were called, became a byé-word with the English; but the reproach came badly from the mouth of those who were open to a counter charge of selfish neglect for having taken no pains to educate or uphold a family, the care of which was in fact accepted by the Company with

---

[99]   Ibid.

[100] Ibid.

[101] Ibid.

the Sannuds or Charter which conferred on them the large revenues of Bengal.[102]

From his observations, it seems that the Mughal princes were deliberately forced to conform to the image of 'wastrels' and 'louts'[103] by not being allowed pursue any useful activity. The Mughals were known to be actively engaged in trading, and many Mughal queens and princess such as Jahan Ara had their trading ships.[104] Begum Zeenat Mahal was a woman of independent means, and it was said at that time that she had the economic resources to pay the soldiers.[105] But all this was denied to the Mughals once they became the dependents of the East India Company.

Montgomery further stated that the British government was indulgent with Mirza Jawan Bakht as he was not implicated, but they had to bow to the sentiments of the English in Delhi, who he wrote were 'eager for retributive justice'.[106] They did not want the English to show any softness to the last Mughal Emperor. Mirza Jawan Bakht showed character when he decided to join his father in exile on account of the king's age and increasing infirmity. No proof of his complicity in the outbreak or in any proceeding that followed was found, and he could have stayed on in India. The Mughal emperor was asked to choose some of his wives to go with him in exile. Several recoiled, but Zeenat Mahal was 'determined to share his fate, and to consummate, in a far-off land, the singular vicissitudes that had accompanied her existence'.[107] Montgomery praised the fidelity of the queen.

---

[102] Martin, *The Progress and Present State of British India*, 33.

[103] Ibid.

[104] Shadab Bano, 'Jahan Ara's Administration of her Jagirs', *Proceedings of the Indian History Congress*, Vol. 66, 205-2006, 430-437, 430.

[105] Martin, *The Progress and Present State of British India*, 33.

[106] Montgomery Martin, *The Indian Empire Illustrated*, 191.

[107] Ibid.

Montgomery also wrote that it was difficult to get the accounts of women 'jealously guarded in the seclusion of an Oriental Palace'.[108] It became easier to get an account of Zeenat Mahal due to 'the comparatively familiar intercourse' for 'the last quarter of a century' that came to exist between the British resident at the court of Delhi. In 1803, the Mughal Empire was reduced to 'the walls that encircled his palace, and whose subjects were limited to the members of his own family, and their immediate personal dependents'.[109] The typecasting of the Mughal queens as secluded women of the 'orient' is no longer tenable with the writings of the Mughal women in the royal courts and their active involvement in the matters of the state.[110]

A gloomy and yet a triumphant description of the downfall of the last Mughal emperor in the British account sums up the English sentiments on the end of the Mughals:

> The palace-itself, as seen from a distance, exhibited a cluster
> of pinnacles and towers, many of which have been shaken
> to the ground, through the terrible occurrences that have
> followed the insane attempt to re-establish the empire of the
> Moguls upon the ruin of that of England, in Hindoostan.

---

[108] Martin, *The Indian Empire Illustrated*, 188.

[109] Ibid.

[110] We have instances of Mughal women who were scholars in their own right: Gulbadan Begum writing a biography of Humayun called *Humayun-Nama*, translated in English by Annette S. Beveridge, *The History of Humayun*, (London: Oriental Translation Fund, Royal Asiatic Society, 1902); Zebunissa, daughter of Aurangzeb, wrote *Deewan-e Makhfi* (Lucknow: Munshi Nawal Kishore, 1876), a collection of poetry in Persian. Makhfi was her pen name, meaning the hidden one; and Jahanara Begum wrote *Sahibia*, translated in English by Sardar Ali Ahmad Khan, (Lahore: Ashraf Printing Press, 1993).

Through the gate shown in the engraving, the infatuated descendant of a worn-out dynasty, on 12th May, 1857, after suffering himself to be proclaimed King of Hindoostan, issued, surrounded by Oriental pomp; and, amidst the salutes of artillery and the clangour of martial instruments, proceeded through the city, to receive the homage of his subjects, and to animate them in their treacherous and rebellious war against the English. Through this gate, also, on the 21st of the following September, the phantom King, intercepted in his useless flight from the retribution he had provoked, was brought back to the Palace he had occupied as ruler of India, a wretched prisoner, divested of rank and title, to await the result of a trial that, in all probability, would consign him, in the extreme winter of his existence, to the doom of a traitor and a felon. It is not in the province of this descriptive work to trace the progress, or to record the triumphs, of the struggle unnaturally forced upon this country by the treachery and vindictiveness of the people of India; and as the subject is fully treated in works devoted to the purpose, to those pages we must refer for details that are now of national importance and of world-wide interest.[111]

The Mughal Empire lay in ruins.

Whether Begum Zeenat Mahal was complicit with the British or negotiating with both sides is difficult to say, with accounts supporting both arguments. What limited sources are available on her convey a conflicting image of her in 1857. She was regarded with suspicion by the sepoys and the English. The accounts mostly project her as playing both sides to ensure the succession of her son. The nationalist and the imperialist historiography also look at her through the same lens.

---

[111] Martin, *The Indian Empire: Illustrated*, 58–9.

Mainodin, a police officer at the time of the revolt of 1857
in Delhi kept a 'roznamcha' or diary of 'daily occurrences.'[112] He
wrote in his diary that the English were regarded as 'trespassers' by
the Indians.[113] Mainodin recollected that after the entrance of the
sepoys from Meerut and the killing of the English, he reached the
palace, and on meeting the emperor, asked him to stop the killing.
The emperor responded; 'I am helpless; all my attendants have lost
their heads or fled. I remain here alone. I have no force to obey
my orders: what can I do?'[114] Mainodin interestingly mentioned
Abdulla Beg as one of the most active mutineers in Delhi. He
was a European—a discharged soldier of the 17th Foot—who
resided at Meerut. He converted to Islam and became a leader
and advisor of the king in the early days.[115] Mainodin narrated
how the king was completely under the control of the mutineers
and, on Abdullah Beg's advice, issued a Perwanahs (notice) asking
regiments to join him. He did not mention Begum Zeenat Mahal.
Bahadur Shah Zafar was surprised when the sepoys from Meerut
marched to Delhi on 11 May 1857, requesting him to take up the
leadership, but he was reluctant and sent for Captain Douglas, the
commandant of the Palace guards.[116]

The imperial accounts projected Begum Zeenat Mahal as
a woman responsible for 'murdering those wretched survivors
of the first day's massacre who had been imprisoned in the
palace'.[117] She was accused of driving 'her reluctant husband
into supporting the mutineers' to 'have the chance to revenge

---

[112] Metcalfe, *Two Native Narratives of the Mutiny in Delhi*, 'Narrative of
Mainodin', 30.

[113] Ibid., 31.

[114] Metcalfe, *Two Native Narratives of the Mutiny in Delhi*, 'Narrative of
Mainodin', 49.

[115] Ibid., 60.

[116] Nigam, *Delhi in 1857*, 47.

[117] Bayley, *The Golden Calm*, 217.

herself' on the British.[118] In Nigam's nationalist perspective, she played a role in the Mughal emperor not agreeing to General Bakht Khan's request to leave Delhi with him.[119] The queen, it seems, was negotiating with Hodson, whom she contacted 'on 18th September 1857, through Elahi Baksh and Hakim Ahsan Ullah for the King's surrender provided he, she, her son Jawan Bakht and her father Ahmad Kuli Khan were guaranteed their lives. This guarantee had been given by Hodson'.[120] According to Nigam, 'The queen played the most important part' in preventing the Mughal Emperor from leaving Delhi and 'eventually Bakht Khan retired with his troops towards Agra and thense to Lucknow.'[121] Another postcolonial representation of Begum Zeenat Mahal is in the novel on Delhi by Khushwant Singh. Singh reinforced the complicity of the begum with the English authorities. He also underlined the difference between the Mughals as the representative of the 'Orient'. He described her, looking from a white woman's eyes, as possessing 'Large almond-shaped eyes, olive complexion and jet black hair'.[122]

The British newspaper *News of the World* condemned Indian women as 'active instigators of the sepoys in their worst atrocities'.[123] 'Mutiny' novels too presented elite women like the Maharani Lakshmi Bai of Jhansi or Begum Zeenat Mahal as actively involved in the massacres of English women and

---

[118] Ibid.

[119] Nigam, *Delhi in 1857*.

[120] Ibid.

[121] Nigam, *Delhi in 1857*, 131.

[122] Singh, *Delhi*, 281.

[123] Indrani Sen, 'Gendering the Rebellion of 1857: The "Loyal Indian Woman" in "Mutiny Fiction"', *Indian Historical* Review, 2007, 34:36, 36–57, 38.

children at Jhansi[124] and at the Red Fort in Delhi. For instance,
N. K. Nigam, from a nationalist perspective, had an equally
unflattering opinion of Zeenat Mahal. He described Zeenat
Mahal as a 'wily queen'.[125] He accused her of 'sounding the
British' and 'misappropriating money that was collected for
paying the troops. The troops came to know of it and would
have looted her house at Farashkhana had there not been
a guard posted there'.[126] At another place, Nigam wrote that
'Zeenat Mahal swallowed Rs. 10,000 received from the Raja
of Ballabhgarh'.[127] On 22 August 1857, Zeenat Mahal wrote
to the British commander to intercede to settle the dispute
between the soldiers and her husband but was refused. She then
negotiated with the sepoys to pay their salaries if they accepted
her son Mirza Jawan Bakht as the commander-in-chief.[128]
Nigam painted a negative picture of the begum, blaming her
for 'the defeat of the Nationalist forces'.[129] He wrote, 'She was
covetous and intriguing. She stooped to meanest tricks to have
her way.'[130] He added that she paid Rs 2 lakh to the British for
guaranteeing the lives of her husband and son.[131]

A few recent newspaper and online articles have given a
more patriotic description of Begum Zeenat Mahal. In an Indian
Muslim Newspaper, *The Milli Gazette*, published online on 14
February 2012, Begum Zeenat Mahal is placed among 'the
most formidable women of her times. She could be categorised

---

[124] Indrani Sen, 'Inscribing the Rani of Jhansi in Colonial "Mutiny"
Fiction', *Economic and Political weekly*, May 12–18, Vol. 42, No. 19,
2007, 1754–1761, 1757.

[125] Nigam, *Delhi in 1857*, iv.

[126] Ibid., 108.

[127] Ibid., 112.

[128] Ibid., 115.

[129] Ibid., 115.

[130] Ibid., 132.

[131] Ibid., 134.

among Noorjahan (Jahangir's wife), Lakshmibai, Razia Sultana, Ahilabai Holkar, and Chand Bibi'.[132] The article goes on to say, 'She was freedom fighter who opened the doors of the Red Fort to the rebel sepoys from Meerut on the morning of 11th May, 1857.'[133] Her haveli at Lal Kuan at the walled city of Shahjahanabad covered four acres at the time of Zeenat Mahal. There was a huge marble fountain. A Nagina Mahal (a jewel palace) had its entrance from the backyard. The rooms were 'carved with Kota stone pillars supporting red sandstone arches'.[134] 'The magnificent house of Zinat Mahal, Begum of the ex-king of Delhi, was granted to the Maharaja' of Patiala,[135] Nirandar Singh 'for his loyalty and attachment to the paramount power'.[136] In an article on Zeenat Mahal in *The Hindu*, there is a reference to the decadent haveli of Zeenat Mahal in Lal Kuan. The writer of the article, R. V. Smith, considered it to be built in 1846. Further, he wrote that 'Beauty, brains and courage were her hallmark then.'[137]

The trial of the Mughal emperor took place at the Red Fort under martial law. He was found guilty of waging war against the

---

[132] Firoz Bakht Ahmed, 'The ruined Haveli of Zeenat Mahal', *The Milli Gazett*, Indian Muslim's leading Newspaper, published online on 14 February 2012, http://www.milligazetter.com/news/3228-the-ruined-haveli-of-zeenat-mahal. Accessed on 9 June 2022.

[133] Ibid. The same point is mentioned by R. V. Smith, though I have not come across the reference of Zeenat Mahal opening the gates of Delhi for the rebels. Smith, R.V. Smith, 'The Sad Plight of Zeenat Mahal', 16 October 2011, http://www.thehindu.com/features/metroplus/the-sad-plight-of-zeenat-mahal/article2543190.ece

[134] Ibid.

[135] Latif, *History of the Panjab*, 329.

[136] Ibid., 328.

[137] R. V. Smith, 'The Sad Plight of Zeenat Mahal', *The Hindu*, 16 October 2011, http://www.thehindu.com/features/metroplus/the-sad-plight-of-zeenat-mahal/article2543190.ece. Accessed on 9 June 2022.

queen of England and of the massacre of British residents who
had fallen into his hands.[138] Lord Canning spared his life; but he
with his son Jawan Bakht and wife Zeenat Mahal, 'who has been
chiefly instrumental in the revolt, and was the rival, in treacherous
intrigue, of Chand Kour (or Jindan) of Lahore notoriety, was
banished to Rangoon'.[139] An impression was created that Begum
Zeenat Mahal in Delhi and Maharani Jindan in Punjab were the
chief conspirators against the British, though both of them denied
their active participation in such conspiracies.

Courtesy: Sir Thomas Metcalfe, 4th Baronet - http://
www.bl.uk/onlinegallery/onlineex/apac/addorimss/
z/019addor0005475u00017vrb.html

Shorn off her jewellery and majesty, the old Queen Zeenat Mahal
seems to represent the lost glory of the Mughal empire.

On 4 December 1858, the king, queen, and Prince Jawan Bakht,
with his half-brother (a mere child) and some of the ladies of the
zenana, were conveyed in H. M. S. *Megoera* to Rangoon, and
thence to Tonghoo, an inland station in British Burma, 'declared

---

[138] Martin, *An Illustrated History of the Empire*, 187–8.
[139] Ibid., 580.

to be the most desolate and forlorn in British Burmah'.[140] Begum Zeenat Mahal lived in exile with her husband. She outlived him and died on 17 July 1886. She was buried near her husband's tomb at Yangon, though the emperor's grave was deliberately left unmarked by the colonial authorities. She too was buried in obscurity. The British Raj till the end distrusted the Mughal dynasty and the possibility of it becoming a rallying point. The obscure life led by Zeenat Mahal in her last years continued in her almost near absence in the history of the period. She and Maharani Jindan emerge to be the most misunderstood queens of their time.

---

[140] Martin, *An Illustrated History of the Empire*, 187–8.

SECTION THREE

Queens on the Margins

5

Guleri Rani of Sirmur

Image credit: Robert Montgomery Martin, The Indian Empire: Illustrated, Vol. III, Print and Publishing Company, London, 1899 (Mayur Publishers, Delhi, Reprint 1983)

The location of Sirmur, with its capital Nahan, had strategic significance for the British with its proximity to Nepal, Garhwal and Doon Valley; a picturesque view.

In order to construct the Rani as an active object of
knowledge, then, it should be grasped that she emerges in the
archives because of the commercial/territorial interests of the
East India Company.[1]

   This, then, is why the Rani surfaces briefly, as an
individual, in the archives because she is a king's wife and
a weaker vessel. We are not sure of her name. She is once
referred to as Rani Gulani and once as Gulari. In general she
is referred to, properly, as the Ranee by the higher officers
of the Company, and 'this Ranny' by Geoffrey Birch and
Robert Ross.[2]

The first critical reference to the rani of Sirmur in contemporary
historiography is in an article written by Gayatri Chakravorty
Spivak. With the advent of the British in the Punjab hill states,
two aspects of the Sirmur state are of critical political and
historical importance. Sirmur's proximity to Doon (the valley)
on one side, and to Garhwal and Nepal on the other. This
location would be of strategic importance to the commercial
and imperial interests of the British East India Company after
the reconnaissance of the Punjab hill states.[3] Another crucial
aspect of the Anglo–Sirmur relations in the early nineteenth
century is the role played by the queen of Sirmur, Guleri Rani.

---

[1] Gayatri Chakravorty Spivak, 'The Rani of Sirmur: An Essay in
Reading the Archives', *Theory and History*, 24, 3, October 1985,
247–72, 263.
[2] Spivak, 'The Rani of Sirmur', 266.
[3] No. 101, From Lieutenant-Colonel D. Ochterlony, Agent, Governor-
General, Loodeana, to C. Lushington, Secretary to Government, No. 63,
dated 18 May 1810, 218: 'the valley of Kaardeh lying between the Jumna
and Sutledge', and 'From the end of the Kaardeh, and running the whole
way from the Jumna to the Ganges and between the two first ranges of
hillsm is the valley of the Dehra Doon'.

Avoiding extreme positions of 'unquestioning deference and violent outrage', she handled the political crises from a 'middle ground in which conformity is often a self-conscious strategy and resistance is a carefully hedged affair that avoids all-or-nothing confrontations'.[4] In his reply to Spivak, Arik Moran argues how the rani of Sirmur negotiated with the British by using the ancient Rajput lineage and tradition to place Sirmur's political importance among the hill states of Punjab. Subsequently, the rani attempted to balance her intricate relationship with the British and her husband, bringing forth her dilemma as a virtuous Rajput wife with its tradition of sati. Her conformity to tradition became her weapon in doing the delicate balancing act. She was not the oppressed or the marginalized voice suggested by Spivak, nor is sati the only defence for her.

The rani and the place are closely intertwined. The relative marginalization of the place in the narrative of history resembles the marginalized position of the rani of Sirmur or Guleri Rani, who is the focus of the present chapter. Just as we know little about Guleri Rani, the history of Sirmur is equally obscure. Sirmur is shrouded in legends. A district in the present Himachal Pradesh, it is known for places like Paonta Sahib and Nahan, which are closely associated with the account of Guru Gobind Singh, the tenth guru. Going back to the historical antecedents of Sirmur, it is believed that it was established by Raja Rasaloo of Jaisalmer, one of whose ancestors was known as Sirmur. Another story is that it derived its name from the fact that it was the most important hill state, as 'Sirmur' means 'head' or 'chief' in vernacular (in a western Pahari dialect).[5]

---

[4] James C. Scott, *The Weapons of the Weak: Everyday Forms of Peasant Resistance*, (New Haven: Yale University Press, 1985), 285.

[5] Thakur Sen Negi, *Gazetteer of India, Himachal Pradesh: Sirmur*, (Aligarh: Oriental Printing Press, 1969, 1).

This chapter is divided into three sections. The first looks at the different versions of the history of Sirmur; the second explores how Guleri Rani emerged in early nineteenth-century British accounts and the third focuses on the negotiations and tensions between the rani and the English officers.

I

According to the 1969 *Gazetteer* of Sirmur,

> The ancient state capital was Sirmur situated in the Paonta valley corner, also known as Kayarda Dun . . . Despite the subsequent shifting of the capital, the original name, Sirmur, has held fast to this day. The original capital, Sirmur, was devastated by a flood in the Giri river about which there are some legends.[6]

The 1904 Sirmur *Gazetteer* begins the history of Sirmur with a particular legend. It states that Sirmur, prior to the present ruling family, was under the Suryavanshi Rajputs. According to the legend, under Raja Madan Singh,

> a woman, an expert in necromancy, presented herself before the Raja, boasting of her skill of crossing the river with an acrobat's rope. The Raja challenged her to cross the river Giri between two ranges, promising her half of his kingdom if she accomplished it. The woman successfully crossed the river, and on her return the Raja fearing her victory had the rope cut, drowning her. The place was cursed, and the old town of Sirmur was swept away, along with the king and his people.[7]

---

[6] Ibid., 45.

[7] *Sirmur State Gazetteer, Part A, 1904* (Compiled and Published under the Authority of the Punjab Government), (Lahore: Punjab

After the end of Madan Singh's dynasty, another lineage was invented associating Sirmur with the Rajputs of Jaisalmer. Following this tragedy, the ruling family claimed descent from Ugar Sain Rawal from the Jaisalmer House in Rajputana. His son Sobha Singh came to conquer Sirmur. The 1969 Gazetteer gives a different version of the present royal family of Sirmur. Here the ruler of Jaisalmer is stated to be Sal Bahan II. The Bhats of Sirmur approached him to send his son to rule Sirmur. Sal Bahan's son died before reaching Sirmur, but his wife delivered a son under the dhak plass tree near the Sirmuri Tal, and he was named Plasoo, and the family called Plassia.[8] The legend of Raja Salwan and Raja Rasaloo invites further investigation, as there is a Raja Rasaloo in the tales of Punjab. Raja Rasaloo or Rasalu was the son of Raja Salwan.[9] He had a son, Puran, from his first wife, Ichhran. Raja Salwan married a younger woman from a hill state, Chamba. Her name was Loona. To cut a long story short, Loona was cursed by Puran as she had falsely accused Puran of having made sexual advances towards her and she got him executed. After Guru Gorakhnath saved Puran, Puran became Guru Gorakhnath's disciple. Raja Rasalu was born to Raja Salwan after Puran forgave both Loona and Raja Salwan. Raja Rasalu is considered to be the first important king in the history of Punjab. It might be possible his influence increased from the western hill areas to the eastern hill areas. It is essential to keep in mind that Himachal Pradesh was carved out of Punjab in modern times in 1966. The legends of the hill areas are common to the tales of Punjab, though the dates of

---

Government Press, 1907), 8; Balgobind, *The Life of Raja Sir Shamshere Prakash of Sirmour*, (Calcutta: Thacker, Spink & Co., 1901), 2–3.

[8] Kunwar Ranzor Singh, *Tarikh i Riyasat Sirmour*, Hindi translation by Amar Nath Walia (Shimla: Himachal Academy of Arts, Culture and Languages, 2007), 197; Negi, *Gazetteer of India, Himachal Pradesh*, 46.

[9] Captain R.C. Temple, *The Legends of the Panjab*, Vol. I, (London: Forgotten Books, 2015),1–65.

Raja Rasalu of Jaisalmer are different from the dates of Raja Rasalu of Punjab.

From the English gazetteers on Sirmur[10] and the popular records available in the local Sirmuri tradition,[11] it seems that the existence of Sirmur can be traced back to the tenth century. In the British account, 'the Jaisalmer Rajputs have been in possession of the State since 1095'.[12] Sirmur seems to have been well-entrenched in medieval polity, in the period of the Delhi Sultanate. In 1254, the Pinjaur village formed the territory of Sirmur, when the Sultan of Delhi, Nasiruddin Mahmud

participated in the Mughal attempt to consolidate the northern territories with frequent incursions into Garhwal. In the mid-seventeenth century, Sirmur was rewarded with the fort at Bairat, and in 1655 with the valuable and wealthy *ilaqa* of Kotaha; this came as a surprise to the ruler, who was forced out by Sirmuri troops. Raja Subhag Prakash was a loyal supporter of the Mughal Emperor Alamgir, and also a great administrator.[13]

---

[10] *The Gazetteer of 1904* and the *Gazetteer of Sirmur State 1934-Part A*, Indus Publishing Company, 1996 (Reprint) by Rai Bahadur Sardar Kahn Chand Kapur.

[11] The Mahant of Jagannath at Nahan has a list of Rajas of Sirmur, 11 of the Gazetteer of Sirmur State, 1934; and Kunwar Ranzor Singh, 19, 196.

[12] *Ruling Princes and Chiefs, Notables and Principal Officials of the Punjab Native States*, (Lahore: The Superintendent Governor Printing, 1918), 3; *The Imperial Gazetteer of India Provincial Series, Punjab, Vol .II*, (Lahore: Superintendent of Government Press, 1908), 357; Balgobind, *The Life of Raja Sir Shamshere Prakash of Sirmour*,4. 'During a period of 700 years the descendants of Raja Badan Singh have been holding the throne of Sirmour in regular succession, Raja Shamshere being the 45th ruler.' 6.

[13] Mark Brentnall, *The Princely and Noble Families of the Former Indian Empire:Himachal Pradesh*, (New Delhi: Indus Publishing House, 2004), 22–3.

The raja's reputation so impressed the 'Emperor that he granted him the *ilaqa* of Kalagarh close to Dehra Dun. The area was retained as the personal property of the Raja even during the British period'.[14] Pinjaur village had been given as the fief to Fidai Khan, foster brother of Alamgir under the Mughals, but in 1675, the raja of Sirmur recovered it from the son of its former holder.[15]

The descent from the Jaisalmer family is common in both the gazetteers. This is probably an attempt to link the hill Rajput rulers to the Rajput rulers of the plains. In the hill states of Punjab too, argues Arik Moran, a pan-Indian Brahmin and Kshatriya identity evolved with the colonial intrusions and the Pahari hill rajas sought association with the Rajputs of the plains. According to Moran, 'The identification of the Pahari elite with Indic civilization'[16] was 'enshrined' in the colonial narrative. For instance, Madan Singh's legend about the fall of his dynasty and the rise of a new dynasty with its association with the Surajbansi Rajputs of the plains aimed at providing legitimacy to the new ruling class among other rulers and the people of Sirmur. The Rajput association with the ruling families of the hill chiefs is significant as Guleri Rani also comes from a prominent Rajput family of the hills.

What is striking in the narratives and a commentary on the colonial records is that the rani's actual name is not recorded. She is only mentioned by the name of the family from which she came, Guler, an offshoot of Kangra state.[17] Despite many

---

[14] Ibid.

[15] *The Imperial Gazetteer of India Provincial Series, Punjab, Vol. II,* 355–64.

[16] Arik Moran, *Kingship and Polity on the Himalayan Borderland: Rajput Identity during the Early Colonial Encounter* (Amsterdam: Amsterdam University Press, 2019), 20–1.

[17] Brentnall, *The Princely and Noble Families of the Former Indian Empire,* 32. The ruler Karam Prakash is mentioned but the author has not

efforts to find her name by looking up the lineages of both
Guler, a line of Kangra royal family, and the Sirmur royal
family, her actual name cannot be traced. 'Tracing the political
biographies,' writes Arik Moran, 'of mid-ranking women of
the Pahari aristocracy . . . remains exceedingly difficult.'[18] The
'the epistemic violence'[19]committed by the imperial archives as
Spivak writes does not occur by not mentioning them. The
rani emerges only when she is needed in the space of imperial
production.[20] The queens are discussed only in generic terms,
and their names hardly feature in the official accounts. One has
to read carefully to find their actual names.

The raja of Sirmur Karam Prakash, a Rajabansi Rajput
with descendants from Jaisalmer, was married to the princess
of Kangra, the Katoch Rajputs, famous by the name of Goler/
Guler Rani. According to Arik Moran, who has worked
extensively on this region, 'The beginning of the nineteenth
century . . . saw Katochi Rajputnis at the helm of the most
substantial kingdoms surrounding Kangra, including Bilaspur,
Kullu, Mandi, and Sirmour'.[21] This makes the position of the
rani of Sirmur or Guler significant in the politics of the hill
states. Her Katochi background makes her pivotal even to the
British. The rani's political presence in the colonial records is
available from 1809. Raja Karam Prakash ascended the throne
of Sirmur in 1793. Unfortunately, the refrences to the rani

---

mentioned the names of his wives, except that the second wife was
from Guler.

[18] Arik Moran, '"The Rani of Sirmur Revisited": Sati and Sovereignty
in Theory and Practice', *Modern Asian Studies* (Cambridge: Cambridge
University Press, 2014), 1–34, 9.

[19] Spivak, 'The Rani of Sirmur', 267.

[20] Ibid., 270.

[21] Moran, 'Rani of Sirmur Revisited', 12.

are intermittent. The queen's regency of Sirmur was during 1815–27.

To understand the political importance of Guleri Rani, we need to understand the political lineage of the Katoch Rajputs in the Punjab hill states. There were two branches of the Kangra Katoch Rajput rulers. The senior lineage was settled at Guler. Vogel records the story of Guler's foundation in 1405. Hari-Chand, the raja of Kangra, separated from his followers while on a hunting expedition and 'fell into a well'. His followers could not find him, and he was assumed to be dead. 'His funeral rites were performed, the ranis becoming *sati*, and Karm-Chand, the younger brother of the Raja, was seated on the *gaddi*.'[22] Hari-Chand was found in the well after 21 days by a merchant, 'who extricated him'. On learning about the succession at Kangra, he decided not to go back and built the new town and fort of Haripur. Guler is, thus, considered to be the senior branch of the Katoch family, and 'on all ceremonial occasions takes precedence of Kangra'.[23] The Muslim chroniclers, according to Hutchins and Vogel, mention that Guler was called the State of 'Gwaliar, from the tradition that a cowherd or *guala* pointed out to Hari-Chand the spot on which the fort of Haripur was built; the cowherd being offered as a sacrifice to ensure the stability of the walls, and afterwards worshipped as the guardian deity of the place'.[24] The account indicates the political prominence of the Guler family and the Katoch Rajputs of Kangra in the Western Himalayan states, and this may help us understand

---

[22] J. Hutchinson and J.P. H. Vogel, *History of the Punjab Hill States*, Vol. I, (Shimla: Department of Language and Culture, 2000) (Reprint), Himachal State Archives, Shimla, 51.

[23] Hutchinson and Vogel, *History of the Punjab Hill States*, 51.

[24] Ibid.

the political role played by Guleri Rani to ensure that the
succession of Sirmur went to her minor son, Fateh Prakash,
despite the removal of her husband as the ruler.

In the eighteenth century, with the Mughal Empire's
declining fortunes, Sirmur was engaged in internecine warfare
with its neighbours. Geographically, Sirmur is near Garhwal,
and the two kingdoms had frequent conflicts, and under the
time of Raja Budh Prakash, Garhwal seized the forts of Bairat
and Kalsi. It was only retrieved after Mughal intervention.[25]
One of Budh Prakash's later successors, Raja Kirat Prakash, had
to face a threat from Garhwal and the Sikhs. He was able to fend
them off, and with his far-sightedness, he was able to discern
the danger from the Gurkha expansion and decided to support
Garhwal against the Gurkhas. This ultimately led to the signing
of a treaty which fixed the western limits of the Gurkha kingdom
at the river Ganges.[26] Dharam Prakash's elder brother was Jagat
Singh, one of the protagonists in the battle of Chinjhiar. He was
married to a sister of Sansar Chand of Kangra. On Jagat Singh's
death, his wife was granted a jagir by Raja Dharam Prakash,
and Raja Karam Prakash respected the same on his accession.
He later withdrew her privileges for meddling in the affairs of
Sirmur to destabilize the raja. She was confined, but she escaped
to Kangra.[27]

It is essential to understand the political presence of the
Katoch princesses through matrimonial alliances with the ruling
families in the hills, in the light of the political dominance of
Sansar Chand of Kangra. The subsequent importance of Guleri
Rani in the political affairs of Sirmur can be also understood in

---

[25] Brentnall, *The Princely and Noble Families of the Former Indian
Empire*, 23.
[26] Ibid.
[27] Moran, *Kingship and Polity*, 93.

the constitution of the political dynamics of the hill states, in which the Katoch princess had the centrality. Queens in Pahari politics were not present for ceremonial purposes. According to Moran, 'By establishing a marital alliance, a rani entering her husband's kingdom not only shared in his family's prestige, but also received land grants, access to *begar* (free labour), luxury commodities, and, once established in her new abode, was free to advance her natal family's interests by influencing the internal workings of the court.'[28] The Katoch royal women exercised a dominant influence in the royal families of many hill states in Simla in the early nineteenth century. Guler Rani herself belonged to the senior line of the Katoch family.

Raja Dharam Prakash had to face invasion by Raja Ram Singh of Nalagarh and Raja Prakram Shah from Garhwal. Raja Dharam Prakash turned the tables on them by defeating and capturing Raja Jagat Chand of Baghal, an ally of Nalagarh. Dharam Prakash got involved with the affairs of the state of Kahlur, as the widow of Raja Devi Chand of Bilaspur 'applied for help to Raja Dharam Parkash', promising to pay him 'a lakh of rupees as *nazrana'*[29]. The raja, with his allies, marched to the border of the Katoch territory, challenging the powerful Kangra ruler, Raja Sansar Chand. Dharam Prakash died in the battle in 1796 and was succeeded by his brother, Karam Prakash, the husband of Guleri Rani.[30] His succession was challenged from within, and he was forced to leave Sirmur. Brentnall does not give the details of why the raja had to leave Sirmur. A Sirmur *Gazetteer* of 1969 shows the details of what transpired at Sirmur under Raja Karam Prakash. In the process, it throws light on his character, leading to the political

---

[28] Moran, *Kingship and Polity*, 95.
[29] Negi, *Gazetteer of India, Himachal Pradesh*, 58.
[30] Ibid.

role of Guleri Rani. The *Gazetteer* mentions the 'incapability' of Raja Karam Prakash resulting 'in mal-administration and many parts of the state slipped out of his possession'.[31] There were mutual jealousies, and the Patiala state record mentions how the state sent an expedition to Nahan in 1796 to assist the ruler in putting down a rebellion.[32] In the beginning, the raja was assisted by Mehta Prem Singh, and for two years he ruled in peace. But later Mehta Prem Singh revolted. Karam Prakash executed Prem Singh and confiscated his property. 'This caused great resentment amongst the subjects of the state and officials belonging to Kanet and Bhat communities became unruly, intending harm to the state.'[33] In this political turmoil, the other chiefs of Sirmur revolted and separated from it. In 1799, the Gurkhas defied the treaties and advanced from the south-east and occupied Dehradun and its forts. The Sikhs also jumped into the fray, taking possession of Pinjaur in the south.[34]

At this time, the Ramgarh state, led by Mian Maldev and Narain Singh, decided to become independent and dethrone the raja. On learning about this conspiracy, the raja and his family moved to the Kangra Fort situated at the hill in Kayada Dun in 1803. Taking advantage of the political disturbance, Ajib Singh, Prem Singh and Kishen Singh, along with his younger brother Ratan Singh, conspired to remove the raja.[35] They besieged the Kangra Fort, and the raja resisted the attack. One of the raja's servants who closely resembled him died fighting, and the rumour spread of the raja's death. 'Taking advantage of this

---

[31] Ibid.
[32] Ibid., 59.
[33] Ibid.
[34] Ibid.
[35] Ibid.

confusion, the raja accompanied by Ranee Guleri, escaped from the fort at night and fled to Kalsi.'[36] In Nahan, Ratan Prakash was made the king. Karam Prakash went to Dehradun to meet Amar Singh Thapa, a senior military commander of Nepal and told him about the trouble created by Karam Prakash's court officials. He also complained that the Ganga was the settled boundary between Nepal and Sirmur, and Amar Singh Thapa had encroached on Dehradun's area. Karam Prakash negotiated with Amar Singh Thapa that if the latter helped him suppress the rebellion and re-establish order in Sirmur, he assured Amar Singh Thapa of good mutual relations. The Gurkhas were looking for opportunities to expand and were also aware of the rising power of the British.[37] Consequent upon the meeting between the two, Ratan Singh was removed; but after Ratan Singh's removal, the Gurkhas did not leave Sirmur. Amar Singh Thapa sent his son, Ranjor Singh, as an administrator to Nahan. 'Ranjor Singh sacked the capital, demolished many a state building and got constructed a fort on the hill of Jaitak towards the north of Nahan where he lodged himself.'[38] The country was conquered by the Gurkhas in 1803.

Another version of the political history of Sirmur is provided by Francis Hamilton, based on his local informant, Harballabh. Sirmur was located west of Garhwal and the Yamuna, with its capital at Nahan. For about fifteen generations, it had 'belonged to a family of the Raythaur tribe', descending 'from a younger son of the Jaysalmer family'.[39] The first raja of Sirmur, according to Hamilton's

---

[36] Ibid., 60.

[37] Ibid.

[38] Ibid.

[39] Francis Hamilton (formerly Buchanan), *An Account of the Kingdom of Nepal, and of the Territories Annexed to their Dominion by the House of*

source Harballabh, was 'Vijay Prakas, who married a daughter of Jagat Chandra of Kumau'.[40] The third ruler of the Sirmur family, Kirti Prakash, was involved in fighting his immediate neighbours and wrested from Bilaspur's superiority of twelve petty chiefs called the Thakur Ranas.[41] He strengthened the western frontiers of Sirmur by taking Jagatpur from the raja of Nurpur. He was succeeded by his equally aggressive son Jagat Prakash at the age of ten. Jagat Prakash set out to marry the sister of the famous Katoch ruler of Kangra, Sansar Chand, at fourteen years of age. The raja of Bilaspur, Hamilton narrates, tried to obstruct him, but he was able to go ahead and marry the Katochi princess. In Hamilton's version, Jagat Prakash's brother-in-law tried to persuade him to avoid any confrontation with Bilaspur on his return. But Jagat Prakash 'disdained to show any mark of fear before his bride', and with an addition of 2,000 men given by Sansar Chand, 'they forced their way back'.[42] Jagat Prakash was keen to take Dun, a campaign left unfinished by his father. But he died at the age of twenty-eight without an issue and was succeeded by his brother Dharam Prakash. At this time, Hamilton states that Sansar Chand (1765–1823), 'having become very violent, made an attack on the Rajas of Mundi and Bilaspur, who applied for assistance to Dharma of Sirmaur'.[43] Hamilton writes that Dharam Prakash received 2,00,000 rupees, 'and having been promised as much more, joined them with his forces, and three Rajas advanced to fight Futeh Chandra, the brother of Sangsar, who commanded the forces of Kangra.

Gorkha (Edinburgh: Archibald Constable and Company, 1819), 302.
[40] Ibid.
[41] Ibid., 303.
[42] Ibid., 303–4.
[43] Ibid., 304.

They were, however, entirely defeated, and Dharma fell in the battle'.[44]

The *jheras* or oral accounts used by Arik Moran provide invaluable information about the battle but interpret it differently. Moran draws attention to the centrality of royal women in the politics of the hill states, despite the *jhera* confining women to the stereotypical 'evil' and 'virtuous'. He highlights the undercurrents of tension between Kangra and Bilaspur due to the regent queen, Nagardevi of the Katoch family, who had been married in Bilaspur. Nagardevi harboured hatred against Sansar Chand's family for dethroning her father and killing her brothers and waged wars against him. While the oral records do not mention Nagardevi of Bilaspur, they narrate the 'evil' role of Raja Jagat Singh's Katoch wife, who he had married so heroically in Hamilton's account. In these accounts, she taunted him with the martial prowess of her brother. She would continue to be malevolent to his successor, according to the oral tradition, despite him giving her a jagir. But it seems that the battle did not end the hostility between Kangra and Sirmur. This infighting among the Rajput rulers of the Western Himalaya brought first the Gurkhas and subsequently the English to intercede. Sirmur is a Pahari Rajput state and, according to Moran, 'the histories of Bilaspur, Kangra and Sirmaur' are intertwined in developing 'Rajput Kingship, polity, and identity on the Himalayan borderland'.[45] In the battle, the young and brave prince dies, and his 'virtuous' wife commits suicide by jumping from the roof.

Dharam Prakash's tragic demise brought to power Raja Karam Prakash II, the third son of Raja Kirat Prakash who was Guleri Rani's husband. According to Francis Hamilton,

---

[44] Ibid., 304.
[45] Moran, *Kingship and Polity*, 24

Sansar Chand persuaded the raja of Hanur, a feudatory of
Sirmur, to turn against the Sirmur ruler, with a promise
of independence and twelve thakurais to him. On these
developments, Karam Prakash invited the Gurkhas under
Amar Singh, 'who commanded the forces of the Nepal
government in Garhawal', for his assistance.[46] Basing himself
on the information shared by Harballabh, Hamilton says that
Amar Singh sent 'Bhakti Thapa with 1000 fusileers, and these,
united to the troops of Sirmaur, advanced to the west in search
of their enemies. They were soon, however, compelled to
retire by the united forces of Sangsar and Hanur'. Hamilton
states that Sansar Chand then entered into negotiations with
Krishna Singh, the son of Ishwari Singh, an uncle of Raja
Karam Prakash, and with his help 'plundered the family
of that chief'.[47] Karam Prakash fled from Sirmur and took
refuge with Amar Singh, who advanced and subdued Hanur.
The estates of Raja Karam Prakash were restored to him.
Subsequently, Amar Singh attacked Kangra but had to make
a disastrous retreat, compelled by Maharaja Ranjit Singh of
Lahore. Amar Singh then approached Raja Karam Prakash,
seeking an audience. It seems that the raja miscalculated the
strength of the Gorkhas after they retreated from Kangra and
gave a bold reply. The Gorkhas under Ranjor, son of Amar
Singh, attacked Sirmur, and Karam Prakash had to leave
Sirmur again.[48] He seeks refuge with a relative near Rayapur,
while 'His wife and son have gone to Lodhyana, in the hope
of procuring assistance from the English'.[49]

---

[46] Hamilton, *An Account of the Kingdom of Nepal*, 304.

[47] Ibid.

[48] Ibid., 305.

[49] Ibid.

II

This section deals with the emergence of Guleri Rani and her interactions with Colonel Ochterlony. The role of Rani Guleri has to be understood in the context of political developments taking place in the region in the nineteenth century. From the correspondence available in the imperial archives, one gets an understanding that the rani approached Colonel Ochterlony sometime in 1811, when the royal family of Sirmur had become a fugitive and sought the assistance of the British authorities at Ludhiana.[50] The British, engaged in a crucial war with the Gurkhas of Nepal, were looking for allies. Sirmur had already been taken by the Gurkhas. After the treaty with Ranjit Singh in 1809, the British were given permission to use the land on the eastern side of the River Sutlej. The diplomatic relations between the British and the Patiala state played an important role after Ranjit Singh's death and the events of 1857. Sirmur, because of its geopolitical position, became important to the British as it allowed them to keep an eye of Nepal.

Simultaneous to the British taking the Cis-Sutlej under their protection, the Gurkha invasion of the Western Himalaya brought the English in confrontation with the Gurkhas. Located between modern Himachal Pradesh, Uttarakhand and the plains of modern Haryana, Sirmur's geopolitical importance in the colonial period is mapped out in the description given in 1814. It was situated between the Sutlej and Yamuna. On crossing the Yamuna, one entered 'the Surmoria country, of which Nahun was the capital or residence of the Rajah'.[51] It was bounded on

---

[50] Kunwar Ranzor Singh, 228; in 1811, General David Ochterlony was the commanding officer of the Ludhina-Karnal Camp. It is here that Rani approached him for help.

[51] *Records of the Ludhiana Agency, 1814-15*, Selections from the Punjab Government Records, (Lahore: Punjab Government Press, 1911), para 7, 396.

the south by the protected districts of the Sikhs; to the east to a considerable extent by the Yamuna; it had a boundary with Kumaon, extending to the east to the Tons and to the north to Bhutan. On the west, the Sirmur state was bound 'by one or other of the Barra Thakoorais or 12 portions, and these are bounded on the south by Sikh districts, on the west by the Ranj of Hindoor, and extend northerly till they join the territory of Bisshaher'. The west of Hindoor was the 'Kehloor country, of which Belauspoor is the capital'.[52] Attacks from Nepal to Garhwal and Sirmur put all the Punjab hill states at risk and extended to the plains of Pinjore, which was also part of Sirmur, to the Punjab region. By the treaty of 1809, the Cis–Sutlej states had come under British protection, raising the stakes of the Company in this area.

Raja Karam Prakash became a fugitive with his family at this time and first interacted with the English officials. He first took refuge in Sabathu, a fief of the Ramgarh family. He had to leave the place and move to Buria as the ruler of Ramgarh, Mian Maldeo Singh, and his brother Narain refused to give further protection. It was in Buria, according to Brentnall, that Guleri Rani decided to approach the British authorities at Ludhiana.[53] However, the available British records of this period do not mention the rani approaching Sir David Ochterlony. There is a reference to the raja of Sirmur writing a representation to him. Ochterlony only mentioned the representation of Raja Karam Prakash of Nahan to him in his correspondence to C. Lushington in 1810. He stated that the raja was 'expelled from his country' and 'lives at a village in the district of Munny Majra, in a great degree, if not entirely dependent on the bounty of

---

[52] *Records of the Ludhiana Agency, 1814-15*, para 7, 396.

[53] Brentnall, *The Princely and Noble Families of the Former Indian Empire*, 23.

Surdar Gopaul Sing'.[54] Ochterlony described 'Surmoreah' with
Nahan as the capital to be 'a country of considerable extent',
governed by the Rajput princes 'who have for centuries
been the rulers of the hills, divided into a number of petty
independent States'.[55]

In his petition to Ochterlony in 1810, Karam Prakash
narrated his version of coming to the throne and his removal
from Sirmur.[56] He stated that he was a son of Raja Kirat Singh
of Sirmur, who died in 1776, leaving behind four sons. Karam
Prakash was the third son. He became the ruler of Sirmur after
the death of his two elder brothers, Jagat Prakash and Dharam
Prakash. They had no male issue. On his accession to 'the
musnud' fourteen years ago, he found himself controlled by the
two principal advisers of his predecessor Dharam Prakash, who
controlled the affairs under his name but without seeking his
opinion. To assert his position, Karam Prakash appointed his
own man and executed the two previous advisers. This action
was seen as tyrannical, creating apprehensions and leading to a
confederacy against him. He was then expelled. His younger
brother Ratan Prakash was appointed in his place. The raja, with
the help of the Patiala raja and some of his supporters at Sirmur,
took the state back.[57] Till 1803–04, when the 'Gorkhas having
attacked and levied contributions from the Gudwal or Serinagar
Rajah meditated a similar attack upon the Surmoreah country
but were for that time prevented by a pecuniary douceur and
by certain stipulations that were made through the medium of

---

[54] No. 101, From Lieutenant-Colonel D. Ochterlony, Agent,
Governor-General, Loodeana, to C. Lushington, Secretary to
Government, No. 63, dated 18 May 1810, in Ludhina Residency
Records, 217.

[55] Ibid.

[56] Ibid.

[57] Ibid.

Maha Chund, Kullolreah'.[58] This treaty was 'highly offensive'[59] to Sansar Chand of Kangra, and other hill rajas, as it opened an easy passage to their territories. They entered into a league to expel Karam Prakash from his country and place 'Rutton Purkas a second time on the *musnud*'.[60] At this time, Karam Prakash stated in his petition to the English authorities, the Gurkhas got a reason to take up his cause and reinstated him. Karam Prakash remained silent on his role in inviting the Gurkhas to help him. He stated that the Gurkhas imposed specific terms on him, 'which bound him to supply them with provisions and to facilitate their progress in their meditated invasion of Kangra and the hill territories beyond the Surmoreah'.[61] Ochterlony's views[62] on the petition was that the raja probably 'evaded' giving assistance to the Gurkhas.

All the imperial records and the account of Kunwar Ranzor Singh have a similar narrative of Raja Karam Prakash as the weak ruler of Sirmur as the reason for his minor son to be given gaddi, with his mother, Guleri Rani as the regent. To be made a regent in the lifetime of Karam Prakash was exceptional. There are many versions with one common factor, the weak character of Raja Karam Prakash.[63] The *Imperial Gazetteer* mentioned that Raja Karam Prakash succeeded his brother in 1793 or 1796. The *Gazetteer* then stated that since he was a 'weak ruler, whose misconduct caused a serious revolt'.[64] According to the imperial records, the raja invited the Gurkhas to assist him, and they

---

[58] Ibid., 218.

[59] Ibid.

[60] Ibid.

[61] Ibid.

[62] Ibid.

[63] Ochterlony considered Raja Karam Prakash as a 'weak and wicked' character, *Ludhiana Residency Records*, 404.

[64] *Imperial Gazetteer*, 383.

'promptly seized their opportunity and invaded Sirmur, expelled Ratan Parkash, whom the rebels had placed on the throne, and then refused to restore Karam Parkash'.[65] Kunwar Ranzor Singh also described him as weak, as being the third son he was not trained for the throne, but he also blamed the local nobility for destabilizing his rule.[66]

It was in this time of crisis, according to the *Imperial Gazetteer*, that 'his queen, a princess of Goler and a lady of courage and resource, took matters into her own hands and invoked British aid'.[67] She appealed to the British commander at Ludhiana, Col. Ochterlony, for assistance to recover the state from the Gurkhas. 'In April 1810 Colonel Ochterlony was appointed Agent to the Governor-General at Ludhiana, in subordination to the Resident at Delhi, through whom he corresponded with government. Captain G. Birch was at the same time appointed Assistant to Colonel Ochterlony.'[68] In April 1810, Col. Ochterlony was appointed A. G. G. at Ludhiana. In June 1815, the designation changed to the superintendent of political affairs and A. G. G. in the territories of the protected Sikh hill chiefs until October 1815, when this office was moved to Karnal.[69] The political officer of Ludhiana Col Ochterlony was given orders to advance against the Gurkhas following the formal British declaration of war on Nepal. The British force advanced towards Nahan

---

[65] The Gurkha army at Dehradun was under the Commander-in-Chief Kaji Ranjor Thapa. The British Army suffered heavy losses of men and material at the Jatak Fort, 7 km from Nahan, and the Gurkhas evacuated it only under the terms of the treaty with the Nepal government with the British India government in 1815.

[66] Kunwar Ranzor Singh, 222-224.

[67] *Imperial Gazetteer*, Provincial Series. Vol. II, 383.

[68] *Records of the Ludhiana Agency*, Preface, ii.

[69] *Punjab Hill States Agency*, 1815-1947, Himachal State Archives, Shimla.

to face the Gurkha army under General Kaji Ranjor Thapa, which was encamped at Jaitek Fort. On 7 December 1814, the British launched their attack, but unfamiliar with the terrain and poorly led, they were routed by the Gurkha force and obliged to withdraw. The Gurkhas retained control of the entire area until the peace treaty was signed with Nepal in 1815.[70] The rani's appeal coincided with the declaration of war against Nepal, and a force was sent to expel the Gurkhas from Sirmur.[71] The East India Company held 'the services of Major General Sir David Ochterlony' in 'high estimation'.[72] After the settlement of the dispute with the Gorkhas in 1815–16, the governor general wrote to the directors of the East India Company regarding the British proceedings with 'the disposal and settlement of the territories wrested from the Gorkhahs in the course of the late War'.[73] The English also arranged to settle those territories 'which have been annexed to the British Dominions and those which have been restored to their native Princes or otherwise disposed of'.[74] There was a strong adverse observation on Karam Prakash of Sirmur 'on account of the incurable depravity of his character and the universal odium under which he laboured'.[75]

---

[70] Brentnall, *The Princely and Noble Families of the ormer Indian Empire*, 23–4.

[71] *Sirmur State Gazetteer*, 1904, 17. The narratives are similar in the state gazetteer.

[72] To the Governor General from Edward Parry, John Morris, East India Office, London, 15 December 1815.

[73] Ibid.

[74] Foreign Political, Letter to Court, 1815-16, 36. To the Honorable Court of Directors for affairs of the Hon'ble the United Company of Merchants of England Trading to the East Indies. From Fort William, Political Department, N.B.E. Edmonstone Archibald Seton and George Davdeswell, 11 December 1816.

[75] Ibid.

The raja was most probably suffering from syphilis, and his public appearance came to be confined, and this led to his queen taking charge of the kingdom and using the royal seal. Karam Prakash was then deposed by the British. The ostensible reason given was that he was barbaric and dissolute.[76] Fraser referred to the 'heartless inaction' [77] by Sirmur in the fight against the Gurkhas, not aiding the British forces under General Gillespie. He further stated that the people also did not want the restoration of Karam Prakash: 'The conduct of the ex-rajah had even made some districts absolutely inimical and active against any measure that favoured his restoration.'[78]

The settlement of the hill country west of the Yamuna was conducted by Lieutenant Ross under the general direction and supervision of Sir David Ochterlony.[79] By 23 January 1810, C. Lushington, acting secretary to government, Fort William, had informed Lieutenant-Colonel D. Ochterlony, commanding at Ludhiana, of the approach of the Gorkha troops under Amar Singh towards the possession of the Sikh chiefs under British protection.[80] At this time, the British were clear that they would not interfere with the Gurkhas' aggression in the hills, but would defend the plains. After the Gurkhas took Sirmur, they claimed territories belonging to Raja Karam Prakash. Ochterlony challenged the Gorkha claims. In response to Amar Singh Thapa's claims, he wrote that 'Chiefs bordering on the hills' were 'under the protection of the British Government'; in particular, 'Punjore, Narrien Gurh and Lahurpoor' were under

[76] Spivak, 'The Rani of Sirmur', 265.

[77] James Fraser, 77.

[78] Ibid.

[79] Cons. 20, Sanads given to the Hill Chiefs, Nos. 44 & 45, October 1815.

[80] *Records of the Ludhiana Agency*, 174.

Sirmur or Nahan district. 'Buddea and Pullasea' were under
Hindour, and 'these places have always belonged to whoever
possessed Surmore and Hindour'.[81] This seems to be the first
confrontation between the British and Gurkhas on the issue of
Sirmur. The Gurkhas had taken Kaardeh in the Sirmur territory.

Based on Karam Prakash's petition, Ochterlony felt that the
raja was not complicit with the Gurkhas. He changed his opinion
in 1814. He wrote that the Gurkhas had not yet consolidated
themselves in Garhwal or Serinagar by 1793. It is in 1803 that
the final subjugation of these places occurred, after the raja of
Garhwal was killed in action with the Gurkhas in the valley
of Dehra. Here Ochterlony highlighted the 'negative' role of
Raja Karam Prakash: 'Antecedent, however to this event, the
weakness, tyranny and mismanagement of Kurrumpurkaush had
excited the general hatred of his subjects and the discontent of
his more immediate dependents, and revolutions unnecessary
to detail had induced him to solicit the aid of the Goorkha
forces to establish his own authority.'[82] A few hundred men
'under Bhugty Sing Thappa were sent to his assistance, but
being surrounded by the troops collected by Kishen Sing and
his own ministers, assisted by Ram Sing, the Hindoor (now
Pulasia) Rajah, and straitened for provisions, he entered into
negotiations which terminated in his being allowed to recross
the Jumna unmolested'.[83] He fled to the low countries. When

[81] In the enclosure No. 91, No. 2, From Lieutenant-Colonel
D. Ochterlony, Agent, Governor-General, Loodeana, to C. Lushington,
Secretary to Government, No. 56, dated 5 April 1810, in *Records of the
Ludhiana Agency*, 197, 198.
[82] No. 176, Col D. Ochterlony, Agent, Governor-General, Loodeana, to
J. Adam, Esquire, Secretary to Government in the Secret, Political and
Foreign Department, No.198, dated 29 August 1814, Enclosure 1 to 176,
'Report on the Hill Districts occupied by the Goorkhas', para 4, 394.
[83] Ibid.

the Gurkhas consolidated their position between the Yamuna and the Ganges, 'he sought their assistance and met their commander at Kalsee, with whom he returned with a large army by Ranjpoor, Kangra, etc., to his own capital of Nahun, having stipulated to let the Gurkhas pass unmolested' through Sirmur. He also agreed to provide troops and provisions to the siege of Kote Kangra, a fort of the Katoch Rajputs, west of the Sutlej.[84] His seeking assistance from the Gurkhas was seen in low light by his adversaries and Ochterlony.

From the time of representation by Raja Karam Prakash in 1810, by 1814, Ochterlony's views on the raja had changed drastically. He was not in favour of restoring Sirmur to 'so weak and wicked a character as Rajah Kurrumpurkaush'.[85] The purpose was not merely to expel the Gurkhas, as that would 'prove rather inimical than beneficial to the views of the British Government', suggesting the enlightened nature of the British rule. Ochterlony decided 'to place his infant son Futteh Sing, a minor of about 11 years of age, on the *guddy*', as the elder son Gopal Singh had died.[86] Here Ochterlony admitted that 'though the imbecility and tyranny of Kurrumpurkash are notorious, much of the information has been obtained from his relation Kishen Sing, and who in fact first caused him to seek the assistance of the Goorkhas'.[87]

The restoration of Sirmur by the British government to Fateh Prakash, the minor son of Karam Prakash, though not mentioned in the correspondences of Ochterlony in the Ludhiana Agency records, stated in files subsequently and in the *Imperial Gazetteer*, was the result of the backdoor diplomacy

---

[84] Ibid., 395.
[85] Ibid., 395.
[86] Ibid., 395.
[87] Ibid., 404.

carried out by Guleri Rani. Karam Prakash abdicated in 1815
and remained in Buria (in Ambala) on a British pension until
his death in 1826. The official accounts repeat Karam Prakash's
'profligacy and imbecility'[88] for setting aside his claim. The
unusual arrangement with Sirmur 'somewhat different from that
made with respect to the other states' in the hill country,[89] was
stated as follows:

> To accomplish these purposes it was proposed to place the
> minor Rajah under the immediate guardianship of his mother
> there being no male relation to which this important trust
> could be confided. The executive authority was to be in
> the Ranee, and the constituted officers of the government,
> subject to the control and direction of Captain Birch acting
> under the orders of Sir David Ochterlony on the part of
> the British government, the military defence of the country
> was to devolve on the British government a provision was
> assigned to Kurum Pergaush on the condition of his residing
> beyond the limits of Sirmore, and engaging never to interfere
> with the affairs of the Raj.[90]

The British officials were at pains to explain that the exclusion of
'Rajah Kurum Purgaush' was 'exclusively personal to him, and
offered no reason for depriving his family of the possession of

---

[88] *Ruling Princes and Chiefs, Notables and Principal Officials of the Punjab
Native States*, 1918, 3.
[89] Cons. 20, Sanads given to the Hill Chiefs, Nos. 44 & 45, October
1815.
[90] Foreign Political, Letter to Court, 1815-16, 36. To the Honorable
Court of Directors for affairs of the Hon'ble the United Company of
Merchants of England Trading to the East Indies. From: Fort William,
Political Department, N.B.E. Edmonstone Archibald Seton and
George Davdeswell, 11 December 1816.

the country, which in fact could not have been appropriated in any other manner so much to the general convenience'.[91] The English authorities underlined the fact that '[t]he restoration of any part of the family was, however, a matter of pure option with the British Government since their own exertions had contributed nothing to the expulsions of the Goorkhas'.[92] In the words of the governor general the restoration was done 'in part to lighten the burden of expense which the defence of the country would entail on the British government'.[93] The 'Goler Rani was appointed the regent' during her son's minority.[94] The British considered it prudent to be allies with the old hill Rajput families, especially when the second queen of the deposed ruler belonged to the influential Katoch Rajput lineage, with her networks within the ruling elite.

The British annexed all the territories east of the Yamuna with Kotaha and the Kiardah Dun. The area of Hanro Gurchari was given to Keonthal. 'It was considered necessary for the British government to retain the Kaardah Doon, the tract between the Jumna and Nahan and the Governor General finally determined on separating the Pergunnahas of Jounsar and Bhawur situated to the eastward of the Thamasor Sonse from Sirmore and annexing them to the British Dominion.'[95] This measure was strongly recommended by Sir David Ochterlony on grounds 'of political expediency as accessory to the maintenance of our ascendancy in that quarter and as contributing in some degree to indemnify us for the charge we should incur in the protection of

---

[91] Cons. 20, Sanads given to the Hill Chiefs, Nos. 44 & 45, October 1815.

[92] Ibid.

[93] Foreign Political, Letter to Court, 1815–16, 36.

[94] *Sirmur State Gazetteer*, 17.

[95] Ibid.

Sirmore'.[96] Military considerations played a role. The land taken
by the British was placed under the management of Captain
Birch and yielded

> a Revenue including Lands and customs of between
> seventeen thousand and eighteen thousand Rupees per
> annum. The Kaarda Doon is very unproductive, but is said
> once to have been otherwise and may again improve. The
> customs of Kaarda to have farmed for Rupees two thousand
> for the current year. The Land Revenue is scarcely worth
> estimating – the Governor General considered the assumption
> of Jaunson and Bhawur to fulfil every expectation. We could
> justly entertain of tribute or any other payment from Sirmore
> as the condition of our protection, the whole of the remaining
> Revenue therefore with the exception of the sum allotted for
> the maintenance of Kurum Purgansh is at the disposal of the
> government of Sirmore. It amounts to about forty thousand
> Rupees per annum, and is appropriated under the supervision
> of Captain Birch to the different branches of the Rajah's
> household and State.[97]

Balgobind in his account of Sirmur's ruling family in 1901,
mentioned that after the expulsion of the Gurkhas from Sirmur,
the throne was given to Fateh Prakash and 'a portion of the
expenses of war, namely, one lakh of rupees, was demanded from
the reinstated ruler, who being unable to pay, mortgaged the
territories below the Jumna'.[98] It was stipulated that he must pay
the money in a certain fixed time. The ruler could not pay and
the territory including Dehradun district was not given back to

---

[96] Foreign Political, Letter to Court, 1815–16, 36.

[97] Secret Cons. 4 July 1815, Foregn Political Department, National
Archives, New Delhi.

[98] Balgobind, 6.

the ruler.[99] Whether Dehradun was part of Sirmur, as claimed by Balgobind, or was under Kangra, remains unclear in the accounts. The Kiardah Dun (or the valley) was, however, restored to the state in 1833 on payment of Rs 50,000.[100] During the first Afghan War, 'the raja aided the government with a loan, and in the first Sikh War a Sirmur contingent fought at Hari-Ka-Pattan.'[101] Under the British Raj, Sirmur or Nahan ranked among the native states in Punjab, with the rulers of Mandi and Sirmur being regarded as equal in rank.[102] In the imperial scheme of things, Sirmur was given an eleven-gun salute. In 1896, the political control of Sirmur was transferred from the superintendent, Simla Hill States, to the commissioner of Delhi (now of Ambala). The state 'furnished a contingent for service in Afghanistan'.[103]

III

It has been a challenge to find the story of Guleri Rani, the main protagonist in the affairs of Sirmur in the early nineteenth century. There is no mention in the genealogical chart prepared by a recent historian of any marriage from the house of Guler with Raja Karam Prakash of Sirmur.[104] What does this indicate? Probably that she was from the extended Guleri family of more obscure origin and not directly from the main royal family of Guler. But the fact that she belonged to the royal family of Guler had substantial political significance in the history of that period. It is due to her royal connection to a powerful Kangra political state that she was able to negotiate with Ochterlony.

---

[99] Ibid, 7.

[100] *Sirmur State Gazetteer*, 1904, 17.

[101] Ibid.

[102] *Ruling Princes and Chiefs, Notables and Principal Officials of Punjab Native States*, 1918, 3.

[103] *Sirmur State Gazetteer*, 4.

[104] Brentnall, *The Princely and Noble Families of the Former Indian Empire*.

In the final settlement with the hill states of Punjab, after the defeat of the Gurkhas, the governor general observed that in the case of Sirmur, the minor son can be the heir under the supervision of a male guardian.[105] There is no mention in the records available in the Ludhiana Agency records of 1814–15 on the Guleri Rani. The British were at pains to disassociate themselves from Raja Karam Prakash based on Ochterlony's views. He did not have any expectations from Karam Prakash, who he describes as a 'mere imbecile, and I fear not at all popular in his own country, where the inhabitants have been of late more reconciled to the Goorkha Government by the milder administration of Runjoor Sing, a son of Ummer Sing Thappa'.[106] Ochterlony shows more faith in a relative of the Nahan Raja Kishen Singh, in the service of Patiala.[107] Based on Ochterlony's observations, J. Adam wrote[108] that in general the hill chiefs were to be restored to their ancient territories, but 'that principle should be modified and tempered in its actual application to the circumstances'. Maintaining a moral stance, it was stated that the governor general would not go against the

---

[105] 'Sanad conferring on Raja Fateh Sing (or Parkash) the lands of Sirmur, dated 21 September 1815 in C.U. Aitchison, *A Collection of Treaties, Engagements and Sanads relating to India and Neighbouring Countries*, Vol. IX (Calcutta: Superintendent of Government Printing Press, 1892), No. XVI, Treaty No. XLIII, 125–6.

[106] No.171, From Lieutenant-Colonel D. Ochterlony, Agent, Governor-General, Loodeana, to J. Adam, Secretary to Government, in the Secret, Political and Foreign Department, No. 193, dated 9 July 1814, in *Records of the Ludhiana Agency*, 383.

[107] Ibid., 382.

[108] No.177, From J. Adam, Secretary to Government, Fort William, to Lieutenant-Colonel D. Ochterlony, Agent, Governor-General, Loodeana, dated Camp on the Ganges near Currah, the 30 September 1814, in *Records of the Ludhiana Agency*, para 18, 414–15.

'character and honor of the British government, to employ its power to restore a Chief of notorious profligacy or imbecility to his former possessions against the will of the majority of the inhabitants.' In this case, for instance, of Karam Prakash, the exiled chief of Sirmur, the governor general fully sanctioned and confirmed any arrangement, in accordance with sentiments of the people to adopt any measures to exclude him 'from all concerns in the government' and find a more suitable heir or an eligible person. This power was given to Ochterlony with his 'personal knowledge' of 'the other members of his family . . . for excluding him personally from all concern in the government and establishing the next heir, or any more eligible person, in the government, under such subsidiary provisions for the administration as you may deem fit'.[109] On 21 September 1816, under a sanad, the British government 'conferred on him and his heirs in perpetuity his ancient possessions with certain exceptions. The Chief is required in case of war to join the British troops with all his forces and also to make roads through his territory'. Under the arrangement arrived at by Ochterlony, Guleri Rani became the regent for her minor son Fateh Prakash from 1815 to 1827.[110] Kishen Singh was set aside for causing Raja Karam Prakash to seek Gurkha assistance.

The court of directors in their reply to the governor general approved the decision to re-establish the 'petty chiefs, although they had not in general strictly entitled themselves to it according to the terms of the Proclamation published in 1814'.[111] They also approved of the decision of Ochterlony and Captain Ross on Sirmur:

---

[109] Ibid.,para 18, 415.
[110] *Sirmur State Gazetteer*, 1904, 17.
[111] Political Letters from Court, 1819-20, Pt I, Answer to Political Letter, 11 December 1816. National Archives, New Delhi.

Justly obnoxious as Kurrum Pergaush had rendered himself
by his cruelties and enormities to the people of Sirmore, it
would have been but an ill-exercise of our power to have
forcibly re-established his authority. The arrangement which
you adopted of elevating his infant son Futty Sing to the
guddy, under the guidance of his mother, was probably the
best which you could have made, although it was attended
with what we consider a great evil, namely, the necessity
of keeping up a vigilant control over the Ranee and the
ministerial officers of the Government. We have little doubt
that this unpleasant duty will be judiciously performed by
Captain Birch, of whose discretion we have reason to think
favorably.[112]

The passage reveals their mistrust of the rani.

Captain Birch was assigned the task of keeping an eye on the
affairs of Sirmur as the Political Agent.

It has been necessary for Captain Birch occasionally to
interfere authoritatively to counteract the facility of the
Rani's disposition and to supply the defects of the ministerial
affairs of the government, but we hope that their experience
and a sense of the real advantages they derive from the present
arrangement will lead to the establishment of a good practical
system of government.[113]

---

[112] Political Letters from Court, 1819-20, Pt I, Answer to Political
Letter, 11 December 1816, London, 20 December 1820.

[113] To the Secret Committee, Foreign Political, Letter to Court,
1815-16, 36. To the Honorable Court of Directors for affairs of the
Hon'ble the United Company of Merchants of England Trading
to the East Indies. From Fort William, Political Department,
N.B.E. Edmonstone Archibald Seton and George Davdeswell, 11
December 1816.

The rani's Rajput lineage may have been a consideration with the English authorities to support her regency, despite the fact that she probably had no experience of running the administration. Moran draws attention to the centrality of women in the political narratives of the hill states. He writes: 'the framing of the narrative by the actions of the Rajputnis hints at their centrality to Pahari politics'.[114] The British, it seems were not happy with this arrangement, as the official records mention undercurrents of tension between the rani and the English officials. The British authorities were apparently not satisfied with the state of administration under her regency. The 1904 *Gazetteer* mentioned the following: 'Under the Goler Rani's regency the affairs of the State were not well administered, owing to the self-seeking apathy of the officials, but Mians Devi Singh and Dalip Singh, sons of the Mians Khushali Singh and Ram Deo, of Ramgarh, executed a deed of allegiance in 1823, thus attaching Ramgarh firmly to the State.'[115] Guleri Rani, despite her diplomatic success with the British, 'proved to be a rather less than adequate administrator, and authority was placed in the hands of Mian Devi Singh and Dalip Singh. They formed an alliance with Mian Devi Singh of Ramgarh in 1823, which firmly established Ramgarh as feudatory of the Sirmur state'.[116] Captain Birch sent Munshi Azizullah Khan to supervise the administration of Sirmur till Fateh Prakash came of age.[117]

Sirmur was made to pay for British protection after coming under the sovereignty of the East India Company. Captain Birch

---

[114] Moran, *Kingship and Polity*, 51.
[115] *Sirmur State Gazetteer*, 1904, 17.
[116] Brentnall, *The Princely and Noble Families of the Former Indian Empire*, 24.
[117] Kunwar Ranzor Singh, 241.

and later Captain Ross restructured the revenue of the state.[118]
James Baillie Fraser considered Sirmur to be an impoverished
state which did not give good revenue to the Gurkhas.[119] It seems
misplaced in view of what Ochterlony reported in 1814–15.
In his enclosure on the estimated revenues under the Gurkhas
from the state of Sirmur was one Rs 1,00,000; Hindoor, 40,000;
Kehloor was 1,00,000; Barra Thakurais, 65,500; Bushair,
60,000.[120] The territories were taken as compensation for
providing assistance and protection to these hill states. A post-
Independence *Gazetteer* of Sirmur underlines this point: 'Before
1815, however, the area of the state must have been larger than
what was restored to it by the British Government, under a
treaty executed in that year, as a compensation for the assistance
rendered by it in the expulsion of Gurkhas.'[121]

Contrary to the British accounts, Arik Moran points towards
the rani's abilities to stabilize Sirmur after years of turmoil. He
finds her a 'phenomenal success as a political leader',[122] but
feels that she carried the burden of her Rajput tradition in her

---

[118] Political Letters from Court, 6 April 1825 to 10 November
1826, S.No.30, 47–9, (London, East India House); the Company's
commendation of Captain Ross's management of Sirmur which have
left the finances of the state 'have been left' in 'the favorable situation'.
[119] James Baillie Fraser, *Journal of a tour through part of the snowy range
of the Himala Mountains, and to the sources of the rivers Jumna and Ganges*
(London: Rodwell and Martin, 1820), 73. The Gurkhas received a
revenue of about Rs 85,000.
[120] No.176, Col. D. Ochterlony, Agent, Governor-General, Loodeana,
to J. Adam, Esquire, Secretary to Government in the Secret, Political
and Foreign Department, No. 198, dated 29 August 1814, Enclosure
(3) to 176, 'Supposed revenue of the Goorkha conquests between the
Jumna and Sutledge rivers', 407.
[121] Negi, *Gazetteer of India, Himachal Pradesh*, 2.
[122] Moran, 'The Rani of Sirmur Revisited', 26.

domestic place, feeling that she was not a good wife in protecting her husband.[123] From reading the different records available on Sirmur, it seems that she revived the Sirmur royal family's fortunes by retaining Sirmur within their dynasty. Moran admires her administrative abilities, where she increased the 'kingdom's annual income from 37,000 to 53,000 rupees between 1817 and 1830 alone'.[124] This made Sirmur a prominent state among the hill states of the Western Himalaya. Hamilton wrote, 'The mountains of this State produced a rent of 70,000 or 80,000 rupees a year. The low country gave 200,000. The chief crops in the mountains were rice and wheat. West from the Yamuna, there are no mines of copper, and few even of iron; but one of these is in Sirmaur.'[125] Going by this narrative, it seems that Sirmur was not an impoverished state, as mentioned in the account of Fraser above. In a recent study, Brentnall observes that the English were happy to give the reigns of regency in the hands of 'the astute Guleri Rani'.[126]

Ochterlony exercised substantial control on the running of the Sirmur affairs. The marriage of Raja Fateh Prakash with a daughter of the raja of Garhwal 'was not carried out as the expenses would have been too great, and General Ochterlony had stopped the levy of the phant-biahlari or benefice, levied to meet the cost of marrying the Raja's children'.[127] The interference of the English authorities continued in the running of the rani's administration.[128] Despite the limitations imposed on her by the British, 'the rani cleverly manipulated

---

[123] Ibid.

[124] Moran, '"The Rani of Sirmur Revisited"', 17.

[125] Hamilton, *An Account of the Kingdom of Nepal*, 305–6.

[126] Brentnall, *The Princely and Noble Families of the Former Indian Empire*, 24.

[127] *Sirmur State Gazetteer*, 1904, 17.

[128] Ibid.

and/or ignored British regulations to empower her kingdom through recourse to her high-ranking benefactor and local customs alike', as Arik Moran rightly observed.[129] She also arranged political marriages of her children to have powerful allies in the hills to prevent any threat of subversion.[130] Kunwar Ranzor Singh mentioned marriages of the four daughters of Karam Prakash into the royal families of Garhwal, Bilaspur and Handur Nalagarh.[131] Fateh Prakash married into the families of Kahlur, Keonthal, Bilaspur, Baghat, Kumharsain, etc.[132] Guleri Rani ensured that her son was well-versed with their ancestors' traditional knowledge and culture, particularly the patronage to Pahari paintings, as Guler has been renowned for 'the finest specimens of Pahari paintings'.[133]

As the regent, the rani was able to hold her power over the British, who had to abide by her wishes till Fateh Prakash became a major. She handled her conflicts with them by the skilful use of the local custom of Sati[134] in the situation of her husband's death. The English authorities acknowledged her situation, observing that 'in the event of his demise, she would be induced to sacrifice herself according to the custom of the country', alluding to the customary practice of the sati.[135] The reason stated in the records is that they needed the rani for the

---

[129] Moran, '"The Rani of Sirmur Revisited"', 18–9.

[130] Ibid.

[131] Kunwar Ranzor Singh, 250.

[132] Ibid., 254.

[133] Moran, '"The Rani of Sirmur Revisited"', 18.

[134] The practice of sati is known to be common among the Rajput ruling families much more in the plains. In the case of Sirur, the widows of Raja Jagat Prakash did not commit sati, and they were given maintenance by the Sirmur state.

[135] Political Letters from Court, 1819-20, Pt I, Answer to Political Letter, 11 December 1816, London, 20 December 1820.

'preservation of peace and good order',[136] and the rani turned the situation to her advantage by consolidating the political position of Sirmur and strengthening her son's position as the ruler. Certainly, she managed to hold her position. It is a credit to her diplomatic skills that in her negotiations with the English, she managed to retain political control over Sirmur.

According to Arik Moran, Karam Prakash had started showing visible signs of syphilis, which prevented his public appearances.[137] In such a situation, Rani Guleri became his public face to negotiate with the British and other men of power. She participated in diplomatic dialogues with the British undercover, which is subsequently mentioned in the later imperial records. Rani Guleri's rise to the regency, her demand for the succession of her son and her decision to stay away from her husband show her decision-making agency. As a Rajput woman, she was expected to follow traditions. She adhered to them, which was a daunting task, considering that she was a regent to her son, displacing her husband as a ruler in his lifetime. Her husband was forbidden to enter Sirmur by the British authorities and continued to reside at Buria till his death in 1826.[138] She emerged as a woman with a shrewd diplomatic mind, who could see that the British would not restore her husband to the throne of Sirmur. She needed to step in to save

---

[136] 'We observe with regret that the ex-Rajah notwithstanding the profligacy of his character and conduct still maintains so much influence over the mind of the Rannee as to render it probable that in the event of his demise, she would be induced to sacrifice herself according to the custom of the country. We trust you persuasions, and those of the Pundits and Brahmins will induce her to forego this horrible purpose.' Political Letters from Court, 1819-20, Pt I, Answer to Political Letter, 11 December 1816, London, 20 December 1820.

[137] Moran, *Kingship and Polity*, 96.

[138] *Sirmur State Gazetteer*, 1904, 17.

her son's political interests and the continuation of her husband's dynasty at Sirmur. Her role in history may not be of confrontation or fighting on the battlefield; she fought a battle of diplomacy to protect the dynastic interests of her family in a situation in which her husband could not. She ensured the continuity of the princely state of Sirmur in the face of strong hostility displayed by all English officials to her husband and later to her. Sirmur was the battleground for showcasing her diplomacy. The British had their interests in the region for strategic reasons, and Rani Guleri had dynastic interests to protect. She succeeded in preventing the direct takeover of Sirohi by the British. The state of Sirmur continued as a princely state henceforth and became a part of the union of India in 1948.[139]

---

[139] Maharaja Rajendra Prakash signed a merger treaty with the Indian Union on 15 April 1948, receiving a privy purse of Rs 1,35,000, in Brentnall, *The Princely and Noble Families of the Former Indian Empire*, 25.

6

Queen Menchi of Sikkim

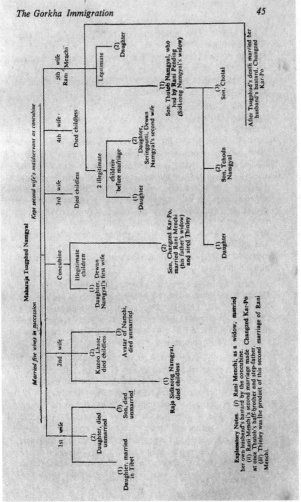

The genealogical chart of Chogyal Tsugphud Namgyal and his five wives is reproduced to locate the position of Queen Menchi within the Sikkim royal family.

Rani Menchi, Tsugphud Namgyal's widow, had remarried,
taking for her second husband Changzed Kar-po, her first
husband's illegitimate son by the concubine. She had
borne him a son, Thinley, alias Lhase Khusho, on whom
the Rani doted.[1]

Queen Menchi belonged to the Tibetan noble family of
Monkyit. She married the seventh Chogyal, Tsugphud
Namgyal (1793–1863), as his fifth wife in 1855. A son, Thutob
Namgyal, was born to them in 1859.[2] In 1860, under pressure
from the English, Tsugphud Namgyal, handed power to his son
Sridkyong Namgyal (1863–74). Before his death, Tsugphud
Namgyal joined his queen, Menchi, with his illegitimate son,
Changzod Karpo, to act as regent to his young son, the ninth
Chogyal, Thutob Namgyal (1874–1914) from 1875–78. Queen
Menchi and Changzod Karpo had a son, Thinley Namgyal.
Changzod Karpo died in 1879. In 1886, Sikkim, China and
Tibet signed the Treaty of Galing, and the maharaja, with
Queen Menchi, stayed at the Chumbi Valley in Tibet. From
1879 to 1888, Queen Menchi countered the pro-English party
with Diwan Namguay (called 'Pagla Diwan' by the English
authorities). Queen Menchi died in 1895.

Sikkim State was bounded in the north by Tibet, in the east
by Bhutan, in the west by Nepal and in the south by the British
district of Darjeeling.

---

[1] L.B. Basnet, *Sikkim: A Short Political History* (Delhi: S. Chand &
Company, 1974), 46.
[2] Secret Department, Register No. 379a, 7 February 1907, Rec.
23 February 1907, Letters from Secretary to the Government of India,
Foreign Department, Records of the 10th Chogyal Sidkeong Tulku
(acquired from London, British Library), Sikkim State Archives, 1676.

Tibet and Cholamoo Lakes from Donkia Pass 18,500ft.

The English travellers mapped out the region and terrain of Sikkim.

Courtesy: J.D. Hooker *Himalayan Journal*, *Vol. II* (London: John Murray,
Albemarle Street, 1854), opposite 124.

'It has an area of 2,818 square miles and a gross revenue of about 10,800 pounds.'[3] Sikkim's political association with the British began with the Treaty of Titaliya, signed between Nepal and the East India Company. In 1835, Darjeeling was ceded to the Company by a treaty disputed by the Sikkim authorities. With the Treaty of Tumlong in 1861, Sikkim became a protectorate of the British. In 1890, Claude White was appointed as the political officer at Sikkim, wielding all decision-making powers. During 1892–95, the British temporarily deposed the Sikkim ruler. In 1895, on the promise of agreeing to British terms, he returned to the throne. Queen Menchi remained uncompromising till the end, never returning to Sikkim.

I

Sikkim has been peripheral in every sense of the word in history. The focus of historians has been on the centres of power in the north and south, but many regions' history remains unexplored. Sikkim is one such region. The political, economic, social and cultural histories of Sikkim, Tibet, Bhutan and Nepal have a close association. The imperial writers and travellers have written on Sikkim, with their interest in Tibet and China.[4] The most famous one was the Younghusband expedition of 1904.

---

[3] Ibid.; also private diaries of the Prince graciously shared by Princess Hope Leezum in Gangtok, Sikkim.

[4] Joseph Dalton Hooker, *Himalayan Journals: Notes of a Naturalist in Bengal, The Sikkim, and Nepal Himalayas, The Khasia Mountain, & c.,* Vol. I, (London: J. Murray, 1855); L.S.S. O'Malley, *Bengal District Gazetteer: Darjeeling* (Calcutta: The Bengal Secretariat Book Depot, 1907); H.H. Risley, *The Gazetteer of Sikhim.* (Calcutta: Bengal Government Secretariat Press, 1891)

In more recent years, a vast range of research has been done in this region.[5]

There is even less information on the queens of Sikkim. It is not easy to write a political biography of the queens, and even more challenging to write their' stories from the periphery. Events and individuals go together, and Queen Menchi's narrative and the events of the late nineteenth-century history of Sikkim are closely linked. Her account is incomplete without the context in which she emerged. But her agency came through in her defence of Sikkim from English influence.

Unpacking Sikkim's history reveals many dimensions of this mountain kingdom, which the Tibetan records describe to be on its southern side. Sikkim as a 'hidden land' has many meanings.[6] It means land for devotion and meditation, a land where many Buddhist texts were compiled and hidden, and land to hide Buddhism's treasures, from persecution in India.

---

[5] Basnet, *Sikkim*; P.R. Rao, *India and Sikkim (1814-1970)*, (New Delhi: Sterling Publishers, 1972); B.S. Das, *The Sikkim Saga*, (New Delhi, Vikas Publishing House, 1983); Alex Mackay and Anna Balikci-Denjongpa eds., 'Buddhist Himalaya: Studies in Religion, History and Culture', *Proceedings of the Golden Jubilee Conference of the Namgyal Institute of Tibetology, Vol. I* (Gangtok: Tibet and Himalaya, 2008); Pranab Kumar Jha, *History of Sikkim (1817-1904) Analysis of British Policy and ActivitiesI* (Calcutta: O.P.S. Publishers, 1985); Alastair Lamb,*British India and Tibet, 1766-1910* (London: Routledge, 1960, 1986); A.K. Jasbir Singh, *Himalyan Triangle: A Historical Survey of British India's Relations with Tibet, Sikkim and Bhutan, 1765-1950* (London: British Library, 1988); Rajiv Rai, *The State in the Colonial Periphery: A Study on Sikkim's Relation with Great Britain* (India: Partridge Publishing, 2015); Saul Mullard, *Opening the Hidden Land: State Formation and the Construction of Sikkimese History*, (Gangtok: Rachna, 2019), among many other anthropologists and historians who, of late, have contributed to expanding the knowledge of the Eastern Himalaya.

[6] Mullard, *Opening the Hidden Land.*

When Buddhism was receding from India, it found refuge in parts of Sikkim and Tibet. According to Sikkim's royal documents, Sikkim's history began when the 'great urgyen Guru Padma Sambhawa[7] in his writings' called Sikkim'hBras-ma Ijongs' and described it as a 'Paradise or a supernatural place'.[8] These sources mention that Guru Padma Sambhawa hid some of the principal Buddhist texts in these areas. The royal records constantly stress Sikkim as a sacred space in the Buddhist world and mention that Bodhisattwa Avalokiteswara and Guru Padma Sambhawa sanctified Sikkim, among other places as 'safe places' for hidden treasures. There is an index of the 'prophesies and the apocalyptical books' of the seers mentioned above. There are guidebooks, giving clues about 'the hidden treasures, and all of these have been hidden in safe places'.[9]

The royal Sikkimese text on the history of Sikkim also mentions how the four important lamas came to Sikkim and assembled at Lha-b-Chen-po. They realized that they needed 'a layman to rule the kingdom righteously' and gave the name of the chosen one—'One named Phuntso from the direction of Gang will appear'.[10] The search party under the hermit Tog-Idan Kalzang Tondup went to Gangtok, and there they were given 'a drink of nice fresh milk' by a man milking his cows, who turned out to be Phuntso Namgyal.[11] From these records, it seems that the lamas consecrated the king at Yuksam Norbugang. This

---

[7] He was an Indian Buddhist and had a great debate with the masters of the Bon religion whom he defeated. Mentioned in Sir Thutob Namgyal, their Highness the Maharaja & Maharani Yeshay Dolma of Sikkim, *History of Sikkim*, trans. Kazi Dousandup (Gangtok: Namgyal Royal Family, Sikkim, 1908), 5.

[8] Namgyal and Dolma, *History of Sikkim*, 5.

[9] Ibid., 6.

[10] Ibid., 18.

[11] Ibid.

coronation took place in 1642, and he was given 'the title of Chos-rGyal (Dharmaraja, king of righteousness)', with two-fold powers (spiritual and temporal).[12]

The records celebrate the ordination and consecration of the Sikkim monarchy by the lamas. They also mention how the Lepchas and Mangars, the inhabitants of Sikkim, 'welcomed' the king of Sikkim. This can be said to be the beginning of a sovereign state in a modern sense. The palace of the ruler was built at Tashi Tengkha. He sought the support of the Bhutias and the Lepchas residing in Sikkim. He 'selected twelve Kazis from amongst the twelve chiefs of Bhutia clans then existing and likewise, he selected twelve Lepcha Jongpons from amongst the superior families of Lepchas of Sikkim'.[13] The Dalai Lama also recognized the ruler, and it was agreed upon between the two that 'whenever this State suffered from any aggression, from the neighbouring States, it always looked to the Tibetan Government for protection and aid'.[14] The most influential lama, who played a political role in bringing Sikkim under Tibetan protection was Lha-bTsun Chenpo. He was the one who made the prophetic pronouncement on the name of the king. The Dalai Lama accepted Lha-bTsun as his guru and gave him an estate in Tibet, and it is through him that the Sikkim ruler also received recognition from Tibet.[15]

Lha-bTsun Chenpo and the first two rulers of Sikkim also built many monuments—the Rabdentse Palace, the Pemiongchi or Pemyangtse Monastery, besides several places of worship, 'and furnishing them with sacred and precious relics'.

---

[12] Ibid., 19.
[13] Ibid., 20.
[14] Ibid., 23.
[15] Ibid.

Courtesy: Richard Temple, *Journals Kept in Hyderabad, Kashmir, Sikkim, and Nepal*, Vol. II (London: W.H. Allen & Co., 1887). On his visit to Sikkim in 1875, opposite 204.

Exterior of the Buddhist Temple at Pemyangchi.

The Peminogchi monastery is among the oldest monastery located near the palace Rabdentse. It signified a close connection between Tibet and Sikkim. Rabdentse Palace was built in the time of the second Chogyal, Tansung Namgyal.

'Thus the great saint Lha- b Tsun by the power of his former wiches and prayers carry on these acts of utility and adornment throughout this land, devoting every hour of his life in its service and benefit.'[16] Under the second Chogyal, the emergence of Sikkim state can be seen. In all these activities, the lamas played a prominent role. Rabdentse Palace was built in the time of the second Chogyal, Tansung Namgyal, on the advice of Lha–bTsung.

---

[16] Richard Temple, *Journals Kept in Hyderabad, Kashmir, Sikkim, and Nepal*, Vol. II (London: W.H. Allen & Co., 1887). On his visit to Sikkim in 1875, 204.

The Sikkim royal family records mention matrimonial relations between Bhutan, Tibet and Sikkim.[17] According to Sonam H. Wangyal, the marriage alliance was possibly meant to secure peace and stability for the fledgling Sikkimese dynasty with their neighbours.[18] There were matrimonial ties with princesses from Bhutan and also from Newar.[19] Women held important political positions in Sikkim. The third ruler, Chagdor Namgyal, was young at the time of his father's death,[20] and power came in the hands of his half-sister, Pende Wangmo, who 'entertained the idea of usurping the throne',[21] creating hostility between the two. With her followers, Wangmo invited Bhutan to invade Sikkim.[22] The young king was saved by Yug-thing Tishey, who took him to Tibet for refuge. The young ruler took shelter in Lhasa under the 6th Dalai Lama, Gyalwa Tsang-yang Gyamtso,

---

[17] Saul Mullard, 'Constructing the Mandala: The State Formation of Sikkim and the Rise of a National Historical Narrative', in *Buddhist Himalaya: Studies in Religion, History and Culture: Proceedings of the Golden Jubilee Conference of the Namgyal Institute of Tibetology, Vol. II: The Sikkim Papers* (Gangtok, 2008), 53–62.

[18] Sonam B. Wangyal, 'A Unique Parallel', *Buddhist Himalaya: Studies in Religion, History and Culture: Proceedings of the Golden Jubilee Conference of the Namgyal Institute of Tibetology, Vol. II: The Sikkim Papers* (Gangtok, 2008), 73–6. The second Chogyal, Tansung Namgyal's first wife was from Southern Tibet, the second wife from Bhutan and the third wife was a daughter of the Limbuwan chief, thereby buying peace in the northern, eastern and eastern sides, 73.

[19] Risley, *Gazetteer of Sikhim*, 11.

[20] The second Chogyal was Tensung Namgyal, son of the first king, Phuntsog Namgyal. He had two wives: a Tibetan and Bhutanese. Mullard, 'Constructing the Mandala', 57.

[21] Namgyal and Dolma, *History of Sikkim*, 25.

[22] Risley, *Gazetteer of Sikhim*, 12.

and the regent, Gyalpo-Lhab Zang.[23] He learnt literature and
astronomy in Tibet. He was given the title of a Thaijee, with
many estates.[24] Later, he married a Tibetan woman of a noble
family of U, known as Lho-Gyelma and the princess of Lowo
Raja, who gave birth to Prince Gyurmed Namgyal.[25] The
Tibetan authorities negotiated with Bhutan for the return of the
king to Sikkim.[26] In 1717, Gyurmed Namgyal succeeded to the
throne.[27] In 1721, he married Mingur Dolma of the Mindrolling
family, but the marriage was not successful.[28] The Chogyal
developed a relationship with a nun of the Sangachoelling
monastery; she bore him a son, Namgyal Phuntsog.[29] In this
period, within Sikkim, two factions emerged: the Bhutias
led by Tamding[30] and the Lepchas under Chagzod Karwang.
The Lepchas supported Namgyal Phuntsog, while Tamding
questioned his legitimacy.[31] Tamding took charge and ruled for
three years in Sikkim.[32] The young Chogyal was protected by
Changzod Karwang. Later, when the Gurkhas rose to power
under Prithvi Narayan Shah of the Shah dynasty of Nepal and

---

[23] Namgyal and Dolma, *History of Sikkim*, 25; Mullard, 'Constructing
the Mandala', 57.

[24] Namgyal and Dolma, *History of Sikkim*, 25.

[25] Jigme N. Kazi, *Sons of Sikkim: The Rise and Fall of the Namgyal
Dysnasty of Sikkim,* (Gangtok: Hill Media Publications and Chennai:
Notion Press, 2020), loc 2056 of 10036.

[26] Risley, *Gazetteer of Sikhim*, 14; Kazi, *Sons of Sikkim*, loc 2056 of 10036.

[27] Kazi, *Sons of Sikkim*, loc 2259 of 10036.

[28] Kazi, *Sons of Sikkim*, loc 2268 of 10036.

[29] Ibid., loc 2312of 10036.

[30] Ibid., loc 2325 of 10036. He belonged to the Bhutia Dzongpons,
the fourteen leading Bhutia families in Sikkim.

[31] Ibid., loc 2330 of 10036.

[32] Ibid., loc 2325 of 10036.

attacked Sikkim, the son of Changzod Karwang, Chothup,[33] repulsed the attack. Chogyal Namgyal Phuntsog had a son, Tenzing Namgyal, from his Tibetan wife in 1769.[34] Thanks to the help given by Changzod Karwang and his son, Chothung, they became powerful and considered themselves on an equal footing as the Chogyal—they even began using the red seal on important documents which was the Chogyal's prerogative.[35] In 1769, Tenzin Namgyal became the Chogyal. He married the daughter of Changzod Karwang, Anyo-Gyal-Yum.[36] She gave birth to Tsugphud Namgyal, with whom the narrative of Queen Menchi is linked.

II

There were constant threats to Sikkim in the late eighteenth and early nineteenth century from Bhutan and Nepal. It was at this time that Sikkim contacted the English. The Gurkha threat compelled the Chogyal, King Tenzing Namgyal, to take flight with his wife and son to Tibet without preparation in 1788.[37] His son and successor, Tsugphud Namgyal, was born in 1785.[38] Tsugphud Namgyal was the husband of Queen Menchi. He became the king in 1793. The Gurkha threat was still present, and the king was living at Yulgyal Palace at Baki. He ordered the Sikkimese leaders to destroy the Gurkhas advancing towards Nagri Jong. The Sikkimese army could not dislodge the Gurkhas from Nagri, so the Sikkimese king approached the East

---

[33] Ibid., loc 2383 of 10036.
[34] Ibid., loc 2426 of 10036.
[35] Ibid., loc 2431 of 10036.
[36] Ibid., loc 2458 of 10036.
[37] Risley, *Gazetteer of Sikhim*, 18.
[38] Ibid.

India Company for a force to help them drive out the Gurkhas. With British help, the Sikkimese were able to prevail against the Gurkhas. King Tsugphud Namgyal decided to shift the capital to Tumlong and built the Wangdutse Palace in 1814, as he considered the Rabdentse Palace to be too close to the Gurkha frontier.[39] In 1815, the British army drove out the Gurkhas.

The king wrote a letter to the governor general, 'acknowledging with thanks the receipt of a *Kharita*, accompanied by the present of a double-barreled gun with ammunition and money'.[40] It was in his time that the East India Company entered into the first important treaty with Sikkim. Sikkim was anxious to fix its borders with the Gurkhas and requested the British to assist. In 1817, the British government made a treaty at Titalia (or Titalya) with Nepal on account of Sikkim, and the territory restored to Sikkim was bounded on the west by Mahanadi and the Mechi river to the east.[41] Under the terms of the treaty, the sovereignty of the Sikkim ruler was 'guaranteed by the Company . . . and Sikkim, including the present district of Darjeeling, was retained as a buffer state between Nepal and Bhutan'.[42] The British authorities assumed the position of the paramount power in Sikkim, 'the Raja being bound to refer to the arbitration of the British Government any dispute between his subjects and those of Nepal or any other neighbouring State.'[43] By the treaty, the British emerged as the arbitrators on behalf of Sikkim, but it was not to the liking of the Sikkim authorities.[44] Ten years later, a dispute arose on the frontier between Sikkim and Nepal. In 1819, serious differences arose between Chogyal

---

[39] Namgyal and Dolma, *History of Sikkim*, 55.
[40] Ibid.
[41] Namgyal and Dolma, *History of Sikkim*, 56.
[42] O'Malley, *Bengal District Gazetteer*, 19.
[43] Ibid.
[44] Ibid.

Tsugphud Namgyal and his maternal uncle, Bolod, son of Changzod Karwang, and brother of Chogyal's mother. These resulted in the execution of Bolod and his family near Tumlong in 1826. The remaining members of the family took refuge in Ilam in eastern Nepal with other Lepchas of their clan. They repeatedly attacked the western border of Sikkim, leading to the frontier dispute between Nepal and Sikkim. Under the terms of the Treaty of Titaliya, the governor general was asked to arbitrate. The British settled the matter in 1829 but asked Sikkim for Darjeeling as it was suitable for a sanatorium for them. The Company officials claimed that in 1835, the Sikkim ruler signed the treaty ceding Darjeeling to them 'unconditionally',[45] but in the official records, the emissary of the Sikkim ruler claimed that he was not aware that he had agreed to this.

On the contrary, the Sikkim ruler claimed some lands in the plains that belonged to him. He thought there would be a discussion on these territories that belonged to Sikkim with the governor general. From the records, it seems that in 1831–35, the British seized the opportunity to intervene 'when some Lepcha refugees in Nepal . . . made an inroad into the Sikkim Tarai'.[46] General Lloyd intervened in the disturbance. According to the Darjeeling *Gazetteer*, 'The refugees were obliged to return to Nepal, and the negotiations ended in the execution by the Raja of Sikkim of a deed of grant of Darjeeling on the 1st February, 1835.'[47] This resentment between the Sikkim authorities and the English official would simmer, and in '1841 the Government granted the Raja an allowance of Rs. 3000 as compensation, and raised the grant to Rs. 6,000 in 1846'.[48]

---

[45] Risley, *Gazetteer of Sikkim*, 20; O'Malley, *Bengal District Gazetteer*, 21.
[46] O'Malley, *Bengal District Gazetteer*, 21.
[47] Ibid.
[48] Ibid.

This started the period of tensions between the Sikkim rulers and the British government. The British records contain peaceful negotiations between them and Sikkim over the giving of Darjeeling to the British for making a sanatorium. But the raja had three conditions for giving Darjeeling to the East India Company.[49] The Sikkim raja wrote, 'The affairs resulting in my country's partition accordingly as it has been lately ordered from the Great Saheb's presidency has been communicated to me by Le'd Major Saheb (Major Lloyd).' The raja expressed his desire to meet Major Lloyd for a long time, but Major Lloyd remained non-committal: 'though I have long declared that I want to meet Major Lloyd, he would not . . .'[50] On meeting Major Lloyd, the Sikkim ruler 'declared that till the arrival of His Lordship's (the Great Saheb Lad of Calcutta's), order from Calcutta, we will make no definitive treaty on the cession of land or district'.[51] The raja was not happy with the manner in which the English took Morung from Sikkim. He stated, 'Now we have put a supplicatory letter, that part of the country which is called Murong, Great Saheb, depends upon your disposition, we have delivered it into your hand, and we have given it over together with the firearms and we have commissioned Dungmo to settle this affair.'[52] He further mentioned, 'The common class of people of this valley could not yet agree about the cession, but they cannot hinder it', as they were no match for the British. At another place, the raja makes a cryptic statement: 'It is not proper in whatever country that the servant distort

---

[49] Foreign Political, 6 April 1835, W.A. Macnaghten, Secretary to Government, Political Department, Fort William, 9 March 1835.

[50] 'Translation of a letter in the Tibetan Language put by the rGyelso of Bras-jong (or the Rajah of Sikkim)', 28 February 1835, Foreign Political, Cons., 101, 6 April 1835.

[51] Ibid.

[52] Ibid.

the answer of his Master – I beg therefore of you, Great Lad Saheb, that you will grant a signed and sealed diploma to the sworn Sungmo and to his brother of Ko-sna, which may come into our hands through Major Lloyd on the day when he will receive the commonalty.'[53] From the Foreign Department file, it seems that the Sikkim ruler had not signed the treaty to transfer Darjeeling. He wanted certain matters to be resolved first, and a confirmation from the governor general to respect the proposed treaty's terms.[54]

In Sikkim at that time, the local Lepchas and the dominant Tibetan groups dominated the Court's politics. The British used this division to get the Lepchas onboard to manipulate them to the advantage of the British. In the Darjeeling *Gazetteer*, O'Malley states that the areas around Darjeeling needed to be cleared, and the English authorities needed to 'attract native settlers'. About ten years earlier, 1,200 able-bodied Lepchas, forming, according to Captain Herbert, two-thirds of the population of Sikkim, had been forced by the oppression of the raja to fly from Darjeeling and its neighbourhood and to take refuge in Nepal. What little cultivation there was had been abandoned; the Sikkim raja had prohibited his subjects from going to Darjeeling and helping in establishing the new settlement.[55] Various expedients were proposed to repopulate the country, e.g., 'to invite the Lepcha refugees to return, to import labourers from the indigo concerns in Rangpur and Ramgarh (i.e., Gaya and Hazaribagh) or to procure settlers from Nepal and Bhutan.'[56] The British poached on the labour resources of Nepal, Sikkim and Bhutan, increasing the population of Darjeeling from 100 in 1839 to about 10,000

---

[53] Ibid.
[54] Ibid.
[55] O'Malley, *Bengal District Gazetteer*, 22.
[56] Ibid.

in 1849. Dr Campbell, the superintendent of Darjeeling, asserted that he could attract the local people, as the English did not practise slavery, which was prevalent[57] in the local states: 'the system of forced labour formerly in use has been abolished, and labour with all other valuables has been left to find its own price in an open market'.[58]

King Tsugphud Namgyal contracted many marriages. He wrote to the Tibetan government 'saying that he wished to marry in Tibet', and the Tibetan government responded cordially by suggesting Lamoi Lacham, a lady of the Lamoi family. He eventually married another lady from the Lamoi family. He also had a child from the maid of honour, who had come with the second lady from Lamoi.[59] She gave birth to a daughter, Pema La, who married Tokhang Don-nyer Namgyal or Namguay (Pagla Diwan) and bore him a son, Changzod Tenzin Namgyal.[60] The ladies of the Lamoi family were the sisters of Tsang Penchen Rinpoche, the Grand Lama of Tashilhunpo named Penchen Tenpau Nyima. The ruler then married a young girl from the Lamoi family, who had become a nun. She died within a year with no issue. Thereafter, the ruler married a lady from the Tanag Dingka family but had no child from her either.[61]

The king then wrote to the Tibetan government intending to marry again as the 'eldest son though living had been recognised as the Avatar of the Dzonchen Lama'.[62] Now began the story of Queen Menchi as the fifth queen of Tsugphud Namgyal. The oracle predicted her marriage, and she was from the Tibetan

---

[57] Risley, *Gazetteer of Sikkim*, 20.
[58] O'Malley, *Bengal District Gazetteer*, 23.
[59] Namgyal and Dolma, *History of Sikkim*, 56.
[60] Ibid.
[61] Ibid., 57.
[62] Ibid., 65.

family of Tanag Monkyit.[63] In the beginning, the fourth queen, who belonged to the Tibetan family of Dinka, prevented the king from meeting the Monkyit queen. So 'the Raja had to arrange a romantic and secret interview with the new Monkyit Rani'.[64] The Dingka queen was struck by lightning soon after and died. The Monkyit queen was given the Jongu lands by King Tsugphud Namgyal, which was previously given to the Dingka rani, showing her rising political presence.[65] The eldest daughter of the raja from his maidservant, Pema La, lived with Monkyit Rani. Pema La was married to Tokhang Don-nyer Namguay, who was of Tibetan origin, and was suspicious of the movements of the British in Sikkim.[66] He became the diwan in 1847.

The rent rolls of the Sikkim had been destroyed in the raids and flight of the royal family. 'In 1847, the Sikkim kingdom received land revenue, cattle tax, timber royalty, pig tax, ferry, duties on goods, and income from lawsuits interstate properties, all amounting to Rs. 19,590,12'.[67] Another rent roll for 1849 showed that the revenue from the above sources 'had fallen to Rs 15876/ 14/ 6'.[68] It is not directly stated in the royal records, but the fall was due to the rise in importance of Darjeeling. Tokhang Don-nyer Namgyal had to negotiate the economic interest of Sikkim. It had become a great market, and 'the slaves

---

[63] Ibid., 57.

[64] Ibid.

[65] Ibid., 135–6.

[66] The diwan is also known as the 'Pagla Dewan' by the British. He had close ties with the Sikkim royal family by being married first to the daughter of Tsugphud Namgyal from a maid servant and later to Princess Tseringputti or Seringputtee Namgyal, daughter of Queen Menchi. The information is from royalark.net, which gives the genealogy of the Namgyal dynasty. Accessed on 11 June 2022.

[67] Ibid., 64.

[68] Ibid.

and menial classes from Sikkim, Bhutan and Nepal all took
refuge there'.[69] It led to tensions between the Sikkimese and
the British authorities. It is mentioned in the Sikkimese records,
'The Sikkim people, not being aware or used to the usages of
a powerful Government, used to pursue their slaves and kidnap
them back from Darjeeling. And criminals from Darjeeling
sought refuge in Sikkim. These things soon brought about an ill
feeling.'[70] The Sikkim durbar wrote to the British authorities at
Darjeeling to obtain the extradition of the runaway slaves from
Darjeeling, but Dr Campbell did not heed their demands.

An interesting pattern that emerges is that the queens played
a crucial political role in the politics of Sikkim. The queens were
invariably chosen from powerful Tibetan families, to keep the
hold of Tibet on Sikkim. They were also married off to the sons
and successors of their spouse in case of his untimely death. This
suggests that their political role was important for the king. While
going through the archival records, my attention was caught by
the mention of a queen who conspired with the 'Pagla Diwan'
to thwart the British attempt to influence Sikkim. This probably
was the first clue to the fact that the queens were not passive in
the royal politics of Sikkim but played an important role. Queen
Menchi (probably from a prominent Tibetan family) was this
queen, whose name I could finally locate with much difficulty.
The imperial records do not name the queens, indicating how
inconsequential they were to the masculine empire. From the
scant sources available on Queen Menchi, she seems to have
been safeguarding Tibet's interest in Sikkim and was not keen
about British presence in Sikkim.

A careful reading of the records indicates that Queen Menchi
was present in the political activities at the Sikkim court in this

---

[69] Ibid.
[70] Ibid., 64–5.

period fraught with tensions with the British. The British records do not focus on her role, but she may have exercised an influential position as the wife of King Tsugphud Namgyal and mother of his son. Queen Menchi was also close to Diwan Namguay, and her subsequent marriage to the illegitimate son of the king, Changzod Karpo or Karpo Tenzin Namgyal, strengthened her position at the Sikkim court. She was close to the wife of Donyer Namguay, who was called Pagla Dewan by the English authorities,[71] an illegitimate daughter of King Tsugphud Namgyal, Pema La,[72] with whom Menchi had resided when she first arrived in Sikkim from Tibet. She later married her daughter Serringputti to Donyer Namguay as his second wife.[73] She was active in the period of the East India Company's negotiations with Sikkim as the fifth wife of the seventh Chogyal, Tsugphud Namgyal.

She played a dominant role in the politics of Sikkim in this period, along with Donyer Namguay and Changzod Karpo, the son of Tsugphud Namgyal from the maidservant. Due to the hostilities with Dr Campbell and Dr Hooker, Donyer Namguay, who was considered the mischief-maker, was banished in the treaty of 1861. He earned the name of 'Pagla Dewan' by continuing to defy the terms of the treaty signed between the *Sikkimputtee* and the Company. In 1868, King Sridkyong Namgyal asked the British government to pardon Donyer Namguay but was refused.[74] Therefore an illegitimate son of the late Maharaja Tsugphud Namgyal was appointed Changzod and was known as Changzod Karpo in 1868. 'This

---

[71] Risley, *Gazetteer of Sikkim*, iv.

[72] Jigme N. Kazi, *Sons of* Sikkim, 199 of 690, location 2805 of 10036.

[73] In Basnet's understanding, it was a calculated move by Queen Menchi to get the help of Donyer Namguay to 'her machinations.' Basnet, *Sikkim*, 47.

[74] Namgyal and Dolma, *History of Sikkim*, 68.

Changzod Karpo and the Monkyit Rani had been enjoined by
the Maharaja Tsugphud Namgyal just before his disease . . . to
help in the administration of the State, during the minority of
the young prince'[75] Thutob Namgyal, who was born with a hare
lip.[76] Queen Menchi and Changzod Karpo also had a son in
1866 called Lhasay Kusho or Thinley Namgyal.[77] The maharaja
died in 1874, leaving the administration in the hands of Chagzod
Karpo, as the young King Thutob Namgyal could not 'carry
on the work himself'.[78] Kusho Changzod or Karpo Tenzin
Namgyal (d. in 1878) was very eminent for his learning in both
secular and religious and ritualistic lore and was very devout.
By his accomplishments, Kusho Changzod 'won the confidence
of the Maharaja Tsugphud Namgyal, who at the point of death
entrusted him with the protectorship of the minor prince,
during his minority, and the administration of the State'. He
joined the Chagzod and Monkyit Rani's hands in marriage, 'and
exhorted them both to carry on the duties of the State jointly
and successfully'.[79] They were to act as the joint regents.

The British narrative is different. O'Malley wrote in the
Darjeeling *Gazetteer* that 'our relations with Sikkim had been
far from satisfactory'.[80] He further stated, 'The Raja, old and
infirm, was a mere cipher in the hands of his minister Namguay,
popularly known as the *Pagla Diwan* or mad Prime Minister of
Sikkim.'[81] The Sikkim royal records mentioned him as loyal to
the Sikkim royal family in their hour of need.[82] The English

---

[75] Ibid.
[76] This disfigurement on his face made Thutob Namgyal sensitive.
[77] Namgyal and Dolma, *History of Sikkim*, 69.
[78] Ibid.
[79] Ibid., 78.
[80] O'Malley, *Bengal District Gazetteer*, 23.
[81] Ibid.
[82] Royalark.net. Accessed on 11 June 2022.

authorities, on the other hand, described him as 'a corrupt and ambitious official' who administered the state, enriching himself at its expense.[83] The English attributed this tension to 'The increasing importance of Darjeeling under free institutions . . . a source of early and constant jealousy and annoyance to the Diwan, who was himself the monopolist of all trade in Sikkim; and it was shared by the lamas and other notabilities, who lost their rights over slave settling as British subjects in our territory'.[84] The English authorities accused the Sikkim officials of scaring and preventing the people of Sikkim from coming to Darjeeling. The British accused the Sikkim officials of 'kidnapping' 'British subjects' and selling them into slavery, 'and there were frequent denials of aid in capturing and surrendering criminals'. Joseph Hooker, the famous botanist, while travelling through Sikkim, reiterated this accusation of the Company officials. He wrote,

> Every obstacle was thrown in the way of a good understanding between Sikkim and the British Government. British subjects were rigorously excluded from Sikkim; every liberal offer for free trade and intercourse was rejected generally with insolence; merchandise was taxed, and notorious offenders, refugees from the British territories, were harboured; despatches were detained; and the vakeels or Raja's representatives were chosen for their insolence and incapacity.[85]

He also accused the conduct of the raja to be untrustworthy, typical of the 'Orient': 'The conduct of the Diwan throughout was

---

[83] O'Malley, *Bengal District Gazetteer*, 23.

[84] Ibid.

[85] Ibid; Hooker in his *Himalayan Journal, Vol. II* described on page 203: 'Campbell had been knocked down, tied hand and foot, and taken to his tent.'

Indo-Chinese; assuming, insolent, aggressive, never perpetrating open violence, but by petty insults effectually preventing all good understanding.' He praised the British authorities in Calcutta for their 'forbearance' and the Darjeeling authorities for their 'patience and passive resistance'.[86] This he considered was read as the sign of weakness by the Sikkim authorities.

Matters reached a head in November 1849, 'when Sir Joseph Hooker and Dr Campbell were suddenly seized and made prisoners', while travelling in Sikkim with the permission both of the Raja and that of the British Government. The object of the diwan was to force Dr Campbell to relinquish claims for the surrender of criminals; to make him, under duress, agree to the dictation of the diwan regarding the giving up of the escaped slaves and to detain him until these enforced conditions were satisfied by the government. According to O'Malley, this method of making 'demands by capture and detention was common with the turbulent tribes east of Nepal,' but in this instance, it was 'aggravated by the violence and various indignities to which the captors subjected Dr Campbell.'[87] Dr Campbell threatened the diwan, saying that this forced concession would be repudiated by the British,[88] 'and intimidated by the characteristic threat of the Governor-General, Lord Dalhousie, that the Raja's head should answer for it, if a hair of the head of either prisoner were hurt, the Sikkimese eventually released Dr. Campbell and Sir Joseph Hooker on the 24 December 1849, a little more than six weeks after their seizure'.[89] The confinement of the two

---

[86] Hooker, *The Himalayan Journal, Vol. II*, 202. Hooker describes the incident wherein he and Campbell were stopped from moving forward and Hooker was kept in confinement.

[87] O'Malley, *Bengal District Gazetteer*, 1907, 24.

[88] Hooker, *Himalayan Journal, Vol. II*, 205.

[89] O'Malley, *Bengal District Gazetteer*, 1907, 24.

English officials became the reason for sending Company forces to Sikkim. They withdrew the grant to the ruler, 'and the Raja was further punished by the annexation of the Sikkim *Tarai*, which he has originally received as the free gift from the British and which was the only lucrative or fertile estate he possessed'.[90] On the pretext of the breach of the terms of the treaty, the British acquired more territories and tax from the people. They maintained that they found only rupees six in the treasury seized from the *Tarai*, which included an area of 640 square miles. The Sikkim ruler was confined to his mountain hinterland. The British projected the conquest as welcomed by the people: 'The change was welcomed by the inhabitants, for it only involved the payment of a small fixed tax in money to the treasury at Darjeeling, instead of a fluctuating one in kind, with service to the Raja and liability to further annoyance from the Diwan.'[91] The British used this act of the diwan to carry out a strategic annexation. O'Malley wrote:

> The whole country thus annexed covered an area of 640 square miles, and its annexation was an important matter; for it made the British boundary march with Nepal on the west and with Bhutan on the east, while it connected Darjeeling on the south with the British districts of Purnea and Jalpaiguri. Previously the district had been an enclave in Sikkim territory, and to reach it the British had to pass through a country acknowledging the rule of a foreign, though dependent, potentate.[92]

---

[90] Ibid.
[91] O'Malley, *Bengal District Gazetteer*, 245.
[92] Ibid., 25.

RAJAH'S RESIDENCE, AND THE HUT ASSIGNED TO US. ARRIVAL OF THE DEWAN.

Image credit: J.D. Hooker, Himalayan Journals, Vol. II (London: John Murray, London, 1854). Illustration of November 1849, 217.

The palace of the Sikkim Chogyal was located at the top at Tumlong. It was here that the Botanist Joseph Hooker and Dr Campbell were detained.

The relations between Sikkim and the British improved briefly after this episode. The British attributed this to the diwan being dismissed, but he found his way into power 'through his wife, an illegitimate daughter of the Raja, and the former outrages were deliberately renewed'.[93] The British accused Sikkim of constant raids in British territory, saying 'property was plundered, our subjects were carried off and sold as slaves or detained in Sikkim, and no redress could be obtained'.[94] The British blamed the diwan's excesses to the ineffectual king. O'Malley wrote: 'The Raja of Sikkim, now an old man of nearly 80 years, had

---

[93] Ibid.
[94] Ibid.

relinquished all cares of State and retired to Chumbi in Tibet, and the Government was entirely in the hands of the Chief Minister, Diwan Namguay, the man who had seized Dr. Campbell and Dr. Hooker in November 1849, and who was the real author of the raids into our territory.'[95]

In 1849, tensions between Sikkim and British government occurred due to the visit of Dr Campbell and Hooker, touring towards the Tsola side close to Tibet. The Sikkim authorities had not permitted them to move towards the northern side, close to the Tibetan border. According to the Sikkimese version, 'The Tibetan Government had issued stringent orders forbidding foreigners to be allowed beyond the boundaries.'[96] The ruler of Sikkim was also allowed to visit Tibet once in eight years. The Sikkim durbar was afraid of incurring the wrath of the Tibetan and Chinese authorities, and as Tsugphud Namgyal was too aged and infirm, Tokhang Donyer Namguay asked the two English men to desist from travelling further. When they refused, the two men were detained. The Sikkimese authorities could not speak English, and Tseepa Adan or Cheeba Lama, who had caused a rupture between the king and his son and could speak English, was appointed as the vakeel or Sikkim agent and posted at Darjeeling. He belonged to the pro-British party. Donyer Namguay was banished and later an illegitimate son of Tsugphud Namgyal, who had been married to Queen Menchi, was appointed as the diwan.

As a consequence of detaining the English officials, the English sent up a force under the Darjeeling superintendent and attacked the *Tarai*, all the land lying below Ramman in the north, the Rangeet and Teesta in the east and the Nepal–Sikkim Frontier in the west and discontinued the annual rent of Rs 6,000

---

[95] Ibid.
[96] Namgyal and Dolma, *History of Sikkim*, 66.

paid to the Sikkim ruler for Darjeeling. O'Malley described the event: 'In November 1860 Dr. Campbell crossed Ramman with a small force and advanced as far as Rinchinpong.'[97] The British suffered defeat, and as 'he had only 160 natives and a complement of English and non-commissioned officers, and when attacked, he was forced to retreat for lack of ammunition and to fall back on Darjeeling'.[98] The British could not take this quietly and sent Colonel Gawler, 'at the head of a force of 2,600 men, including 2 mountain howitzers and a detachment of artillery, with Sir Ashley Eden as Envoy and Special Commissioner, started from Darjeeling on the 1st February and reached Tumlong, the Sikkim capital, early in March 1861'.[99] The use of superior war weapons to extract diplomatic victory at Tumlong went hand in hand, called the 'gunboat diplomacy'[100]—a strategy of intimidation frequently used by the European powers against the local princes. The treaty obligations between Sikkim and the Company were enforced by violence. The diwan fled, the British force was disbanded and the old raja abdicated in favour of his son, Sridkyong Namgyal. The British forced the new king to sign a fresh treaty on 28 March 1861. Sridkyong Namgyal was a lama, who was persuaded by the Cheebu Lama to leave his spiritual quest and succeed to the Sikkim throne, at the behest of the British. The British did not want the son of Queen Menchi to succeed the king—he was a minor and also considered to be under the influence of the pro-Tibet group.

In the Sikkim royal accounts, the entire episode was blamed on the infighting between Cheebu Lama and Donyer Namguay,

---

[97] O'Malley, *Bengal District Gazetteer*, 25.

[98] Ibid.

[99] Ibid.

[100] A common term where a threat of military force is used to demand acquiescence.

which compromised the interests of the Sikkim royal family. The royal accounts were not incorrect, as Sikkim lost both politically and economically under the Treaty of Tumlong of 1861. The British authorities, who had been trying to make inroads into Sikkim for commerce and trade with Tibet and China, gained substantially. 'The treaty stipulated that full compensation should be made' to the British subjects

> who had either been kidnapped or pillaged by the Raja's people: it provided for full indemnification for the losses sustained in Dr. Campbell's retreat; it guaranteed the opening out of the country to trade, and the removal of all restrictions on travellers and merchants; it fixed the maximum rate of transit duties to be levied on goods between British India and Tibet; it provided for the construction of roads, and the security of those who traversed them; and lastly, it contained provisions for the banishment of Diwan Namguay, and for the future good conduct of the Sikkim Government.[101]

In the period of King Sridkyong Namgyal, the real power was exercised by Queen Menchi's husband, Changzod Karpo, who had been appointed as the diwan after the expulsion of Diwan Namguay. In the treaty of 1861, Tokhang Donyer Namguay was blamed for the misunderstanding between Sikkim and the English authorities and he 'was banished from Sikkim'.[102] Donyer Namguay took the matters to the Tibetan government, and they rewarded him with marks of distinction, making him an officer of the 4th grade and granting him an estate.[103] The British were aware of the tensions between the local Sikkim

---

[101] O'Malley, *Bengal District Gazetteer*, 26.
[102] Namgyal and Dolma, *History of Sikkim*, 67.
[103] Ibid.

gentry, primarily the Lepchas and the Tibetan group, and they exploited the divide in the politics of Sikkim by playing up a group of Lepchas against the pro-Tibet group.

Under King Sridkyong Namgyal, the relations remained by and large cordial, and in 1873, the king visited Darjeeling, along with his sister and brother Thutob Namgyal. Sikkim's allowance was increased from Rs 9,000 to 12,000. In 1873–74, Mr Edgar, the deputy commissioner of Darjeeling, 'was deputed to visit Sikhim and the Tibet frontier to enquire into the condition and prospects of trade with Tibet, and the advisability of making a road through Sikhim to the Tibetan frontier'.[104] Mr Edgar visited all passes of the Chola range and met the King, his officers and some officers of the Tibetan district of Phari. The Tibetan and the Chinese authorities were wary of these movements of the English, and the Chinese Amphan, or the resident of Lhasa, wrote to the Sikkim king in the name of the emperor of China, 'reminding him that he was bound to prevent the "Peling Sahibs" (Europeans) from crossing the frontier of Tibet, and warning him that if he continued to make roads for the Sahibs through Sikhim, "it would not be well with him"'.[105]

Queen Menchi and her husband Changzod Karpo acted as regents for Thutob Namgyal from 1874 till 1878. She wanted her son by Diwan Karpo to play a dominant role in the political affairs of Sikkim. The British records portray her as supporting her son to be the king. It is possible that Queen Menchi was concerned about protecting her disfigured elder son, who was an heir to the Sikkim throne, and keeping him out of public view. Risley wrote: 'Raja Sikyong Namgyel died in April 1874, and unsuccessful intrigues were attempted to set aside the accession of Thothub Namgye in favour of Tinle Namgye (born

---

[104] Risley, *The Gazetteer of Sikhim*.
[105] Ibid.

in 1866), but were defeated by the prompt action of the then Deputy Commissioner of Darjeeling, Mr. J. Ware Edgar (now Sir John Edgar).'[106] Edgar wanted to thwart a pro-Tibet faction under Diwan Namguay's influence: 'Edgar suspected that an attempt might be made to set aside the succession of Thothab Namgyal in favour of Tinley Namgyal, since the former had a hare-lip which was considered a disqualification by the ex-Diwan's faction on the alleged ground that it indicated a want of intellect.'[107]

Queen Menchi was part of the sacerdotal court, called Tashi Llunpo Labrong, which also included Lhassay Kusho Thinley Namgyal (the rani's son from Changzod Karpo) and the Tokhang Donyer Namguay and a few lamas. A Tibetan subject, Kampa Gyatso, refused to allow the Sikkim subjects to graze their cattle on the Tibetan frontier. The queen, along with other members of the court, went to Zhigatse to settle the matter.[108] At this time, in 1877, Deputy Commissioner of Darjeeling Sir John W. Edgar approached Maharaja Thutob Namgyal to allow Nepalese settlers to settle in Rhencock. The Sikkim ruler replied that 'the small bit of Rhencock land was situated in such a way as to raise disputes and questions on all sides, being the pasture ground of Tibetan subjects and well as Bhutan boundary'.[109] The real reason was that both his predecessors, Tsugphud Namgyal and Sridkyong Namgyal, strongly opposed the settlement of the Bhutias and Gorkhas on Sikkim land, due to their constant attacks on Sikkim. But the English authorities kept pressuring the Sikkim court. Most likely, the rani and Changzod Karpo, along

---

[106] Ibid., 24.
[107] P.R. Rao, *India and Sikkim (1814-1970)* (New Delhi: Sterling Publishers, 1972), 63.
[108] Namgyal and Dolma, *History of Sikkim*, 74.
[109] Ibid., 79.

with the Donyer Namguay, were also against the settlement of the Nepalese and the Bhutias on their land.

Meanwhile, a delegation of Lepchas and Bhutias of Sikkim approached Sir Ashley Eden in Darjeeling to intercede on their behalf as 'the Maharaja Thutob Namgyal, being young and inexperienced, the Phodong Lama Karma Tenkyong and the Khangsa Dewan Lhundup' were breaking the commands of the previous rajas, allowing 'Paharias to settle in Namthong and Tchadam, and now Namchi has also been handed over to the Newars'.[110] The British used the differences at the Sikkim royal court to their advantage. Ashley Eden, then lieutenant governor of Bengal, met the young maharaja and Changzod Karpo at Kalimpong. He instructed Changzod Karpo to regard the general body of the 'Sikkim people with impartial justice and protect them alike'.[111] Karpo was later pressured by the Khangsa Diwan and Phodang Lama Brothers to give in writing authorization to settle the Gurkha settlers in Sikkim.[112] He refused to give this order, and at Gyantse met Chinese Resident Sung Amban or Amphan and the Tibetan official Shape Rakasha, negotiating for the enlargement of the Tibetan estates granted to Sikkim after the investiture of Thutob Namgyal with a Chinese button of the first rank (plain coral). Unfortunately, Changzod Karpo, Queen Menchi's husband, died in 1879.[113]

Within two years of his death, Rani Pending (from the Tibetan family of Tashelhunpo), who was the wife of the previous king, Sridkyong Namgyal and after his death married to King Thutob Namgyal, died in 1880. With these two deaths, the British records mention that the 'whole power of

---

[110] Ibid., 76.

[111] Ibid.

[112] Ibid.

[113] Ibid., 78; Risley, *Gazetteer of Sikkim*, 25.

the State' came 'into the hands of the old Rani Men-chi and Dewan Namgay', who was living at Chumbi and 'favoured Tibetan interests and the cause of young Tinle, then growing up to manhood'.[114] Diwan Namguay and Queen Menchi would control the affairs of Sikkim till the death of the diwan in 1888.

King Thutob Namgyal did not show any inclination to remarry. According to Risley,

> pressure seems to have been brought to bear on him, and so having obtained two elephants from the Government of Bengal in 1881, he sent them to the Grand Lamas at Tashelhunpo and Lhassa, in charge of Nudup Gyaltsen (brother of the Phodang Lama) and the Rhenok Kazi. These officers, when at Lhassa, arranged a marriage between the Raja and the daughter of Shafe Utok, one of the leading men in Tibet.[115]

Here, the British accounts mention that Queen Menchi broke off the marriage alliance of Thutob Namgyal in order to place her younger son Thinley on the throne. Risley wrote:

> the old Rani and her son Tinley, accompanied by Dewan Namgay, followed shortly afterwards in 1882-83, and, apparently in furtherance of their design to place Tinle in direct succession to the Raj, broke off this match, and secured as a wife to the Raja the daughter of an inferior officer in the Dalai Lama's Court, known as Leden-se. It is said that the old Rani had to execute a bond, guaranteeing that the Raja of Sikkim would receive the girl as his Rani;

---

[114] Ibid.
[115] Ibid.

but without the slightest attempt at a show of decency, the
girl immediately went to live with Tinle, and by the time
the party returned from Lhassa to Chumbi, she was very
far gone in pregnancy, and in fact bore two children before
Raja Thothub ever saw her. All this helped the intrigues in
favor of Tinle, as his joint marriage with Leden-se's daughter
is pointed as proving Thothub and Tinle are legitimate
brothers, and so both of the royal family, polyandry being
permissible under Tibetan law.[116]

The Sikkimese royal records also give details of the matrimonial
alliance between Thutob Namgyal and Yeshe Dolma. The records
state that in 1881, the ministers and lamas of Sikkim collectively
submitted a request to the maharaja and the dowager rani (that
is Queen Menchi) 'praying that His Highness should think of
marrying another Rani'.[117] This was accompanied by a 'sevenfold
Nazar, so the Durbar addressed a request for two elephants from
the British Government'.[118] These elephants and some buffaloes
were to be given to the Tashi Lama and the Dalai Lama for two
purposes: to grant an extension of the Tibetan properties and to
ask for the hand of a suitable rani for the Maharaja. According to
the Sikkim royal records, names of a few girls from respectable
Tibetan families were written and submitted for divination. From
these, two names were finally shortlisted, one of them being the
maharani, Yeshe Dolma. These facts were reported to the king
and Queen Menchi. Here the records mention that it was agreed
by the king, his mother and his half-brother, Thinley Namgyal, to
propose for the hand of one rani. 'In pursuance of the prevailing
custom of two brothers having one wife jointly the Maharaja

---

[116] Ibid., 25–6.
[117] Namgyal and Dolma, *History of Sikkim*, 81.
[118] Ibid.

consented to marry one wife for both brothers. Accordingly, the Dowager Monkyit Rani and Lhasay Tinlay Namgyal set out from Sikkim towards Lhassa.'[119] The two names were again submitted after a lot of divination. It was then that the name of Yeshe Dolma came out most favourable. This was considered final, and the Chinese Amban, Soong-Amban and the Ka-shag-Lhagyayor the body of Tibetan Council were addressed on this subject. Donyer Namguay, according to the Tibetan custom, formally approached the Lhayding and asked for the hand of the lady. It was laid down in the marriage certificate of her marrying the two brothers jointly.[120] The nuptial ceremony was performed at Lhasa itself, publicly proclaiming her joint marriage.[121] In 1883, Queen Menchi arrived at Chumbi palace with her younger son, Lhassay Kusho. The Khangsa Diwan brothers,[122] who controlled the affairs in Sikkim as diwans, were informed that the rani was with child, and they decided to create discord between the king and his family. The relationship between the king and his wife remained strained for five years. After his meeting with Queen Yeshe Dolma when he realized that he had agreed to this arrangement and the relationship became cordial.[123]

Queen Menchi was active in safeguarding the interests of both her sons. She married both of them to the same woman, Yeshe Dolma, to firmly bind the brothers together. Polyandry was a common practice in Tibet and in the Sikkimese royal family, especially when it involved the Tibetan queens. Alice Travers argues in her paper that the connection of Tibet and Sikkim

---

[119] Ibid., 82.

[120] Ibid.

[121] Ibid., 83.

[122] The Khangsa diwans were the descendants of the sopan, who had helped the father of Psugphud Namgyal flee from the sudden Gurkha attack in the 1880s.

[123] Ibid.

through matrimonial alliance went back sixteen generations, and around twenty Tibetan women were married into the Sikkim royal family.[124] They seem to have enjoyed political eminence, as they were subsequently married to the princes on the deaths of the king. In the case of the Monkyit queen, Menchi, a similar pattern existed. Even before the death of her husband, King Tsugphud Namgyal, she was married to his illegitimate son, Changzod Karpo, to act as regents for her son from the king. I feel that Queen Menchi, along with Donyer Namguay, who was married to the illegitimate daughter of the King Tsugphud Namgyal, Pema-la, who in turn was close to Menchi when she came as a new bride, constituted a powerful Tibetan group and made attempts to thwart the British encroachments in Sikkim, to safeguard the Tibetan interests. Later, Queen Menchi would marry her daughter Serringputti with Donyer Namguay. Queen Menchi played a politically dominant role in Sikkim till 1890. To strengthen their ties with Tibet, Queen Menchi, with prince Thinley, a son from her marriage with Diwan Karpo, visited Tibet in search of a common bride for both the brothers in a polyandrous marriage. Yeshe Dolma was not the initial choice, but later the marriage was performed. Queen Menchi played a decisive role in establishing a political arrangement in Sikkim through a common marriage between her sons to keep a degree of political hold on them.

---

[124] Alice Travers, 'Women in the diplomatic game: Preliminary Notes on the matrimonial link of the Sikkim royal family with Tibet (13th–20th centuries) (in French), in *Bulletin of Tibetology,* Vol. 42, No.1 and 2, 2006, Namgyal Institute of Tibetology, Gangtok, Sikkim, 91–134, 94: 'The matrimonial alliances between the royal family of Sikkim and the great Tibetan families, religious and secular, have structured the relations of these two countries over sixteen generations, since the beginnings of the foundation of the Sikkimese royalty, but above all from its actual foundation.'

The tensions between the British and the Tibetans worsened in the 1880s. In 1884, the king, along with his brother Lhassay Kusho or Thinley (Queen Menchi's son from Diwan Karpo), were asked to remain at Tumlong and not to leave for Chumbi by Colman Macaulay and Oldham.[125] In the meeting, Macaulay told the king to administer Sikkim from Tumlong and that he should select Lachen or Lachungas his summer residence.[126] At this time, Paro Penlop of Bhutan plundered Phari, which brought the Chinese and the Tibetan officials to Phari. Thinley and Donyer Namguay suggested to the king to wait upon these officers as was the custom. The maharaja agreed, and the two went to Phari on behalf of the king. The Chinese and Tibetan officials enquired why the king had not come personally and why he discontinued spending the summer at Chumbi. The king had been honoured with the button of rank by the Chinese government, and the Tibetans were also angry at his absence. 'The Maharaja then sent Shew Dewan Phurbu to Darjeeling, with letters to the Commissioner and Deputy Commissioner, asking whether his highness might not be permitted to visit his summer residence.'[127]

The British agreed on the condition that he must find out the real facts of what had occurred between Tibet and Bhutan and to use his influence to reopen the trade that had stopped. The king was further ordered to extend his stay in Chumbi as Colman Macaulay would arrive there for a Tibet mission in 1886. Macaulay asked the 'Sikkim Durbar to write and inform

[125] Namgyal and Dolma, *History of Sikkim*, 83; Colman Macaulay, *Report of a Mission to Sikkim and the Tibetan Frontier, with a Memorandum on our Relations with Tibet* (Calcutta: Bengal Secretariat Press, 1885), 15–6.

[126] Namgyal and Dolma, *History of Sikkim*, 83; Macaulay, *Report of a Mission to Sikkim*, 15–6.

[127] Namgyal and Dolma, *History of Sikkim*, 84.

the Tibet Government about the peaceful intention of this projected Mission'.[128] The letter was communicated to the Phari Jongpon, who sent it to Shape Rampa. Rampa replied that 'there had been a general resolution passed that no English Gentleman should be permitted to cross the boundary, he hoped that they would not start from Darjeeling at all, but if they did so, yet the Sikkim State must do its utmost to ask them not to cross the boundary of British and Sikkim Territories'.[129] The Tibetan government reminded Sikkim that it was 'giving an annual grain subsidy of 1000 score measures per year' only for the purpose of safeguarding the boundaries. The English officials in Darjeeling pressured the king to stay in Chumbi till the mission arrived, and if he could hand over the letter to the Chinese Amban in person, 'it would please the Lieutenant Governor exceedingly whereas if His Highness failed to do so, it would displease the government'.[130] A Chinese resident or Amban had moved his post closer to the Tibetan frontier to prevent any British movement. Sikkim was caught between two great powers. The British were insisting on sending a peace delegation under Mr Macaulay to Tibet and China. The Tibet government refused such a commission outright. In 1886, the British authorities threatened the Sikkim authorities that they would annex Sikkim if their wishes were not complied with.[131]

The Phari Jongpon refused to take the letter from the English, stating that he had no such orders. The Khangsa Diwan communicated the refusal to the British. The deputy commissioner of Darjeeling then requested the king to allow them to build a few dwelling houses in Kophup in Sikkim.

---

[128] Ibid., 85.
[129] Ibid.
[130] Ibid.
[131] Ibid., 86.

The king replied that it would be better to delay such a project that year due to the suspicions of the Tibetan officials, unless consent was obtained from Tibet. He also requested the British to consider the Rishichu as 'constituting the boundary between the British and Sikkim territories'.[132]

Meanwhile, the Tibetans started building a fort at Lingtu to fortify themselves against any British attack. The Sikkim ruler requested the Tibetan officers not to build the fort as it would aggravate the matters with the British government.[133] The Tibetan officials replied that the land above Rhencock belonged to Tibet and they were well within their rights to build a fort on their land. They also taunted them, as recorded in the Sikkim account, saying 'that you Sikkimite need not light the lamp, while it is clearly to be seen by the eye'.[134] The English authorities disputed the boundary, replying 'that above Jelep La, the land belonged to Tibet and they might go and come or do anything as they pleased, but below Jelep the Tibetans must not be allowed to settle down there, and that they must be asked to go away'.[135] The king's officials enquired from the people of Tromo under Tsanpa Tshring 'as to the actual boundary of Tibet and who was in possession'.[136] Tsanpa Tshring wrote that 'below Jelap and above Rhencock the land originally belonged to Tibet. But the Tibet Government had given Rhencock to Sikkim, so the land above Ganyak the line above which bamboos grow could be claimed by Tibet because, it was the grazing ground of the Tromowas'.[137] From

---

132 Ibid.
133 Ibid., 87.
134 Ibid.
135 Ibid.
136 Ibid., 86.
137 Ibid.

this statement, it seems that Tibet wanted to protect its grazing lands, while the British intended to deny them such mobility. Tibet accused Sikkim of 'acting as guides for the British'[138] by opening roads and building bridges up to Kophup near Jelep. They also accused Sikkim of not explaining to the British 'that Rhencock was the Tibet Sikkim boundary' and that Tibet was compelled to take back what it had given to Sikkim. Further, the lands above Ganyak, beyond the boundary line were used as pasture lands.[139] The Sikkim government admitted that Rhencock was given to them by Tibet. The king extended his stay in Tibet, while the English asked him to return, else his annual subsidy would stop.[140] The king explained his position by stating that he was asked to stay on in Tibet by the English officials. Later, seeing the heightened state of tension between Tibet and the British, he made attempts at reconciliation. The Sikkim ruler wrote: 'Ours is a small State, and all that we can do in case of a rupture between two such powerful Governments, we can only pray that we may be allowed to preserve neutrality.'[141] In December 1887, the king returned to Gangtok, where a palace was newly built, along with the Yeshe Dolma and Thinley Namgyal.

Meanwhile, in March 1888, an expeditionary force was sent to Lingtu, forcing the Tibetans to evacuate, and in September 1888 the campaign ended with the complete expulsion of the Tibetans across the Jelep.[142] In December 1888, Chinese Resident Sheng Tai arrived at Gnatong to settle the Tibet–Sikkim dispute

---

[138] Ibid., 88.
[139] Ibid., 87–8.
[140] Ibid., 90.
[141] Ibid., 92.
[142] Risley, *Gazetteer of Sikkim*, 26.

with the English authorities. Mr Paul was already there.[143] But the talks were unsuccessful. Finally, with the arrival of James H. Hart of the Chinese Imperial Customs Service, fresh attempts at solving the Tibet–Sikkim problem were opened, culminating in the signing of the convention in Calcutta on 17 March 1890.

Prior to this, in 1888, the king was informed that the troops were seen advancing towards Gangtok, under J.C. White, without a prior intimation to the Sikkim ruler. This seemed suspicious, as there was no intimation of his purpose of visit. Queen Yeshe Dolma showed presence of mind at this time and told the Sikkim officials to have a word with White regarding his advance, while the king, queen and few officers retired to Lagyap. Immediately after their departure, the troops arrived and 'fired off a gun and took possession of the Palace'.[144]

As the king and his party were proceeding to the Chumbi Palace, they received a message from Queen Menchi that Mr Paul and the British forces had arrived at Rinchenpong. The British forces entered the Chumbi Palace, asking Queen Menchi about the whereabouts of the king, and 'threatened her saying unless he came forward himself troops would be sent to search him out'.[145] Queen Menchi handled the situation diplomatically by stating 'that the Maharaja had not yet arrived at the Palace, and that if troops be sent to search him, it would only serve to frighten him the more, she would rather get him to come of himself to see Mr. Paul, and asked him to go back to Rinchenpong taking the troops with him'.[146] Queen Menchi warded off the serious confrontation between her son and the English authorities. She also got an opportunity to inform the

---

[143] Ibid.
[144] Ibid., 97.
[145] Ibid., 98.
[146] Ibid., 98.

King about these developments and decide accordingly. In this moment of uncertainty, Queen Yeshe Dolma advised the king to proceed to Chumbi as his mother, Queen Menchi and the princes were in the palace. Queen Menchi handled the situation with tact and political sagacity, sending another messenger to inform the king that she had told Mr Paul

> that the Raj party had been lost in the jungle, she would go in search, and asked permission to approach with them when found, to which Mr. Paul had answered saying that the British Officer would be at the Langrang for that night, so that if the Rani succeeded in finding them, they might come there, and that the Sahebs had returned.[147]

The tactical manoeuvring by the queen at the delicately poised moment helped the Sikkim ruler to negotiate with the British. The king asserted that he had done no wrong. Mr White became the political officer, and the Tibetan influence at the palace was reduced. While Queen Yeshe Dolma was forced to come to Gangtok, Queen-mother Menchi continued to reside at Chumbi, with the elder son of the king, Thutob Namgyal. The British sent some representatives from Sikkim 'to fetch the elder Kumar from Chumbi, where he was living with his grandmother'.[148] Queen Menchi was told of the precarious position of her son by the representatives of the British. She held her ground, despite knowing about her son's confinement by the English authorities, and argued

> that when His Highness was taken down, it was in a friendly manner and good faith, with promises of kind favour but that

---

[147] Ibid., 98.
[148] Ibid., 103.

he had been shifted to Kalimpong without any certainty as to what might be done to him. On the top of this to ask that the two sons be sent down, without her knowing what might be their fate, was too painful to her. In short, being aged, she could not afford to lose sight of the children.[149]

They returned to Kalimpong unsuccessful.

The king was kept a virtual prisoner, humiliated and pressed to send for his eldest son, Tsodak Namgyal. For this reason, he was not allowed to meet his other son, the Avatar Kumar. His allowance was reduced to mere Rs 500. The king fled from Gangtok but was caught and kept in total disgrace at Darjeeling and in Kurseong as a prisoner. He was not allowed to enter Gangtok till he agreed to the British terms. At Kurseong in 1894, Mr Nolan met the king, who tried to explain his position in the Tibetan–Chinese affair, stating that he was only trying to prevent the rupture between the two governments. Mr Nolan's reply is interesting. He said that the king tried to act like a mediator, 'which should not have been his position, as little States must always depend on more powerful governments'.[150] He was also compelled to apologize to the British. Only after that was he allowed to go to Gangtok in 1895. In the same year, Queen-mother Monkyit (Menchi) died. 'The funeral ceremonies and charities to different monasteries would require some Rupees two thousand which was procured on loan from Kayahs and distributed to all the monasteries in Sikkim and those of U and Tsang in Tibet'.[151] Thus ended the life of a queen who was never shown in imperial records as important in resisting the British

---

[149] Ibid.

[150] Ibid., 114.

[151] Ibid., 120.

intrusions, but her presence in the politics of Sikkim in the late nineteenth century cannot be ignored.

III

The ruler of Sikkim mentioned that they were unfamiliar with the title of 'Sikkimputtee' or raja, but it seems to be the title used in the Indian plains. In the 1835 treaty with Sikkim, the British authorities used the title of 'Sikkimputtee' and 'raja' in the terms of the treaty. The ruler of Sikkim was unfamiliar with what was considered the final treaty, and he was unaware that he had given away the lands in the plains to the Raj for the nominal amount of Rs 3,000. The Sikkim durbar was unhappy and raised objections with the British authorities. Since that time, there were undercurrents of tension between the British Raj and the Sikkim ruler. The authorities in Tibet were unhappy with the treaty and felt the breach of Tibetan sovereignty over Sikkim. As the diwan and the queens came from Tibet, many tried to stop the British intrusions in Sikkim.

Monkyit Rani gave birth to Thutob Namgyal and two daughters.[152] The sixth Chogyal Tenzing Namgyal married a daughter of Changzod Karwang, called Anyo Gyal-Yum (the lady dowager or the mother of the prince) and Chogyal Tsugphud Namgyal.[153] Changzod Karwang was an influential official, and in the lifetime of King Namgyal Phuntso, he had 'obtained so much power that he used to affix the red seal'. Later, his sons Changzod Chogtup and Changzod Bolod used the red seal, 'thus putting themselves upon an equal footing with the Raja'.[154] Their father had given protection to the fifth Chogyal Namgyal Phuntso,

---

[152] Ibid., 57.
[153] Ibid., 45.
[154] Ibid., 44.

who was a minor at his ascendancy to the throne. Power was usurped by one of his nobles, Changzod Tamding, in 1738–41. At that time, Changzod Karwang backed the young king and took him to safety to Sinchel, near Darjeeling.[155] They were the Kazis or the Jongpons of Lepcha extraction.

In the time of the seventh Chogyal, Tsugphud Namgyal, the younger son of Changzod Karwang, Bolod, proud of his association as the 'maternal uncle'[156] of the king, misappropriated funds and the red seal. In 1819, the Kazis and Lamas tried to bring about an amicable settlement between the king and Changzod. This kept on happening for a couple of years. The ruler was offended by the repeated disregard of the settlements by his uncle Bolod and his rebellion, in which he lost a son and the second lady of the Lamoi family due to sorcery. In 1826, the king ordered Bolod to be killed as a consequence. This started a feud with the nephew of Bolod, settled in Ilam in the Terai. He was appointed as Kotah Jongpon. Bolod's family started the Kotapa insurrection with the help of Nepal. J.W. Grant, the British officer, wrote to the Sikkim ruler in 1831 that the insurrection by Yug Dathup would be immediately suppressed.[157]

The British accounts underline the 'foreignness' of the Sikkim royal family and their increasing remoteness from the people of Sikkim. Richard Temple described the raja of Sikkim as impoverished, with a limited revenue source of about 1,000 pounds a year from the agricultural produce and transit duties. He further stated, 'The Raja himself is a foreigner, i.e., he is a Tibetan residing half the year in the Chumbi Valley, which belongs altogether to Tibet, and where he has a house.'[158]

---

155 Ibid., 39.
156 Ibid., 58.
157 Ibid., 58.
158 Temple, *Journals*, 164.

According to Temple, who visited Sikkim in 1875 and traversed different routes to Sikkim from Darjeeling, 'The population of Independent Sikkim is naturally very small, about 5,000 only. Of these 2,500 are Lepchas, 1,000 Limbus, and 1,500 Bhutias.'[159] He did not include Tibetans in this enumerated list. He observed that the diwan, who was a near relative of the king, was also a foreigner. Citing Joseph Hooker, Temple said that Sikkim rulers were not held in high esteem in Tibet and China, and none of the best Tibetan and Chinese families 'considers them worthy of notice'.[160]

The distancing between the ruler and the people was linked by Risley to the Tibetan wives of the rulers. He argued,

> Such marriages introduced a new and important factor into Sikhim politics. Women brought up in the dry keen air of Tibet could not stand the moist warmth of the Sikhim hills, drenched by the immoderate rainfall which prevails on the southern slopes of the Eastern Himalayas. Their influence, coupled with the Tibetan proclivities of their husbands, promoted by the Nepalese invasion of the country, induced the Rajas to transfer the head-quarters of their Government to the valley of Chumbi, one march to the Tibetan side of the Jelap pass.[161]

The prolonged absence of the king from Sikkim resulted in the neglect of the internal administration of Sikkim, and according to Risley, 'Lepcha interests were neglected, and Chumbi became the Hanover of Sikhim.'[162]

---

[159] Ibid., 161.
[160] Temple, *Journals*, 164.
[161] Risley, *Gazetteer of Sikkim*, iii.
[162] Ibid.

J.D. Hooker constantly refers to the unsatisfactory state of affairs between the British authorities and Sikkim in the 1840s.[163] He mentions the influence of the Diwan over the old raja, who estranged him from his eldest son. According to Hooker, the king's eldest son was 'said to possess much ability and prudence, and hence to be very obnoxious to Diwan, who vehemently opposed his marriage' as he was a monk. But the monks procured a dispensation from Lhasa for his marriage and were able to 'undermine the influence of the violent and greedy stranger'.[164] Hooker mentions that the diwan was related to one of his wives.[165] The diwan 'had established his influence over the youngest' son, Thutob Namgyal from Queen Menchi.[166] Hooker refers to the power of amlah or the councillors over the king,[167] and he reiterated that 'the people had long given evidence of their confidence in the English.'[168] The same was repeated by Colman Macaulay.

There is a constant comparison between the civilized and progressive world of the English with the backward ways of the rulers of these mountain states. While the ruler of Sirmur Karam Prakash was treated with disdain, they acted as the 'saviours' of the rani, promoting her as the regent to her minor son, in the lifetime of her husband. The Sikkim ruler was bullied and forced to accept English terms, in the guise of the civilized behaviour of the king. The treaty negotiations between Sikkim and Major Lloyd, the English representative, were detailed. Contrary to the English position that the raja gave the Darjeeling territory

---

[163] Hooker, *The Himalayan Journal*, Vol. I, 167.
[164] Ibid., 288.
[165] Ibid., 281.
[166] Ibid., 288.
[167] Hooker, *The Himalayan Journal*, Vol. II, 192.
[168] Hooker, *The Himalayan Journal*, Vol. I, 283.

unconditionally in the official British records, the Sikkim king's responses state otherwise. The ruler was reluctant to part with Darjeeling by stating that his country was 'small', but he was aware of the power of the British and wished to have 'friendly' relations with them. Further, in exchange for Darjeeling, he asked for territory in plains, the settling of Eklatok Kazi and his party in Sikkim, with a promise that they would stop plundering Sikkim and take the revenue of Morung in alliance with the Rumman Zemindar, who was troubling the Sikkim ruler.[169] In his letter to Macnaghten, Major Lloyd stated that he met the ruler of Sikkim on the banks of the Teesta at a place called Took Sampo. He also acknowledged receiving Machaghten's letter seeking the 'cession of Darjeeling'. He further stated that he received the governor general's letter while returning to the plains after his meeting with the king, and he could only forward it to the ruler. Since then, he did not hear from him. This indicates that the raja's meeting remained inconclusive, and he did not respond to the communication from the governor general. He then went on to mention that the raja received him in full durbar, and 'presented me a written paper stating that he had many grievances to make known'.[170] He mentioned that at the commencement of the meeting that the 'Raja seemed rather alarmed' as he has been told 'not to meet any of the English gentlemen for if he did they would take his country from him as they had done to all the princes of Hindostan'.[171] He stayed on the opposite bank of the Teesta and had to cross the river on a bamboo raft every time he wished to meet the

---

[169] To W.A. Macnaghten, Secretary to Government, Political Department, Fort William, from Major Lloyd, in Foreign Department, 9 March 1835.
[170] Ibid.
[171] Ibid.

raja; the ferry was provided by the ruler. In his second meeting with the king, the Sikkim ruler made three requests. First, that his western boundary should be extended to the Ronki, but on Lloyd's refusal, he asked to be assured that the boundary fixed by Lieutenant Weston would be honoured; second, that Rummonao and Kazis be seized and delivered to him. Lloyd craftily replied that he had no power to do so, but the king could write an application to the governor general, drawing the ruler into the trap by stating that he wished Major Lloyd to 'mediate between him and his opponents to put an end to the unsettled state of the country'.[172] The third request of the King was to add Dabsong to his lands in the Morung. Lloyd answered diplomatically, stating that he had received orders from the governor general 'to request the Raja to cede Darjeeling to the British sovereignty in exchange for land in the plains or for a sum of money'.[173] The raja asked for time and did not meet Lloyd for three days, but sent his emissaries across for discussion to settle the dispute between him and the Karjees. In this meeting, the raja told Lloyd of many instances of favour given to Eklatok Kazi by him and his ancestors, and he wanted to put him to death, but acceding to Lloyd's request, he would allow them to settle in Sikkim territory. The king was convinced that they would never settle quietly, 'but would be continually intriguing with the goorkas'. The king, therefore, requested the English to re-establish a guard post at Naggree. Lloyd insisted that the raja forget past issues and pardon them and agree 'not to punish or oppress the Lepchas in any way'. Then they could return and settle themselves to the east of the Teesta and be loyal to the king. But if they continued 'to make incursions' from Nepal into Sikkim territory, the Nepal government 'should be requested to

---

[172] Ibid.
[173] Ibid.

remove them from the vicinity of the frontier if they could not otherwise restrain them'. Further, respecting Rummoa, Lloyd was asked to exercise his authority

> to demand from him an account of the last three years' revenue of the Morung which he had embezzled and proceed against him agreeable to the customs in the Company's territories for the same and make him refund the plunder he had made of the property of various inhabitants of that country and prohibit him from returning to it and also make a proper settlement of the revenue for the Raja.[174]

Regarding Darjeeling, the raja said it was a small matter and he would give it to the company out of friendship and 'build houses there for the people who might resort there'. From the language, it seems that the raja was not giving up his claim on Darjeeling entirely, as he suggested that he would give them residence for the sick. The king's concluding remarks make this clear, as he said, 'if his requests were complied with he from friendship would give Darjeeling to the British government but that his country was a very small one'.[175] Lloyd understood the implication of the king's remarks as he elaborated that 'meaning I suppose that he could not afford to part with any of it', and requested it to be continued to his son after his death.[176] The king also made it clear that he would not be seeing any of the English gentlemen again. He was civil throughout the discussions and gave Major Lloyd several presents, which included 'a silk dress, which I beg permission to keep, two ponys, five cows, two showl goats . . . a chowry, wase, a bundle of gold dust &

---

[174] Ibid.
[175] Ibid.
[176] Ibid.

c'. In return, Major Lloyd gave the king his watch and sword, 'to which he had apparently taken a fancy', and later he sent a shawl. Such was the unequal exchange. In the end, as per Lloyd's account to his vakeel, the raja stated that if all his demands were met, 'Then my Dewan will deliver to Major Lloyd the grant and agreement under my red seal of Darjeeling that he may erect houses there which I have given in charge of the said Dewan to be delivered.'[177] This was on 25 February 1835, and the red seal of the Sikkim ruler was missing on the treaty. Yet, the British took it as his official approval and simply showed it as the final transfer of Darjeeling unconditionally to the English authorities. The duplicitous character of the British treaty-making repeated itself again and again in 1861 and 1889.

In June 1889, J.C. White, executive engineer, was appointed assistant political officer at Gangtok to advise and assist the maharaja in his administration of Sikkim. A representative council, which included a few influential people of Sikkim, was appointed to guide the King.[178]

The plight of Tsugphud Namgyal in 1861 and his son Thutob Namgyal in the 1880s were similar—both were humiliated and hounded from place to place. In 1890, with the signing of the British-Chinese Convention of 17 March 1890,[179] Sikkim was incorporated into the British Indian Empire, to make administrative, foreign and border-related decisions. During 1893–95, the Chogyal and his wife Yeshe Dolma were under house arrest at Kurseong and Darjeeling. Sir Charles Elliott, the

---

[177] Ibid.

[178] Risley, *Gazetteer of Sikhim*, 26.

[179] Secret Department, Register No. 379a, 7 February 1907, Rec. 23 February 1907, Letters from Secretary to the Government of India, Foreign Department, Records of the 10th Chogyal Sidkeong Tulku (acquired from London, British Library), Sikkim State Archives, 1676.

governor of Bengal, appointed a council to govern Sikkim under
the chairmanship of John Clyde White, who acted as the de facto
ruler of Sikkim. He also exerted pressure on the king to bring
back his eldest son from Tibet to be groomed by the British as
the heir, weaning him from the Tibetan influence. The British
were apprehensive that the second son was considered an avatar
of Phodung Lama, and the people of Sikkim would not accept
him as a ruler. The Sikkim ruler repeatedly resisted the pressure
to bring back his eldest son. He knew that the British might
remove him and place his son on the throne. Thutob Nagyal
was restored to his state in 1895 on the condition that he would
write to his eldest son to return. He agreed and wrote to him,
but the prince refused as it would hamper his education. The
eldest son, Tsodrak Namgyal, remained with his grandmother,
Queen Menchi, at Chumbi, receiving his education in Tibet.
The British then decided to groom the second son, Sidkeong
Tulku, as the heir apparent.

Thutob Namgyal, the ruler of Sikkim after his mother Queen
Menchi's death, was among the last of the anti-British and pro-
Tibet party. He was left alone to tackle the English. Later, the
English compelled Yeshe Dolma to join him with his second son.
He and Rani Yeshe Dolma had very few alternatives under the
autocratic hold of the British resident. The king, and later his wife,
spent their time trying to evade the English officials at Gangtok.
Just as Major Lloyd bullied King Tsugphud Namgyal, similarly
White bullied King Thutob Namgyal. It was only Queen Menchi
who refused to be subdued by the English, not giving in to their
intimidation, refusing to give her grandson or letting the English
take them to Sikkim from Tibet in her lifetime.

Yeshe Dolma also made attempts to resist, but in deference
to her husband's political circumstances, handled the British
officials diplomatically. The British attempted to weaken the
Tibetan influence by providing Sidkeong Tulku with an English

education. He was educated at St. Paul's School in Darjeeling and spoke English fluently. Later he went to England, studying at Pembroke College, Oxford.[180] The British encouraged the heir apparent to explore marriage prospects outside Tibet.[181] With his western education, he needed a wife well-versed in the English ways and with a good knowledge of English. To find a wife from Tibet with such requirements became difficult. Further, the English were careful about their strategic considerations in Sikkim. Any marriage that the heir apparent contracted 'would not be permitted to impair the plenary rights of the British Government to regulate and limit the entry of aliens into Sikkim'.[182]

Queen Menchi's loyalty to the Sikkim–Tibet relations was non-negotiable. She was among the last queens (except Yeshe Dolma, selected by her) to politically align with Tibet. Queen Menchi and Donyer Namguay were strongly anti-British. They could sense the dangers of the British presence in the Sikkim hills. The British strongly denounced Donyer Namguay as 'Pagla Dewan'. I tried to trace the antecedents of the Donyer Namguay but could not find any in the available records. But what emerged in the records is the sharing of power between the Bhutanese and the Lepcha clans with the Sikkim royal family.[183] All these political alignments in Sikkim were

---

[180] India Office, March 1907, Secret Department, Register No. 379a, 7 February 1907, Rec. 23 February 1907, 1672.

[181] 'Proposal to marry a Japanese lady', in Secret Department, Register No. 379a, 7 February 1907, Rec. 23 February 1907, 1676.

[182] No. 379, Calcutta, 7 February 1907, J.C. White, Political Officer in Sikkim, in Secret Department, Register No. 379a, 7 February 1907, Rec. 23rd February 1907, 1676.

[183] Hong Tran, 'Chogyal's Sikkim: Tax, Land & Clan Politics', *Independent Study Project (ISP) Collection*, 1446, 2012, https://digitalcollections.sit.edu/isp_collection/1446. Accessed on 11 June 2022.

gradually eroded by the British, and the differences between different court factions and clan politics were played upon by the English officials to loosen their support to the Sikkim royal family. Queen Menchi's role in this period needs to be placed in the perspective of the movement of the British in these hills with an eye on trade and commerce with Tibet and China. Queen Menchi, along with a group of Sikkim officials, resisted the efforts of the English to weaken Sikkim's ties with Tibet, and make inroads into Sikkim territory. The English needed a pliable and a dependent government in Sikkim, to ensure that their commerce and mobility in Sikkim would not be hindered by the Sikkimese authorities, and they could control the trade outposts and trade activities on the borders.

Conclusion

One is confronted with many challenges while tracing the history of the queens discussed in this book. There are not just silences around them; they are invisible. Finding out their names in the archives became akin to solving a puzzle. While the men were all named, the constant use of the term 'rani' or 'maharani' without these women's names made it difficult to understand whom the imperial records were referring to. In recent years, the forgotten names of women, such as Uda Devi, Azizan Bai, Rani Draupadi of Dhar, Habiba, Bhagwati Devi, etc., many of whom belonged to marginal castes and communities and who played an important role in resisting the British Raj, have started to resurface. Women faced double exclusion, one because of gender and the other because of their social status. The Marxist and subaltern approaches have challenged the perspectives of imperialist and nationalist historiography. More research is needed on the question of women. We still have gaps in knowledge regarding their domestic lives and how they navigated traditional social structures. These are the limitations of the imperial archives, as their objective and focus are different. The large-scale production of knowledge by the colonial departments and officials violently displaced the existing knowledge tradition in India. They gave primacy to recorded history much more than was done previously. It also led to homogenization and standardization of knowledge, which was written from the perspective of the colonists.

The Western imperialism of the nineteenth century has left behind the debris of destruction, which includes these knowledge traditions. The forces of imperial ambition and capitalist acquisitiveness came together to wreak political, economic and social havoc on the lives of the colonized. Armed with the modern weaponry and the power of documentation, the imperialists wove a narrative to convince the readers of the appropriateness of their actions against bad native rulers with their irrational laws of succession and dated traditions. The British (which included more Scots and Irish) emerged as the God players who tossed aside the Indian rulers of the nineteenth century.

How is the discipline of knowledge applied to power structures, especially in the manner in which the princely states were either seized or made subordinate or subservient to the interests of the colonial state? The entire indigenous tradition of the law of succession was moulded into a colonial way of acquiring and understanding the rules of succession, which suited the needs of a colonial power. In many ways, Agamben's concept of the state of exception is appropriate to describe the machinations of the colonial state.[1] Every time the colonial state faced opposition from the princely states, it made the excuse of being threatened, and they justified the extreme measures used under what can be termed as the 'State of Exception'. If Kittur was rebellious, then the entire state, its

---

[1] Giorgio Agamben, *State of Exception*, trans. Kevil Attell (Chicago: The University of Chicago Press, 2005), 38. Here Agamben compares the 'force of law' and the 'state of law', in which in the first norms are not applied, while in the 'force' 'acts that do not have value' acquire force.

fort and people had to be pounded into submission. The rules of combat did not apply in this state of exception. Similarly, in Jhansi, successions could be set aside by epistemic violence to the Indian laws on succession.

Today, colonialism has left behind unresolved problems. These colonial debris lead to despair and new directions. Today, countries with a colonial past are simultaneously trying to climb out of the complex web of power configuration of the British. Colonial power discourses and narratives have also found new voices from within. Many Indian princes who resisted the British have become part of the national saga and glorious chapters in the nationalist struggle. A post-independent nationalistic surge has seen many queens joining the national pantheons of hero. Among them, Kittur Rani and the rani of Jhansi are the front runners. But they are not alone. Modern politics and popular imagination associate their heroism with the bravery shown by the heroes of the lower castes, for instance, Jhalkari Bai in Jhansi and Sangolli Rayanna in the case of Kittur. In the people's songs, there is a valorization of the martial tradition. Primarily, the queens with a martial bent of mind, confronting the opponents without surrendering, made it to the annals of folk tradition. In Kittur, both the rani and her trusted subordinate's heroism are spoken in the same breath. In the British records, Guru Siddhappa was seen as the primary foe, and he was executed immediately after suppressing the rebellion by being blown up with the canon. But in the popular imagination, it is Sangolli Rayanna who plays a pivotal role in this rebellion. So, while Lakshmi Bai and Chennamma, along with their associates, are immortalized in the folk tradition, there are no songs that I could find on Maharani Jindan, Begum Zeenat Mahal, Guleri Rani or the Sikkim queen.

A common strand in these queens' lives is the succession of their sons, natural and adopted. These queens play a critical political role, yet there is a common thread that runs through all of them. All of them fight to ensure the succession of their sons or adopted sons, and for this, they enter into diplomatic negotiations with the imperial authorities. Almost all of them are enigmatic personalities. What seems fascinating on reading about them is that they ought not be fitted into any category, as they refuse to conform to what was considered the norm of their times. To ensure the continuity of their dynastic line they either enter into negotiations or compromise or resist and finally rebel against the Raj. Unfortunately, the loyalty of the ranis remains confined to their family or the place. The ranis are associated with the place, usually their marital home. The place and the queen together define that historical moment, which brings them to the centre stage of history. Queens, place and identity are intrinsically linked. These women are thrust into difficult positions by their husbands' deaths. Sirmur is an exception—it was remarkable for the times for the queen to become the regent in her husband's lifetime. The survival of their kingdoms became dependent on their negotiations.

Barbara Ramusack classifies the princely states into three categories: antique states, successor states and conqueror states.[2] The first type of state is similar to what Colonel Tod used to describe primarily the Rajputana states. I disagree with the usage of the term 'antique' for the Rajputana states—they are dynamic and actively engage in the medieval polity of their times, both as independent entities and as partners in the Mughal Empire. To an extent, she supports the classification of the colonial officials. The English officials justify taking over Jhansi as their 'dependency', in other words, their creation, and hence their right of takeover, while Orchha, and Datia were Rajput states, existing before the British expansion. This is an effect of romanticization of

---

[2] Barbara N. Ramusack, 43.

Rajputs by Tod in his works on Rajputana. Most of the Rajput states were subordinate rulers of the Mughals and part of the Mansabdari system. The colonial officials similarly held the Maratha states as the ones where the leaders had carved out independent principalities through conquest. This is again similar to what Ramusack calls the warrior states. All these classifications are problematic. The British did not stick to such classification after 1858. In my understanding, all such classifications were convenient strategies to co-opt and annex the princely states on one pretext or the other in the pre-1857 period. What emerges from the archival records is that the British created a hierarchy among the princes before 1857, and they treated them accordingly. They gave precedence to the Rajputs and Thakurs as the oldest ruling lineages. Then came the Maratha chiefs extending Maratha power to north India. The Maratha officers appointed by the Peshwas and made autonomous principalities under the Raj were placed in a separate category. The Raj was eager to take direct charge of the smaller principalities like Kittur and Jhansi. However, they had entered into pacts with the rulers, assuring them of the continuity of their line. Yet, the English authorities did a complete about-turn and decided not to honour their agreements on the flimsy ground of adoption, knowing that adoption was common among India's ruling class.

The violence of 1857 benefited the English loyalists, which included some princely states. The peasantry, the rebel leaders and the lower caste leaders on the margins were hounded and publicly hanged. Queen Victoria's Proclamation only rewarded the pacifist princes and ensured the offensive end of those who fought the British. They were to be hunted and publicly punished so that the consequences of their defiance of the imperial state got embedded in the psyche of the colonized. All English officials were not prejudiced, but the broader perception, further aggravated by the popular

European perception, judged the rebellious queens to be evil. For instance, Maharani Lakshmi Bai's association in the English press with the Jokhum Bagh Massacre, which was later proved incorrect, led the British to disgrace and hang her father at the same spot where the massacre had taken place. The act was also repeated in Delhi in the brutal massacre of Mughal princes by Captain Hodson, and their bodies were left in the open—a reprisal for the killing of English women and children inside the Red Fort. The intensity of hate and mistrust that the Company authorities had evoked among the erstwhile Company soldiers ensured that the Mughal Emperor was also held guilty, despite accounts of his efforts to stop the killing of the English inside the fort. The British, with their projections of civility, were no less brutal in retaliation.

Another aspect that distinctly emerges from the study is that these queens did not deal with issues of nationalism. There is no nationalist consciousness in them—they are fighting for what they consider right for their principality. It is a question of political expediency against a power that does not adhere to the rules that they themselves formulate. A common pattern is discernible in the narratives of these six queens. Their position was complicated and their actions complex. All of them were fighting to ensure the succession of their sons, who were heartlessly wrenched from their arms, in one way or the other. While the official records detail the heart-rending stories of the massacre of the English men, women and children in many instances in the course of the rebellion, the description of the acts of the Indians was couched in legalese, the moral and the ethical. The accent in all such records is on the moral turpitude of the Indians—Hindus and Muslims—and the righteous indignation of the evangelizing English.

There is a strong condemnation and an accusatory tone about the acts of the Indian rulers, conveniently downplaying the fact

that it was the British who not only imposed unfair treaties upon
the princely states but misled them with false promises. They
also misinformed the rulers by couching them in administrative
language—a language unfamiliar to the Indian rulers. The
English also arbitrarily broke their terms and conditions. When
the Indian rulers, such as Rani Chennamma, reacted against
this breach of promise by fighting the English, the blame was
squarely placed on her for killing the English. Hence the British
got an excuse to attack Kittur and annex the territory. During
the second Anglo-Sikh battle, Lord Dalhousie wrote to Lord
Gough, the commander-in-chief 'that H.E. is responsible
for the army, but that I am responsible for the Empire'[3]. It is
apparent that by the 1840s, the British were already considering
themselves as the imperial sovereigns of India, despite the titular
presence of the Mughal emperor in Delhi. The British Raj did
not only leave the monuments of commemoration, but the
monuments of destruction such as the pounded forts as a symbol
of their might and a reminder to the Indians of what the Raj
could do.

One can link ambivalent subjectivities of these queens to
the moment of transition in the nineteenth century. When
compared to the women in India's freedom struggle, these
queens were not fighting for India's Independence, but to
protect the interest of their sons and retaining the power in
their family. But these queens, caught in a time warp, were
serving the cause of patriarchy. It is only in the late 1970s that
women's issues and their struggles gained public recognition.
So, one cannot judge these queens of the nineteenth century, at
a time of transition from the pre-modern to modern, from the
lens of the present. The ranis have largely been seen as fostering

---

[3] *Private Letters of the Marquess of Dalhousie,* 40.

a conservative upper caste vision[4] of the role of women in the public and private sphere. Without denying the conservatism of the ranis, one can see the skilful use of Indian customs and practices to their advantage. For example, Maharani Jindan's use of the veil as a political weapon foxed the British. The queens operated within a patriarchal frame, yet they were subversive. On occasion, they used the traditional roles and customs defined for the woman to negotiate with the Company Raj. Take the instance of Sirmur, where Guleri Rani threatened the British authorities with sati to get her way with regard to the control of Sirmur and the support of the British for her cause. Similarly, Maharani Lakshmi Bai constantly urged the British authorities to allow her to go to Varanasi to perform the rites of a widow. She knew that the people of Jhansi wanted her as the ruler and were not happy with the takeover by the company officers. The officers needed her presence in Jhansi, and the rani was negotiating from this limited vantage position. This may also be the reason for Captain Ellis being soft on her, but which was frowned upon by the higher levels of the English authorities. Ellis approved of encouraging the rani to harbour the wish of ruling Jhansi. It isn't that all English officers supported the arbitrariness of the British Raj. Many like Ellis were uncomfortable with the arbitrary decision-making; some like Montgomery Martin questioned the mercenary character of a few, sensitive to the excesses of the British in India; and another one like J. D. Cunningham, was critical of the unnecessary war of the British in Punjab.

The silences in the imperial records on the ranis is a challenge to historians today. Certain queens are marginalized in the imperial records. The rani of Sirmur is a case in point.

---

[4] As argued by Mary E. John, Tanika Sarkar and many other women scholars.

During my research, I came across another queen from Sikkim who was on the margins of history, located in a remote corner of India. In the nineteenth century, while the British Raj was expanding, it followed a similar modus operandi in acquiring domination over the princely states. Sikkim was no exception. Even if the polities of the princely states were dissimilar, the British exhibited a common pattern of acquiring these states. There was a certain pattern that connected the political positions of these 'native' Indian rulers. The histories of the Sirmur and Sikkim are no different. There is little information about them and even less about the role of certain queens in the political life of the state. Very little is known about the rani of Sirmur and even less about the rani of Sikkim. A careful reading of the imperial archives reveals undercurrents of tension, especially in Sikkim, and an attempt has been made to unearth the tensions and her role at a time when the British authorities were also negotiating with the ruler of Sikkim for commercial reasons. In Sirmur, there was archival information on the deposition of Karam Prakash in his lifetime and the succession given to his son; there is a silence in the imperial records on how this unusual development came about.

While in recent times there has been research beyond Maharani Lakshmi Bai, on Maharani Jindan in particular and to a lesser extent on Rani Chennamma, there is still a dearth of both sources and research on the rani of Sirmur, the rani of Sikkim and Begum Zeenat Mahal. My work only points to some of the challenges and scope for further research on them. What is apparent, yet not underlined, in the British records is the heavy financial burden on the princely states in the form of peshkush (fixed tributes) and the revenue of the most lucrative land, in the case of Jhansi, for the maintenance of the British army. Due to these financial burdens and demands of the Raj, the Indian princely states were in debt to the Company. Maharani

Lakshmi Bai was left with hardly any pension by imposing liabilities, purportedly the dues which Raja Gangadhar Rao owed to the British authorities. Rani Lakshmi Bai was reduced to a state of penury.

The oblivion of the ranis of the nineteenth century does not end with the Raj. The archival records developed the narrative along the lines by using terms like 'traitors' or enemy against their toughest opponent, Guru Siddhappa. Rani Chennamma finds very few mentions, reflecting the patriarchy of the Raj, which finds it unnecessary to mention women. Even Maharani Jindan is mentioned sporadically in the official records, but there are many lurid accounts of her in other unofficial records. The oblivion continues in postcolonial times. Their ruined forts are visible proof of that oblivion. Their families left far behind, their stories coming alive only in some moments of nationalistic fervour, but otherwise a silence.

The resistance of the ranis to the Raj rests on a moral position, 'forcing a moral confrontation'[5] of 'a shared humanity' between them and the colonial authority. An important point is that the nineteenth century witnessed many insurgencies; some were large in scale like the one in 1857, while some were more local. Maharani Lakshmi Bai and Begum Zeenat Mahal were a part of this grand rebellion of 1857. The reprisals against them were brutal and unforgiving, but they, along with the other rebels of 1857, gave a lease of life to the remaining princes, continuing in one way or the other till 1947 and beyond. But as consequence of their resistance, their characters were tarnished. Their moral excesses were tied to an 'oriental' imagery of sensuality and indolence. The eccentricities of the princes and their effete character fit the orientalist frame and provided legitimacy for an imperial takeover.

---

[5] Gopal, Location 608 of 12705.

One common and unyielding rule of the Raj, be it before or after 1857, was the non-negotiability of the white man's killing. In that regard, the Raj was uncompromising right till 1947. Nowhere is this particularistic application of law more apparent than in crisis situations, when a so-called universalist principle of law became particularistic. A killing of the white populace provoked an immediate violent reaction, and the 'moral' indignation of the whites found 'retribution' in the large scale blood-letting of the Indians to quench the thirst of revenge. The white world could not be challenged. This was apparent in Kittur when the collector of Dharwad, John Thackeray, died due to his act of aggression against Kittur, impervious to the sentiments of the people. The annihilation of Kittur was irrevocable. The fortitude and courage of the English men and women were juxtaposed against the brutalities and savagery of the Indian sepoys and the eccentricities of the rulers. All these became the legitimate grounds for possessing the Indian territories. The position of the Raj was clear — acquisitiveness, both territorial and monetary. In both Jhansi and Kittur, the first act of the British was to take the treasury and the fort.

A point that emerged in the course of my research was the continuity of imperial policies in the pre- and post-1857 period, with the Raj continuing with similar imperial policies against the princely states throughout the nineteenth century. Only an aura of benevolence or paternalism was assigned to the empress as benefactress in her 1858 proclamation, as if with this, the Raj became genial. On the contrary, contradicting the assertion of discontinuity before and after 1857, Sikkim's political position was eroded in a manner similar to the other princely states till they agreed to a subsidiary position in 1890. The only difference was that the imperial authorities avoided direct annexation and confrontation after 1858, aligning themselves with one of the most regressive elements of Indian society. They did not forgive and reinstate those who directly challenged white supremacy. The strategy of status quo politically and culturally suited the white Raj in India.

The colonial records constantly mention the treachery and deception of the Indians, which underlines the strong mistrust that emerged between them and the Indians. The Indian queens questioned the ethics and the morality of the English officials. How could the Indians trust the unreliable and mercenary white people? They only submitted to the might of their battering guns and canons, which pounded the Indian fortress towns with impunity. In the imperial records, there is not a word of concern or remorse on how many ordinary men, women and children would die. But the count of white men, women and children is recorded in careful detail, as in the case of Jokhum Bagh in Jhansi. This episode stripped the rani of all 'civilizational' values. The imperial archives were presented in a trial mode, and the resistance was already condemned without any trial.

A story of the arbitrary and violent dispossession of the ruling families and separating mothers from their children are placed in the paradigm of the evil machinations of the queens. The colonial representation strategically typecast the resisting queens under the fairy tale archetype of an 'evil queen'. The narrative of Maharani Jindan subtly foregrounds such a representation. No sympathy is accorded to the maharani. Rather, it seems that the benevolent colonial officers did a favour to young Maharaja Duleep Singh by taking him away from her 'malevolent' presence and putting him in the warmth of a loving Christian family. Similarly, Maharani Lakshmi Bai is vilified in the English tabloids as 'evil' after the Jokhum Bagh incident, in which unarmed English men, women and children were killed, despite a promise that on their peaceful surrender they would be unharmed. For this her father was executed with equal brutality in the same spot. It was a clear case of revenge, and it was based on a primitive code of conduct—an eye for eye. Most of the colonial responses are based on a similar code of violence, especially at the death of a white European. The reprisals were a butchering of thousands of colonized.

In the nationalist representation, queens were either seen as divine or as mothers to make them non-threatening. What these queens played upon is the definition of femininity in the nineteenth century. In this, their role as a mother and protector of their child and the honour of their family is the theme that has been exemplified in their actions and strategies. The themes of 'love, morality and maternity'[6] are prominent. The nationalist historiography also picked up this definition of femininity to idealize women in Indian society. None of the queens challenged the existing traditions and patriarchal norms, but they exercised their agency in the matters of the state. They took up the reigns of the administration when their husbands were indisposed and also showed vigour in the upkeep of the dynasty. They were actively involved in the interplay of power at the royal courts and showed firm decision-making. They also navigated the different pressure groups and political affiliations at their husband's court, to protect the interests of the dynasty. They were dispassionate and strategic and at times shrewd negotiators. The rani of Sirmur illustrates such shrewd negotiations with British officials to ensure that in her husband's lifetime she became the regent of the minor king. She not only saved the Sirmur dynasty, but also ensured the continuity of the family succession despite her husband being held in great contempt by the English authorities.

---

[6] Joan W. Scott, 372.

From the narratives of the ranis, the ranis seem to have handled the situation in a similar way as the men handled it in other princely states. If some men revolted, so did the ranis, and similarly, if men engaged in diplomatic discussions with the Raj, so did the ranis. They acted rationally and after careful deliberations on the nature of the threat. They weighed their odds carefully, eschewing the emotional, as did the rani of Sirmur when she set aside her husband's claim to the gaddi in favour of her son. She not only became the regent of Sirmur with the support of Lord Ochterlony and his subordinate, but she also ensured that they supported her by playing to the sentiments of tradition.

The unequal relationship of the king and the queen and the centrality of the king in the political and social hierarchy left the queens in a vulnerable position. As women, they were deprived of their right over property and right to be citizens or subjects, to make a choice about their lives after the death of their husbands. Yet, from the limited space available to them, they tried to create a political space, negotiating traditional Indian patriarchy as well as British patriarchy. Maharani Jindan had to negotiate this constantly. More than the queen of Maharaja Ranjit Singh, she had to play upon her identity as 'Mai' Jindan, the mother not of the minor king, but of all of the kingdom of Lahore and its people. The British attempted to rip off this identity by representing her as a sensuous and promiscuous woman. Her personal acts were embroidered and presented as being untrustworthy and unsuitable.

Folk narratives have kept the history alive; but where there is dearth of folk sources, many historical characters have been reduced to obscurity. There aren't many folk narratives or indigenous records on Begum Zeenat Mahal, Maharani Jindan, Guleri Rani of Sirmur or Queen Menchi of Sikkim. This raises other questions. Why did they not capture the popular imagination in the way Rani Kittur and Maharani Lakshmi Bai did? Why were such folk songs and stories not woven around them? In the folk tradition, there is a certain valorization of the 'martial' and the 'tragic'. There are no simple answers. What is interesting in the folk records is that they match the events with the official narratives. Some of the recent Bundelkhandi and Bhojpuri folk songs on Maharani Lakshmi Bai verbatim tally with the official records, even matching the exact dateline. This suggests that the oral tradition today reflects an awareness of the official written records. Could we say the same for the rendition of folk songs from the period when the actual events occurred? Were the popular traditions familiar with the official records at that time? It seems very doubtful.

The queen as a widow had no subjectivity of her own, and hence no representation because, as Spivak observed, the subalterns cannot represent themselves. Women are voiceless. Such presumptions are echoed in the case of Jhansi, where the British dismiss the presence of the widowed rani. Her capability as an administrator for Jhansi was not considered despite her talent. But these women voiced their opinions emphatically, challenging the colonial and Indian patriarchy. Many of these queens did not overtly counter traditions, but their position become clear from their acts. Maharani Lakshmi Bai did not perform any rites of the widow. Maharani Jindan came forward as the regent to attend the durbar to discuss the matters of the state. It has been mentioned in many English records that the maharani was considered to be the only effective threat within the Sikh leaders. That speaks a lot about her political acumen and explains the anxieties of the British authorities to remove her influence over Maharaja Duleep Singh and Lahore politics.

Many Indians resisted British rule. Some of them have been selectively appropriated in the present political scenario as the icons of a certain kind of nationalism. Kittur's Rani Chennamma and Maharani Lakshmi Bai of Jhansi have been appropriated as the ideal Hindu women. In today's times, their stories have been associated with not just their heroism, but also with lesser-known historical characters, such as Sangolli Rayanna and Jhalkari Bai. These are people from the humbler castes. During my field research to Kittur, I found the name of Sangolli Rayanna being taken in the same breath as that of Rani Chennamma. There are as many memorials of Sangolli Rayanna as that of Rani Chennamma. The modern age phenomenon of identity politics has affected the popular histories of the place.

There is a legal dimension in both the cases, but interestingly, the legal question involving the law of succession was not taken up by a judicial proceeding in a court of law but negotiated by the colonial administrators. Instead of fighting a legal battle, the British fought an armed war to deny the queens' representations for legal succession. This questions the widely stated position of the British that they introduced the 'rule of law' in India— where the company's economic interests were involved, no law was followed. Legal issues were not resolved in courtrooms, but in battles. Princely territories were acquired through administrative manoeuvring and by the outright use of force. The princes were pounded into submission.

Reading beyond the moral transgressions upon which many of these contemporary accounts touch, one can see them as signs of independence and challenges posed by these women within the confines of a male-dominated society. They were fully aware of their conduct, and yet they defied the norms. They may have been aware of the price they might have to pay, but this did not prevent them from breaking taboos and defying moral injunctions. Their actions indicate their strong agency in making decisions to fulfil their personal requirements. Begum

Zeenat Mahal retained her distinct identity as she preferred to stay independently in her haveli.

Kittur and Jhansi have to be included in the broader histories of the nation in the making under the nationalist frame. Individuals, events and places are intertwined in one frame, and the individuals are placed as the heroes of the freedom struggle. Undoubtedly, these are stories of rulers fighting for freedom, but in the particular context of individual kingdoms and dynastic succession. The queens discussed in the book were fighting for the survival of their dynasties.

Maharani Lakshmi Bai is the most popular 'warrior' Queen of India. Stories of her valour are part of popular culture and people's imagination from the very beginning of India's fight against colonial rule. Rani Chennamma of Kittur is a predecessor of Maharani Lakshmi Bai. She resisted the takeover of the principality of Kittur by the East India Company. The two stories are similar. Both queens wanted their adopted sons to be recognized as the successors after the demise of the existing ruler. Both were refused by the Company without any convincing answers, and that became a cause of contention.

The forts of Kittur and Jhansi were deliberately left in the state of destruction as an example of what a mighty empire does to those who dare to rebel against them. In today's India, these sites of destruction are the symbols of resistance to foreign rule. These sites have emerged as an unfinished agenda in postcolonial India, which appropriates them as heroes. These rebellious ranis are feted and glorified by the political players, but, ironically, those who sided with the Raj are still part of the ruling power groups of one or the other political affiliation. The descendants of these ranis are unheard of, and their properties are not restored to their descendants.

In postcolonial India, the 'rebels' against the imperial Raj have not found any place in the political frame of an independent nation-state. The sagas of their courage and their resistance are part of the nationalist imagination. Still, they remain strictly confined to the dead past, whereas the 'supporters' and collaborators of the British Raj flourished then and now. Many occupy a centre stage in India's mainstream political parties. Many political parties are resurrecting the bogey of old political rivalries, for instance in Mysore, playing the old and familiar game of the colonial rulers propping up some ruler at the expense of another. The relics of the colonial past are amplified by the communal overtones in such cases to only confirm the fact that past debris becomes an explosive issue in present-day India. These Indian princely states are remnants of the past. They continue in the changed political situation of independent India, with new political roles. They are a part of many political parties and have successfully engaged with the democratic process in India. Old feudal loyalties jostle with the highly competitive electioneering process of modern-day Indian democracy. Interestingly, the main protagonists of the early to the mid-nineteenth century Indian rulers, who negotiated with the patriarchs of the East India Company, do not find any place in contemporary India. In the postcolonial political imagination, primarily women warrior queens find place.

Epilogue

We look for Ranis in our present. Do they exist, or are they a figment of our imagination? We have idealized a few of them and erected innumerable statues of them.

On the other hand, the colonist who treated them unfairly has been forgotten. In Dharwad, during my research, I had a tough time locating the English cemetery used by the colonizers. We used local transport, thinking that the driver of the auto-rickshaw we used might know. He didn't. As a Christian, he knew of a new cemetery where the Indian Christians were buried. We were given a clue by a historian of the city, Dr Shadakshari, to go to the fish market. Finally, we left the auto-rickshaw and walked on foot looking for the cemetery. Another local vaguely mentioned a butcher shop adjacent to it. Finally, the butcher, on hearing our inquiries, came out. He was suspicious of us, thinking that we were from the government, and came to inspect that no cow had been butchered.[1] He asked

---

[1] In 2020, the Karnataka Government passed the Prevention of Slaughter and Preservation of Cattle Law, widening the ambit of anti-cow slaughter law. The previous laws on the prevention of cow slaughter in existence in the state were the 1964 and 2010 laws. For details see, 'Karnataka widens ambit, passes tough anti-cow law', 10 December 2020, *The Indian Express*.

for the whereabouts of the body. When we looked puzzled, he
immediately changed his position, asking us about our visit.

When he was assured that we were only interested in seeing
the graves of the British period, he took us to the land next to
his shop. All the memory of the British rule was lying effaced in
front of our eyes.

The ruins of the English cemetery at Dharwad, 2019, wiping out
all the memory of the colonial past, reducing it to the debris of the
colonial past.

The old British cemetery at Dharwad with cows all around, 2019.

An indifference to the colonial presence at the old British cemetery at Dharwad, 2019.

Once-beautiful marble graves inlaid with epitaphs are ruined by animals lying over the stone. Most of these graves, some of them with intricate architectural designs, are now broken. Most of the graves are covered with cow dung, and the smell is unbearable. Some of the local youths also use the place to sleep, and they helpfully removed the cow dung for us to read the epitaphs. They seemed amused and bemused by our interest. The Raj is not even a memory there.

What remains in Kittur is a park in John Thackeray's name, now called Kittur Rani Chennamma Park, the man who tried to take the fort of Kittur but was killed by the loyal supporters of the Kittur royal family. Rani Chennamma and her warriors, who fought the Raj valiantly, are now celebrated throughout Kittur and to an extent in Dharwad. Honour has been restored to the local heroes, and the 'villains' are defiled and pushed to the margins. A local legend is that the 'traitors' who betrayed the cause of Rani Chennamma and the Kittur royal family have not been forgiven—their families remain cursed. According to the local people, the park is where the Kittur officials left the 'headless body of John Thackeray'.

Image credit: Vivek Sachdeva

A memorial in black stone in the name of Thackeray
stands inside Rani Chennamma Park.

They retell the story with enthusiasm, uncaring about the gory
details. According to the local tale, the British got their just dues.
The descendants of the royal family, to whom the principality was
never restored because they openly rebelled against the British,
remain at the periphery. The rani and her most loyal supporter,
Sangolli Rayana, have memorials, but the descendants have not

been reinstated to their social position in postcolonial India. It is postcolonial politics that decides who is to be remembered and who is not to be remembered. Kalamath, the seat of the Lingayat spiritual head in Kittur with a common boundary wall to the fort, has maintained a continuous tradition, despite the political oblivion of the Kittur royal family. It maintains the graves in continuity of all the rulers of Kittur, from the time Kittur became the capital. Today, the Lingayats are powerful in the changing political landscape of postcolonial India.

The colonial narrative of destruction is graphic in the condition of the forts of Jhansi and Kittur. The conquest was irrevocable. But today the narrative has changed, and the same sights are a mark of courage and valour shown by these queens. They are remains of the past, which are preserved as a testimony of colonial violence. The same sites have become symbols of courage and resistance of these queens, changing the narrative today. What was irrevocable has been replaced by a new narrative of the people and the state. In present times, one can see a reification of the symbol of destruction. The site of ruin has emerged as a site of resistance today.

Image credit: Vivek Sachdeva

The ruins of Kittur Fort pounded by the English battering guns in 1824.

The cemetery at Dharwad symbolizes the indifference or perhaps even the insignificance of the Raj today in the minds of the ordinary people.

The ranis had no power and property except what was bequeathed to them by their husbands as rulers, and on their husbands' demise, they were at the mercy of the patriarchal system of the East India Company. The Company did not recognize the ranis as political leaders in their own right, and they were to be consigned to obscurity by conveniently taking refuge behind the Indian 'tradition'. The ranis were hemmed in by patriarchy on both sides—pressured into the position of helpless dependents, when they were capable of running the estates. When the ranis challenged the British assertions of their 'weakness', they were portrayed as being scheming, manipulative and characterless and without any integrity. They were shown to be malicious and emotional, as if they could not see beyond their vested interests. If this was the imperial discourse, the nationalist historiography foregrounded their maternal behaviour to counter the imperial projections. The projection of motherhood, of a virtuous wife stemming from a particular cultural tradition, trapped these women into a particular role. They seem to have oscillated between one of the two extremes. Why is it not possible to see them as the product of their times, as women who acted in accordance with the code of honour and conduct applicable to their male counterparts? Moreover, these are fragmented tales of the queens, as only fragments of their lives are available in the official narratives while some are available in popular culture.

Mahasweta Devi wrote: 'In front of the Phulbag Palace', in Gwalior, 'is a small raised platform at the side of the road, where the tongawallah will stop his carriage for the curious tourist. There is a tiny flower garden there and an insignificant-looking memorial marked "The Chhatri of Maharani Lakshmibai of Jhansi".'[2] It was on this spot that the rani was killed and cremated, but there was no memorial till Independence. Even in the post-Independence period, there is an abject neglect of Zeenat Mahal's haveli or the ruined forts of Kittur and Jhansi. A girls' school runs in Zeenat Mahal's haveli.

Maharaja Ranjit Singh and Maharani Jindan are now part of a shared history of India and Pakistan. Maharani Jindan finally came home after leaving Lahore in 1847, when her grand-daughters, Bamba Sutherland, Sophia and Catherine brought her ashes to Lahore in 1924, 'interred in the grand mausoleum (of Maharaja Ranjeet Singh) in the heart of Lahore'.[3] In Sikkim, I found some awareness of Queen Yeshe Dolma's resistance, but no clue on Queen Menchi. It is as if Queen Menchi and Guleri Rani were phantoms in the histories of their regions. Invisible, they played a crucial political role far beyond what is known in history about them, with their progeny continuing to be part of the history of their places.

If we look at the narratives of Jhalkari Bai or Mangla or the queens fighting battles diplomatically or on the battlefields, these women of the nineteenth century challenge the stereotypical notions of femininity, which confined them to domestic spaces or in conventional roles. They come across as feisty and resilient women, who actively engage in political manoeuvring and power games in the courts and negotiate with the English company officials. There is scope for research on the women who fought alongside these queens.

[2] Mahasweta Devi, 286.
[3] Anita Anand, *Sophia: Princess, Suffragette, Revolutionary* (London: Bloomsbury, 2015), 385. 'The thought of Jindan's eternal exile from Punjab had always troubled the daughters of Duleep Singh . . . Sensing the symbolism of the act, Bamba decided it was time to bring Rani Jindan home.'

Select Bibliography

Archival Records

Foreign Political Department Proceedings, National Archives of India.

Mutiny Records Correspondence, Part II. Lahore: Punjab Government Press, 1911.

Records of the Ludhiana Agency, 1814–15, Selections from the Punjab Government Records. Lahore: Punjab Government Press, 1911.

The Asiatic Journal and Monthly Register for British and Foreign India, China, and Australia: Vol. 19, 'Disturbance at Kittoor, Death of Mr. Thackeray, in Asian Intelligence, Miscellaneous, Bom. Cour. Nos.3, 1825, 474–5.

The Asiatic Journal and Monthly Register for British and Foreign India, China, and Australia: Volume 3. London: Parbury, Allen, and Company, 1830.

Gazetteers

Dhariwal, L.C., *The Indore State Gazetteer*, Volume I-Text (Under the authority of the Government of His Highness the Maharaja Holkar). Indore: Superintendent Holkar Government Press, 1931.

Himachal State Archives Records (under Department of Art and Culture), Kasumpty, Shimla.

Negi, Thakur Sen, *Gazetteer of India, Himachal Pradesh District Gazetteer: Sirmur*. Aligarh: Oriental Printing Press, 1969.

O'Malley, L. S. S., *Bengal District Gazetteers: Darjeeling*. Calcutta: The Bengal Secretariat Book Depot, 1907.

Punjab State Gazetteers: Phulkian States Patiala, Jind and Nabha, Vol. XVII A, Punjab Government Press, Lahore, 1904.

Ramaswami, A., *Tamil Nadu District Gazetteer: Ramanathapuram*, Director of Stationery and Printing, Madras, 1972.

Sirmur State Gazetteer, Part A, 1904 (Compiled and Published under the Authority of the Punjab Government). Lahore: Punjab Government Press, 1907.

Sirmur State Gazetteer, Part A, 1934. Lahore: Superintendent, Government Printing, 1939.

Sikkim State Archives Records, Gangtok.

The Gazetteer of Sikhim, Introduction by H. H. Risley. Calcutta: Bengal Secretariat Press, 1894.

The Imperial Gazetteer of India Provincial Series, Punjab, Vol. II. Calcutta: Superintendent of Government Press, 1908.

Unpublished Work

Diaries of 10th Chogyal Sidkeong Tulku (unpublished, Private Papers with Princess Hope Leezum).

Mallikarjun I. Minch, Rani Kittur Channamma: Her Revolt Against the British Rule, Ph.D. Thesis, Karnatak University, Dharwad, 2001.

Books

Agamben, Giorgio, *State of Exception*, trans. Kevil Attell. Chicago: The University of Chicago Press, 2005.

Anonymous, *Ruling Princes and Chiefs, Notables and Principal Officials of the Punjab Native States*. Lahore: The Superintendent Governor Printing, 1918.

Ahluwalia, M. L., *Maharani Jind Kaur (1816-63)*, ed. Prithipal Singh Kapur. Amritsar: Singh Bros., 2001.

Ahluwalia, M. L. and Kirpal Singh, *The Punjab's Pioneer Freedom Fighters*. Bombay: Orient Longman, 1963.

Aitchison, C. U., *A Collection of Treaties, Engagements and Sanads relating to India and Neighbouring Countries*, Vol. IX. Calcutta: Superintendent of Government Printing Press, 1892. No. XVI and No. XLIII (For Punjab and Sirmur).

Anand, Anita, *Sophia: Princess, Suffragette, Revolutionary*. London: Bloomsbury, 2015.

Anghie, Antony, *Imperialism, Sovereignty and the Making of International Law*. Cambridge: Cambridge University Press, 2004.

Atwal, Priya, *Royals and Rebels: The Rise and Fall of the Sikh Empire*. London: C. Hurst & Co., 2020.

Baird, J. G. A., *Private Letters of the Marquess of Dalhousie*. Edinburgh and London: William Blackwood and Sons, 1910.

Balgobind, *The Life of Raja Sir Shamshere Bahadur of Sirmour*. Calcutta: Thacker, Spink & Co, 1901.

Balikci-Denjongpa, Anna & Alex Mckay (ed.), *Buddhist Himalaya: Studies in Religion, History and Culture* (Proceedings of the Golden Jubilee Conference of the Namgyal Institute of Tibetology, Gangtok, 2008), Volume II-The Sikkim Papers. Gangtok: Namgyal Institute of Tibetology, 2011.

Ball, Charles, *The History of the Indian Mutiny: Giving a Detailed Account of the Sepoy Insurrection in India; and a Concise History of the Great Military Events which have tended to Consolidate British Empire in Hindostan, Vol. I*. London: The London Printing and Publishing Company Limited, 1858-59.

Bayley, Emily, ed. M.M. Kaye, *The Golden Calm: An English Lady's Life in Mogul Delhi: Reminiscences*. New York: Viking Press, 1980.

Basnet, Lal Bahadur, *Sikkim: A Short Political History*. New Delhi: S. Chand & Co., 1974.

Bates, Crispin ed., *Mutiny at the Margins: New Perspectives on the Indian Uprising of 1857*. New Delhi: Sage Publications, 2013.

Bell, Major Evans, *The Annexation of the Punjab and the Maharaja Duleep Singh*. London: Trubner & Co., 1882.

Belmessous, Saliha, ed., *Empire by Treaty: Negotiating European Expansion, 1600-1900*. New York: Oxford University Press, 2015.

Benton, Lauren and Lisa Ford, *Rage for Order: The British Empire and the Origins of International Law, 1800-1850.* Cambridge: Harvard University Press, 2016.

Benton, Lauren, *A Search for Sovereignty: Law and Geography in European Empires, 1400-1900.* Cambridge: Cambridge University Press, 2010.

Bhattacharya, Sabyasachi, *Archiving the British Raj: History of the Archival Policy of the Government of India, with Selected Documents*, 1858-1947. New Delhi: Oxford University Press, 2019.

Brentnall, Mark, *The Princely and Noble Families of the Former Indian Empire, Volume One, Himachal Pradesh.* New Delhi: Indus Publishing Company, 2004.

Bose, Melia Belli and Cathleen Cummings eds. *Women, Gender and Art in Asia, c.1500-1900.* New York: Ashgate, Routledge, 2016

Cesaire, Aime, *Discourse on Colonialism.* New York and London: Monthly Review Press, 1972.

Campbell, Christy, *The Maharajah's Box: An Imperial Story of Conspiracy, Love and a Guru's Prophecy.* London: Harper Collins, 2000.

Chandra, Satish, *Medieval India.* New Delhi: Orient Blackswan, 2018.

Chandra, Satish, *Medieval India*, Part II; A textbook of class XI (Old series), (New Delhi: NCERT, 1983) (Reprint).

Chapman, Lebra Joyce, *The Rani of Jhansi: A Study of Female Heroines in India.* Honolulu: University of Hawaii Press, 1986.

Cooper, Fredrick and Anne Laura Stoler, *Tensions of Empire: Colonial Cultures in a Bourgeois World.* Berkeley: University of California Press, 1997.

Copland, Ian, *The Princes in the Endgame of Empire, 1917-47.* Cambridge: Cambridge University Press, 2002.

Dalrymple, William, *The White Mughal.* London: Bloomsbury, 2009.

Dalrymple, William, *The Anarchy: The East India Company, Corporate Violence, and the Pillage of An Empire.* London: Bloomsbury, 2019.

Dalrymple, William & Anita Anand, *Kohinoor: The Story of the World's Infamous Diamond.* New Delhi: Juggernaut, 2018.

Datta, C. L. & Surinder Singh, eds., *Crisis in the Western Himalaya: Reports of J. D. Cunnigham 1841-42.* New Delhi: Aakar Books, 2015.

Dehlvi, Zahir, *Dastan-e-Ghadar: The Tale of the Mutiny*, trans. Rana Safvi. New Delhi: Penguin Books, Random House India, 2017.

Devi, Mahasweta, *The Queen of Jhansi*, trans. Sagaree and Mandira Sengupta. Kolkata: Seagull Books, 2010.

Dhillon, Harish, *The First Raj of the Sikhs: The Life and Times of Banda Singh Bahadur*. New Delhi: Hay House India, 2013.

Dirks, Nicholas B., *The Hollow Crown: Ethnohistory of an Indian Kingdom*, Second Edition. Ann Arbor: The University of Michigan Press, 1993.

Dutt, Jogesh Chunder, *Kings of Kashmir being a translation of the Sanskrita Work Rajatarangini of Kalahana Pandita*. Calcutta: Trubner and Company, London, 1879.

Edwardes, Major Herbert B., *A Year on Punjab Frontier in 1848-49, Vols.I & II*. London: Richard Bentley, 1851.

Edwardes, Lieut. H.B. Edwardes, *Political Diaries of Lieut. H. B. Edwardes, Assistant to the Resident at Lahore 1847-49*. Allahabad: Pioneer Press, 1911.

Ernst, Waltraud & Biswamoy Pati, eds. *India's Princely States: People, Princes and Colonialism*. London and New York: Routledge, 2007.

Fanon, Frantz, *The Wretched of the Earth*, trans. Richard Philcox. New York: Grove Press, 2004.

Farooqui, Mahmood, *Besieged: Voices from Delhi 1857*. New Delhi: Penguin Books, 2010.

Fraser, Antonia, *The Warrior Queens: Boadicea's Chariot*. London: Phoenix Press, 1988.

Fraser, Baillie, *Journal of a tour through part of the snowy range of the Himala Mountains, and to the sources of the rivers Jumna and Ganges*. London: Rodwell and Martin, 1820.

Fraser, George Macdonald, *Flashman and the Mountain of Light* (From the Flashman Papers, 1845-46). London: Harper Collins, 2005.

Forrest, George W., *The Indian Mutiny 1857-58, (Selections from the Letters, Despatches and other State Papers Presented in the Military Department of the Government of India, 1857-58), Vol. IV*. Calcutta: Superintendent Government Printing, 1912.

Forrest, G. W., *A History of the Indian* Mutiny (Reviewed and Illustrated from Original Documents). Edinburgh and London: William Blackwood and Sons, 1912.

Gardner, Colonel Alexander, *Soldier and Traveller: Memoirs of Alexander Gardner* (Colonel of Artillery in the Service of Maharaja Ranjit Singh), ed. Major Hugh Pearse & Introduction by Sir Richard Temple. Edinburgh and London: William Blackwood and Sons, 1848.

Ghosh, Durba, *Sex and the Family in Colonial India: The Making of Empire.* Cambridge: Cambridge University Press, 2006.

Greenblatt, Stephen, *Marvellous Possessions: The Wonder of the New World.* Chicago: The University of Chicago Press, 1991.

Grewal, J. S., *Maharaja Ranjit Singh: Polity, Economy and Society.* Amritsar: Guru Nanak Dev University, 2001.

Griffin, Lepel H., *The Rajas of the Punjab being the History of the Principal States in the Punjab and their Political Relations with the British Government.* Lahore: Punjab Printing Company, 1870.

Gopal, Priyamvada, *Insurgent Empire: Anticolonial Resistance and British Dissent.* New Delhi: Simon & Schuster, 2019, electronic publication.

Gupta, Archana Garodia, *The Women Who Ruled India.* Gurugram: Hachette India, 2019.

Gupta, Subhadra Sen, *Mahal: Power and Pageantry in the Mughal Harem.* Gurugram: Hachette, 2019.

Haldar, Piyel, *Law, Orientalism and Postcolonialism: The Jurisdiction of the Lotus-Eaters.* London and New York: Routledge, 2007.

Hallisey, Robert C., *The Rajput Rebellion against Aurangzeb: A Study of Rajput-Mughal Relations in Seventeenth-Century India.* Columbia: University of Missouri Press, 1977.

Hamilton, Francis (formerly Buchanan), *An Account of the Kingdom of Nepal, and of the Territories Annexed to their Dominion by the House of Gorkha.* Edinburgh: Archibald Constable and Company, 1819.

Hodson, The Rev. George H. ed., *Twelve Years of a Soldier's Life in India: Being Extracts from the Letters of the late major W.S.R. Hodson (including a Personal Narrative of the Siege of Delhi and Capture of the King and Princes).* London: John W. Parker and Son, 1859.

Hooker, Joseph Dalton, *Himalayan Journals: Notes of a Naturalist in Bengal, The Sikkim, and Nepal Himalayas, The Khasia Mountain, & c., Vol. I.* London: John Murray, 1855.

Hooker, J. D., *Himalayan Journals, Vol. II.* London: John Murray, London, 1854.

Hutchison, J. & J. P. H. Vogel, *History of the Punjab Hill States, Volume I.* Shimla: Department of Language and Culture, Himachal Pradesh, 1933, Reprint 2000.

Innes, Lieutenant-General J. J. McLeod, *Sir Henry Lawrence: The Pacificator.* Oxford: Clarendon Press, 1898.

Ishwaran, K., *Speaking of Basava: Lingayat Religion and Culture in South Asia.* London and New York: Routledge, Taylor and Francis, 2019.

Jahanbegloo, Ramin, ed., *Talking History: Romila Thapar in Conversation with Ramin Jahanbegloo with the Participation of Neeladri Bhattacharya.* New Delhi: Oxford University Press, 2017.

Jhala, Angma Dey, *Courtly Indian Women in Late Imperial India.* London: Pickering & Chatto, 2008.

John, Mary E. ed., *Women's Studies in India: A Reader.* New Delhi: Penguin Books India, 2008.

Joshi, H. G., *Sikkim Past and Present.* New Delhi: Mittal Publication, 2009.

Kazi, Jigme N., *Sons of Sikkim: The Rise and Fall of the Namgyal Dysnasty of Sikkim.* Gangtok: Hill Media Publications and Chennai: Notion Press, 2020, electronic publication.

Kohli, Sita Ram, *Catalogue of Khalsa Darbar Records, Volume I.* Lahore: Superintendent, Government Printing Press, 1919.

Kolff, Dirk, H.A., *Naukar, Rajput, and Sepoy: The Ethnohistory of the Military Labour Market of Hindustan, 1560-1850.* Cambridge: Cambridge University Press, 1990.

Kosambi, Meera, *Crossing the Thresholds: Feminist Essays in Social History.* Ranikhet: Permanent Black, 2007.

Krishna Rao, M. V. & G. H. Halappa, eds., *History of Freedom Movement in Karnataka, Vol. I.* Mysore: Government of Mysore Publication, 1962.

Lamb, Alastair, *British India and Tibet, 1766-1910.* London: Routledge, 1960, 1986.

Latif, Syad Muhammad, *History of the Panjab: From the Remotest Entity to the Present Time.* Calcutta: Calcutta Central Press Company Limited, 1891.

Login, E. Dalhousie, *Lady Login's Recollections: Court Life and Camp Life, 1820-1904*. London: Smith, Elder & Co., 1916.

Mbembe, Achille and Steve Corcoran, *Necropolitics*. Durham and London: Duke University Press, 2019.

Macaulay, Colman, *Report of a Mission to Sikkim and the Tibetan Frontier, with a Memorandum on our Relations with Tibet*. Calcutta: Bengal Secretariat Press, 1885.

Col Malleson ed., *Kaye's and Malleson's History of the Indian Mutiny of 1857-8*, New Edition, In Six Volumes, Vol. III, London, New York and Bombay: Longmans, Green & Co, 1897.

Mantena, Karuna, *Alibis of Empire: Henry Maine and the Ends of Liberal Imperialism*. New Jersey: Princeton University Press, 2010.

Martin, Robert Montgomery, *The Indian Empire: Illustrated*. London: Print and Publishing Company, 1899.

Martin, Robert Montgomery, *The Progress and Present State of British India (A Manual for General Use, based on Official Documents, Furnished under the Authority of Her Majesty's Secretary of State for India)*. London: Sampson Low, Son, & Co., 1862.

Martin, R. Montgomery, *Our Indian Empire and the Adjacent Countries of Afghanistan, Balochistan, Persia, and Depicted and Described by Pen and Pencil*, Vol. II, The London Printing and Publishing Company Ltd., London & New York, 1879–81, 1879.

Martin, R. Montgomery, *The Indian Empire: Illustrated,* Vol. III, Print and Publishing Company, London, 1899 (Mayur Publishers, Delhi, Reprint 1983)

Metcalfe, Charles Theophilus, *Two Native Narratives of the Mutiny in Delhi*. London: Archibald Constable & Co., 1898.

Metcalf, Thomas R. *Ideologies of the Raj*, New Delhi: Cambridge University Press Foundation Books, 1998.

Michael of Greece, Prince, *The Rani of Jhansi: A Historical Novel*. New Delhi: Rupa, 2013.

Mill, James. *The History of British India*. London: Piper, Stephenson and Spence, 1858, 4 volumes.

Moore, Lucy, *Maharanis: The Extraordinary Tale of Four Indian Queens and Their Journey from Purdah to Parliament*. London and New York: Viking, 2004.

Moran, Arik, *Kingship and Polity on the Himalayan Borderland: Rajput Identity during the Early Colonial Encounter*. Amsterdam: Amsterdam University Press, 2019.

Moran, Michelle, *Rebel Queen*. New York: Touchstone, 2015.

Mukhoty, Ira, *Heroines: Powerful Indian Women of Myth and History*. New Delhi: Aleph Book Company, 2017.

Mukhoty, Ira, *Daughters of the Sun*. New Delhi: Aleph Book Company, 2018.

Mullard, Saul, *Opening the Hidden Land: State Formation and the Construction of Sikkimese History*. Gangtok: Rachna, 2019.

Mullard, Saul and Hissey Wangchuk, *Royal Records: A Catalogue of the Sikkemese Palace Archive*. Andiast: International Institute for Tibetan and Buddhist Studies (IITBS GmbH), 2010.

Naikar, Basavaraj, *The Rani of Kittur: A Historical Play*. New Delhi: Gnosis, 2012.

Naikar, Basavaraj, *The Rani of Kittur* (A Historical Play). Bangalore: CVG Books, 2015.

Naikar, Basavaraj, *The Rebellious Rani of Belavadi and Other Stories*. Bangalore: CVG Books, 2018.

Nair, Janaki, *Women and Law in Colonial India*. New Delhi: Kali for Women, 1996, Second Impression, 2000.

Namgyal, Sir Thutob, their Highness the Maharaja & Maharani Yeshay Dolma of Sikkim, *History of Sikkim*, trans. Kazi Dousandup. Gangtok: Namgyal Royal Family, Sikkim, 1908.

Narayan, Badri. *Women Heroes and Dalit Assertion in North India: Culture, Identity and Politics*. New Delhi: Sage Publications, 2006.

Nigam, N. K., *Delhi in 1857*. New Delhi: S. Chand & Co., 1957.

Nijjar, Bakhshish Singh, *Maharani Jind Kaur: The Queen Mother of Maharaja Dalip Singh*. Delhi: NBS Revised Edition, 2003.

Osborne, The Hon. W. G., *The Court and Camp of Runjeet Sing*. London: Henry Colburn Publisher, 1840.

Parvez, Aslam, *The Life and Poetry of Bahadur Shah Zafar*, trans. Ather Farouqui. New Delhi: Hay House India, 2017.

Pai, Anant ed., *Amar Chitra Katha, Incredible Women of India, The Rani of Kittur: The Defiant Queen, Vol. 748*. New Delhi: India Book House, 1967.

Pati, Biswamoy, ed., *The Great Rebellion of 1857 in India: Exploring Transgressions, Contests and Diversities*. London and New York: Routledge, 2010.

Pillai, Manu S., *The Ivory Throne: Chronicles of the House of Travancore*. New Delhi: Harper Collins India, 2015.

Pitts, Jennifer, *Boundaries of the International Law and Empire*. Cambridge: Harvard University Press, 2018.

Rai, Rajiv, *The State in the Colonial Periphery, A Study on Sikkim's Relation with Great Britain*. Gurgaon: Partridge India, 2015.

Rajan, Saketh (Saki), *Making History: Karnataka's People and their Past: Colonial Shock, Armed Struggle, (1800-1857), Vol. II*. Bangalore: Vimukthi Prakashan, 2004.

Raman, Bhavani, *Document Raj: Writing and Scribes in Early Colonial South India*. Ranikhet: Permanent Black, 2018. Originally produced by the University of Chicago Press, 2012.

Ramusack, Barbara N., *The New Cambridge History of India: The Indian Princes and their States, Volume 3, Part 6*. Cambridge: Cambridge University Press, 2004.

Rana, Bhawan Singh, *Rani of Jhansi*. New Delhi: Diamond Pocket Book, 2016.

Rangachari, Devika, *Invisible Women, Visible Histories: Gender, Society and Polity in North India, 7th-12th Century*. New Delhi: Manohar Publishers & Distributors, 2009.

Rao, P. R., *India and Sikkim (1814-1970)*. New Delhi: Sterling Publishers, 1972.

Renders, Hans, Binne de Haan, Nigel Hamilton, *Theoretical Discussions of Biography: Approaches from History, Microhistory, and Life Writing*. Leiden and Boston: Brill Academic Publishers, 2014.

Richardson, Hugh, *Richardson Papers* (Contributed to the Bulletin of Tibetology, 1965-1992). Gangtok: Sikkim Research Institute of Tibetology, 1993.

Roy, Tapti, *The Politics of a Popular Uprising: Bumdelkhand in 1857*. Bombay, Calcutta, Madras: Oxford University Press, 1994.

Saggu, Harbans Kaur trans. Jagjit Kaur, Mahinder Kaur Gill, 'Punjab ki Pratham Nari Swantrata Senani: Maharani Jindan', in *Punjab Ki Raniyan*. New Delhi: Vijay Publication, 1997.

Said, Edward, *Orientalism*. New York: Pantheon Books, 1978. New Delhi: Zubaan, 1989.

Sangari, Kumkum and Sudesh Vaid, *Recasting Women: Essays in Colonial History*, New Delhi: Zubaan, 1989

Scott, James C., *The Weapons of the Weak: Everyday Forms of Peasant Resistance*. New Haven: Yale University Press, 1985.

Scott, Joan Wallach, *Gender and the Politics of History* (Gender and Cultural Series). New York: Columbia University Press, 1999.

Sengupta, N., *State Government and Politics: Sikkim*. New Delhi: Sterling Publishers, 1985.

Seetal, Gyan Sohan Singh, *Maharani Jindan (A Novel)*. Ludhiana: Lahore Book Shop, 2013.

Singh, Ganda ed., *History of the Freedom Movement in Punjab: Maharaja Duleep Singh Correspondence, Vol. III*. Patiala: Punjabi University, 1977.

Singh, Kunwar Ranzor, *Tarikh i Riyasat Sirmour*, originally published in Persian in 1912; Hindi translation by Amar Nath Walia. Shimla: Himachal Academy of Arts, Culture and Languages, 2007.

Stokes, Eric, *The Peasant Armed: The Indian Revolt of 1857*, ed. C. A. Bayly. Oxford: Clarendon Press, 1986.

Singh, Harleen, *The Rani of Jhansi: Gender, History, and Fable in India*. New Delhi: Cambridge University Press, 2014.

Singh, Khushwant, *Ranjit Singh: Maharajah of the Punjab*. London: George Allen & Unwin, 1962.

Singh, Khushwant, *A History of the Sikhs, 1839-1964, Vol. II*. London: Oxford University Press, 1963.

Singh, Khushwant, *Delhi: A Novel*. New Delhi: Penguin Books, 1990.

Singh, Kirpal (ed.), *Hardinge Papers Relating to Punjab*. Patiala: Publication Bureau, Punjabi University, 2002.

Singh, N. William, Malsawmdawngliana & Saichampuii Sailo eds., *Becoming Something Else: Society and Change in India's North East*. Newcastle upon Tyne: Cambridge Scholars Publishing, 2015.

Singh, Sarbpreet Singh, *The Camel Merchant of Philadelphia (Stories from the Court of Maharaja Ranjit Singh)*. Chennai: Tranquebar, Westland Publications Limited, 2019.

Smyth, Major G. Carmichael, *A History of the Reigning Family of Lahore, with some Account of the Jummoo Rajahs, the Seik Soldiers and their Sirdars*. Calcutta: W. Thacker and Co., 1847.

Stoler, Ann Laura ed., *Imperial Debris: On Ruins and Ruination*. Durham and London: Duke University Press, 2013.

Suri, Lala Sohan Lal, *Umdat- ul-Tawarikh, An Original Source of Punjab History, Chronicles of the Reign of Maharaja Ranjit Singh, 1831-1839, Daftar III, Part V*, trans. V. S. Suri. Chandigarh: Panjab Itihas Prakashan, 1972.

Suri, Vidya Sagar, *Some Original Sources of Panjab History: Analytical Catalogues of Some Outstanding Persian Manuscripts and Annotated Translations into English of Contemporary Chronicles Entitled Dewan Ajudhia Parshad's Waqai-i-Jang-Sikhan (Pheroshehr and Sobraon, 1846) and Muhammad's Naqis' Sher Singh Nama (Tarikh-i-Punjab)*. Lahore: Keeper of Records to Government, 1956.

Sylvester, Assistant Surgeon John Henry, *Recollections of the Campaign in Malwa and Central India under Major General Hugh Rose*. Bombay: Smith, Taylor & Co., 1860.

Tahmankar, D. V., *The Ranee of Jhansi*. London: Macgibbon & Kee, 1918.

Temple, Richard, *Journals Kept in Hyderabad, Kashmir, Sikkim, and Nepal, Vol. II* (Introduction by Richard Carnac Temple). London: W.H. Allen & Co., 1887.

Temple, Captain R.C., *The Legends of the Panjab*, Vol. I, Bombay: Education Society Press, London: Trubner & Co.1884: Forgotten Books, London, reproduced in 2015, 1-65

Trouillot, Michel-Rolph, *Silencing the Past: Power and the Production of History*. Boston: Beacon Press, 2015 (20th Century Edition).

Vaggar, A. B, ed., *Kitturu Samsthana: Dakhalegalu, (under Chief Editor, Prof. Mallikarjun Hiremath) Volume-I*. Belagavi: Prasaranga, Basavaraj Kattimani Pratisthana, 2019.

Versaikar, Vishnu Bhatt Godshe, *1857: The Real Story of the Great Uprising*, trans. Mrinal Pande. New York and New Delhi: Harper Perennial (HarperCollins), 2011.

Wodeyar, Sadashiva Shivadeva, *Rani Chennamma*. New Delhi: National Book Trust, Reprint 2016.

Articles

Anagol, Padma, 'Agency, Periodization and Change in the Gender and Women's History of Colonial India', in *Gender and History*, Vol. 20, No.3, November 2008, 600–27.

Bailkin, Jordanna, 'The Boot and the Spleen: When Was Murder Possible in British India?', in *Comparative Studies in Society and History*, Vol. 48, No.2, April 2006, 462–93.

Bannett, Judith M., 'Women's History: A Study in Continuity and Change', in *Women's History Review*, Vol. 2, No. 2, 1993, 173–84.

Bano, Shadab, 'Jahan Ara's Administration of her Jagirs', in *Proceedings of the Indian History Congress*, Vol. 66, 205-2006, 430-437.

Benton, Lauren, 'From International Law to Imperial Constitutions: The Problems of Quasi-Sovereignty, 1870-1900', in *Law and History Review*, Vol.26, No. 3, Fall 2008, 595–619.

Bhukya, Bhangya, 'The Subordination of the Sovereigns: Colonialism and the Gond Rajas in Central India, 1818-1948', in *Modern Asian Studies*, Vol. 47, No. 1, January 2013, 288–317.

Chakravarti, Uma & Kumkum Roy, 'A Review of the Limitations and Possibilities of the Historiography of Women in Early India', in *Economic and Political Weekly*, 30 April 1998, WS2–WS10.

Chakravarti, Uma & Kumkum Roy, 'In search of Our Past', in *Economic and Political Weekly*, Vol. 23, No. 18, April 30, 1988, WS2-WS10.

Chandha, Suresh K. 'Opinions: Vanishing Values-Economic Growth alone not Enough', *Tribune Chandigarh*, 20 May 2013.

Datla, Kavita Saraswathi, 'The Origins of Indirect Rule in India: Hyderabad and the British Imperial Order', in *Law and History Review*, Vol. 33, No. 2, May 2015, 321–50.

Deshpande, Prachi, 'The Making of an Indian Nationalist Archive: Lakshmibai, Jhansi, and 1857', in *The Journal of Asian Studies*, Vol. 67, No. 3, August 2008, 855–79.

Fisher, Michael H., 'Indirect Rule in the British Empire: The Foundations of the Residency System in Dia (1764-1858), in *Modern Asian Studies*, Vol. 18, No. 3, 1984, 393–428.

Forbes, Geraldine, 'Reflections on South Asia Women's/Gender History: Past and Future', in *Journal of Colonialism and Colonial History*, Vol. 4, No. 1, 1–18.

Gerwin, Martin and Christoph Bergmann, 'Geopolitical Relations and Regional Restructuring: The Case of the Kumaon Himalaya, India', in *Erdkunde*, Bd. 66, H.2, April–June 2012, 91–107.

Inden, Ronald, 'Orientalist Constructions of India', in *Modern Asian Studies*, Vol. 20, No. 3, 1986, 401–46.

Jekila, A. and P. Barathi, 'Queen Velu Nachiar: First Woman against British', in *Infokara Research*, Vol. 9, Issue 3, June 2020, 891–897

Kapila, Shuchi, 'Educating Seeta: Philip Meadows Taylor's Romances of Empire', *Victorian Studies: A Journal of The Humanities, Arts & Sciences*, Vol. 41, No. 2, Winter, 1998, 211–41.

Mani, Lata, 'Contentious Traditions: The Debate on Sati in Colonial India', in *Cultural Critique*, No. 7, The Nature and Context of Minority Discourse II, Autumn, 1987, 119–56.

Moran, Arik, '"The Rani of Sirmur" Revisited: Sati and sovereignty in theory and practice', in *Modern Asian Studies*, Cambridge University Press, 2014, 1–34.

Mullard, Saul, 'Constructing the Mandala: The State Formation of Sikkim and the Rise of a National Historical Narrative', in *Buddhist Himalaya: Studies in Religion, History and Culture: Proceedings of the Golden Jubilee Conference of the Namgyal Institute of Tibetology*, Vol. II: The Sikkim Papers (Gangtok, 2008), 53–62.

Nair, Janaki, 'On the Question of Agency in Indian Feminist Historiography', *in Gender & History*, Vol.6, No. 1, April 1994, 82–100.

Prakash, Gyan, 'Postcolonial Criticism and Indian Historiography', in *Social Text*, No. 31/32, Third World and Post-Colonial Issues, 1992, 8–19.

Rajan, Meenakshi, 'Spiritual Warriors: The Role of Women in the Sikh Religion', in *Proceedings of the Indian History Congress*, Vol. 68, Part Two, 2007, 1445–6.

Roy, Pinaki, 'Alternative History: A postcolonial rereading of Naikar's 'The Queen Of Kittur', in *Indian Journal of Multidisciplinary Academic Research (IJMAR)*, Vol. 1, No. 2, August 2014, 105–15.

Saksena, Priyasha, 'Jousting over Jurisdiction: Sovereignty and International Law in late Nineteenth-century South Asia', in *Law and History Review*, Vol. 38, No. 2, May 2020, 409–57.

Sarkar, Tanika, 'Nationalist Iconography: Image of Women in 19th Century Bengali Literature', in *Economic and Political Weekly*, Vol. 22, No. 47, November 21, 1987, pp. 2011-2015.

Sen, Indrani, 'Gendering the Rebellion of 1857: The "Loyal Indian Woman" in "Mutiny Fiction"', in *Indian Historical Review*, 2007, Vol. 34, No. 36, 36–57.

Sen, Indrani, 'Inscribing the Rani of Jhansi in Colonial "Mutiny" Fiction', in *Economic and Political Weekly*, Vol. 42, No. 19, May 12–18, 2007, 1764–61.

Shubert, Adrian, 'Women Warriors and National Heroes: Augustine de Aragon and Her Indian Sisters', in *Journal of World History*, Vol. 23, Issue 2, June 2012, 279–313.

Singh, Sardar Ganda, 'Three Letters of Maharani Jind Kaur', in *Proceedings of the Indian History Congress*, Vol. 13, 1950, 304–13.

Spivak, Gayatri Chakravorty, 'The Rani of Sirmur: An Essay in Reading the Archives', in *Theory and History,* Vol. 24, No. 3, October 1985, 247–72.

Spivak, Gayatri Chakravorty, 'Can the Subaltern Speak?', in Cary Nelson & Lauren Grossber eds., *Marxism and the Interpretation of Culture*. Urbana: University of Illinois Press, 1988, 271–313.

Travers, Alice, 'Women in the diplomatic game: Preliminary Notes on the matrimonial link of the Sikkim royal family with Tibet (13th-20th centuries) (in French), in *Bulletin of Tibetology,* Vol. 42, No. 1–2, 2006. Gangtok: Namgyal Institute of Tibetology, 91–134.

Trevithick, Alan, 'Some structural and Sequential Aspects of the British Imperial Assemblages at Delhi, 1877-1911', in *Modern Asian Studies*, Vol. 24, No. 3, July 1990, 561–78.

Wangyal, Sonam B., 'A Unique Parallel', in *Buddhist Himalaya: Studies in Religion, History and Culture: Proceedings of the Golden Jubilee Conference of the Namgyal Institute of Tibetology*, Vol. II: The Sikkim Papers (Gangtok, 2008), 73-6.

Online Sources

'Alha Deshraj Paterya, Jhansi Ki Rani Laxmi Bai, Vol. I and II', YouTube, https://youtu.be/JdiU48E31MQ. Accessed on 17 June 2022.

Ahmed, Firoz Bakht, 'The Ruined Haveli of Zeenat Mahal', in *The Milli Gazett*, Indian Muslim's leading Newspaper, 14 February 2012. https://www.milligazette.com/news/12-special-reports/3228-the-ruined-haveli-of-zeenat-mahal/. Last accessed on 14 July 2022.

'*Kar Gai Amar Kahani Jhansi Ki Nar* (Rani aur Vir Bhesh Ghoda Pe Baithi Kar Gayi Amar Kahani', YouTube, 18 October 2017, https://youtu.be/4epsK5nsPic and https://youtu:be/e-KcBNSVWKU. Accessed on 17 June 2022.

Mishra, Kailash K., 'Abbakka Rani: The Unsung Warrior Queen', *Vihangama*, Vol. I, January-February 2002, ignca.gov.in/PDF_data/Abbakka_Rani.pdf

Smith, R. V., 'The Sad Plight of Zeenat Mahal', 16 October 2011, *The Hindu*, https://www.thehindu.com/features/metroplus/the-sad-plight-of-zeenat-mahal/article2543190.ece. Last accessed on 14 July 2022.

Tran, Hong, 'Chogyal's Sikkim: Tax, Land & Clan Politics', *Independent Study Project (ISP) Collection, 1446, 2012*, https://digitalcollections.sit.edu/isp_collection/1446. Accessed on 17 June 2022.

Venturi, Franco, 'Oriental Despotism', in Journal of the History of Ideas, January -March, 1963, Vol. 24, No. 1, 1963, pp.133 -142; Rolando Minuti, 'Oriental Despotism', in European History Online, http//www.ieg-ego.eu, ISSN2192-7405.

Royalark.net.